AND TOMORROW . . . THE WORLD?

AND TOMORROW . . . THE WORLD?

INSIDE IBM

Rex Malik

millington

For Nicholas and Marcus,
who will one day I hope
appreciate what drove me to write this.

Copyright © 1975 by Rex Malik
All rights reserved
ISBN 0 86000 043 5

First published 1975 by
Millington Ltd.
109 Southampton Row
London WC 1B 4HH

Printed in Great Britain
at The Pitman Press, Bath

Contents

IBM v. Telex. Argument and evidence in court, a contrast between legal process and reality. The history of the computer and evidence of the process of invention and development. From Babbage to Turing. IBM's entry into the field.

The genesis of IBM. Computing, Tabulating and Recording Company. Thomas Watson Snr, from NCR to IBM. The growth of IBM at home and internationally. The rewards of success.

The Cold War and IBM's final decision to build a computer. The generation clash. IBM and Federal Government. 700 Series and SAGE.

Contents

Contents

vii

Contents

Author's Introduction

This book is about control. It is about a sham: an American company which masquerades as a multinational and has dozens of foreign subsidiaries, each with a board packed full of local worthies and executive flunkeys, but which in reality is a company, in all meaningful senses of the word, *consolidated*, and in which power is about as widely distributed as is power in the Kremlin.

It is essential in such a book to distinguish clearly between the organ grinder and the monkey. This book is primarily about the decisions made by a handful of men, all of them American, and why those decisions are made. It is about the control that they exercise over the destinies of a so-called multinational company, The IBM Corporation, and indirectly over the development of a world-wide industry: computing. This is a control which has been exercised by them for the best part of a quarter of a century.

To understand IBM, then, it is necessary first of all to understand American IBM, and it is with the activities of that part of the corporation that these pages are mostly concerned. But unless the reader keeps firmly in mind the notion that what we are dealing with here is the reality of control, and not its public face, he or she will not really understand what this book is about. (For the control that is exercised over American IBM is no different from that exercised over its foreign subsidiaries.)

This book is also about the IBM of the past, of the near present, and of the near future, and deals with some of its problems, hopes, plans, expectations—and aspirations. It is the result of one man's attempts to get close to a corporation, attempts which took place over many years and which nearly always ended in failure and exasperation. That any human being, at all intelligent, should devote so much time to trying to understand any corporate animal might seem odd, even futile. However, the computing industry and the sciences and other 'ologies' on which it is based and by which it is surrounded form a large central role in my life. For the possibilities inherent in computing are of revolutionary potential (a statement now of obvious triteness, which was not quite so obvious or trite when I first wrote it during the fifties).

Essentially then, computing is about politics, and as I am a political animal (because, to quote that friend of former IBM Chairman Tom Watson Jnr., the late President Kennedy—and I hope the quotation is not apocryphal—'all the other games are for kids'), it is an activity with which it is fitting that humans become emotionally involved (or it should be. Why so much of the computing is in reality so boring and so repellent can be found here).

IBM is not just a major international company, in the area of computing, it is the international environment. This has important consequences and effects, not the least of which is that, whatever the prophets of technology may write, or the science fiction writers propound, the likelihood of some of the possibilities inherent in computing actually happening are dependent upon IBM seeing if, how, and when, it can make a profit out of them. I have no objection to profit, much the reverse. But a situation in which one single corporation can have such an unrestrained influence on the direction in which computing, and thus industrial societies, evolve, is not one that I face with any equanimity, whoever runs the corporation involved.

What you are witnessing, then, as you go through these pages is the spectacle of a writer who has over many years been reluctantly pushed into a position which he did not initially seek. I wish IBM were a different sort of corporate animal, and for a long time I thought it was: but I was wrong, and this is in some ways an attempt to make up for it.

This book has other origins, and they are perhaps worth mentioning.

There is for a start the surprising lack of a book on IBM,

creator of computer systems, manufacturer and marketeer; a book which concentrates on what IBM is really about.

There is an attempt by this writer to put together a history of computing, an attempt which foundered after some months of work simply because he could not see a market large enough to support the effort and time that would be involved in finishing the research and writing it up. Some of the results of that research have, however, found a home in Chapters 2, 3 and 4.

As a work specifically concerned with IBM, the book's origins lie in a period of convalescence I had to endure in the autumn of 1973. I was under instructions to take it easy: superfluous instructions as I was at the time incapable of doing anything else. That summer, legal processes had led to a massive release of IBM internal papers into the public domain there were, for instance, nearly three thousand pages of IBM management committee's minutes.

Checking through these alone had seemed a daunting proposition: however, I now had the time. I managed to lay my hands on some of them in London, and started reading. I thought they would tell me quite a lot about the internal workings of IBM: I was right. Here laid out before me was the rationale which underlay many IBM actions, rationale often totally unsuspected—at least by me, and it is my job to know what goes on in the computer industry.

It is from that initial reading that this particular book stems. Originally I had intended to write about IBM purely (sic) as revealed by the Papers, but it soon became apparent that there was a much larger story to tell. To write about IBM in any meaningful way would lead me to use material not found in the Papers themselves. The end result is that it is this other material which forms the bulk of this book. To assemble it, I have not just had to go back through my files and clippings, I have also trespassed on the time and patience of many people, both in Europe and America. I have used the material acquired during many visits to the USA (three of which were made especially for these pages), have travelled well over forty thousand miles, and have over a hundred hours of interviews on tape, mostly with IBM executives both past and present, but also with civil servants, lawyers, politicians, executives in other companies involved in the computing industry, and fellow IBM-watchers, of whom there are many.

I have had to be careful with some of my IBM friends, and with those IBM acquaintances with whom IBM management know I have had dealings in the past. Indeed, in many cases because the executives and I have met through the auspices of IBM, I have gone out of my way to avoid discussing the corporation with them: I have no wish to put their livelihood at stake. If any of them should find this book a surprise, I hope that they will not think I have abused any of their confidences of the past.

I am grateful however to the other senior people in IBM—past and present—who, taking due precaution, have talked to me.

Most of the research is original: I have relied on few books and clippings by others. I have however drawn extensively on material written over the years for such outlets as the BBC, *The Financial Times*, the *New Scientist*, *The Observer*, *The Guardian*, *Computer Weekly*, *Computer Digest*, *Computable*, *01 Informatique*, *Data Systems*, and many more, some of them unfortunately now defunct.

I have used few references from other journalists, and where I have done so they are attributed in the text. I have, however, made extensive use of legal documents; trial transcripts, depositions entered in evidence, judgements and appeal documents prepared by the various parties in a number of cases, among them the cases of the Justice Department, Control Data Corporation, the Greyhound Computer Corporation, Telex Computer Products, all versus IBM, and the judgement given in the patent suit between Honeywell and Sperry Rand.

Finally, I must discuss my use of human sources. In a book relying so much on excerpts from a large number of interviews and discussions, some of them going back many years and most of them unattributed, it is necessary to explain why, and how, the quotations were selected.

It was important from the start that those being interviewed were promised anonymity where they wanted it: and nearly all did so. The reason is to be found in IBM's ability to influence their employment or promotion prospects, either current or future. As I did not wish to put any of my sources at risk, anonymity was a necessary precaution.

But I was faced with a set of problems which arose from the

promise of anonymity. This can lead to a situation where the writer becomes the repository for a lot of hitherto suppressed bitterness, hostility, and animosity. Except where I had relied on the judgement of my source in the past, I used an interviewing technique which has served me well over the years (and not only me), interspersing the discussion with an interest in the relationship of the interviewee with IBM, his present and former bosses, his frame of mind, his rationale for talking at all, and his general well-being. All these helped to provide guides to motivation, and thus an indication of the calibre of the material I was receiving.

Where there was doubt, I cut it out. Regretfully I have had to leave out many good stories—some of which threw light on important areas of IBM—simply because the motives behind them were suspect, and the stories were not supportable, though they might well be true. In most of the substantive matters I have used the quotation giving me the consensus of agreement, if not necessarily the one from the most senior employee or former employee. What was surprising was the degree of agreement I obtained, and how personally marked former employees had been by IBM, a company they will all willingly talk about. There has been no tampering with the substance of any of these quotations, though sometimes I have removed identifying data, or altered it. (So that if anyone in IBM Corporate wishes to identify someone who, the indications are, is in Tomsk, it may well be that the person concerned is actually in Minsk. But since this was purposefully done without regularity, he may well be in Tomsk after all.)

I am grateful for the help and encouragement received from many sources. Jim Bonnett, Managing Director of EDP Europa, and Christopher Hipwell, Editor of *Computer Weekly*, both gave me help in providing access to material of record, some of which I had missed or forgotten. Otherwise I wish to acknowledge the help of the following who read the manuscript in whole or in part—and at various stages: Ted Schoeters, joint editor of the Technology Pages of *The Financial Times*, Pearce Wright, Science Correspondent of *The Times* and a former European Editor of *Datamation*, Dr Herbert Grosch, formerly of IBM and the National Bureau of Standards, Washington D.C., and at the time of writing Editor in Chief of *Computerworld*, and Paul Armer, former head of computation at the RAND Corporation, and an ex-President of the American Federation of Information Processing Societies. The last two in particular allowed me to raid their memories. It should be unnecessary to add that the fact that they read the manuscript in whole or in part does not imply that they approved its contents. But no doubt it is necessary to so write. More important, they saved me at times from making critical mistakes, particularly of interpretation.

It should also be unnecessary to state that this book was written without the help, cooperation or encouragement of IBM, which, from what I gathered during the course of my research and writing, would have been much happier had I chosen to look at some other corporation. As for the material, I am of course grateful to IBM, if grateful is the word I want, for providing it, though I would have been much happier had I been able to come to different conclusions.

Lastly, much of the material, particularly in Part One, is replete with numbers: references to machines, pieces of equipment and calculations concerned with cash and profit. The second will be easier to cope with than the first, but neither unfortunately is avoidable if the story is to be properly understood.

It will help to think of those numbers as characters. I know I do. For to think of numbers as characters is perhaps a good preparation for the future that many of IBM's machines make, not simply possible, but likely.

For those who wish for a lighter start, I would suggest beginning with the prologues and chapter one, and then going on to chapter eight, and continuing from there. Which may give them the strength to come back to the beginning to see how it is really done.

Rex Malik
Nassau, The Bahamas, March 1975.

Prologue One

The theme of the 1972 IBM World Trade systems engineers' sym-
posium held in Amsterdam—some 2,000 IBM employees attending   was 'The Social Role of IBM' The then President of IBM
World Trade, Jacques Maisonrouge, the token European in the
ranks of IBM senior management (now chairman of IBM World
Trade, Europe/Middle East/Africa, which in 1973 grossed
around $3,400 million) spoke on the future role of IBM in the
developing countries, and of how IBM might help in the education
of their populations.

Monsieur Maisonrouge normally speaks flawless, if
Americanised English. Indeed, his control is such that he can
play-act at will: he can become more American, or more
French—and thus more European—according to the audience
he is facing. However, at one point in his speech, his subconscious
seemingly took over. What it is thought he meant to say was: 'We
shall send in IBM teams.' What he actually said was: 'We shall
send in IBM troops.'

A minority of his audience laughed or groaned, according to
their temperament; mostly, as sources present indicate, an
irreverent minority of Englishmen and Frenchmen. The majority
response, however, was enthusiastic; indeed, the sentiments were
loudly cheered and applauded. Nobody has recorded the composition of that enthusiastic majority; however, as the turnover of
IBM Germany was roughly $1,700 million in 1973,* a substantial
number must have come from there. (IBM seem to bring out what
outsiders sometimes feel is the worst in the German character.)

*This should not be construed as if IBM Germany has half IBM's external European
sales. There is much intercompany billing between the subsidiaries, and IBM Germany
is a major supplier to the rest of IBM World Trade.

Prologue One

This is the story of the background which led to that Freudian slip, the rise during the sixties and early seventies of the world's most overvalued and richest manufacturing corporation, a corporation at the heart of a creation/usage industry which is now taking a substantial and steadily growing percentage of Gross National Product of the industrialised countries, providing products and services on which all major organisations are now critically dependent*: the most vertically concentrated and well organised—some would say over-organised—corporation in history.

This is the tale of how IBM became a major force in our lives; of its rise to power and riches, and of the changes that happened in IBM during that time, changes which Lord Acton for one would have recognised and understood.

* 2% of gross is not unusual in major corporations. At the governmental level, the percentage is higher: U.S. Federal computing expenditure is now (1973–4) around $6 billion a year.

Prologue Two

UNITED STATES GOVERNMENT
Memorandum
DEPARTMENT OF JUSTICE

To: Files   DATE: October 30, 1970

                                 FILE: 60-235-38

FROM: Burton R. Thorman, Assistant Chief,
            Special Litigation Section

SUBJECT: U. S. v. IBM

    A xerox copy of the following document was found by me on
October 29, 1970 in the files of R. A. Pfeiffer, IBM Director of
Marketing. A stamp indicated it was a "CSM Study" not to be
reproduced. The initials "HAF" are probably those of Hillary
[sic] F. Faw, IBM Director of Business Practices, part of the corporate staff. Text follows:

HAF   11/21/69

Thoughts for Consideration

The liability of IBM's risk lease is dependent on price leadership and price control.

By means of price leadership, IBM has established the value of data processing usage.

IBM then maintains or controls that value by various means: (timing of new technology insertion; functional pricing; coordinated management of delivery; support services and inventory; refusal to market surplus used equipment; refusal to discount for age or for quantity; strategic location of function in boxes; "solution selling" rather than hardware selling; refusal to support subsequent use hardware, etc.

Unbundling has created a new threat to IBM's price control.

By eliminating fixed price solution selling of hardware eventually leading to increased price competition.

Functional pricing already under pressure because of OEM activity. Unbundling will increase that pressure.

Equalization of subsequent use adds value to existing third party inventories.

Seriously reduced capability to maintain
[This is pencilled in. Couldn't decipher.] ahead of supply.

Legal problems are emerging as a result of certain practices which are key underpinnings to price control.

Refusal to market used machines and parts.
Refusal to sell bills of material.
Maintenance parts prices.

The key underpinnings to our control of price are interrelated and interdependent. One cannot be charged without impacting others.

These interrelationships are not well or widely understood by IBM Management. Our price control has been sufficiently absolute to render unnecessary direct management involvement in the means,
[the next five or so lines were deleted from document].

The D. J. Complaint specifically covers varying profit margins and an intensive investigation of this issue would reveal the extent of our price control and its supporting practices. Such a revelation would not be helpful to our monopoly defense.

If IBM's price control is seriously threatened, either from the market or (because of unbundling) or from legal exposure (because of the supporting practices) or from the D. J. (because of demands for remedy) It Is necessary that IBM Management fully understand its import in order to decide.

　　Negotiations' strategy with D. J.
good vs. bad practices remedies
good vs. bad structural remedies (or)
decision to litigate.

Pricing Approach to New Systems.

　　Reduction of Legal Risk relating to practices.

Recommendation

　　Assemble a small, knowledgeable, secure group to think through these issues, particularly in their interrelationships—define the emerging environment and the various new forces which indicate significant new change—and map the rudimentary elements of strategy or alternative strategies for consideration by Management.

It is to be noted that the deleted portion above probably is based on a claim of privilege, counsel's usual basis for excluding material.

A xerox copy of the document has been ordered.

　　[Bold emphases are mine. R. M.]

Prologue Two

This document was first found in IBM files during the processes of legal discovery in the four-year-long (December 1968–January 1973) Control Data Corporation versus IBM anti-trust suit, a suit which was settled out of court in CDC's favour (see page 66*ff*). During that case, its admissibility was surrounded by much legal argument. However, it was reproduced in the Telex trial brief for the Telex versus IBM anti-trust suit, and has been entered in evidence in the case of U.S. (Anti-trust division, Justice Department) versus IBM.

The initials 'CSM' stand for Cravath, Swaine and Moore, a well known New York law firm, who has long been IBM's main outside counsel. CSM is deeply embedded in IBM's internal workings, to a far greater degree than one suspects was ever envisaged when the doctrine was established that client–counsel relationships are privileged. CSM has done well out of IBM, so much so that at one time some of its partners were thought to be considering setting up a separate law firm just to handle IBM's business.

CSM. speaking for IBM, has talked of Hilary Faw playing the role of 'devil's advocate' and has tried to have many of the documents prepared during the course of the study referred to in this Justice Department Memorandum declared 'legal work product', thus bringing them under client–counsel privilege and extending it even further, even though Faw is not a lawyer.

There were five CSM study teams—or, in IBM nomenclature, 'Task Forces'—set up, beginning back in 1962 and extending through into 1970. They were basically teams of lawyers and IBM executives charged with looking at the anti-trust implications of IBM practices. It is believed that one of the reasons that Cravath, Swaine and Moore reacted so huffily after the initial Telex Case judgement went against them was because the practices of which IBM had been found guilty were practices that one task force in particular—and thus Cravath, Swaine and Moore—had indicated they could get away with (though no doubt they did not state it as crudely as that).

The 'Faw Memorandum', as it has become known, was associated with CSM Task Force V. The memorandum is interesting not just because of its cool approach and the way it clearly spells out exactly what the problems are and how they are caused, but also because of the reputation, expertise and past history of the man who wrote it.

Hilary Faw joined IBM in 1946, was in its senior echelons throughout most of the early sixties, and was passed over into one rank below during the middle to late sixties. He was a protégé of A. L. Williams, a former IBM President (see Chapter 8), was for a time Controller, and seemed headed for the top. The controller is a key and senior member of the corporate financial staff; the post is a jumping-off point for a senior vice-presidency at least, and for the role of chief financial officer, a position till recently held by Paul Rizzo, who came up by this route, and has now gone on to even higher things.

Then bad luck set in: in 1963/64, before the 360 Series was announced, things started to go wrong for Faw, including ill health: Faw dropped out. When he returned, he had lost his position in the mainstream and was shunted sideways. (In the annual report for 1973 he was listed as Assistant Treasurer, a post he has held for some years.) Faw, according to some of those who have known him, is essentially a shy man, a quiet man with a considerable intellect and, as important, honesty and commonsense. ('How on earth he ever got mixed up with that galère,' says one who has known him for many years, 'I shall never understand.')

When Faw returned he was for a time heading what was known internally as 'Faw's Stable'. From it have come many of IBM's current senior financial men, including its present controller, and the senior financial executives in the Data Processing Division and the European part of IBM World Trade.

The point of all this is that in the idiom current at the time of writing, Faw is a man who tells it like it is. And, as will be shown, the situation covered by the memorandum at the time of writing was precisely as described.

In his deposition in the case of Control Data Corporation versus IBM (see Chapters 5 and 14), Hilary Faw was questioned about the document's origins and indicated that it was an introductory instruction to the CSM task force. With blatantly leading questioning, counsel for IBM made sure that Hilary Faw answered correctly by getting him to agree that the memorandum was prepared in contemplation that there would be a task force. It could now be declared legal work product, though as the terms of the memorandum make clear, to consider it as such is stretching credulity a little far, even for lawyers. One can make the point even more forcefully: how can counsel, supposedly officers of the court, faced with a document containing virtually a litany of every practice at some time or other adjudged illegal under American anti-trust laws, have any option but to tell their client that he is breaking the law and that his practices should cease forthwith. If any such advice was given it was not acted upon, as subsequent events make clear.

There is, however, another possible explanation: through indiscretions of senior IBM corporate officials in early 1970 it became apparent then that IBM was considering settling its suit with the Justice Department and entering into another Consent Decree (see Chapter 14). In the light of this, the task force is thought to have had a different brief: it was to explore how a settlement could be made which would satisfy the Justice Department without affecting IBM's ability to control those same prices. It appears that this task might have been assigned to Faw to handle—which is not, however, something that can be said in court.

PART ONE

The Defendant

CHAPTER ONE

In the Beginning

A provision in American law allows parties in a suit to appear before a court after judgement has been given in order to try to make the Court change its mind. They can then argue the relevance of the Court's findings of fact and of law, and the resultant judgement.

On 16th October 1973, the United States District Court for the Northern District of Oklahoma, Tulsa, Judge Sherman A. Christensen presiding, heard such argument. The case had been one in which the Telex Corporation of Tulsa and its major subsidiary, Telex Computer Products Inc., had sued the IBM Corporation under the Sherman and Clayton Anti-Trust Acts, alleging monopolistic and predatory commercial practices, which practices IBM had denied. IBM had counterclaimed that Telex stole IBM trade secrets and copyrights, which Telex had in turn denied.

These were the central issues. The trial began on 16th April 1973 and lasted twenty-nine days; a hundred-and-sixteen days later a judgement was given. The Judge put a stop to most of the practices complained of by both sides, and granted legal injunctions accordingly. He then awarded the plaintiff, Telex, $325 million, and the defendant, IBM, $21,193,776.

That $325 million award was the largest sum ever awarded in American anti-trust legal history. It was a dubious distinction for IBM, and though the Judge was to change his mind and later reduce the award to $259·5 million, the revised award was still to be the largest ever made.

3

But it was not the only precedent that IBM established. The trial brought the biggest release into the public domain in history of any corporation's senior corporate confidential documents. Now popularly known as 'The IBM Papers' (and not, as M. Maisonrouge refers to them in a typical piece of IBM ellipsis, the Telex Papers), they contain the majority of the minutes of the two top IBM corporate committees for nearly four years, hosts of product assessments and reports, planning and financial documents, presentations to management on a wide range of topics, letters, memoranda and the like. These document many of IBM's past and present practices and give some insight into some of its future intentions. They serve here a very useful purpose: they make it possible to document and contrast the argument over findings with the material that was in evidence at the trial.

That a document was in evidence does not mean to say that it was much debated or relied upon: the trial was fought over quite narrow territory, and the findings stage restricts the argument even further to the issues that the judge has ruled on. However, here we need face no such restriction. What should interest us is the truth, not only the law, for the two may not necessarily be concomitant.

The argument on that October day was being put forward for IBM by Mr Nicholas de B. Katzenbach, IBM's Chief Counsel, a Vice-President and Director of the Corporation. Mr Katzenbach has considerable legal prestige: he succeeded Robert Kennedy as President Johnson's Attorney General, thus becoming the leading law officer in American Government. (Indeed, he was Attorney General when the investigation of IBM which led to the current U.S. Justice Department v. IBM anti-trust suit began.)

The Court was well aware of his prestige, and much of the time the Judge was most complimentary—and deferent—to Mr Katzenbach, his position, and his undoubted legal skills.

It was Mr Katzenbach's first court-room appearance in the case: a calculated appearance, for he did not make it without a really impressive audience. The key personalities of IBM (and their flunkeys) were present in court in large number. The psychological sandbagging of the judge was in full swing. Attempts to influence judges in this way are legitimate, at least in the sense that there is no law to cope with them. If the Judge is to continue to rule against IBM, then let him do so in front of the leaders of that hitherto most admired, rich and powerful corporation.

IBM had clearly not expected to lose the first round: it tried to make sure that it did not lose the next. Mr Katzenbach came to court, bringing all his considerable prestige, to try to recover as much as possible.

He said several things that day which are worthy of notice, including: 'I did sit in and do sit in on the decisions of top management. I do know what is presented there.'

Even had he not said so, the IBM DP (Data Processing) Group Financial Procedures Manual, which was in evidence, stated it for him: 'The IBM Vice President and General Counsel (Legal Staff) is to review pricing policy, the pricing of products and services and any changes thereto, to determine their compatibility with the Consent Decree and the anti-trust laws in general.'

Thus, whatever had been going on, Mr Katzenbach could not plead ignorance nor take the other tack, that 'counsel was misled by client'.

Mr Katzenbach also stated: 'When one acts against one's own self-interest in the normal competitive situation, one's own self-interest, that is if one prices below costs to take a very clear example, it seems to me *that in and of itself given any kind of position is predatory.*' [Italics added.]

Mr Katzenbach was saying that if you price a product at less than it cost you to make, and if you do this because it is the way you are going to be able to sell it in competition with someone else's product, then this conduct is such that it contravenes the anti-trust laws; you are trying unfairly to poach business which should be going to your competitors.

Among the trial exhibits was an 'IBM Confidential' document entitled 'Grey Book Management Summary Update', April 1st 1970. The Grey Books are company product 'bibles'; each major product will have one. Grey Book circulation is restricted in IBM: they list what the product is to do, the expected numbers that IBM expects to shift, how the product compares with others on offer by IBM and other companies, the component parts, IBM's cost data, forecast earnings, profit expected from the product, and the like. This is obviously confidential information in any company. It is obviously also the type of material a court would like to see introduced in any monopoly case.

The Management summary updates are a collection of basic

data from all current Grey Books dealing with announced and on-the-market product: they are summaries of revenue and expected profit.

Page 11 of that April 1970 summary deals with a computer system known as the 360/67. It is an atypical case in IBM's history; however, Mr Katzenbach's remarks were all-embracing, there can be no exceptions, atypical or not.

Latest Financial Projection: Million $

Unit	Revenue	Profit	Per Cent
CPU (Central Processor Unit)	$ 30·1	$(78·0)	(258·8)
Reader/Punch	1·3	0·4	30·1
Printers & Controls	5·0	1·9	37·5
Files & Controls	19·5	4·9	25·2
Tapes & Controls	7·9	2·8	35·6
Channel	13·6	3·1	23·0
Storage	35·7	17·5	49·1
Other	7·2	(2·0)	(27·8)
Total System	$120·3	$(49·4)	(41·1)

New Build Quantity.   31.

The brackets indicate a projected loss over the total life of the product of $49·4 million: that it is over the total life of the product can be established from what Mr Katzenbach said: '. . . The financial analysis of *every product* is subjected to precisely the same process and the same standards in order to project revenue costs and profit *for its entire life*.' [Italics added.]

To make sure there was no misunderstanding, he also said elsewhere: '. . . every product not only has to be estimated to make a profit, but it has to carry its full share of direct and indirect costs associated with it . . .'

There is a viewpoint which would state that to make the case absolutely watertight, one would need the initial forecasts and those would have to show that IBM initially expected to make a loss. I do not have them, but it is not as essential as that line of argument might seem to indicate.* The thrust of Mr Katzen-

---

* However, estimates of the initial figures were introduced in the Justice Suit.

bach's remarks is that every product will make a profit. The thrust of the IBM forecasting and costing methodology is that management is continually kept informed of the situation: the remedy, if IBM is to live up to its protestations in court, is to raise prices, and that remedy has been available to IBM at any time in the life of the programme, some four years of it. IBM has chosen not to do so. Indeed, the 360/67 is a classic example of a blocking move aimed mainly at keeping competition out of a sector of the market in which the competition is technologically stronger. IBM 360/67s sat around customers' premises, the customers obtaining minimal use and IBM obtaining no rent because the software to make the system work was not available. As a result many of IBM's orders were eventually cancelled. However, during the time the 360/67 system was on the premises, other would-be competitors were locked out of this market sector.

But IBM is in no position to alter substantially the bases on which it will charge for the various parts of the system. While the 67 programme is in progress, other manufacturers are charging that IBM has prematurely gone into parts of the computer market for which it is ill equipped, at prices which are unrealistic. Any changes in rentals, then, not in line with inflation or an improved performance would be an admission that this is true, and not exactly helpful to a defense against a charge of 'monopoly'.

The projections, however, reveal another IBM practice: the tendency of IBM, at the time, to underprice the computer proper (the CPU) and recoup through the units that surround it, particularly storage. It's a classic example of the loss leader. The expected revenue on storage is greater than that on the CPU, and for that there is a further reason: IBM, whether by technological inability to solve the problems involved or by management initiative, will have software created which requires extensive storage. Consequently the user's storage requirements will be way out of line with those he would probably have incurred had he obtained a system of similar performance from elsewhere. The emphasis of IBM's data processing sales force has always been on what they call 'shifting iron', and software which requires twice as much storage to achieve the same ends is as good a method as any of shifting it.

None of this was mentioned by Mr Katzenbach. What he did was generally to try to obscure the real pricing and costing issues

by a discussion of the time products will stay out on the market:
'. . . if you overestimate the rental life, the average rental life, then
what was envisioned as a profitable programme can become less
profitable, and if the product stays out on rent longer than you
expected, then it will become more profitable.'

Page 43 of the IBM System 370/165 Grey Book, dated
January 1971 (this is for a major product: the second largest computer system in IBM's then range) shows the following:

Forecast Rental Life	54·9 months
Pricing Life	48·0 months
Physical Life	12·0 years
Economic Life	90·0 months
Committee Rental Life	72·0 months.

The key to these is simple; the explanation is easy to check by
reference to the IBM DP Group Financial Procedures Manual
which is in evidence. The two key 'lives' are forecast rental life and
pricing life.

The manual describes the difference between them: 'Any
difference between the two is caused by judgemental factors
which may enter into the final resolution of a rental pricing life.'
What the manual does not state is that there is one critical
difference between the two. IBM will calculate a price covering
both costs and profit over the shorter of the two periods, the
pricing life; a price which will be presented to management in
terms of so many months' rental at so many dollars a month.
Management will take that monthly rental and build on it.

The judgemental factors are a simple way of stating that
forecast life is an estimate honestly arrived at from the figures by
low echelons; pricing life is the figure arrived at by top management taking into account what they think the market will bear, the
cost of competitive equipment, and how the equipment compares
on a price performance basis with other IBM product of greater
or lesser capability. In producing a project primarily for a rental
market, one obviously does not wish to destroy those one has on
the market already, at least not until one is ready to do so.

However, that is still not the rental that IBM will obtain. For that you have to go to the committee rental life: the time the average machine of a given type will be out on the market before IBM starts to replace it. As for economic life, that will determine how long IBM will be prepared to support such a machine, a measure of importance to those who have bought, instead of renting, it.

IBM has every intention of replacing that equipment. The timing is indicated in the Committee Rental Life estimates which, the manual states, is 'the time that the Economic and Rental life committee estimates the average machine of a given type will be on rental.'

What we have is a situation in which IBM costs and obtains a fair profit on a computer system over 48 months; a system which it expects to stay out for at least 72 months before replacement. The actual life, were IBM not to produce an 'improvement', would in fact be 144 months.

It is on this sort of basis that IBM's profits are earned, a remarkable whirlygig in which those who rent IBM's computer systems are often paying inordinately highly for the privilege of the dividends and stock growth they expect to receive, for, as we shall see, many of IBM's customers are also its own shareholders. It is this income above and beyond the forecasts which will in part give IBM the power and resources to go on to develop the systems which will obsolesce the product the Grey Book discusses. In other words, those users/shareholders are paying out more than they should for the privilege of eventually paying out even more. Naturally, Mr Katzenbach did not mention this. Instead, he went on to say the following: '. . . Most of the costs on a product, most of the costs are incurred before any revenue at all is produced and then you have to wait overtime to get back the investment that you made in that product.' Apart from the fact that this is not strictly true, since IBM 'front loads' its costs, i.e. it tries to recover as much cost as possible in the early life of a product, it also gives an impression of hundreds of millions of dollars being gambled, of financial risk of a high order. And that is nonsense. The Grey Book for the 370/165, page 36, shows otherwise (see next page).

This indicates that IBM's direct cash contribution to the development of the 370/165 will total some $50+ millions over two-and-a-half years before revenue begins to outstrip expenditure. During that time IBM will gross over $25 billion, and at no

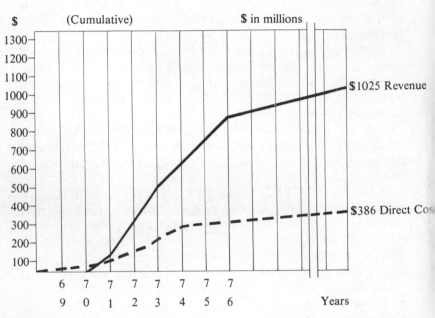

System 370
CPU
Program Turn Around Analysis
Revenue/Direct Cost—(Cash Contribution)

REGISTERED IBM CONFIDENTIAL

time will IBM have at risk more than $40 million, some 0·4% of its then annual revenue, on this product. It might be argued that this could be said of any company, but it is not so. IBM's production costs as a percentage of total revenues are, as we shall see, almost trivial. Indeed, IBM probably has the lowest such costs of any complex technology producer anywhere.

What the above does not show is how much IBM expects to make from this product. A System 370 Financial Analysis prepared on 8th June 1970 and presented to IBM's Management

Review Committee (see Chapter 9, p. 228) gives the following analysis:

($ millions)

	Rev.	Profit	%	Accpts.
NS2-CPU & Mem.	$ 3453	$1340	38·8	3234
553-CPU & Mem.	2201	623	28·3	963
Console Printer	122	33	27·0	16027
2000-LPM Printer	704	200	28·4	5514
Merlin File	4452	1589	35·7	16205
Total	$10932	$3785	34·6	

This was prepared for the Series 370 announcement. It shows the expectations for the two new large IBM systems, the 155 and the 165, here disguised as the NS2-CPU with Memory and the 553-CPU with Memory. It becomes quite obvious that for the expected rewards, the IBM outflow is miniscule, that IBM is in an almost no-risk situation. Of course, it all depends how those figures are interpreted, and what IBM's full and total costs are . . .

During Mr Katzenbach's presence, the argument over pricing and its relationship to costing was to take up much of the court's time. And it led to the following remarkable exchange between Mr Katzenbach and the Judge [referred to throughout the transcript as 'The Court'].

The Court: Would it be feasible . . . for you to refrain as between boxes, peripherals and integrations—to refrain from intentionally establishing a differential that would accomplish a market advantage?

Mr Katzenbach: Yes, Your Honour; between the integrated product . . . [deletion of technical terms] . . . and the same box on the outside.

The Court: Yes.

Mr Katzenbach: Yes, Your Honour, it would be possible—

The Court: In other words, you do pricing all the time, and you do a wonderful job, and you try to have each product carry its weight—

Mr Katzenbach: Right.

The Court: —together with a reasonable profit margin.

Mr Katzenbach: Yes Sir.

The Court: And you're constantly engaged in that, and it isn't a hit and miss, as we discussed before, and you know when you're simply adding a loading factor on for some extraneous purpose.

Mr Katzenbach: Yes, Your Honour, I—

The Court: You should know that and you should bear the consequences of failing to heed it, if there is an injunction which prevents you from failing to heed it.

Mr Katzenbach: It would be possible, Your Honour, to attempt—and the decree used actual costs, and I assume, on that the word 'estimate'—

The Court: It would be a fair, good faith—

Mr Katzenbach: Fair estimation.

The Court: Approximation.

Mr Katzenbach: You could, with such products, attempt to price to the same profit margin on each product.

The Court: Yes.

Mr Katzenbach: I would be less than candid with the Court if I said I thought you could achieve it.

It may be that this dialogue is a little too obscure to take in quickly, but what it indicated was this. Mr Katzenbach began by agreeing with the Judge that yes, IBM could so price its products that each showed a similar profit percentage, but as soon as the discussion progressed he realised the implications. For the heart of the Telex case was that IBM selectively and specifically priced so as to injure its competition. IBM was not simply trying to compete: it was using the price–profit ratios to put its competitors out of business.

But what makes a man wriggle so? For in less than a couple of minutes, Mr Katzenbach stated that IBM is both competent and incompetent, and that in precisely the same area: pricing. What is it that put Mr Katzenbach into a position that, however hard he may try, the language he uses in court and the evidence can exist side by side in such flagrant contradiction? A former distinguished Professor of Law (Harvard), one might well think, would have more respect for the content of language than to betray it at its most basic: that he should try to pull Humpty Dumpty's trick in *Alice Through the Looking Glass:* 'When I use a word, it means precisely what I want it to mean, neither more nor less.'

Is it just money, the mores of the particular side of the American legal profession he has chosen, the character of the man—and the company he is keeping—or is there more?

Is there perhaps more, within the specific context: perhaps a recognition that though IBM's position is in equity indefensible, equity has little to do with the law, or the reality of the marketplace, and that while it may have mattered what was said in that courtroom, it did not matter that much. For IBM had the legal* and financial resources to be able to stretch the case out to suit its convenience: it had done so before, and no doubt noticed the competitive benefits.

It was quite prepared to stretch this—and any other case—out again, using every legal trick that came to hand (and why, if the law is an ass, should IBM not take advantage of it?). And, perhaps as important, Mr Katzenbach knew quite well what his masters sitting in that courtroom would have to say back within

---

* After all, that senior partner of Cravath, Swaine and Moore, Judge Bromley, former honorary IBM director and member of IBM's advisory board, and long-time legal adviser to IBM in its dealings with anti-trust law, has said—in respect of another case—the following: 'Now I was born I think to be a protractor... I quickly realised in my early days at the bar that I could take the simplest anti-trust case that Judge Hansen could think of and protract it for the defense almost to infinity... If you will look at that record (*United States v. Bethlehem Steel*), you will see immediately the Bromley protractor touch in the third line. Promptly after the answer was filed I served a quite comprehensive set of interrogatories on the Government. I said to myself, "That'll tie brother Hansen up for a while," and I went about other business.'

the sanitised sanctity of their own corporate offices to anyone seriously putting forward proposals for equal profit on all products. The ability to manipulate prices has been behind the rise of IBM—it is one of its major weapons, and everybody in Corporate who matters knows it.

Why, after all, should Mr Katzenbach not know Corporate reactions? As he has said and the evidence has already made clear, no major pricing decision is ever made without Mr Katzenbach—or whoever is IBM General House Counsel—being present.

But what is wrong in IBM's position, what is there that, at its mildest, is open to doubt, that should lead it into a situation where management is likely to have to devote much of its time to the problem of legal challenge?

For, as this book is being written, IBM faces probably more anti-trust actions than have ever been brought against any company at any time. IBM has waived the statute of limitations in a number of suits, so that the corporations concerned can see how the courts treat those now before them, before deciding in their turn whether or not they are to bring one of their own.

To understand why this should be so, one must first of all start with a sensible discussion of the computer industry, its antecedents, the markets that IBM was accused of dominating, and how all this came about. The word 'sensible' is carefully chosen, for the development of the computer and the computer industry is surrounded by much mythology and PR 'flackery'.

These are to be expected, for much was and is at stake, and till recently both had seemingly been rewarded with the seal of respectability by the judgement of the courts, whether legal, or of public opinion, neither of which had enough knowledge of the history of the development of the technology to be able to sort out truth from public relations (or fact from fiction, depending on the terminology one wishes to apply).

Why should it have been otherwise? Much of that mythology was carefully created and/or expensively acquired by inventors and computer manufacturers—among them IBM. Naturally enough, in an industry almost totally dependent on a 'new' technology, an industry which from its early days has shown astonishingly high growth rates, the electronic and mechanical expression of the key basic ideas were patentable, and those patents were likely to be worth a lot of money to the holders, both in the short and long terms.*

It can then become, and did become, in the interests of inventors and companies in the field to claim and to try to prove that they and they alone were the father of this, that or the other, and that this, that or the other was and is crucial and critical to the development of computing and the industry, and consequently they should be rewarded accordingly. This claim is worth not just the licence or royalty money that a company may expect to take in or pay out: it is important from the public relations standpoint. There is, and why should there not be, a general respect for experience. That a company had the wit and foresight to somehow develop or acquire key patents at the right time can be turned into a marketable asset and a source of profits.

This has been particularly so within the computer industry and its predecessor, the business machines industry. Indeed, one can say that the development of the industry has been plagued with more than its fair share of patent and patent-licensing arguments and claims (sometimes legal claims, sometimes not) and 'we were first' public relations. The result is that a quarter of a century later most people even in the industry are now no longer sure where fiction ends and fact begins.

* * *

IBM has done more than its fair share of creating myth, and sometimes that myth creation has been compounded by the very companies with which it is in disagreement. Thus in the Telex versus IBM suit, it was agreed by both sides—and accepted by the Court—that a number of statements about the industry were true. It was in the interest of IBM to prove that it had a substantial 'track-record' in the industry, that it was a leader and that its expertise was fairly acquired. If this were so, Telex could then be counter-sued and accused of stealing that expertise, above and beyond the knowhow license it held from IBM. It was in the interest of Telex to agree that IBM was very much the market

---

* After the 'final' granting of the ENIAC computer patents in 1964, for instance, Sperry Rand sought an estimated royalty from Honeywell which would eventually have cost the latter $250 million.

leader, a dominant force, and that while some of its past experience might have been fairly acquired, its size and strength put it into a special position of responsibility. It should not have abused that position.

Both sides called upon the mythology of American history for support. What seemed strikingly apparent from a reading of the trial briefs was a set of shared assumptions, an agreed line, that the computer was an invention which owed everything to native American genius, the free enterprise economic system, and to mores and virtues peculiar to America. The computer was an invention out of Mark Twain, and encompassing in passing Alexander Graham Bell, Thomas Edison, the Wright brothers *et al.:* one was almost surprised that no one dragged in the name of Benjamin Franklin.

It was in effect, said one side, those very American virtues which were being abused. It was also, said the other, those very American virtues which they were trying to defend.

The mythology of American knowhow, Yankee shrewdness and foresight can stand on its own quite effectively without having to be stretched to encompass things which were, and are, manifestly not true. It is necessary to point out that the computer is by no means the unique invention of America and Americans, as seems to be generally believed on both sides of the Atlantic.

The first computer to be put to practical use, the first *working* machine, came out of a totally different society, one with different mores and 'virtues', and, what is more, one which the Yankee inventor, manufacturer and trader of mythology would have found singularly repellent. It was the product of a then ardent Nazi,* ardent to the point that he was a believer in the possibility of the final stand, who went into hiding in 1945 and did not surface to be interrogated till 1948. His name was Konrad Zuse, and he first began to try to build a computer in the mid-thirties. He built four machines, calling them Z1, Z2, Z3 and Z4. Z1 never really worked. Z2 worked after a fashion. Z3 and Z4, however, were different propositions: Z3 was in use in 1941.

As for Z4: 'I built it with the help of the German Aircraft Research Institute. By then I was fully engaged in computing. It

---

* Established in a conversation in 1970 with the former British intelligence officer who carried out his interrogation.

was used extensively in the aircraft industry, as were some other calculating devices I built. Z4, which was destroyed in a bombing raid, was among other things used in the development of the HS 293, a sort of flying bomb carried by an aircraft, which after launching was guided to its target by radio control.

'When I started, I had no connection with any of the literature in the field—with the exception of Leibnitz, and I used his notion of going to binary. I didn't know of Babbage, so I re-invented his idea of programming. I settled on floating point arithmetic early on. I even came up with the notion of a universal algorithmic language very early on—back in 1945. I called it "Plankalkul".'

And just to emphasise the nature of the Zuse accomplishments, he also said: '. . . in 1944, we were running production processes directly from the computer.'*

The early Zuse work was to have no effect at all on the direction and progress of computing in the post-War era, for Zuse's absence and the different path followed in the then West were to make his solutions practically obsolete. Zuse was to return to the computer business in 1950 when he started his own small company in West Germany, a company which was eventually to end up as part of the much larger German computer and electrical/electronics manufacturer, Siemens AG.

It is important to note, however, that Zuse's machines were operational a few years before the ENIAC (Electrical Integrator and Numeric Calculator) of the Moore School of Engineering, University of Pennsylvania, popularly believed to be the first electronic computer, began operations.

It was accepted in America, and till fairly recently in Europe, that the ENIAC was the precursor of today's computers—'till fairly recently' because, in the autumn of 1973, an American Court ruled otherwise. We need not take the part of the judgement concerned with attribution of the invention to another American too seriously, because, as we shall see, in attacking the public's belief that the ENIAC was the first computer and that it was 'invented' by Drs John W. Mauchly and Presper J. Eckert, and in attributing the invention elsewhere, the Court still managed to get it wrong.

---

* The quotations are taken from an interview with the author published in *The New Scientist*, 16th July 1970.

The Court decided that credit belonged to Dr John V. Atasanoff. In the early forties Dr Atasanoff was an Associate Professor at Iowa State College, Ames, Iowa. He had invented a 'computer', some elements of which were working in 1941. It was a machine whose existence was known to Dr Mauchly, who had been to see it in June 1941.

Dr Atasanoff's machine had its origins in problems he faced in 1937, when he wanted to create a machine to solve a specific type of equation known as linear. To do that he had to think through the principles involved and how they might be realised: in other words, the technology that would have to be used.

He plumped for the digital on/off principle known as binary (now at the heart of the present digital computer), and the use of vacuum tubes for his logic circuits: the circuits which give the machine the appearance of 'thinking'. He also plumped for the principle of regenerative memory, the basic technique used in radar to keep the trace on the screen. The problem that faced him was one that faced the computer industry to be for the next ten to fifteen years: there was no electronic store that could hold the data indefinitely without its degradation and disappearance. The trick involved in the regenerative memory was to keep that data cycling around till required.

Dr Mauchly has since commented that the resultant machine bore no relationship to the ENIAC, and Dr Mauchly is right. It was not automatic and it was small, almost desk-top, whereas the ENIAC (of which more later) was a monster, thirty tons of it, with rows and rows of valves, 19,000 of them. But the ENIAC, too, differed from what was to come, and in one respect Atasanoff was on the right lines—a value judgement—where the ENIAC was not. Atasanoff used binary; ENIAC used the more usual base ten notation, the normal human scale for counting.

However, the critical point is, where did all this originate? There is no question that it originated with Charles Babbage. Hence the constant preoccupation of those with an interest in computing history in asking the early twentieth-century workers whether they had read Babbage. Often their reply was that yes, they had, but not till afterwards. This matters in the context of the American computer industry and was to lead to considerable argument over the years and to the filling of lawyers' pockets.

Already, as one can see, the waters are being muddied. Other people had also hit upon the idea of the computer, some contemporaneously, others even earlier, much earlier. Dr Atasanoff put his finger on it when he said: 'Everything has been around a long time, you know. Nobody really invents anything. We all lean on the works of others.'* In fact, Dr Atasanoff is right. It has all been around a long time and was all done before, and that mostly in Europe. The Zuse example gives some indication of this; however, Zuse himself was not the first to think in this way: many had been there before him.

The long tradition of invention in the field of calculation has involved men of wide and diverse background, often philosophers, usually mathematicians, always practical engineers; inventors in the true sense in that they have not simply theorised, they have also tried to build something. And a cussed lot they have been too: intemperate men, argumentative men who took great delight in doing each other down. This was so in the early days: it was also so in the twentieth century and has practical implications.

An arbitrary start must be made somewhere. Perhaps the best time is the seventeenth century, with many workers in the field. In particular two stand out. One is the French philosopher, Blaise Pascal, and his calculator, a machine first exhibited in Paris in 1642. Essentially this was an adding–subtracting machine, coping with multiplication by the addition of the number to be multiplied the correct number of times. The other is that mathematician and political fixer, Wilhelm von Leibnitz. He produced his first calculator in the early 1670s. It included the invention of the stepped wheel, still in widespread use in industry today. The Leibnitz solution followed a more elegant route than Pascal's. It duplicated the normal processes of addition and multiplication as they were (and are) taught in schools, by being able to fetch and carry mechanically, and it had a built-in division capability.

The next advance came from Alsace with Joseph Marie Jacquard's creation, the Jacquard loom. He took the idea of punching holes in tapes and cards and then using them for control, ideas that had been used to work musical boxes and the like, and devised a control system for a loom enabling complex pic-

---

* Interview with *Datamation*, February 1974.

tures to be mechanically woven. He is important here because the holes were punched in cards and this idea was to be taken up—in 1832—by the most ambitious and yet unsuccessful machine creator of them all, the one to have probably the most long-term influence on the direction that computing would take: Charles Babbage, Lucasian Professor of Mathematics at Cambridge (1828 to 1839), a seat at one time previously held by that other remarkable creator, Isaac Newton. Later, too, it was the punch-card route which was to lay the foundations on which IBM was to build its fortunes and eventually its computing business.

Babbage designed two machines: the Difference Engine and the Analytical Engine. The first was a calculating device for mechanically computing and printing tables of mathematical functions, a model of which was demonstrated before the Royal Society in London in 1822. Though the full machine was never completed, the British Government spent some £17,000 on its development, an unprecedented sum for the times. It was an interesting forerunner of the close financial relationships that were to arise between the public purse and computer scientists and industry more than a century later.

In 1832 Babbage developed the Analytical Engine, the true precursor of the computer. He thought of it as an automatic universal computer, one that could handle all kinds of calculations. His technology was very different, however, being dependent upon rods, gears, wheels, and the links between them—yet we still have not moved too far away from the essential Babbage layout. He foresaw a store or memory, an arithmetic unit which he called a mill (now called a central processor), a control unit, and input and output devices. Input was in punched card form, output could take many forms including a direct printing operation. It is to Babbage's proselytising on behalf of the Analytical Engine that we owe the birth of programming. The world's first programmer, Ada, Countess of Lovelace, daughter of Byron, in a translation of a lecture concerned with Babbage's work, proceeded to add notes of her own. And it is to Lady Lovelace that we owe that modern comforting fiction that the computer only does what we tell it; she, however, phrased it with much more elegance: 'The Analytical engine has no pretensions whatsoever to originate anything. It can do whatever we *know how to order it to perform.*' [The italics are her own.]

Babbage died embittered in 1871, with many inventions to his credit, but not a working calculating/computing engine. (It is worth noting here that in his attempt to build it, his engineering demands advanced the state of the art of metal machining considerably, and one can fairly claim on his behalf that he is one of they key progenitors of machine tool industry of today.)

The ideas immanent in the Difference Engine, however, were to be taken up by a Swedish engineer, George Scheutz. Helped by the Swedish Government and the Swedish Academy he was eventually to build two machines. One was to be bought by the Dudley Observatory in Albany, New York; the other, eventually, by the British Government's Registrar General's Office: its job was to be the preparation of life tables.

The Scheutz machine perhaps deserves more importance than it has no far been given by technological historians. The reason concerns usage. Up till the time of the Scheutz machine, calculating machine developments had been aimed at other fields of endeavour, primarily the elimination of drudgery in the preparation of astronomical and navigation data and tables. With Scheutz, one begins to see the application of machines to calculate in more mundane fields, in the routine of administration.

As for Babbage, he was to have little influence on the direction of calculating machine developments until well into the twentieth century. Calculation was to take a different route until the technology available caught up with his ideas: then Babbage was to be much admired.

Babbage, in his *Life of a Philosopher* published in 1864, foresaw that too: 'If unwarned by my example any man shall undertake and shall succeed in really constructing an engine embodying in itself the whole of the executive department of mathematical analysis upon different principles or by simpler mechanical means, I have no fear of leaving my reputaton in his charge, for he alone will be fully able to appreciate the nature of my efforts and the value of their results.'

The next major and practical advance came from a statistician on the staff of the U.S. Bureau of Census, Herman Hollerith. He developed an electrical tabulator which extended some of the ideas present in the existence of the punch card, using the absence and presence of holes to sort and count electrically.

The first Hollerith machine was developed as the result of a competition for a census-taking system, and the early machines were to be used in the analysis of the 1890 U.S. Census. Hollerith went on to be chief engineer of a company called the Computing, Tabulating and Recording Company, IBM's precursor. It was a case of remarkable prescience, for the one thing that Holleriths and the other machines which the company was to sell did not do was to *compute*: instead, they calculated. Indeed, the word computer was a term used to describe the work done by humans: it was a job title for a lowly class of mathematicians (or part of the title of the organisations employing them) who did simple routine calculations. These calculations could not be done by a machine without bringing it to a stop after each sum, feeding in new instructions, repeating the process and so on, until completion. The critical difference then between calculator and human computer or mechanical computer was that the second stored internally the instructions which enabled the steps to be taken, and could execute them without reference to any external agency.

This is closely analogous to the way in which people compute: to calculate is to move step by step, to compute is to come up with the desired answer, whatever that answer may be, by referring to instructions held internally in the memory.

(The difference is critical: to calculate had been a machine function, to compute a human function. Indeed, as Captain Grace Hopper, U.S.N.—the first American programmer in the sense the term is used today—has pointed out, computers came to be called by that name because it was the obvious description of the jobs that the machines were now doing.*

The name change began in the forties with the Automatic Sequence Controlled Calculator, a machine devised by Howard Aitken and built by IBM as a gift for Harvard—where it was known as the Harvard Mk 1. Thoses working with it found themselves almost unconsciously referring to it as a computer, for that was the job it was doing.)

And so we come to the nineteen-thirties and the tangled skein of invention which led to the rise of the computer industry we know.

Arguably the key event took place in 1937; the publication in the Proceedings of the London Mathematical Society of a paper

---

* Conversation with the author.

(written the previous year) by a twenty-five-year-old British graduate student in mathematics, Alan Mathison Turing. The paper was entitled 'On Computable Numbers with an application to the Entscheidungsproblem'. The literal translation of that last word need not concern us. However, what Turing tried to do should, since the paper was to have a profouund influence on the early development of modern computing. It was to excite interest among many mathematicians, for it raised the possibility of replicating human computing processes in machine form.

Perversely, this was not what Turing had set out to do. Following the work of another eminent mathematician, Alonzo Church, he had aimed to counter a then conventionally held view that all mathematical problems were capable of solution. To do that he had to discuss the processes by which problems were solved, and to demonstrate that there were problems which could not be solved by any fixed and definite process. In order to get that far he had to describe such a process. It would have to be universal; there was no point in inventing a process which was not all-inclusive, for if it was not so Turing would not have his proof. But, such a process, to quote Turing, was obviously 'something which could be done by an automatic machine'.

He set out to invent one—a paper 'machine', now known as the Turing Machine. It was a design for a machine he was to call 'universal', in that, when supplied with suitable instructions, it would imitate the behaviour of any other machine. The carrier of those instructions was to be paper tape along which the machine would move.

It was a paper precursor of what was to come. And, interestingly enough, the Turing tests which went with it are still all-encompassing. No one has as yet managed to get around the theoretical limitations that Turing set, and Turing's 'rules' are still the standard by which what is possible is measured.

Turing was soon to go on to Princeton to take his PhD (and to be offered a job by John von Neumann, to be his assistant. Turing was effectively to reply that whatever he was going to do with his life he was not going to start out as anybody's assistant). The Turing paper was to have a marked influence on events. Von Neumann and Turing were to discuss it before the thirties were out, and it is mostly as a result of those conversations that von Neumann was eventually to think through the concept of the stored program, the method by which an electronic computer would hold and call up its own instructions. It is important, however, to remember that von Neumann was not the first. In principle, Babbage, Turing and Zuse had been there before him.

The work on which von Neumann was directly to build was the ENIAC. The ENIAC had begun life as a project to build a large advanced calculator for working out ballistic tables, a subject with which the U.S. Army was vitally concerned, and it was therefore Army financed. The result, the ENIAC, might be faster than any previous calculator then generally known and also be capable of carrying out a wider range of calculations, but it still had great limitations. Unlike today's programs which can be almost infinitely flexible, those for the ENIAC had to be set every time the machine was given something different to do—a laborious process, for initially it meant that the machine had to be altered and differing connections made every time new problems were set up.

In 1944 von Neumann came on the scene. With the Moore School he was given a contract to go further than ENIAC: to design a computer. From this was to come his paper, 'The First Draft Report on the EDVAC', published in 1945, in which the stored programme is spelt out in terms of an *electronic* computer.

Much of this history has been extensively discussed before. However, it has usually been told in black-and-white terms, with the computer springing new-born out of the exigencies of World War II. What has seldom been mentioned is the critical part played in permitting scientists and engineers to do more than think and struggle by events which preceded that war.

As a practical methodology, binary had been around a long time, and the pulse technology while new in computing practice was well understood in radio, radar and communications, understood enough, that is, to enable it to be adapted to computing practice.

Binary around a long time? Forget Leibnitz and Babbage: one does not have to go back as far as that. The notion of the valve as a binary or on/off device had been originally demonstrated in 1919, while in 1929 American General Election researchers had shown that it was possible to use a thyraton valve as a relay, thus making counting practicable.

The further notion that Atasanoff or indeed almost anybody

else was the true and only inventor is now beginning to look increasingly unrealistic. In 1931, an Englishman, Dr Wyn Williams, showed how to count very rapidly using an array of thyraton valves and no moving parts. Moreover, in 1936, contemporaneously almost with Turing's work, William Phillips, a London Chartered Actuary, put forward a paper in which he advocated the   of this technology to achieve counting in binary.

However, hardly anyone listened to them. Zuse and Atasanoff might be using binary,* but the two big machine developments, the ENIAC and the IBM-built Harvard Mk 1, were scale-of-ten, decimal machines. The American version of the truth is that binary or base two as the standard was eventually set by John von Neumann. Rudimentary stored programs, and binary might already have been in use elsewhere; von Neumann was to put together a package and spell out a design framework, an architecture, which was to be with the industry for a long time to come. What von Neumann did was to work out how the data and the instructions could be held in the computer at the same time. And suddenly, one was at the level of a low-order brain: no more would problems have to be laboriously set up from the outside. But all this of course was in theory: practice was still some time off.

In August 1945, the ENIAC team held a conference at the Moore School. The conference brought together experts in computation and calculation to discuss the proposed EDVAC design. IBM was not represented, though not for want of trying. Much of IBM's talent had been involved in military calculation, preparing trajectory tables and the like for the Aberdeen Proving Grounds, the military establishment which had sponsored the ENIAC development. Many of the defence calculating contracts were tied in to Aberdeen and so all the specialists in the field knew that ENIAC was being built. Indeed, one of the Stibitz machines was housed in the same building.

IBM's specialists wrote to Eckert and Mauchly asking if they could send a few people. They got a letter back saying that the

---

* George Stibitz, another 1930's–40's large calculator pioneer—for Bell Laboratories—was to use *bi quinary*, a mixture of 2's and 5's.

conference was not open to manufacturers.*

Turing had had an advance copy of the von Neumann Draft Report on the EDVAC and, being Turing, his immediate reaction was to rethink the proposed design and draft his own version. It was eventually to be a most ambitious version, for Turing's principle was that anything anyone in this field could do, he could do better. Thus, for instance, where the EDVAC design had fifty storage delay lines, the Turing design proposed five hundred.

It is about here that one needs to point out that if one wishes to be formally legalistic (Dr Atasanoff and American Courts notwithstanding), all the critical working firsts in the direct ancestry of current computers originally appeared in Britain. And not only those in the direct ancestry. With the exception of the work of Zuse, and a claim in America by the late Professor Norbert Wiener (popularly known as the father of cybernetics) to have thought up the concept of the stored program computer in 1940 (though nothing came of it), the field was to be bracketed in almost every possible combination by the British. There has been much argument in Britain about who was first; the agreement is that the first operational stored program computer in the direct ancestry of today's machines *was* British.

The cause was Alan Turing, and here one needs to digress from the Moore School Conference. According to his mother, the late Alan Turing had first thought of the idea of a computer—complete with stored program—not long after the paper came out. The claim is unsubstantiated, but largely as a result of the paper tape notions of the 1936 paper, Turing had become involved in the work of the Department of Communications of the British Foreign Office, a euphemism for World War II British cryptoanalysis centre. This was based at Bletchley in Buckinghamshire. The first machine was the 'Heath Robinson', operational in 1940, followed by the 'Peter Robinson' and then the 'Robinson and Cleaver' and the 'Super Robinson': it made use of the Turing notion of a fixed format tape and a data tape, trying to read one against the other: counting was electronic.†

---

* This prohibition was to be got round in the future; most of the participants were eventually to end up as consultants to, or on the payroll of, the computer manufacturers; among them, Eckert and Mauchly with Remington Rand, eventually Sperry Rand UNIVAC, and von Neumann and Goldstine with IBM.

† In the outside world Heath Robinson was a designer and illustrator who 'invented' many natty and funny machines. Peter Robinson and Robinson and Cleaver were famous British department stores.

The Robinsons were nothing to what was to come. The successors, called Colossi, were developed by a team led by a Cambridge logician, Professor M. H. A. Newman. The claim has been made that Newman was inspired by Turing's 1936 work. This is quite possible as the two were close and had, pre-Bletchley, already jointly collaborated on a mathematical paper.

However, it is known that Turing was involved in the design of the Robinson Series, and was one of those providing the requirements for the Colossi. The first Colossus was installed in December 1943, and before the war's end some ten had been brought on site. In many ways the Colossi were similar to the ASSC (Harvard Mk 1) or the ENIAC in that switching functions were performed by valves, about 2,000 of them. Data was entered by punched paper tape where it was worked on by stored patterns (a similar notion to that in the Robinson method. Control was exterior via a plug-in system.

The Colossi were limited machines for a specific purpose, but then so was everything else. And the same thing was to happen to the Bletchley workers as to those involved on the ENIAC: once the war was over, they were generally to go on to work on computer projects elsewhere.

We can now return to that Moore School Conference: though Turing did not attend, one who did was Maurice Wilkes, the newly-appointed head of the Mathematical Laboratory at the University of Cambridge. A distinguished war career in radar had led to his appointment (as had disagreements among those responsible for the appointment about the other possible candidate: Alan Turing).

Wilkes was looking for something to do, and it took him some thought to come to the conclusion that computing might be it: the U.S. trip was exploratory. The Cambridge Laboratory had had some experience with mechanical systems, particularly with a calculating device known as a Differential Analyser. So why not computers?

He arrived late at the conference. He spent the sea journey back to England trying to design a computer, his version of the EDVAC. Meanwhile, separately at the University of Manchester, other ex-Bletchley researchers under M. H. A. Newman were also approaching the stage of devising and building their own machine. It was going to turn out to be a race, one which new participants entered almost every week. The von Neumann Report had really been about principles: in practice, there seemed to be many possible solutions.

The race was to include Bell Laboratories, a group headed by John von Neumann at the Institute of Advanced Study at Princeton, the ENIAC team (but now no longer at the Moore School) and a group at MIT led by Dr Jay Forrester. At the time Forrester was working on a military contract. (It eventually led to the development of what is known as real-time computing, the outcome being the Whirlwind computer, but that is another story.)

In the process Jay Forrester invented and with MIT eventually patented core storage, which was later to be critical in the development of computing. MIT did its financial and legal work well both for itself and the inventor. Most of the early inventors have done handsomely in terms of honours and prestige, sometimes they have done well in terms of salary, stock-options and the like, but Jay Forrester was the only individual to make cash as the direct result of specific invention: otherwise the real monies were to be made later by those exploiting the work of the original inventors.

'But then,' said one of the early participants, 'Jay understood money, and both he and MIT played their cards well. They just sat there quietly and waited till everyone was committed to the type of core storage that he had invented, and then they moved in.' Moving in included filing suits for patent infringement. The one against IBM was filed in 1962 and settled in 1964 with Jay Forrester reputedly getting $10 million for his share plus royalties thereafter. Core storage, in some cases, is still with us.

Alan Turing, meanwhile, was at Britain's National Physical Laboratory and his work was leading to the NPL's own machine, the 'Pilot Ace', which was eventually to be used in the design of the wings of the first commercial jet aircraft, the De Havilland Comet.

Not until 1950 was Pilot Ace operational. It was preceded by both the Manchester MADM and Cambridge EDSAC computers. From the Manchester machine was to stem the world's first commercial computer offering, by Ferranti Limited of Wythenshawe near Manchester, and for a time Dr H. Bowden (now Lord Bowden) had the distinction of being the world's only official commercial computer salesman; a sales force, as he has said, then outnumbered even by that of the British lighthouse manufacturing industry, which employed two representatives.

So advanced was the work in computing in Britain that when Ferranti sent a consultant, Dr Prinz (the first man to write a computer chess program), to look at the progress of work in America, wherever he went he was told to go back to look at the work being done in Manchester University, only a few miles away from Ferranti's head office: so advanced that within a short time, Dr F. C. Williams of the Manchester MADM team was to be employed by IBM as a consultant.

The development that stemmed from the Cambridge machine was even more striking. From it came LEO, the Lyons Electronic Office, the first computer ever installed in a commercial office setting, becoming operational in January 1954, at the head office of Lyons Ltd in London. In terms of operation, it preceded the first UNIVAC commercial installation by some six months, and the first IBM by even more.

From Ace was to stem Deuce, the computer which took Britain's English Electric into the computer business, its operations now being part of International Computers Ltd.

Meanwhile, back in America, what of the work of the ENIAC team? During the autumn of 1944 Eckert and Mauchly had discussed the prospects of creating commercial versions of the ENIAC with potential customers. They were in an odd situation. Though ENIAC had been publicly funded through an Army Ordnance contract which required the University of Pennsylvania to grant a royalty-free license on all patents arising from the work done, the University had not made an assignment agreement with Eckert and Mauchly and so was not in a position to grant such a licence to anyone wanting it. The 'inventors' were in a good position then to exploit their invention—or so it seemed.

Eckert and Mauchly resigned from the University of Pennsylvania at the end of March 1946, with the specific intention of building machines on a commercial basis, and formed the Electronic Control Company.* By the autumn of 1946 they had ob-

---

* Among the backers they were talking to at the time was Ernest Cuneo, a former Roosevelt aide who had been involved in the wartime beginnings of what eventually became the CIA. He was some fifteen years later to become much more famous as the man to whom Ian Fleming dedicated *Thunderball*. All very appropriate as eventually the CIA became one of the computer industry's—and IBM's—best customers.

tained a study contract from the Census Bureau.* Their report
was submitted a year later.

By early 1948 the machine was under construction and parts
were being demonstrated. By now the Company had become the
Eckert and Mauchly Computer Corporation. By the middle of
1948 EMCC had contracts to build two machines, called
BINACs, for Northrop (they eventually built only one), and
during 1948 they finally entered into an agreement to sell a
UNIVAC system to the Census Bureau. That machine went into
operation in early 1951, by which time Eckert and Mauchly Computer Corporation had become part of Remington Rand. For the
main backer of EMCC had been killed in an air crash, and his
successors and heirs—in one of the great missed opportunities—wanted nothing to do with computing.

*   *   *

Where was IBM while all this was going on? Some large special
calculating machines apart, the main thrust of IBM's development was still pre-electronic. The Mk 1, the large calculator that
Howard Aiken had built for Harvard using IBM funds and equipment, had been succeeded by an even faster and larger calculator,
the SSEC, the 120,000 vacuum tube Selective Sequence Electronic Calculator, which went into operation in New York in 1948
and was to be in use till 1952. It had a limited capability to change
its instructions in mid-flow and was somewhat faster than the
Mk 1, nearly as fast as the ENIAC. It was also more flexible and
was used on a wider range of scientific problems; but, it was still
not really a computer.

Mr Thomas Watson Snr, Chairman and Chief Executive of
IBM, had specifically rejected the notion that IBM might build
such a thing commercially. He had been approached by Eckert
and Mauchly when they ran out of money, but had turned them
down. Indeed, they never got through his door. (There exists a
story that IBM offered to hire them, but only if they dropped their
silly ideas about electronic computers.) What is definite is that one

---

* This, it is claimed by IBM, was one of the events that was eventually to trigger
them off to enter into the computer business. For the Census Bureau was not just a 'Blue
Chip' account, it was looked on almost sentimentally, as the account which had made
IBM possible in the first place.

John Macpherson, at this time the senior IBM authority on computing and its possibilities—a sort of coordinator of wartime projects—told them on behalf of IBM, and on authority from Mr Watson, that IBM would not back them. He did not tell them that an uncommitted IBM was quietly tinkering away on a contingency basis. But turned down they were. The refusal came, and a week later Eckert and Mauchly went to see James Rand on his yacht off Florida, subsequently selling their company to what was then Remington Rand.

The reason they were turned down was two-fold. IBM was convinced that it had just as good products on the way: they might not be technically as advanced but they seemed, to a conservative management, to be more suited to its market. By then IBM had some commercial electronics experience; there were electronic valves in its Model 077 collator, and in some of its 600 series and calculators, notably the 603 (300 valves) and the 604 (1,400 valves). The 604 should not be ignored; IBM delivered the first in 1948, and by 1958 over five thousand had been installed. The 604 is a key machine in keeping IBM afloat while it made the transfer to computers as the base of its business. Northrop Aviation were to take a 604 and lash it to an IBM tabulator, to produce the prototype Card Programmed Calculator, which IBM then took up and of which it built some seven hundred. With these developments on the way, it seemed to many in IBM as if conventional if advanced products were going to be good enough for IBM as far off into the future as anyone would wish to look.

The second reason had to do with the general disagreements about whether computers had any future. Howard Aiken, creator of the ASSC or Harvard Mk 1, and the SSEC, had stated that the market was unlikely to be there—if one was thinking in terms of more than six machines. IBM's internal reports had indicated that Aiken might be wrong by 100%; even so at twelve machines it did not seem very attractive.

How IBM missed the boat the first time round was eventually to be recounted by Thomas Watson Jnr in his 1962 McKinsey Foundation lectures. He began by referring to the ENIAC:

'Many people in our industry, and I was among them, had seen the machine, but none of us foresaw its possibilities. Even after Eckert and Mauchly left teaching to begin manufacture of a civilian counterpart of the ENIAC, few of us saw the potential.

'Their company was absorbed by Remington Rand in 1950 and the following year the first production model of UNIVAC was delivered to the Census Bureau where it replaced some IBM machines.

'Throughout this entire period IBM was unaware of the fact that its whole business stood on the threshold of momentous change ... we didn't jump to the obvious conclusion that if we could feed data faster we would increase computational speeds 900%. Remington Rand had seen just that—and with Univac they were off to the races.'

To be fair to IBM, they were not the only people who thought it was not going to fly. Alan Turing had also said that there were unlikely to be many computers created and sold (three was his number for the U.K.). He claimed there just weren't the mathematicians around to cope with the output. And there was a long stream of other expert authorities also going around saying never ...

Appearances as ever were deceptive, and two factors were to intervene on IBM's behalf to make certain that they were not overtaken by events. One was that—in a memorable phrase that Herb Grosch* continues to be fond of using—Remington Rand were to take up Eckert and Mauchly and then spend much time 'snatching defeat from the jaws of victory', before settling down and stabilising. By the late fifties, IBM was again number one and Remington Rand, as it had been in the punch card machine field, once more number two.

It was war and the possibilities of war which was to tip the scales. IBM was to be rescued by the combined efforts of Kim Il Sung, Chairman Mao, Comrade Stalin and his many divisions, the Cold War and the seeming defence needs of America, particularly in the intelligence, cryptoanalysis, and aviation sectors. By 1949 IBM was receiving visits from within the American defense establishment and was being asked to develop and market a faster machine than the projected UNIVAC.

It was by now not simply UNIVAC that IBM had to think about. The von Neumann Report had led to a build-your-own-computer movement, and there were the best part of a dozen projects in

---

* Dr Herbert Grosch was an early worker in the field at IBM, and no book on the origins of the computer industry would be complete without his presence.

hand across America, including development at the RAND Corporation, the AEC Los Alamos, and the National Bureau of Standards—two machines. Though it was not to acknowledge it in public and though it was without official management sanction itself, by 1950 IBM was already developing a computer.

CHAPTER TWO

Megalomania Unlimited ...

To the public at large, the computer has a unique image. It is a machine of the order of a low-level brain which is at the heart of technological progress, one used for tasks of incredible complexity which it handles at just as incredible speed: controlling moon shots and anti-missile defences, monitoring patients in intensive care units, creating three-dimensional pictures of immense complexity for design engineers and the like.

It will cope with almost any mathematical formulation, enables information to be found in an instant, and has great potential in education. True, its existence and further development raise problems; for instance, for the first time we have to think seriously about the individual's right to privacy in contrast to the society's needs for information. But generally, the computer can be made to seem beneficial and economic, a remarkable product of the inventive genius of man.

Problems apart, however, most of this is but the surface gloss on a different reality. Those uses are to the majority of computers what Grand Prix racing is to the automobile industry. Most computers are used for very boring things concerned with accountancy, e.g. calculating the payroll, billing the customer, generating paper to do with money, cost analyses, stock recording and the like. It is these accountancy uses that account for the majority of high-value computer sales on both sides of the Atlantic, and it is the provision of computers for these kinds of tasks which provide the bedrock of IBM's business.

This is a necessary prelude to any attempt to understand how IBM came to dominate the computer industry: it did so because it

dominated the industry that preceded it—the account-
ing/tabulating machine industry—which, naturally, gave IBM a
major advantage in the conversion of users from one system to
the other. It was easier for IBM's salesmen to convert customers
from existing equipment than it was for new entrants in the field to
take away those customers. Furthermore, IBM salesmen had an
incentive to do so; their rewards were so structured that the loss of
an existing account to a competitor led to a drop in the salesman's
income.

Initially, there was little chance of such a loss. IBM had one
major advantage: IBM service was superb, and that service was
in part responsible for IBM's stranglehold on the punch card
equipment business. The service was like that of the telephone
company: IBM employees were always on duty. A chance
remark at a party that you were having trouble with an IBM
machine would lead to a service engineer camped on your
doorstep first thing the next morning. IBM and IBM employees
took great pride in the corporation and in its service, and were
rewarded accordingly.

It was this loyalty that was initially transferred to the computer, and was soon reflected in the sales figures. IBM and its
main competitor, Remington Rand, were immediately to dominate the computer business, as they had done the business which
preceded it. At the start, the proportions were different,
Remington Rand being the leader, but the seemingly natural
order of things soon reasserted itself.

To understand how IBM came to dominate the computer industry, one must also have a feel for how IBM came to dominate
its predecessor, the business machines industry, and how that
became the launching pad for its world dominance in business
computers.

*   *   *

The highly condensed and very short history of IBM's pre-
computer years that follows is best handled in two parts: a short,
formal history of IBM, pinpointing the high spots of its growth in
terms of personnel, revenues, profit and the like; and the more in-
formal history of its creator, the man who built IBM: Thomas
Watson Snr.

The formal history is quite clear, simple and unusual for a company of IBM's size. IBM is one of the few very large companies to grow primarily through internal processes, not through acquisition. This, however, was not its origin, which lies in three companies (themselves the amalgamation of some fifty companies) which were merged in 1911 to form the Computing, Tabulating and Recording Company. One of the three was the company founded by the Dr Herman Hollerith mentioned earlier, and it was this company that Mr Watson was really to expand.

For the first three years, CTR did not do at all well. A forty-year-old Thomas Watson was appointed General Manager in 1914 to reverse that trend. It was then an early, if small and unprofitable, conglomerate, dealing with time clocks, weighing machines, and the Hollerith machines. By the end of Watson's first year, CTR had nearly 1,400 employees and a gross income of $4 million, with gross profits around $1·3 million—just over thirty per cent.

There is a theory, to which we shall return, of organisational trajectory: the initiated policy brings in results which are then looked upon as the expected norm and which become the targets of tomorrow, until, in other words, that policy becomes both conventional wisdom—and conservatism. The theory was not to be formally expressed for some time, but sixty years later that thirty per cent is still the desired norm, even if it is not always achieved.

From the earliest days, Watson understood that if the company was to grow it would require a policy of high ploughback into expansion, and plough back he did, which was to give IBM so much of its later strength.

In 1915, Watson moved up to become President, and by the end of World War II, the company had nearly quadrupled sales. Profits might not have kept pace with ambition, but they were still a respectable two million dollars plus.

In 1924, the company was renamed International Business Machines. By 1929, the year of the Stock Market crash, IBM was grossing $18 million, and that year it still managed to pay out a dividend, albeit a small one. IBM was to continue to grow through the thirties and the Depression. There is a tendency to forget that the Depression, though widespread, did not affect society in equal proportion—part of society continued to get richer. The thirties also saw the real start of what we call the consumer society, the beginnings of large-volume production and the mass marketing associated with it. It saw, too, in America, the beginnings of an embryonic welfare system, through the Social Security Act of 1935, and an attempt to pump funds into the economy through the National Reconstruction Act. Any volume business or legislation which required that records be kept in large numbers was obviously of benefit to IBM, which saw the thirties through in the end by cuddling up to Washington, and building for stock. It could afford to. Customers might not be taking the large volumes of machines that IBM would wish; however, the policy of rental only—without a purchase option—meant that at least there was income.

That income was only in part obtained from machine rental, it also came from punch cards. The last were all-important. The 'official' biography of Mr Watson Snr was to maintain that over the twenty years from 1911 to 1930 twenty-five per cent of IBM's profits came from the sale of such cards.

The estimate is thought to be much too low an averaging of profit over the period. In fact, the profit contribution of punch cards was believed to be much higher in the late thirties and during the war period than in previous years.

IBM's punch card machine near-monopoly and its tie-in of punch cards and machines—you used one with the other, or the machine rental contract was terminated—was to lead to an anti-trust suit (see Chapter 14), the results of which IBM was to avoid for twenty years more. And the combination of tight hold over patents and tie-in of punch cards were to be at the core of IBM's dominance for years to come.

In the meantime IBM was changing and adapting its technology—though not very fast. It brought out a horizontal sorting machine in 1925, an eighty-column punch card in 1928, and in 1931 introduced its 600 Series of calculators, the first machines it made which were eventually to handle both multiplication and division: IBM was catching up with Leibnitz (but it was 1943 before that happened; with a special order for Los Alamos).

The 1930s saw a number of other developments which were to prepare it for the paper-shuffling economy that was to come. In 1933 it acquired a typewriter manufacturer, and two years later produced if not the first electric typewriter, at least the first one on which anybody made a profit. By 1937 it had over 10,000 employees, its gross income had passed $30 million, and its paper-shuffling activities had been extended to produce a collator, extensively used in the social welfare programme. In 1939 IBM grossed $41 million and declared profits were back near that 30% goal, over $12 million.

IBM did well out of the war. By the end of 1945 it had more than tripled its revenues—to $140 million. It had achieved growth within five years that had taken twenty years of peace to obtain.

The corporation came out of the war also much strengthened: where other typewriter manufacturers had been made to switch their production to war products, IBM had realised, and had sold to Washington the notion that an army also marched on its orders, and that as a small and unique electric typewriter manufacturer it should be allowed to continue its production. As for its existing product, that had been intensively used by the Armed Forces; also IBM had got involved in cryptography.

However, peace came, and over the next three years the company could only add some fifteen or so million dollars in turnover, yet bringing it up to a still respectable $156 million. But boom times were coming again. Between 1946 and 1956, which covers the start of the Cold War, the Korean War, the re-equipment of America's Armed Forces and IBM's entrance into the computer business—IBM grew from 22,000 employees to 72,000 and its gross income to not far short of $600 million. In eighteen years the company had increased its revenue fourteen-fold: growth unprecedented but not unnoticed.

These are the bare bones of the overall story. Within it there was a subsidiary tale, the rise of world-wide IBM: the company had not been called International Business Machines just because Mr Watson had delusions of grandeur. Mr Watson really believed in what he said, even where reality might indicate the reverse. From the earliest days he was to exhibit a useful capacity in a leader—a capacity for self-delusion and an ability to make everybody else believe that, because he believed something to be so, it was so.

CTR had inherited contacts with the world outside America. There were already a number of agreements existing between the Hollerith company and Continental—primarily German—Europe before CTR was formed: for international meant primarily America plus Europe. When Mr Watson came in, he started to formalise those external relationships (and in 1917 tried out the name IBM in Canada, where he opened a card manufacture and product assembly plant—long before the parent company made its own name switch).

In 1919, it was thought advisable to centre most Continental operations in Paris. In 1922, the French company, Société Internationale des Machines Commerciales, established its own assembly and card manufacturing plant. Representation elsewhere quickly followed. That representation, however, was largely for what were still known as Hollerith machines, the name by which the customers thought of them.

By the early thirties IBM straddled the globe, at least in representation—then in over seventy countries—if not in sales, though most of those sales were American exports.

Growth in the rest of the world parallelled that in home in everything except profits. Mr Watson was interested in growth, and ploughed everything back until the point in the late thirties where more than minimal profits had to be shown; there was just too much business going abroad.

In 1949 the IBM World Trade Corporation, a wholly-owned subsidiary, was formed, and the process of name-changing* and rationalisation started. IBM had so far kept out of the British and British Empire markets. It had an agreement with the then British Tabulating Machine Company whereby that was its agent. In 1950, however, IBM decided to move into Britain and those linked overseas territories, and made a deal whereby it would compete against its licensee.

By the mid-fifties there were few places on the planet in which IBM was not represented (or had not at some time been represented, for the map of the world had by then substantially changed). The IBM companies might be dormant, as in the case of IBM China, but IBM lived, and no doubt still lives, in the hope that one day it would once more operate there also.

This was the formal legacy that Mr Watson had left his inheritors, but what of the not so formal?

*   *   *

* See page 48.

If it is impossible to disentangle the growth of IBM World Trade from the growth of its parent, it is also impossible to separate the growth of either from the mores, philosophy and practices of their boss, Mr Thomas Watson Snr. From 1914 till 1952, his influence was all-pervading. It was to linger on till his death in 1956, for to the end no one knew where he would next turn up—or on whom he might descend. And, as had been said of kings of older times, his wrath was wonderful to behold.

It would not be unfair to call the elder Thomas Watson, IBM's creator, the Charles Foster Kane of the business machine industry, with this difference: where Kane was an exaggerated fictional version of William Randolph Hearst, Thomas Watson's version of Kane was real.

It must be remembered that he did not take charge of what was to become IBM till he was forty. He had already been successful: as he was to duplicate at IBM the techniques that had brought him that success, to expand and embellish them, it would be reasonable to presume that his character was by then fully formed.

The early career of Thomas Watson Snr has been extensively documented. It was too remarkable a life to remain hidden from the public gaze, even if by temperament Mr Watson had so wished, though he did not. It has, however, been amply embellished by the mythmakers.

Some facts are undisputed. His family came from Scotland, via Ireland, eventually settling down in New York State in the 1840s. He was born in 1874. Hence we have recently celebrated—if that is the word—the hundredth anniversary of his birth.

His business career began in 1892. He became a salesman, starting off, interestingly enough, with mechanical devices; with sewing machines, pianos and the like. He had some elementary commercial knowledge, having attended a business college, a euphemism in those days for courses in book-keeping, simple accountancy and the like.

From the start his business life was bound up with sales, whether peddling stock, running a butcher's shop or selling cash-registers. It was this last experience which was to establish him, for after struggling, sometimes successfully, sometimes not, with other ventures, he was eventually taken on by the National Cash Register Company.

It was at NCR that he learned the basics of the techniques which he was later to use to build up IBM, and it was fitting that his mentor was to be John Henry Patterson, NCR's founder, a man who combined benevolence with ruthlessness in a way which would have made him stand out even at the Court of the Borgias.

In Patterson Mr Watson had found his mentor, and he was to be marked for life. The Watson sales record in NCR was a good one, the product of the training and atmosphere of NCR at the time. It was to lead to a scheme of Patterson's which was to make Mr Watson a national figure, if not exactly a national hero.

Patterson made Watson an offer: NCR would finance the setting up of a dummy corporation, theoretically in opposition to itself, in practice owned and controlled by NCR. It would then be used to take over and if possible eliminate the non-NCR used cash-register business.

The money was clearly illegal, and the defence that Watson was at the time a young man in a very rough era under the influence of one of the industrial legends of America is inadequate. For the deception was blatant. Mr Watson, however, was already exhibiting a capacity for self-delusion, for conveniently forgetting what he had said the previous week, for rewriting history to suit himself, all of which were to serve him in great stead.

The venture almost succeeded, and by 1910 Mr Watson was effectively sales manager of NCR. But by 1912 NCR's methods finally caught up with Patterson, Watson and NCR. They were indicted on charges of criminal conspiracy, monopoly and restraint of trade. The last two were to be familiar recurring themes throughout Watson's career. What was different in this case was that the defendants were not able to settle short of a Court judgement. A clutch of NCR employees, including Patterson and Watson, were convicted and sentenced to terms of imprisonment—the first anti-trust case in which prison sentences had been awarded.

Then luck intervened. The cause of that first piece of instant luck was an 'Act of God'. NCR's plant was built on high ground in the city of Dayton, Ohio. In the spring of 1913, while the anti-trust judgement and convictions were being appealed, Dayton was hit by floods and NCR found itself with the only base in the area from which relief could be organised. Patterson moved into action, using the plant, the offices and his cash to organise emergency facilities, while Watson, then in New York, organised relief trains. The result was predictable: almost overnight Patterson and Watson became near-heroes.

This did not happen of course without some help. Extensive press coverage arrangements were made, NCR picking up the tab for journalists who went to Dayton, and Patterson was to be shown in pictures with anybody who was anybody and who could be press-ganged to appear—which was not difficult. However, public plaudits, judiciously aided by 'facilities for the Press', in the euphemism of the trade, were one thing: the courts were another. The machinery of the law could be relied on to drag things out. The original verdict had been appealed, the penalties altered, appealed again and a new trial granted. Eventually, it was all to peter out in a Consent Decree. (This, too, was a foretaste of what was to come. IBM in its turn was to make more anti-trust 'firsts', and luck was to intervene more often than not to nullify the convictions or agreements reached between the parties, each time seemingly in favour of Watson and his interests.) Mr Watson refused to sign this decree, for by that time he had left NCR and gone to what was to become IBM. He argued (roughly) that the decree bound him only in the context of NCR, not elsewhere.

This was to be the story of Mr Watson's life; indeed, in a close parallel to events more than half a century later, Mr Watson's counsel was to argue at that trial on roughly the same lines as were taken by IBM's counsel, Cravath, Swaine and Moore during the pre-trial proceedings of the Control Data Corporation case of the late 60's. Lawyers have tabbed the tactic The Inverted Nuremberg Defence: 'It wasn't us guys at the top who were to blame, it was all those fellows down below who out of zeal, their own understanding of what was good for the company, love even if you like, had exceeded the limits of their authority. And if they didn't have the authority, then we at the top were obviously blameless. If we'd only known, we would have stopped it.' It was a defence which has since proved popular in America, and not just in the trials and troubles of the business machines or computing industry.

What then had Watson learnt at NCR which was to be useful later, and on which he was to build?

Perhaps the first thing was his predilection for a uniformed and disciplined work-force, a predilection taught him by Patterson.

Patterson did not invent the notion of the short-haired, clean, sober-suited, disciplined and regimented work-force, treated with the care with which a gentleman treats his dog, his horse or his gun, a work-force in which every man knows his place and duty, a duty clearly and carefully defined and circumscribed.

That had been formulated not too long ago in 1870 and by the military. It had been made fashionable by the victory of the Prussian King Wilhelm over the Emperor Louis Napoleon at the battle of Sedan. The battle may have come thirty years too soon, but it marks the real start of the twentieth century. As ever in these things, the birth of a new era was surrounded by misunderstanding and confusion.

It was not the field-grey, short-haired, tightly-disciplined Prussians who beat Louis Napoleon—it was their guns. The French were cut to pieces almost before the battle proper, what little there was of it, begun. An advance in technology had once more changed the history of the world.

The confusion began there. What was initially transferred to civilian life was the look, not the technology. (One of the major causes of confusion in twentieth-century industrial society is a tendency to equate order with efficiency, and style with performance. Order may lead to efficiency, but it does not follow that it always will or that efficiency may result in the required economic performance. However, successful economic performance is almost always wrongly attributed.) As ever, it was the middle classes who were most awed by the Prussian success and proceeded to emulate what they thought they had understood. Almost everywhere armies started changing their uniforms from the riotous assemblage of colours, reds and blues and golds, to sober field-grey and the like. New technology was introduced, but much more emphasis was placed on the first than the second.

In civilian life, it was the organisations staffed and run by the middle class, particularly in finance, which began to set rules concerned with the appearance of their employees—rules which implied that neatness, cleanliness, sobriety and uniformity of appearance were if not somehow next to godliness, at least a lot nearer mammon.

But to exert these sorts of controls meant that the organisation had to become much more all-encompassing: it led to the growth of personnel departments. This was something that Patterson learnt early. It was this Watson was to develop further at IBM. His twist was to seemingly change the status of his employees. Until Watson came along, the daily clean white shirt was one of the marks of the middle class. Watson was to take this and other distinguishing badges and apply them downwards—and thus right across—the social scale.

Having removed the outward distinguishing marks of society, Watson substituted his own. He abolished staff/worker differentiations, by making everybody into both at once. Time clocks were used all round, and separate facilities were abolished. Since everybody much of the time looked the same, a lot of social uneasiness disappeared.

Patterson taught Watson many other things. He learned how to move men. Once their individuality had effectively been broken down by putting them into quasi-uniform, they had to be shaped. He applied the techniques of the Quota Sales Club, the boy-scout presentations and competititions, the rah-rah routines, the trick of constant outpouring of simplistic messages, the earnest presentation of elementary, and often rather boringly simple, precepts as if they were the tablets brought down from on high.

Even the techniques of presentation since made famous in IBM's flip charts (see Chapter 10) were to originate in NCR, though the flip charts came later. At the start blackboards were used.

He had learnt a crucial lesson: that if you looked after your own, it could be made to pay. If you gave job security, wages calculatedly just above industry norms, fringe benefits better than those offered by the competition, you could demand extra performance from your men that was worth considerably more than the extra all this would cost.

He had learned the valuable technique of the 'Open Door', the direct access of the leader to his followers. This was useful technique: to junior staff it gave the appearance of reducing remoteness, giving access to management and thus infusing the warm glow of the family togetherness; at the top it also gave him a chance to monitor their activities. The people who had to worry seriously about the open door after all were those in the middle: his 'managers'.

He had learned that these things made it possible for him to be master in what he regarded as his own house; IBM was a greater extension of the Watson ego. If there was competition to his authority, it could only come from a greater loyalty, and that was certainly not a union loyalty. It would never do if there was competition for loyalty from trade unions, which were anathema and have remained so to this day (though IBM cannot help but be part unionised in many countries, such as Japan and Sweden). However, as Mr Watson once expressed it, if one had to have unions, then the company leadership had failed.

Above all he had learned one thing: how to make other people's inconvenient judgements go away. If you just stood there long enough, refused to accept that other people's judgements might make sense, and kept on denying that it was so, sooner or later they would lose interest, move on and allow you to accomplish your ends.

Mr Watson had also learned that he could cope with the competition in almost any way he chose, so long as he was reasonably discreet about it. He had learned that for his competition recourse to the law was an after-the-event thing, by which time if he had done his work well, the company should be in a position where it could fight back from even greater strength. He had at NCR closely observed the techniques of legal harrassment of competitors in otherwise meaningless patent infringement suits which would tie up their resources and manpower for a long time to come, until they could be made to cry 'enough'.

He had learned how to look at competitors' equipment, take it apart, improve it, and then market it as his own.

He had learned that there was no point in improving product unless he was otherwise forced to do so either by the competition or by the company's own internal needs for greater volume and profit. He had learned that it was essential to get into a dominant position, so that he could charge what he liked and could tailor the market to his own requirements.

Almost all the precepts that Watson preached, and the techniques he was to apply at IBM, originated elsewhere. The Watson genius was adapting and refining them to work within an organisation which was not really a family, a tribe, a nation nor a state, one which did not have the same emotional pull or the ability (and power) to call on the sanctions of the ultimate loyalty.

*   *   *

From the early days, Mr Watson's IBM contract, as befitted
one steeped in the salesman's ethic, gave him both a salary and a
percentage, in his case a percentage of net profit. By the mid-
thirties this had made him a rich man and allowed him to cultivate
his tastes.

These did not include the proverbial wine, women and song,
and unhealthy living. They were instead the tastes of the born in-
terferer. What Mr Watson wanted was that the world should be
allowed to get rich, though no doubt he regretted that he didn't
have a percentage on that generally. The pursuit of riches, as he
saw it, also meant the pursuit of peace; and to this end one had to
cultivate the great. Surely what had worked in IBM was capable
of being transferred elsewhere on to a wider stage?

Of course, for the word to spread, he would have to be
recognised. He liked recognition. Recognition had its uses: here
was an itty-bitty company, not even in the *Fortune* top 500 in any
of the recognised terms of employees, assets, turnover. Yet its
chairman was the highest-paid executive in America, floating
through the late thirties and for long afterwards on an annual
salary and commission of over $300,000. And IBM, in part
because of its multinational operational nature, seemed to have
the entrée almost everywhere, access to the great.

The resultant 'Who's Who in America' entry was to be up-
roariously funny. Goering might collect medals, Watson collected
everything. At the end of his life, the biography ran twenty-two
lines before it mentioned that he was married. Most of those lines
were taken up by a list of honorary degrees. Between 1934 and
1951 he was to collect twenty-nine of them from places as far
apart as California, Canada, France, Belgium and Peru (though
the majority came from universities and colleges of the second
rank in the north eastern United States).

He also picked up a number of other academic honorifics,
among them the Honorary Rectorship of Dubuque University.
This would have been remarkable enough had those honours been
the rewards of a lifetime of public service or for statesmanship
above and beyond . . . Or had the degrees been concentrated in
any area in which he could be said to have expertise or to have
made contributions. Instead they covered a wide territory.
Ironically, the majority were Doctorates of Law; there were also
doctorates in the literary humanities, engineering, science, even in

business administration (where he might have claimed to have advanced the state of the field). Also, the social sciences, where if he had not exactly advanced the field, he could claim to have achieved one thing which merited recognition and which went a long way towards explaining why IBM was noticed at all: its lay-offs in the Depression had been minimal compared with most of the other companies of IBM's size or above.

He also collected decorations. From 1934 to 1950 he was to be awarded them by thirty countries,* among them the United Kingdom (an Honorary CBE), the Kingdom of Cambodia and a clutch of Latin American countries including Panama, Bolivia, Brazil, Chile, Colombia, Cuba, the Dominican Republic, Haiti, Mexico, Paraguay, Peru, Venezuela; nobody can say why he didn't get the remaining three and sweep the continent. He did, however, sweep Scandinavia: Finland, Norway, Sweden and Denmark.

America was not to reward him quite as well; the best he could do there was the Medal for Merit of the U.S. War Department in 1947. However, he made up for it by collecting memberships: in associations, committees, and anything else that could be organised: the Carnegie Endowment for International Peace: Joint American–British Commonwealth, French, Norwegian, etc.; Chambers of Commerce abounded, after all, he had also been President of the International Chamber of Commerce. But his memberships were not confined to business or directly linked to it; they included the Boy Scouts, the Presbyterian Church and almost every other extant Protestant religious body. The Air Force, Army and Navy had his support, as did Ordnance (Council Member: American Ordnance Association), and they were neatly balanced with the sponsorship and patronage of Disabled Veterans and Order of the Purple Heart organisations.

Still there were more. The list was not quite endless, but long: hospitals, eye disease, infantile paralysis, Travellers Aid, poetry, Shakespeare, modern art, music, opera, symphony orchestras.

And as he had more than a dozen clubs to go to, it seemed that wherever it was at, Mr Watson was likely to be there also.

Mr Watson was beginning to believe in his own myth—and

---

* The entry only records, however, twenty-nine. The thirtieth, the Order of Merit of the German Eagle, presented by Hitler, had become an embarrassment.

that could be dangerous. Indeed, there came a point in the late thirties where Mr Watson's more than incipient megalomania almost went entirely beyond the bounds of reality. He began believing that he and the company were seemingly interchangeable.

'No one ever talked frankly to him, he was simply too powerful and too rough. If you did talk frankly to him, that was the end of you, so no one did. I think that the incidents of accepting Nazi decorations, and the Depression suicides* in the company when the sales pressures got too much all got a very bad response. In each case you knew he was going to brazen it out. There was officially no PR Department to stop him. But somehow or other he would get shipped out on the Queen Mary or down to Palm Beach to simmer a little bit. They used to control him, and it must have been a very delicate operation indeed.'

In 1937, at the height of the delusion, he started to re-name many of IBM's overseas subsidiaries. In Sweden, Switzerland, Japan and Colombia, they were retitled Watson Business Machines, followed by the local equivalent of Incorporated. In 1938 he did the same thing in Finland, Turkey and Uruguay. In 1939, he took this process one step further: he began to delete the Business Machines part of the title, substituting the name of the country, the operation in Turkey now became known as Watson Turk, and that in what was then the Netherlands East Indies, now Indonesia, became Watson Java. Others to be given similar accolades included Sweden, Switzerland, Italy and Mexico.

Had the war not intervened, this process might have continued, with no doubt interesting consequences. But war did come, and that, though IBM is still a little coy about some of its international operations in those years (particularly of the subsidiaries in those countries America was now fighting) was to be its salvation.

---

* There were only a couple of admitted suicides, supposedly caused by IBM's high sales quotas. However, one happened in the New York area and was widely reported and commented on.

CHAPTER THREE

IBM Takes Over the Computer

War has served IBM well. World War II was to take it out of the ranks of those illy-billy companies and begin to turn it into an American giant. The Cold War was to take it into the computer business and turn it into a multinational giant.

It was not to be a process of simple organic growth without resistance, the filling of a vacuum. It was to be growth through combat, combat in which IBM seemingly played by different rules from everybody else.

Mr Watson had left his successors an IBM well equipped to fight, an organisation indeed so tuned that it needed to fight somebody if for no other reason than to demonstrate its virility. IBM was organised on centralised lines with good communications between the leader and his troops, and the troops were accustomed to reacting to the whims and wishes of the revered leader.*

The leadership had been patriarchal, despotic and benevolent, indeed had been publicly called by the last two terms by a senior IBM executive. The labour force was well-paid, knowledgeable, disciplined and effectively organised to execute any given orders. The corporation too was rich, had substantial income and product, and knew how to sell more. Its service and maintenance were more than competent, they were of high quality. IBM's people were always on duty and seemed to take the idea that

---

* Revered is the right word to choose. Mr Watson's visits to IBM establishments used to be preceded by new paint, the frequent cleaning of fabrics, and the daily delivery of fresh-cut flowers, all of which ceased as soon as his appearance was over.

something was unserviceable, or not up to standard, as a personal affront.

Mr Watson had also created a system where IBM did not sell product outright—it leased it. It exhibited the signs of a monopoly, if an unusual one. The only competition then to be taken seriously would come from technological and price advantages of a substantial order. And as IBM's intelligence system, while capable of improvement, was better than that of anyone else around, IBM seemingly had little to fear.

During the fifties, sixties and early seventies, IBM was to mount three major wars against its competition. There was the war against the manufacturers of very large computer systems, which was to culminate in the CDC anti-trust suit. There was the war on the peripheral device manufacturers which was to bring on the anti-trust suit of the Telex Corporation; and there was the war of IBM versus seemingly everybody else, which brought on the suit of the Justice Department, in which Justice sought—and still seeks—to have IBM broken up.

But before IBM could fight a war over computers and their markets, it first of all had to get into the computer business. Not surprisingly, it was a war which was to provide the pretext. Officially, IBM was on the side of peace: was not everybody? Had not Mr Watson emblazoned the slogan 'World Peace Through World Trade' over IBM's Madison Avenue headquarters during the thirties? (Mr Watson was no historian, otherwise he would have realised that the slogan was meaningless. Trade between Great Britain and the Kaiser's Germany, for instance, reached its peak in the year immediately prior to the start of World War I.) Mr Watson had preached against war, especially in the years running up to World War II (in this he was not alone—so had the men who caused it).

According to IBM, the event that was to lead to its real growth happened in 1951. A 1973 issue of THINK, American IBM's house journal, commemorating the twentieth anniversary of the delivery of the first IBM computer to appear on the market, the IBM 701, records that Mr Watson asked the American Government what IBM could do for the 'war effort'.

The answer came back: 'Build a large computer.'*

---

* One wishes that IBM would make up its mind. It also tells another story: that the major reason for IBM's entry into computing was due to the loss of that sentimental-

There's only one thing wrong with this story: it is only partly true, and grossly oversimplified; it is a tidying up of history described by one of those around at the time as 'Corporate bullshit'. The truth as ever was much more interesting.

The computer that Washington wanted IBM to build might be intended for the war effort, but it was not bound for the firing line, nor even the rear echelons of the battlefield. It was needed by defence planners and by defence related industry. It would be essentially what we now think of as a scientific computer, a machine used for large-scale computation, whether by mathematicians or engineers, or, particularly, designers of nuclear weapons.

Mr Watson's experiences with large machines for scientific work had not conditioned him to like the reality of the scientific environment. The creation of such a device would involve IBM seriously with scientists and other individualists who didn't obey the normal rules of conduct. they spoke before they were spoken to, had little regard for the rules of dress and seemed to have even less regard for the nicely defined hierarchy of IBM. Real scientists, it seemed, didn't know their place. Nor did the machines they wanted, machines which took up a disproportionate amount of time for the rewards they brought in, whether kudos or money.

Nor did Mr Watson like to be under pressure; however, pressure he encountered, and from the only man he could not fire—his eldest son, Tom Watson Jnr. TJW Jnr had recently been

---

value prestige account, the Census Bureau, to the first UNIVAC computer then being built by Eckert and Mauchly ... Actually, this widely-believed story is a phoney. IBM did not have much of the Census Bureau installation. The Bureau had been good to IBM, not the other way around.

To steep oneself in IBM is often to get the feeling of *déjà vu*. IBM repeats its successes and its mistakes with seeming regularity. But in this case *déjà vu* contains a touch of irony. The machines which had led to the creation of the Hollerith Company—to which IBM was the successor—had been used in the 1890, 1900 and 1910 censuses. However, the first batch of contracts with Hollerith had come to a stop in 1905 on the grounds that dealing with Hollerith was too expensive. Thereafter, from 1910 to 1950, there had been little change in Census Bureau methodology. However, it had created its own development division. This had developed a Census unit-counter, and by the thirties the Bureau had a mix of kit of its own and IBM's. IBM was to hire one of the Census Bureau's divisional heads (Lawrence Wilson, chief of its Machine Tabulating Division) and, in part on the basis of that Census Bureau know-how, he was to head the development of a combined unit-counter and multicolumn sorter, which IBM was to market successfully as its 101.

It would not be unfair to write that what prodded IBM was not so much that it had lost the Census Bureau account, but rather that someone else had gained it: that was galling.

promoted to President of IBM, a post which had been part of Mr Watson's title for over a quarter of a century; father moved on to become Chairman and Chief Executive Officer.

Surrounding TWJ Jnr were many of the youngish World War II veterans who had some idea that change was on the way, though they might not have had a clear idea what that change was to bring. Around Mr Watson Snr, too, and scattered elsewhere throughout the company, were men of a much higher intellectual calibre than the company had previously employed. The company was better staffed than before the war, for its production was now nowhere near as simple or homogeneous, and the new conditions had led to the hiring of substantial numbers of university graduates, particularly from prestigious engineering schools such as MIT.

IBM too was facing another more normal clash, to be expected soon after a major war. More than most, IBM had been a predominantly male company; World War II had seriously depleted IBM of its younger executive ranks. The wartime growth had come from a largely female labour force run by old men. Now the young men were back . . . The generation clash spread far beyond the area of headquarters or the locations immediately visible from Galactic Headquarters.* The management, in practice largely Mr Watson, could not help but look back on the IBM of earlier times with nostalgia—the days when products were simpler, technological change was slower, and there were few requirements for machines to do very complex tasks. For Mr Watson was now taking less and less interest in the newer products; he might understand them, but he didn't feel them.

However, after much argument, Mr Watson gave his qualified approval to go ahead with the market 'research' to precede development of the computer that Washington wanted. For this was still IBM. Enthusiasm, however forced (and IBM is always enthusiastic once a decision to go ahead had been made), might get IBM started, but no one was going to go ahead without some idea of numbers.

As THINK tells it, the then director of product planning and market analysis, Jim Birkenstock, set out to visit defence and aircraft companies to look at the probable demand. He came back

---

* The name is Grosch's.

with numbers: seventeen was his estimate of demand. IBM was to build twenty 701s in all. It intended to build nineteen, seventeen for the market and two for itself, but then someone went and sold another, which had to be hurriedly assembled from spares, so hurriedly that it took storage away from one of its own machines. However, 'We will take one if you build it' is one thing, actually building it so that it works satisfactorily and is capable of delivery is another, and not simply for IBM.

There were many internal arguments. 'They seemed,' said one of the participants much later, 'to be on generation lines. The old hands were saying "It's ridiculous to think of building seventeen of these, we will never in a million years sell that many", and the new hands were saying the reverse. "Seventeen? We shall sell a lot more than that." '

That the clutch of decisions which finally took IBM into the community market place were not made unaided, and that had it been left to Mr Watson the decision would probably have not been made at all until much later, was to be eventually recognised by IBM, even if that recognition was not widely publicised.

At the end of the fifties, Corporate management held a dinner to which a handful of outsiders were invited. They had one thing in common; all had been connected with the organisations, mainly concerned with defence, which had been pressing IBM to get into the computer business, and they were the people who had been doing the pressing. That communality of interest was recognised: they were each presented with a watch for having goaded IBM into entering the field of electronic computers.

They might goad, but an internal IBM decision had to be made: this final decision (heavily influenced by TJW Jnr and one A. L. Williams, both of whom we shall meet again) is arguably the last serious product decision that Mr Watson was to make in his life. From here on the future was to pass into other hands.

From that decision was to stem the particular style and form of the computer industry. A computer industry of course already existed, albeit a small one: IBM, however, was to set the patterns for the development of the industry. It might not initially have the leadership in the laboratories, but it was soon to establish it elsewhere through its ability to market.

The weight of its marketing effort was to lead to its competitors having to advance the state of the art in order to retain some market share. As soon as IBM saw that its market was likely to be eroded, it was then forced to release the same advance or its equivalent.

This was to lead to the concept of computer generations. A generation is one in which a change in the basic components, the circuits on which computing capability rests, leads to a sizeable jump in performance. In terms of speed of transport, comparable generations would be the horse, the steam engine, the internal combustion engine and the jet, covering a period of over a hundred years. The computer on the market was to be advanced comparably in its technology in less than twenty years.

The generations are vacuum tube, transistors, MSI (or Medium Scale Integration of circuits) and LSI (or Large Scale Integration). Vacuum tubes were comparatively slow and unreliable, transistors were faster. All the generations after the first are essentially transistor generations, the difference being in the end degree of integration. The more one can integrate, the faster the system can become, for less distance do the signals need to travel.

Naturally the change in components was to make possible changes in machine organisation, or what is called architecture. Speed was not to be achieved simply by faster components, but by the way in which they were put together. Architecture, of course, would also depend upon advances in the theory and practice of computing. Pulling these notions together, the significant IBM machines in the generations that followed become apparent. In the first generation they were the 701, 704 and 709, all scientific machines; and the 702 and 705, business machines.

The 709 led to the transistorised 7090 series, and with the computer numbered the 7094 IBM entered the second generation, which was also to include the 1401 and STRETCH.

The third generation is that of System 360, beginning in 1964, since when IBM had been evolving its systems so that they are a mixture of MSI and LSI: System 370 introduced in 1970 was initially known to the sceptics as Generation $3\frac{1}{2}$.

The 701, introduced in 1952, owed something to the von Neumann-designed computer then being built at the Institute for Advanced Study at Princeton. The 701 was to be devised within IBM, but not by old IBM hands. The researchers were post-war entrants. Some of them had been involved in wartime calculator developments, some indeed having worked on machines such as the ENIAC. And what had they been doing in IBM before Mr Watson had given his controversial go-ahead to computers? The 701 might be IBM's first computer to appear on the market, but strangely, Mr Watson's opposition or not, it was not the first machine that IBM was to start developing. Those newish IBM-ers had already been devising a computer, an IBM computer aimed at the commercial market and organised on very different lines to the von Neumann machine.

The 'secret' predecessor to the 701 was called the TPM, Tape Processing Machine. (There is in fact nothing secret about it, except that it does not fit the mythology, for the head of the project, one Ralph Palmer, has in fact discussed it in public.)

TPM was a modified 604 calculator developed at Poughkeepsie. A version of it was in existence and on display within IBM in 1950, and there had been at least a year's development effort behind it before anyone outside the team associated with its creation was allowed to see it.

TPM was an attempt to explore the possibility of using magnetic tape as a storage medium. It was aimed at commercial data processing and it was from this development that eventually was to spring the IBM 702 computer, though by that time, development experience with the 701 was to ensure that the result was a much larger machine that initially foreseen.

On the completion of the 701 development, the team were allowed to return to the development of the TPM or 702. The interval, however, had been critical: the 702 was almost immediately outclassed. It was facing a machine from UNIVAC which had *buffered input/output*, a technique which allowed the computer's performance to be more efficiently organised than otherwise.

IBM was not to make that mistake with the 702's successor, the 705. That too was buffered. By then they had dropped the Williams storage and its regenerative memory and switched to core memory (see page 28). Meanwhile, an Electronic Data Processing Machine Division under Executive Vice-President Louis H. LaMotte* was created to produce the 701, and a head of marketing appointed. The sales manager of the Electric Accounting Machine Division was to be Thomas Vincent Learson (see Chapter 8). Soon after, in 1954, he was to be promoted to Direc-

---

* Still on IBM's Advisory Board in 1974.

tor of the EDPM division and put in charge of engineering, manufacturing and sales.

'From the start,' recalls one of the participants, 'Learson used to come up to Poughkeepsie and bounce on the engineering people all the time: Hurry! Get the machines out.'

But Learson's prime responsibility was marketing, and in IBM's terms, marketing was sacrosanct. The machines were built to marketing requirements. Where market reasons are apparent, IBM has seldom been afraid of change providing it can be convinced that change will work in its interests.

The 701 was aimed at a market clustering round defence—it was initially called the Defence Calculator—which would ensure that eventually the taxpayer would be paying for it. Defence, however, also meant prestige. The first machine was delivered to Los Alamos in March 1953, and in April was introduced to the public at a New York luncheon in which every mathematically-minded eminent American scientist who could be persuaded to be paraded was paraded.

Already IBM was image-building. The THINK article commemorating the 701 may not say much, but it does give some revealing glimpses of IBM internal method. Richard Whalen, designated 701 production manager, was given some starting advice by the then General Manager of IBM's Poughkeepsie plant, Smith Holmans: 'Lay out the department so it looks like a manufacturing set-up. It's the first one in the world. I can't tell you how to do it. But customers will be coming to visit us, so you've got to make it look like we know how to build computers.'

It was advice that IBM was to follow ever after. It was not simply that IBM did not know how to build computers on a production line basis: after all, no one else did either. Whalen could not be told how to do it because there was a more fundamental lack of know-how: this was to be IBM's first real taste of the production end of the electronics business. At this end it knew little about vacuum tubes and even less about electronic storage media, even magnetic tape. But here was IBM suddenly involved in the manufacture of its own tubes (the designer of its storage system, Phil Fox, states in that article: 'As far as I know, this was the first electronic component that we made and used commercially') and the assembly of all sorts of unfamiliar components.

As for magnetic recording tape, Whalen recounts the tale of the time he was called to the inspection area, where an inspector had unrolled about a hundred feet of magnetic tape on the floor to check the quality. On asking the inspector what was the matter, Whalen was met with the immortal reply: 'It's no good, there's no adhesive on the back.'

Little things such as lack of experience, however, were not going to stand in IBM's way: nobody else after all knew much more.

Almost overnight IBM became committed to the computer business: the cause was the reception that the 701 was given.

It is a cliché of image that the computer industry tries to present, that the computer we have today is the result of competitive free enterprise and the market system: by acumen out of foresight. That Mr Watson was finally pushed into the production of computers as the result of a Washington initiative tarnishes that image a little, but not as much as the reality that was to come. For, though IBM did not then realise it, its early computers were superbly timed. They hit the market at the peak of the curve in every profit-conscious free enterpriser's dreams; it was almost the ultimate in sellers' markets. For the Cold War was at its height. It did not matter much what tab was put on computers, those with access to the public purse were prepared to buy.

The management of Douglas Aircraft, for instance, was debating whether or not to order the 701, and when the word came through that Lockheed had ordered one Douglas signed an order the same day.*

The machines which had been transitional to the electronic computer had largely come out of defence expenditure, and the computers that preceded the 701 had all been devised for uses which the government was happy to support. Where it was not, they were university give-aways,† tax deductible, a magic phrase to the spirit of any corporate accountant.

---

* It was also needed by the intelligence community, particularly the National Security Agency and the CIA. Cryptoanalysis and intelligence data filing was to become a large source of IBM income. Of course IBM did not sell directly, initially other names were usually put on the contract. There was a point in the fifties indeed where cynics used to make comments of the sort that judging by the contracts awarded, the U.S. Navy had more computers than it had ships.

† Thus the IBM-built ASSC designed by Aiken had been a gift to Harvard. The talk had been three to five million dollars; but the cost to IBM had been between one and two.

ENIAC had been sponsored and paid for by the U.S. Army, Whirlwind by the Navy, Eckert and Mauchly's first contract had come from the Census Bureau, and their next from the aircraft industry. The work in Germany had had military connections as had the work in Britain. The components, too, had all mostly been developed with taxpayers' support: even the Williams tube had originated in Research & Development done for military purposes.

IBM had had its share of R&D dollars, but much of the funding had not been directly concerned with its main business. However, it was now going to make up for the past. It was to attract a lot of R&D funds under one heading or another, and it was for a few years to be faced with a government market in which expense hardly counted and formalities were minimal. Due to the exigencies of defence, it was going to be able to write its own contracts with hardly any interference or policing.

Within a couple of years some people were waving more than just blank cheques around. One then would-be customer remembers going to IBM with a two-page order letter signed by his treasurer. The first page was blank, the second page typed with their standard terms of contract. The customer knew what he wanted the machine for, what he did not know was exactly what the machine and its subsidiary units would cost. So the blanks included the space for the figures. He agreed with IBM exactly what it was he was buying and at what price, and then the first page was typed up in a matching type-face: IBM had its order, and they were both happy.

The reason for that happiness was that IBM's deliveries were scheduled from the time the order was received. Of course, this did not necessarily mean that the customer would get delivery of that order, for with the 701 the government was just as likely to reschedule—as it did in the case of Los Alamos.

There was the customer who wanted a high-speed storage unit, one larger than IBM then marketed. When told that it would cost half a million dollars, he replied that at that price, he would take two. As he said later, he knew enough about the technology to know that at half a million dollars, it was underpriced.

IBM would not accept the order for two. It took an initial order for one, and stated that price for subsequent units would be set later. Eventually that user had three of the units, the second and third each rented from IBM at a purchase price equivalent to a million dollars.

In late 1954, there came what was to become known in computer circles as the second Oklahoma Land Rush. This was the competition for the 701's successor, the 704. The rules were still basically simple: that the first customer order to be received in IBM New York, complete with all the appropriate signatures and precise figures, would be the first in the delivery queue, and so on thereafter.

(The rules originally stated that the order was to be delivered at the local IBM office. Then somebody said: 'Oh, my God, what do you do about California versus New York, all those different time zones?')

One of the first major users was American General Electric, whose computing activity was headed by Herb Grosch. He recalls being no boat Pratt & Whitney out of that pushed through cleverness and chicanery' with the help of his local Cincinnati IBM salesman. IBM sent out the prices on the Friday night. 'My guy went down to his office on the Saturday, taking with him the order I had given him, all pre-signed and ready to go, regardless of price. He was going to take it and stamp it in his own office. He read the new rules and on his own initiative went down and bought an airplane ticket and flew to New York. So did the Pratt & Whitney salesman, who was just as clever. But he had not worked in New York City, so he went to World Headquarters, which was the obvious place to go, and was waiting outside the door at 9.15 when they opened.

'However, my guy knew that it said New York, it didn't say World Headquarters, so he went to the downtown office which opened at 8.30 and time-stamped it there: and won by 44 minutes.*

'I ordered three 704s simultaneously ... in the end I got numbers 3, 20 and 60. I stretched them out in order to get a later model ...'

In little more than a couple of years, Grosch had taken GE's

---

* It is a good story, and for years Grosch believed that he had been the first, only to find on reading the draft of this manuscript that someone else had been there before him. The RAND Corporation's order had been time-stamped in New York at between 7.0 and 7.30 a.m. that same morning. But it did not make any difference, because here too government had interfered and re-scheduled deliveries.

computation requirements from something which brought IBM in a rental of $3,000 a month for business machines to $50,000 a month with the 701, and then $120,000 a month with the 704s. Other people were operating similarly, if not on quite as large a scale.

And yet this was nothing compared to what was on the way. MIT's Whirlwind had metamorphosed into the basis of one of the major defence contracts of all time: SAGE. Whirlwind had led to Project Charles, which in turn led to the establishment of MIT's Lincoln Laboratory (a collaboration with the U.S. Air Force's Cambridge Laboratory, which was heavily involved in data transmission techniques and concerned with how to get the information from radar scanners to computers). This was followed by the Cape Cod air defence experiment of 1952, which used Whirlwind linked to radar. The results of that led to the decision to build SAGE, for which IBM was to build the computers. It was to be a multi-billion dollar decision: an air defence system which was to cost America in the region of ten billion dollars over the next ten years. Although most of this went into weapons systems, IBM's contracts were substantial: that first SAGE computer came out of the direct line of development of the 701. It was called the Q7, and with its surrounding kit weighed over 110 tons and contained nearly 60,000 vacuum tubes.

Each SAGE installation required two computers: in the terminology, the computers were 'duplexed' to allow continuous operation in case of a breakdown of either one.

The SAGE system took many years to develop. Though delivery of the first machine was scheduled for 1955, it was to be 1958 before the first installation went live and 1963 before SAGE was fully operational. But by the mid-sixties there were nineteen computer centres based on the Q7. And the average cost of each computer had been around $20 million.

Yet once again the unhappiness of IBM with new and changing technology was to be demonstrated, even where the settlement cheques were open-ended and government-guaranteed. The bidding procedures might be more complex than those of wartime, the days when some defence sales were simply negotiated between IBM senior sales executives and Armed Forces personnel during morning canters on the outskirts of Washington. IBM had to be sold SAGE, it did not welcome it with open arms. The same

Birkenstock, this time accompanied by T. V. Learson, had to go round the defence establishment asking for advice: Should IBM build the SAGE computers, and if so, what advice would people give them?

As so often happens with defence, cost figures are scrambled. But within a short time, IBM was making at least a hundred million dollars a year from the defence budget, and that was to climb considerably before the fifties were out. But what defence paid covered much of IBM's R&D, and that was to be put to more commercial use. For, apart from the civil market, there were also civil government orders . . .

Some idea of what was at stake was to be noted by Hilary Faw in a 1965 internal IBM memo, where he noted that the high-end (large, fast and complex) scientific machines alone, the 701's successors the 704, 709 and 7090 91 had brought in $130 million in net profit before tax through 1963.

As to the *development* of the computer generally, there was long a belief in the computer industry that during the fifties the U.S. Government spent around $250 million on development directly relating to computers.* Component development, too, spreading over more time into the sixties, was widely estimated to have cost another $250 million. Much of the first went to IBM, in part through the SAGE contract, much of the second went to IBM, in part through the components that IBM was buying in.

The majority of the 701 customers might not come directly within the straight government development-order-delivery cycle, but the majority were still to be paid for by the taxpayer. And they were to have one effect: they were to lead to the taxpayer being called on to spend even more, though no one might tell him so directly. The 701 was almost too successful in the sense that the machines almost everywhere were immediately running as continuously as their not very good reliability would allow. Thus, Herb Grosch recalls that in the mid-fifties at GE, he was using 160 to 170 hours of machine time a week, on his own machine and on any other machine where time was available for hire. He was anxiously awaiting the arrival of the 704 (then still known in IBM as the 701A).

---

* Whether or not this includes the CIA's expenditures, I have been unable to establish. But it is worth noting that the first of the large information retrieval system, WALNUT, was to be built by IBM for the CIA in the fifties.

Dr Grosch was not alone: this was the situation almost everywhere computers were in use. Computing requirements were beginning to exhibit their familiar tendency; whatever the time available, it was not enough. There would not be the capacity to do what was required till the appearance of the next machine; that, in turn, would also exhibit the same tendency.

The situation was tailor-made for a growth-oriented company like IBM: but reliability was a problem. To obtain reliability and faster performance, IBM was to switch to core memory which was to be at the heart of both the 704s and of SAGE. With that switch in 1954 the real rise of IBM begins. IBM had never let its lack of technology defeat it before. It was not going to do so now.

One of the strengths of IBM had always been its grip on the relevant patents. IBM understood then, as it does now, the use to which patents can be put. Unfortunately it did not own the core patents, nor had it a license. At the start of the fifties, it had few patents which were relevant to the technology central to the computing part of electronic computing. It was now to make up for it.*

To get into core memory IBM had to buy up patents—and there seemed to be a lot of them on the periphery, all having to be individually negotiated. It was costing time, and it was costing millions of dollars.

The key core memory patents concerned with the creation of a three-dimensional array which would allow more than limited storage to take place were to prove the biggest problem. These were owned by Jay Forrester and MIT. The situation became very complicated and expensive, so much so that at one time IBM nearly decided not to go ahead with core technology. Had it not done so, IBM would not have been in the computer business on the scale we know today, for in the short term there was just no way around. But IBM has seldom ever admitted that it was wrong: management decided to persevere, using its cash to make up for its lack of know-how.

Core might add to IBM's costs; it was not, however, to add as substantially to IBM's prices as might be thought. For it was

---

* So much so, indeed, that in the 1956 Consent Decree settlement the list handed in showed that its computer patents by then far outnumbered its tabulator and accounting machine patents, the reverse of the situation that the Justice Department expected.

about this period that IBM began to arrive at a new basic pricing technique. Computers were not to be sold or rented at prices which bore much relationship to what they cost to produce, but according to performance ability. This was a further extension of prior practice with business machines, a practice equivalent to metering, in that the rental charged was tied to what went through the system.*

From the start, the ability of a computer to perform calculations in a given period of time had been used as a technological measure of capability. And it was to discover a major similarity between computers and power stations, the more the throughput the more devices could be slung round them. As each computer model was a unique entity with its own peripheral devices, IBM could charge roughly what it liked. And it did.

This pricing technique was to make the growth of IBM possible. It was a subtle a superb technique, providing that one can had the right type of user to play it on: reasonably well off, inexperienced and dumb.

And initially not just the dumb and inexperienced. There were those about who were as aware as IBM of the costs of computing. 'We knew,' as one put it, 'exactly how IBM were raping us.' But that did not really matter: it had set the price levels around which everybody operated, and it still ended up with the best price/performance ratios. So the users paid, sometimes grudgingly, but they paid.

However, when one turned to commerce, it would be fair to state that the majority of initial users were well off, inexperienced and dumb. By the late fifties, the majority of users were no longer defence-oriented: they were commercial, companies wanting that computer to do simple things, lots of dumb things. And they

---

* Much later T. V. Learson was to propose that IBM add a new twist to the form of metering that IBM had long practised. Limiting users to the purchase of punch cards from IBM had itself been a form of metering by monitoring the numbers users took. IBM had a different and even greater producer of revenue in what was known as extra shift rental, in which if the renter wanted to use the machine above a standard number of monthly hours, 176 hours being a standard sort of figure (which meant that the user had a possibility of 22 eight-hour shifts a month), he had to pay more. What Learson was to propose was essentially a scheme which would effectively monitor the number of operations taking place within the computer: the greater the number of operations, the greater the rental. It was never seriously considered, not due to anti-trust implications, but because it was supposed to have become apparent that had any such scheme been seriously introduced, IBM's revenues would have gone down, not the reverse.

suffered, often without realising it. Yes, the computer could work at the promised speed, and the delights of computing were there for all to try. But nobody actually indicated that to make effective use of that throughput capability would require that the user have a lot more software covering many more applications than IBM or any other manufacturer was offering.

IBM could keep such users happy, but the defence and scientific users were another breed. IBM might initially have been 'the best game in town', now this was becoming debatable. It was to be argued on the high-technology market more seriously than it had been in the past, for the open cheque-book customers of the early and mid-fifties were no longer so eager to go along with IBM as sole supplier: they were often looking at other options.

That difference between the two breeds of user was to lead IBM into the first of its major electronic computer wars: IBM was now to try once more to achieve a situation similar to the one Mr Watson Snr had accomplished with punch card machines.

CHAPTER FOUR

Round 1: The War on Control Data Corporation

The IBM war on CDC is important, and not just as history. It may have started over ten years ago and officially have been finally settled 'with prejudice' (a phrase used when two parties by coming to an agreement have debarred themselves from taking action against each other ever again, at least over the same facts and territory) in early 1973. It is important, however, because the events that surround the case are a critical part of the Justice Department suit against IBM, and thus we have not heard the last of them.

The actions that IBM took against CDC were in substantial measure responsible for much of IBM's growth thereafter: how much so it is, for this author at least, impossible to quantify. Much of the data needed to base conclusions is either still in IBM or barred by legal privilege. All that can be said from the events of the market-place is that IBM's gains thereafter—and everybody else's losses—can probably be counted in billions of dollars.

On Wednesday, 11th December 1968, the Federal District Court in St Paul, Minnesota, was handed one of the most massive and comprehensive private anti-trust suit filings in America's history, and that from one of Minnesota's most prestigious technological companies: Control Data Corporation, best known as a manufacturer of large scientific computers, a company which was soon to report (excluding activities centred outside computing) 1968 revenues of nearly $440 million and earnings around $20 million.

CDC was taking on IBM. There had been rumblings from CDC for a long time about IBM's market-place behaviour. Two years before, in reporting a small net loss for 1966, CDC's Chairman William Norris had publicly stated: 'IBM has been out to get us, and you can print that.' Now at last CDC was striking back—and with superb timing at that. It had just announced its CDC 7600, claimed to be the largest and fastest computer in the world.*

It was obvious that in filing its suit, CDC was protecting itself from any counter-moves that IBM might make on the market, the sort of moves to which it objected in the complaint, which it claimed were monopolistic in intent and anti-competitive in practice—and which were spelt out in the filing presented to the Court. As important, the filing was made soon after IBM had let it be known to the industry generally in a 'we don't mean you any harm', gift-horse type of gesture that it was considering the separation of some of the services it was offering from the total package it had on the market: it was considering what became known as unbundling, the separation of the pricing of the computer system and the software that went with it, so that users buying one would not have to pay for the other whether they wanted it or not.

That bundled practice was beginning to look suspiciously like a tie-in sale, an 'if you take one, you must take the other' behaviour which could be seen to offend against existing anti-trust legislation. It was just one, and by no means the only or even major, aspect of IBM's practices which had led to vociferous and lengthy complaints about IBM's behaviour by almost all of its major competitors (including CDC: this was also to feature in its suit), behaviour which in 1966 had led the Justice Department to start investigating IBM for possible anti-trust violations.†

But still Justice had not filed its suit. The CDC suit also looked

---

* This time CDC was wrong. The 7600 was to replace the CDC 6800, a computer system which CDC had in its turn announced prematurely in reaction to IBM's 90 Series moves, but had never been able to deliver—though some CDC sources maintained that many of the program problems and delays had been caused by the way CDC had been 'bled' by IBM.

† IBM's 'unbundling' task forces quite specifically attribute unbundling to the suit filed by Justice—and Justice in its turn was triggered off by CDC. It is believed that CSM advised IBM that the practice of unbundling was illegal under Section One of the Sherman Act as far back as 1965.

like a forcing move, for even if a small percentage of the measures that CDC claimed IBM had taken really had occurred there was a much broader charge to answer. Justice would have no option but to go ahead and file.*

The case was defined by the Sherman Act, Section Two: IBM had monopolised and attempted to monopolise various markets and sub-markets defined in the complaint. CDC sought to have IBM broken up and asked for punitive triple damages (three times the damages adjudged suffered), the standard plaintiff's remedies. However, the key complaints were those for which it sought restraining injunctions. It listed thirty-six practices of IBM, mostly out in the market-place.† They included such activities as interfering in customers' negotiations with competitors and intimidation of would-be customers' personnel—standard routines as far back as Mr Watson's NCR days. But more important, they also included another group of practices. As a result of the CDC case a set of twentieth-century industrial marketing phenomena enter the economic language: paper machines, fighting ships and phantom computers. It was these last that CDC was really after.

The ability to sell something you do not have and cannot create is not strictly a twentieth-century phenomenon: people have been peddling nostrums for man's incurable ailments, and even more incurable greed, probably since the first barter transaction was made. The twentieth century's main variant, however, is not quite as hit or miss, though it still retains a large element of faith: the faith of the purchaser that the one offering the nostrum will be able to create it. The variant is a phenomenon based on one proposition, that the solution that does not exist today can be made to exist, if not tomorrow at least within the foreseeable future, and that the purchaser should therefore wait. The reason the purchaser is willing to wait is known as technological change, the ability to solve a set of problems from technology which has not yet been tried on the market because it is new.

In the hands of most supplier companies, this is a perfectly legitimate operation. They begin with the notion of creating

---

* And so it proved. Justice filed a month later.
† The thirty-six practices complained of were so stated that CDC covered everything that could be considered, so that if IBM wriggled out from under one charge it could be caught under another.

something to fill a presumed need. They may fail; failures for instance, in the defence field are legion. They do not set out to fail, however, for they advance their own interest by succeeding.

At the heart of the CDC charges, however, was the IBM twist on that technique. IBM was using the expectations of proposed customers, and its own reputation, to create products which were products only in name; they were paper phantoms. It was contracting to deliver those figments of IBM imagination at specific prices, and those prices would not be set or tailored around what the product cost to manufacture, but to the prices that were being charged by its competitors.

It was using these techniques to buy itself time while it developed machines that might conceivably work and hold off competition. It was holding off the competition for different machines and had little intention of delivering the offers it made on the market at the prices stated.

The CDC suit was to be progressed by the lawyers for over five years, until what became known as "Black Friday", the 12th of January 1973.* Shortly after, it was announced that a settlement had been revealed—the largest private settlement in such a suit in American anti-trust history. The settlement contained the usual disclaimer of admissions of guilt: nobody admitted anything. But legal precedent and common sense, as ever, differ: there was no question who had won. IBM paid CDC $15 million to cover its legal costs and agreed to sell CDC the IBM Service Bureau Corporation for $16 million, which was SBC's depreciated book value and as such was a 'steal'—and both IBM and CDC knew it. (The previous year SBC had grossed over $60 million and showed

---

* The CDC story comes under the heading of 'the one that got away'. A month before the settlement, I went in to CDC to discuss several matters, among them the progress of the suit. Unusually, there hadn't been a journalist in the place for weeks. The now deceased CDC Vice-President in charge of press relations proceeded to explain to me why little could be said. However, he suggested that I talk to Dick Lareau, a CDC officer and its Chief Counsel. The meeting was fixed on the spot. This should have alerted me. I was a little tired, and I knew that there was something unusual about the meeting, particularly when most of the time was spent in making me talk. It was not till a few weeks later that it became apparent that I had gone into CDC at a time when they had just completed a round of the negotiations, were working out their position for the next, and were more interested in finding out whether I had stumbled across what was going on than in answering any questions.

But you can't win them all.

profits of $1·5 million.) IBM further contracted to use SBC services at $5 million a year for five years and covered the retirement benefits of former IBM-owned SBC employees at $2·6 million a year for ten years. IBM also awarded CDC four five-year R&D contracts worth in total around $24 million.

What did IBM get out of it? Part of the settlement agreement was that CDC should destroy its legal work product, the CDC created index to the critical IBM documents it had obtained through legal process. It was widely assumed that the publicly expressed IBM satisfaction with the settlement (IBM's Chairman Frank T. Cary: 'This settlement . . . gives fair value to both sides') was due to the removal of this serious IBM embarrassment, taking away one of the main tools that could be used by others also in the process of suing IBM, particularly the Justice Department and the Telex Corporation

In the short term, this might be so. With IBM, however, one must always think about additional considerations, and those got surprisingly little attention. The two companies signed a worldwide patent cross-licensing agreement covering computer networks and such areas of technology as magnetic storage, special software called transaction oriented and terminals. The first area was one in which IBM skills were woefully deficient. It was concerned with operations in a communications environment, an area where IBM was not as commercially strong as it could be; having decided, however, that this was the direction in which computing was going, IBM was going to make sure that its patent position was strong. This was, in fact, no more than a repetition of the moves IBM had made in the fifties to make sure it had access to the technology it needed to make IBM computer manufacturer possible.

However, the CDC case and the events which led to it are interesting not just in themselves or for these issues but as an example of IBM's practices and behaviour towards the rest of the computer manufacturing industry. What IBM did to CDC, it had done towards everybody else, though not in such a consistent, cover-all-options fashion. This tells us a lot about IBM as a monopoly, *de facto* if not specifically *de jure*. It provides insight into the character of the men who ran and still, in the main, run IBM. It gives indications of the economic power that IBM wields and reveals some of its mechanics: the cleverly, almost intuitively designed structure; the internally buttressed machine that the Watsons built.

First it needs to be pointed out that the behaviour of IBM during the period of the presumed CDC challenge was remarkably similar to the behaviour of IBM throughout its history. The reactions were normal, though the techniques might be updated. The 'phantom computers' and 'paper machines' were subtle adaptations of ideas with which Patterson and the elder Watson were familiar. They would have approved of the variations, had they thought of them.

Both also would, no doubt, have approved of the end of the suit, an out-of-court settlement, concerning which neither party would say anything more than the formal statements and agreements they put into Court. That further explanations were not to be given may not be part of a written agreement between the two, though in view of the agreement they made while the case was in progress, it may well also exist.

Ten months prior to the final settlement the two suitors (a *post-hoc* description which seems appropriate in the circumstances) had entered into an information-exchange agreement which guaranteed confidentiality on both sides. IBM and CDC were 'desirous of exploring in detail the feasibility of consummating certain suggested commercial transactions between them'.

They were, in other words, trying to come to a settlement. Yet at the same time the CDC case was being progressed, and the Justice Department and Telex suits had been joined with CDC's for document discovery by the very court that was due to hear CDC's suit. A court obviously prefers that litigants come to a settlement, amicable or otherwise, one which seems to indicate that some form of justice has been done, before the court needs to rule. In this particular situation it was also obviously sensible for the parties to wish to keep quiet about their desire to arrive at such a settlement: publication of this news could, after all, affect the stock market price.

This kind of settlement, then, might be legal, but this one made a nonsense of justice. Moreover, the parties involved, one can infer, knew it. The document itself is quite interesting. It forbade either party from volunteering to the Court or to the Justice Department the knowledge that such an agreement existed between IBM and CDC. It carefully stated, however, that if the

Court made a specific request, then the existence of the agreement could be admitted.

The agreement is similar to the types of agreement that IBM generally makes or tries to make with its would-be competitors, which leads quite naturally to the story of IBM's reactions to the challenge that CDC was to pose. What follows is primarily concerned with the moves IBM made; however, to understand the suit at all, one must obtain some understanding of CDC.

*   *   *

CDC is headquartered in a tinted-windowed, white tower which dominates part of that fast-developing area lying between St Paul and Minneapolis, Minnesota. The tower is no longer quite as dominant as it was when it was created in the early sixties and CDC is no longer the same company. When that tower was built, CDC was a small company about which little was known, except that it was in an industry dominated by IBM, so dominated indeed that few gave CDC much chance of survival, and the building was jocularly and widely referred to as Norris's Folly.*

CDC's origins are in an early and small Minnesota-based computer manufacturer, Electronic Research Associates, which in 1952 was bought by Remington Rand (now Sperry Rand); like the Eckert and Mauchly Computer Corporation, Remington Rand ran ERA independently of its own mainstream activities until 1955, when the two computer interests were brought together and became the basis of what in now the UNIVAC Division of Sperry Rand.

At that time Remington Rand was treating the computer manufacturing business with low priority. It had started off with almost all the business, but Remington Rand's management seemed unaware that the computing technology was evolving

---

* One afternoon while the suit was in progress, William Norris was reputedly looking out of one of the windows when an aide pointed out a passing funeral procession, a seemingly never-ending line of black Cadillacs.

'Some funeral,' said the aide.

'That's no funeral,' snorted Norris, 'that's the IBM legal department returning from lunch.'

There are other versions of this story, including a statement attributed to Norris that 'I looked out of the window one day and saw a long line of cars approaching. I thought at first a funeral had lost its way. But they turned out to be IBM lawyers.'

rapidly as industry grew. In 1975, a dissatisfied William Norris, ERA's founder and by then a Sperry Rand Vice-President and General Manager of the UNIVAC division, left to found CDC, taking with him a clutch of senior associates. They started with little cash, and with one major intention: to build large, fast, scientific computers. And, in a repetition of history, with one major customer, the National Security Agency via the U.S. Navy (soon to be followed by the AEC).

It might seem odd that CDC was aiming for the scientific market; it seemed open to the fiercest of competition. It was the market in which IBM and UNIVAC had both had their biggest success, even if 'scientific' should turn out to be defence or defence-inspired.

But their competitors were not quite so well entrenched. By the mid-fifties both IBM and Remington Rand had realised that the major market of the future was going to be the business market, and they had switched their main drive accordingly. By 1956, the total U.S. civil/defence market already amounted to 500 million dollars a year, of which IBM had claimed half (according to T. J. Watson Jnr, in a talk he gave to his development scientists and engineers). In terms of usage, the business administration market was already outstripping the scientific.

There was another significant difference between the two which also needs to be brought out, one apparent from the early days. Business computing was naturally an extension of the tabulator–accounting machine business of the time. Here the computer was used for paper shuffling and printing; its output dealt mainly with simple answers to simple questions and the product of just as fundamentally simple analyses. In computing terms the tasks performed were trivial, but they led to a heavy utilisation of paper, to lots of storage,* to records of all kinds being kept in machine-readable form, and to a lot of input/output devices. Business computing also required that customers' hands be held; the customers might not be the great unwashed public, the costs of computing

---

* It could be argued that had there been minimal change imposed on the industry by the threat of competition, there would have been just as minimal advance. IBM storage was expensive—and of limited capacity. The IBM RAMAC 305 disc system, for instance, held around 10,000 'entries' or records. But a major insurance company might have a million such records. It seemed that a lot of RAMACs could be sold.

ensured that those could not afford it, but they were generally the great unskilled. Precisely in that lack of skill lay IBM's profits.

'Scientific' computing was much different. Much of the time its output could be handled by one printer. What scientists wanted was a machine which could chug along calculating the answers to a problem and which could then simply spew them out: one fast printer might do it. The print-out might be cluttered up with housekeeping and other data to enable one to find out how much time the run had taken and cost, but really the scientist was likely to get the meat of his needs without a large requirement for output devices. He might want it in a form which gave not just the answer but also the various steps taken on the way to achieving it, so that the results could be checked. Or he might, as in weather-forecast calculations, require the answers as lists of spot figures, each representing a point on a weather observation grid. He might even be satisfied by the statement of the final problem followed by the answer, requiring as little as a single sheet of print-out. But the demand for output devices to go with 'scientific' computers was low.

The requirement, then, was for large, fast, central processors with loads of main memory, of core storage. As for the software requirements, they might be large, but they were specialised, they did not cover the wide spread of territory that business administration led to. The hand-holding required was often unique and individual to each case—not then an IBM type of operation at all.

That CDC might grow into a company aiming at more commercial markets might be discerned from the markets initially aimed at. Mechanical calculation and machine computing has shown one major characteristic throughout its history. If you wish to know what techniques the businesses of ten to fifteen years in the future will be using, look to see what is being done within scientific installations, particularly defence-related: look within the prestigious engineering and science laboratories, the often government-funded research 'Think-Tanks' and similar institutions. Thus, modelling, computerised simulation and business games originate in a non-commercial environment, that of defence research.

The business game, indeed that most popular of executive training tools, comes out of the work of the RAND Corporation on military gaming. The key and initial work transforming war gaming into business gaming was done by Dr Richard Bellman, one of the world's leading applied mathematicians. It was an extra-curricular activity, tossed off quite quickly in his spare time.

These were techniques for using a computer. But nuclear physicists and weather scientists—also initially funded by military research —had an even greater influence on mainstream computing. They were the first to work with immense carefully structured files of data; they were the first also to have a need for software which would allow that data to be accessed and searched at rapid rates in a multiplicity of combinations. This was to be one of the major pressures on the development of computer languages, the devising of instructions which would enable the data to be manipulated and which in turn could bring out of that computer the information required in whatever combination specified as quickly as possible. There was almost always a good economic rationale behind that search, and no more so than in the use of computers in that most 'scientific' of tasks, weather forecasting. The problem there is simple to describe: it was useless trying to forecast the weather twenty-four hours ahead of time if, once you had collected the data, it was going to take thirty-six hours to process and compute it. The scientific requirement was simple: if it took two instructions to get something out, that was one too many: make it one operation and do not lose any accuracy. This principle has been the generally unseen and un-suspected driving force behind much of computer development.

It was the technological skills to make such computers work that CDC would have to obtain to stay in these 'science' markets. These skills in turn would give it valuable expertise which could be transferred to the commercial market, to the rich companies who were the source of IBM's steady profits. IBM knew that without the largest and fastest, most reliable machine, there was little in-centive for the large users to do business with IBM. Whoever had that machine should eventually be able to move down into the markets of the commercially hard-headed companies, often technologically innocent, in the *Fortune* 500.

The point was to be well put by IBM's chief scientist, Dr Emmanuel Piore, in a memorandum to T. V. Learson; indeed, it has probably never been better summarised: 'There are a number of scientific institutions in the world that require very large in-stallations to make progress on their problems. These institutions are easily identified; they work very closely together; they all have the point of view that their current installations will be too small for, or lack the power to solve, their future problems. These future problems also can be identified. Thus when these institutions obtain a computer complex; they are always projecting what will come next that is more powerful. *These same scientific institutions set the tone for industrial users requiring a large amount of scientific computation.*' [Italics added.] He might have added that in the long term they set the pace for those requiring any facilities for computation.

Still, given that CDC concentrated its efforts—and that they kept a profile low enough to keep them from irritating Galactic Headquarters, then they might do well. And initially, so it proved.

CDC delivered that first computer, a CDC 1604, to the U.S. Navy in 1960. The initial IBM reaction to CDC and its 1604 was confused; there seemed no way to compete which did not involve a major change in IBM policy, the separation of the charges for the machine and the services, maintenance and software which went with it. That change—the 'unbundling' previously described—was not to be announced for a further nine years. Initially, IBM did almost nothing, except to mount a study.

Within two years, CDC had moved into fourth place in the sales league of American computer manufacturers. By the end of 1964, after picking up a number of computer operations on the way (among them CEIR, and Bendix—for which CDC paid $10 million; a substantial acquisition for a company which six years before had had four employees and cash assets of under $20,000), CDC was in third place, behind IBM and UNIVAC.

The disparities, however, were large. By 1962 IBM had just over 70% of the market (incremental*) and was earning rental revenues of nearly $52 million a month, UNIVAC had over 11%, RCA nearly 3% and CDC something less, that last worth not much more than $2 million a month. The rest was spread over a large number of other would-be entrants in the field.

At the start of 1964, IBM's incremental market share had increased to 72+%, worth over $1,200 million a year; UNIVAC with 9% was running at around $155 million a year (and showing a

---

* There are two serious ways of measuring market share: cumulative, the current year plus all previous years; and incremental, the current year alone.

loss); and CDC, though it might be showing a profit, had roughly half that turnover. The difference, then, in the gross between IBM and CDC was approximately fifteen to one.

The 1604 was targeted on the then-largest machines around, including the IBM 704 (soon to be supplanted by the IBM 7090 Series) as well as the computers of other manufacturers; some, such as Philco, were soon to leave the business as they could not stand the pace. (Philco sold out to Ford.)

Between 1960 and 1964 CDC was to stretch computing considerably by increasing both speed and capacity. It came out with the CDC 3200 and then with a commercial-market version, the CDC 3600. Later it launched the CDC 6600, which was really to provoke IBM pressure. The CDC 6600 almost overnight upped the calculation possibilities in any given period of time, ironically also by fifteen, this time fifteen to one in CDC's favour—thus outperforming IBM and everybody else by a substantial margin.

IBM might have been able to contain the impact of a machine like the 3200—but the 6600? The performance gap between the 6600 and its nearest competitor was very wide; and the nearest competitor, to the chagrin of IBM—and according to its own calculations—also came from CDC: it was the CDC 3200.

This gave CDC room to manoeuvre. Suppose that CDC were to make the same move with its 6600 monster as it had done with the 3200? It would then have a range aimed at both scientific and commercial markets, and could target on IBM's main and most profitable business, particularly the richer corporations who were the most impressed by size and performance.

IBM was to overemphasise CDC's capabilities: it thought CDC was technically proficient right across the board. CDC knew differently, but IBM panicked. Panic was caused by a memo from IBM's Chairman, T. J. Watson Jnr, to his senior Corporate officers. In most organisations, a sarcastic memo from the chairman leads to something happening, and that reasonably fast. In IBM such a memo indicates that the Almighty is displeased and the necessity to eliminate the source of that displeasure, quickly.

Chairman TJW Jnr's memo was sarcastic in the extreme, and was to have precisely these consequences. (See Appendix.) The memo and its contents did not spring entirely from his own appreciation of the probable result. Its contents had been prompted by Dr Piore, who in turn had been stirred by one of IBM's senior scientific researchers, Harwood Kolsky. He had sent a paper upward arguing that, STRETCH fiasco or no STRETCH fiasco (see page 78), IBM had to show leadership at the high end of the range or else unpleasant consequences would follow, and those consequences would be felt in IBM's 'Gold Chip' accounts.*

Tom Watson Jnr was also being unfair to IBM. Change was on the way, but IBM was displaying its usual characteristic of keeping a number of projects—among them a large machine development called Project X, started in October 1961, in which government defence funding had a hand—quietly simmering, though not all with the same degree of urgency, in case the whims of those at the top indicated that IBM needed to move, and move relatively fast.

That the CDC 6600 announcement was on the way was well known to IBM, as it was known throughout the industry. As the CDC announcement drew nearer, the heat was turned up: the reason for it was not simply the prestige involved or what might indirectly or in the long term stem from it.

Prior to Tom Watson Jnr's memo, Vice-President T. V. Learson had written a few of his own, and their contents were causing concern in IBM's senior ranks. The first of them stated that a machine similar to the CDC 6600 had been estimated to have a market of fifty-three machines. 'If the market is anywhere near this number, we will be committing *a very serious crime* [italics added] in not moving Project X by some other solution at a more rapid pace.' The name Project X was, though it might not have been so recognised at the time, soundly chosen if X stands for unknown.

The second memo, acerbic in tone, was addressed to Dr Piore. In part it stated: 'Your position has always been crystal clear with relation for the need for Project X to move faster. Mr Hume

---

* The memo has since surfaced in the Justice Department trial brief—though its existence was never any secret in IBM as there was much argument among IBM's senior designers and researchers about what should be done, and that argument spread out into the computing community. Among other things, the memo contained the following statements: 'It should be deliberately done as a competition stopper . . . It should be a deliberate prestige gainer . . . It should be deliberately done as a money loser . . .' In the IBM reply, the IBM brief in the Justice suit, the importance of Dr Kolsky is downgraded and a note states 'his recommendations were not acted upon by IBM'. Nevertheless, there was a large machine programme, and it was for years pursued, though IBM's forecasts indicated that a loss would be made.

[1974—a Senior Corporate Vice-President] would be in complete agreement with you as to the need. Our problem is not this, our problem is resources ... Your letter of the 13th adds nothing to the situation which has been discussed with CMC [Corporate Management Committee] over the past 12 months. Don't you think that you and I owe CMC advice and counsel on the solution rather than a statement of the problem?'

Learson's memos might be fair, which is doubtful, but Tom Watson Jnr's was not. He had been responsible for pulling IBM out of the serious development of large machines for the better part of two years. But in the technologically advanced end of the computer business, this is precisely what a company cannot do. The reason is understandable. A computer system can take anything from two to six years to develop. If a manufacturer is to stay in that technologically advanced end of the market, development must be continuous and must at least match the capability of those companies fully committed. One cannot follow the then IBM practice of reacting to the market and expect to stay in front. But IBM had for all practical purposes, done so, primarily because the internal IBM advice had stated that the market just was not there for IBM, which was reason enough for Tom Watson Jnr to emulate his father.

The cause of that withdrawal had been a computer system called STRETCH, a project initiated in 1955 (STRETCH as in 'Stretching the state of the computer development art'). Initially it was developed under an AEC Los Alamos contract. The IBM authorised version of the STRETCH failure (as near authorised as these things ever are) was to be described in *Fortune* in 1966:

'The [STRETCH] computer had been designed to dwarf all others in size and power, and it was priced around $13,500,000. But it never met more than 70 per cent of the promised specifications, and not many of them were sold. In May, 1961, Tom Watson made the decision that the price of Stretch should be cut to $8 million to match the value of its performance—at which level Stretch was plainly uneconomic to produce. He had to make the decision, it happened, just before he was to fly to California and address an industry group on the subject of progress in the computer field.

'Before he left for the coast, an annoyed Watson made a few tart remarks about the folly of getting involved in large and overambitious projects that you couldn't deliver on. In his speech, he admitted that Stretch was a flop. "Our greatest mistake in Stretch," he said, "is that we walked up to the plate and pointed at the left-field stands. When we swung, it was not a homer but a hard line drive to the outfield. We're going to be a good deal more careful about what we promise in the future." Soon after he returned the program was quietly shelved; today only seven of the machines are in operation. IBM's over-all loss on the program was about $20 million.'

The article then went on to point out that two years after the STRETCH fiasco, Tom Watson had to say in IBM that 'his strictures against overambitious projects had not been meant to exclude IBM from this scientific market'.

What we have here is the story of STRETCH as seen through the filters that management imposes: an honourable failure in which real trial is made good. There is, however, another way of looking at it, which is not quite so flattering.

What IBM did with STRETCH was to devise a large machine for what it thought was a small market, and naturally enough it tried to price that machine against its expectations in that market. In reality the machine had been priced too high for its performance. The design intention had been to produce a machine a hundred times faster than the 704. However, the computer system that was produced was only thirty-five to forty times as fast. It had, however, been priced and sold as if it had more than twice that speed, and though some people in IBM maintained that once it was understood how to use the machine, it would reach around 75% of original design expectations; it was not to be given the chance. IBM had in fact spent about $50 million developing STRETCH, a derisory percentage of which was on its software: and IBM was not prepared to add substantially to the software expenditure.

The Watson intervention has been held up as that of an honourable man who, on hearing of user dissatisfaction, takes decisive action. Nobody has ever asked—at least in public—whether the action taken made sense. But there were those who thought TJW Jnr was wrong.

Had STRETCH been marketed as if it were forty times faster than the 704, the market would have been seen to be far larger. Those $13-million machines might have been produced in much greater numbers than the nine eventually manufactured, and for even less than $8 million; IBM might still have come out directly ahead. For though STRETCH was to be much maligned in IBM (nobody after all wanted to be associated with what management considered a disaster), technically that $50-million development expenditure was to be a cheap price to pay for a long-term result.

The 7090 had been the first IBM computer to make use of transistors: STRETCH was to add substantially to IBM's experience. From it stemmed some of the organisational concepts to be present in Series 360, many of which are still present in IBM's products today. From STRETCH was to come the development of the Series 360 standard channel, and that channel was to make the development of the Plug-Compatible-Manufacturer peripherals industry possible [see next chapter].

STRETCH is the first major example of a large computer development to go wrong within IBM, at least of a machine of which IBM was scheduled to build more than one. It was not to be the last. Yet, after STRETCH, TJW Jnr was to keep quiet about IBM's large computer mistakes.

The tale of IBM and the large machines is the perfect antidote to those who believe in the mythology of the large corporation as the solution to the problems of managing advanced technology, a mythology of which IBM is one of the stoutest advocates.

After TJW Jnr's memo, the story of IBM and the large machine market was, for the rest of the sixties, to be the story of mismanagement on a grand scale. Management was to indicate a surprising lack of understanding of the technology it was investing in and of which it was supposedly in control. Management too was to vaccilate between incompatible objectives.

Particularly at the top, as TJW Jnr's memo indicates, there is immense pride in IBM about the corporation's technological competence and capabilities. That memo was to start IBM on the road of trying to compete with the CDC technology which was targeted at the prestige customers: CDC had no option, those initially were the only organisations with a need for a large computer. It was natural then that the moves IBM would take would be aimed at CDC.

On the one hand, IBM wanted to save face: it did not want it said that CDC produces the fastest machines in the world. On the other? Tucked away in Corporate was a committee whose job was simply to consider the moves IBM was making on the market and their probable impact on companies such as CDC. It did not really matter if IBM drove, for instance, Sperry Rand, General Electric or RCA out of the computer manufacturing business —and its policies were eventually to eliminate the latter two. Those corporations were large and diverse enough to survive. However, the failure of the CDCs and other small companies was a different matter. The job of the committee was to ensure that the small corporations survived, not necessarily to achieve riches but at least to prosper well enough to keep IBM from having to face anti-trust problems as the result of their collapse. It was a committee which was to be singularly powerless, and no more so than when T. V. Learson and Frank T. Cary were to be in the IBM Data Processing marketing driving seat

However if the market was to be treated, IBM would require at least one large working, successful computer system. IBM was now to start investing heavily in the development of giant machines in its search for a winner. Many years elapsed, however, before such a working machine was to be delivered. During the interval Project X—for a computer with 10 times the performance of STRETCH—was to be transformed into the genesis of the 90 Series. Over the next six years, IBM was to introduce to the market the 90 Series, the 91, four versions of a system designated Model 92, and three versions of a Model 95.* Linked to Series 360, though much of the time the machines bore little relation to it, were to come the 360/64, 360/65, 360/66, 360/67, 360/70, 360/75, 360/81, 360/85 and, eventually, a really large system, the 360/195. And of these only three were to show a profit, one of them a derisory profit.

To get the 360/195 to market, and to try to develop its successor, IBM made three separate attempts at giant computer development (one of them, at Menlo Park in California, was an attempt to duplicate the methodology of CDC using a small, highly-motivated laboratory cut off from the rest of the corporation. Small in IBM's terms, however, meant starting off with a

---

* Ironically, in some of the accounts for which these machines were intended IBM lost out to CDC's 6800. This was the case in two Atomic Energy Commission prestige accounts. It needs to be recorded that, at the time, CDC did not have a 6800 either.

hundred people), and one attempt to bring out an even more advanced version of the 195, the 195-II, all of which came to
nothing.*

But all this was later. Back in late 1963, the problem out in the
market-place seemed to be that CDC needed to be stopped at all
costs. The basic Kolsky, Piore, TJW Jnr line had been endorsed
by the rest of IBM's management. As seen from those Corporate
heights, CDC was targeted on the advanced edge users; education, aerospace, nuclear research, space, weather, the oil industry
and the like. These were the prestige accounts, the pace setters. If
CDC became entrenched in these markets, could it conceivably
move down io the really profitable commercial markets? And
what would happen to IBM if it did?

IBM refused to consider such a possibility. Instead, it set out to
affect a situation where CDC would not be capable of moving
down, by making sure that it would have little or no place to move
down from.

IBM went back to Project X. And, what had happened to his
father was now to happen to Tom Watson Jnr: he was to be overtaken by events. IBM would react according to its own internal
dynamic, and its success at containing the opposition, particularly CDC, would help bring to the top the man who had
been carefully clawing his way up for nearly twenty years,
T. V. Learson.

Prior to the CDC 6600 announcement, Learson had been wary
of Project X. In December 1962, the Project X programme was
slow and unhurried. The first system was scheduled for announcement in December 1965 and for delivery in January 1968. The
programme was expected to cost $46 million, with the majority of
the costs—$25 million—being incurred in 1964/65. Learson in-
dicated that the programme did not look profitable and wanted to
slow it down. Four months later, in April 1963, Learson wrote to
Dr Piore that 'ultimately Project X will cost $30 million before we
receive any revenue. How much of this $30 million will ever be
recoverable is certainly very indefinite'.

By July, Learson was talking of costs of '$42 million to do an A
Test† and programming, product test, and engineering', going on

---

* Though a large computer derived from this is still eventually expected to surface.
† Alpha Test. One of a set of standard procedures that IBM goes through in bringing
equipment to market.

to state that other computers—which were late—were the key to IBM's business, and that Project X could be talked about in mid-1964 with orders being taken from early 1965. Already the schedule had been advanced more than a year. However, by late September, the situation had changed. Watson's memo had done its work, the conference having taken place at Jenny Lake in Wyoming, and the executives having been galvanised as to the criticality of what was at stake, Learson was receiving memos stating that 'DSD [Data Systems Division] was immediately moving to get one and preferably two contracts for a super machine', while B. O. Evans (Vice-President: Engineering) was being told: 'We have a clear mandate to move ahead on Project X as rapidly as possible', and that the mandate meant that they should be in an 'announceable' (they had the grace to put it in quotes in view of what followed) position 120 days on, with a firm machine at a firm price.

The memo continued: 'This obviously means that we must define a machine, do the best pricing that we can, define a market, and be able to announce a machine with performance and price by the end of the year.' The schedule had been moved forward one year more for good reason: the AEC was due to make a decision about a large computer for Los Alamos.

IBM was thinking in terms of a computer of 2·5 times the performance of the CDC 6600, to be marketed at $7 million. But it soon became apparent that $7 million would be far too high.

IBM was now going to start playing the numbers game. It was going to create those paper machines, phantom computers and 'fighting ships' (Vice-President F. T. Cary—now IBM Chairman, was eventually to use that phrase in an internal memo), loss leaders meant to 'unhook' customers from would-be competitors.

The techniques to be used might not of themselves be illegal—it depends on how the Consent Decree of 1956 was interpreted—they were, however, illegal within the company, in that IBM thought that a Court, faced with such manoeuvres, might well declare them to be illegal and on paper at least was not prepared to take any chances. The corporation had instructed its salesmen they were not to go around telling other companies' prospective customers 'Hold on, we may not have anything for you at the present time, but we do have something coming out in the future which will fill your needs,' particularly when nobody really knew whether or not that something would actually ever appear. Indeed, the *Fortune* piece was later to state that some employees who had practised this technique and had so told a customer had been fired. (But not by any means, all: at least one senior employee used to go out remarking, 'I'm off to break the Consent Decree again'.)

IBM had a rule book: 'Business Conduct Policies: Responsibilities and Guide'. And that book was well-known within IBM's senior management. On 22nd March 1961, speaking to a dinner meeting which included all the members of IBM's then Corporate Management Committee, the Divisional Presidents, General Managers and Staff Heads, i.e., most of the executives concerned with policy, Tom Watson Jnr had made a policy statement on anti-trust responsibilities. It is reproduced towards the start of the rule book. Among other things, after covering what was clearly illegal, it also states:

'The second class [of actions likely to be in violation of the anti-trust laws] consists of those acts which, though not themselves illegal, may create a pattern of apparent monopolistic practices. Even though no one will probably start a lawsuit over any one of them, these acts may accumulate ito an anti-trust action brought either by the government or by an aggrieved competitor. Examples of this category are:

'a. Unhooking—that is the inducing of a cancellation of a firm competitive order prior to installation.

'b. Proposals or mention to a prospect of a commercial product before it has been officially announced when done to thwart a specific competitor.

'c. Subtle disparagement of a competitor's products by suggesting for example that his cards may not work so well in our machines.

'Acts in this second category standing alone technically may not be a violation of the anti-trust laws. But when judged by hindsight, a series of several of these acts might be regarded as an indication of an over-all attempt to monopolise and provoke the institution of an action.'

That last sentence particularly was remarkably prescient. For this was to happen; IBM was to engage in what could only be described, to quote Tom Watson Jnr, as 'a pattern of apparent monopolistic practices'. The rules and guidelines were to be broken, and not simply by salesmen acting on their own initiative. Within weeks of TJW Jnr's memo reacting to the CDC 6600, IBM was to be marketing computers of unfixed characteristics, systems of a very flexible price, of which only one thing could be said with any certainty: there was no one in IBM who could give any guarantee that anything IBM produced would bear any resemblance whatsoever to anything that was being touted.

Why this powerful reaction? IBM might have a problem with CDC, but it was not facing CDC alone. American General Electric was offering a system at the top end of the range which also looked as if it would compete, and this system offered the new principle of time-sharing. In the more commercial smaller machine market, IBM was also under pressure from Honeywell. These pressures might not be reflected in the profits that CDC, GE or Honeywell were making; those— where any profits at all were being made—were derisory. They were, however, indicated by the orders being taken on the market. True, those orders were not that large in number, but the trend line looked wrong.

Even after IBM's anti-competitive moves begin in 1963, moves which put a stop to much of the competition's growth, one gets some idea of the way things were going by looking at comparative increases in turnover. During the years 1964 to 1966 IBM's computer system turnover was roughly to double. However, CDC's was to grow two and a half times, GE's fourfold, and Honeywell's four and a half times.

But by 1966, IBM in terms of annual rental received was still to pull in roughly five times the total of the other three combined ($2,500 million versus approximately $500 million).

That was not, however, how IBM Corporate executives saw the situation at the time. One of them remembers some of his senior colleagues wandering around the corridors saying: 'We're dead, we're going to be wiped out.'

Morale was also low out in the field, for good reason. As previously mentioned, the structuring of IBM's salesmen's pay meant that they were credited only with new business: where they had replaced prior IBM equipment out on rental, IBM subtracted from the commission the amount of rental lost by that replacement. And if they lost an account? That was also debited against them. CDC, GE and Honeywell efforts meant that many might well find themselves operating on negative commission, not the most inspiring morale-booster.

So IBM reacted. It started moving to knock off the competition. The knocking off of that competition began with the evolution of Project X into the 90: before long the 90 was to become the 90 Series: series, because each proposal was just not good enough and had to be superseded by another. Series 90 is of interest for many reasons, not the least of which is that it cut right across IBM's then current philosophy. At the time, IBM was in the throes of planning and developing Series 360. The rationale for this series was that there were too many incompatible IBM computers around. What IBM wanted to produce was a series of computers carefully graded in size and performance in order to have something available to suit any prospective user, irrespective of the size of his operations and budget. The series was intended to have a new capability: a user moving from one 360 to another would not, as hitherto, have to worry too much about the problems of conversion from one computer to another; the machines would be tailored so that such movement should be easy, requiring minimal software changes—if any at all.

But the 90 did not fit into the 360 framework: it was a machine out on its own. About the only long-term logical decision that had been made with the 90 was the numbering: it would fit at the top end of the numbering range for Series 360—whether or not the computer was compatible.

In many ways the situation had a hilarious side to it: here was IBM, $6 million invested in Project X development expenditure, with a schedule moved forward by over two years, sounding out possible users and preparing to launch a machine in the $7 million range, and no one in IBM knew exactly what it was that was to be produced. However, a Data System Development Division Status Report (June 1964) on the 604 project indicated differently. It is indeed a good example of the 'new economics' in action: the more you sell, the more you lose.

The report deals only with CPU and memory, and states the following (in millions of dollars):

'(a) At a price of $4·5, we could sell 26 systems and our total loss would be $41.

(b) At a price of $5·7, we could sell 12 systems and our total loss would be $45.

(c) At a price of $4·5, and limiting our sale to 12 systems, we would lose $56.

(d) At a price of $4·5, and limiting our sale to 2 systems, we would lose $39.'

The report then goes on to destroy one of the major IBM defences; that even had the programme been planned to show a loss, it needed to be looked at in the light of the contributions it would make to other future IBM product, such contributions far outweighing any probable loss to be expected. It does so by stating the following:

'(e) Although there was some disagreement on the point, the Financial people say that taking all development costs not attributable to the 604 and applying them somewhere else, would still not show a profit on the programme],'

Whichever way one plays with these figures, IBM still comes out making a loss.

The 90 was not to go through IBM without resistance. The corporation contained those who could in fact add when required and many of them were in its senior ranks in the Data Processing Division and Corporate headquarters. Their duties were to look at proposed future product, make market projections, calculate costs and expected revenues, examine the proposed technology, and then draw the appropriate conclusions, whatever those might be. But, to be able to draw conclusions, they must first of all receive proposals. Proposals for the projected 90 were put forward and were received with the kind of internal reactions one would expect.

Corporately IBM might wish to develop a computer deliberately created as a money loser (or more tactfully as one internal memo put it: 'a shared-cost development' for the benefit of the government), but if that was to be the case, then the decision to proceed would have to be made—and be seen to be made—at the top.

Non-concurrence is a dreaded word in IBM's management terminology. It means that someone somewhere down in the hierarchy does not agree with a formal proposal, on the basis that it clashes with what is laid down in his listed duties: it does not fill the criteria which must be fulfilled if a project is to receive a go-ahead. Among the non-concurrences that the 90 programme brought forth were those of Corporate Finance (including the then Assistant Treasurer, Hilary Faw), Financial Analysis—which saw the programme leading to a loss—and Product Testing—because there was no guarantee that performance would reach what was offered. There were those in IBM who had not forgotten the STRETCH fiasco, and they were in no hurry to repeat it. But Data Processing Division had its way. (It is worth noting that the management of DPD was to change hands that summer of 1964; it was to be taken over by Frank T. Cary, and his performance during the next four years was a key step on his route to the Chairmanship.)

In August 1964, three months after announcement, the Model 90 was withdrawn, and IBM seriously began to consider every possible move to destroy the competition's market prospects. First, IBM released news of its replacement, the Model 92, which was to come in two versions: the Model 92I and the Model 92J. The 92I was priced at \$4·38 million, the 92J at \$5·88 million,* the first having twice the memory of the second.

The 92 CPUs were really the same as those of the 90: the difference lay in the memory. But this change was not enough to meet the challenge on the market. In November 1964, IBM announced the 91, again with two versions, I and J the same processor as the 92 but this time with slower, separately-priced memory. This, in turn, enabled them to market it as a still cheaper computer system, \$3·517 million for the I version, \$4·795 million for the J, which had twice the memory of the first.

Still they had not got it right. IBM's management had overridden the non-concurrences: they were now to go further and ignore almost all figures dealing with the 90s, except one: What would the price have to be for IBM to get orders? IBM management now played with prices solely in relation to its opposition. There were to be eleven major price changes over those eighteen months with the 90 Series (but no changes in the rest of

---

* Even at \$5·88 million, the 92J showed a forecast loss. This is what one would expect. Management had made a decision to market 6/10 machines—but nobody was going to tell that to the sales force. Next, they projected 24 systems, which forecast eventually grew to around 100.

the line). CPU and memory speeds were juggled as if according to the wishes of the last customer an IBM salesman had spoken to. Even the salesmen sometimes were confused.

One month later, in December 1964, they rang the changes on the prices of the 92, chopping more than a million dollars off the 92J and half a million off the 92I, bringing the prices down to $4·4 million and $3·8 million respectively, while having speeded up the CPU. By January 1965, the price on the 92J had come down to $3·3 million and that on the 92I to $2·7 million. Yet even this was not enough. Frank T. Cary knew that the levels which would ensure that IBM obtained the orders were lower still, so he initiated instructions to Forecasting to work on the basis of a new bottom price of $2·3 million.

It was the classic loss leader situation. IBM's internal forecasts indicated that even were IBM to obtain 100% of what it judged the market to buy the losses would be heavy, for each machine would have to be sold at a minimum price of $4·792 million to recover costs, not $2·3 million.

IBM never delivered any 92s. Instead, having done their anti-competitive work well, in July of 1965 they were withdrawn and replaced by the 91/95, with three versions ranging in price from $4·05 million to $5·1 million.* The 91/95s had thin film memories, then a good sales point because much of the future of memory looked as if thin film was going to be a long-term answer: thin film seemed bound to continue to be intensely developed. Everybody was wrong.

By December 1965, the Series 90 programme was for 22 machines with a projected loss of $79·3 million. By July 1966, the programme had extended to 25 machines, with a loss projected at $108·9 million.† By the end of the year, IBM was announcing that no further orders would be taken. Within nine months, in the autumn of 1967, the series was finally withdrawn. All that IBM delivered were two 95s and approximately fifteen/91s.

---

* In another remarkable Freudian slip, the January 1975 IBM trial brief in the Justice case was to carry the following: 'Plaintiff correctly states that IBM manufactured 17 of its Model 91/95 "fighting machines".'

† IBM just did not care whether it made money on the machines, though naturally it wanted to minimise the loss. In 1965 T. V. Learson wrote to the president of IBM's SBC asking whether he had been advised to cancel his order for a 92.

The 91 should not, however, be allowed to sink into obscurity without recording a more than unusual failure (which also occurred on some other systems). There had been much internal debate about large machine programmes; it was a basic clash between two views of the world. On the one side there were those who wanted a set, properly organised programme of development, a lengthy operation; on the other, the usual marketing approach: we need a machine and we need it now.

It was the second route that had been chosen, and the waste associated with crash programmes was to happen. Some 91s were delivered, and before very long the first batch started to go seriously wrong. The 'cracked stripe' problem appeared. The transistors started to shed their working parts. Take off the back of the computer cabinet and one was likely to find bits of transistors all over the floor. What had happened was that the aluminium layer which carried the current round to those transistors was not thick enough, resulting in unexpected molecular level reactions.

This gives a good indication of the rush that IBM was in: the systems that started shedding were already in customers' premises, they were in intensive use, so much so that the shedding was first reported by a customer and was not found to happen on IBM's own internal engineering model till after the field failures had occurred. One gets some idea of the scale of the failure from an IBM employee's later comment that it led IBM to junk $15 million worth of components into the River Delaware. It was an underestimate: an IBM internal 1966 note put the loss at $24·3 million.

It was the rock-bottom $2·3 million System 92 price, however, which, in my opinion, was to show quite clearly IBM breaking the law. Instructions were issued stating that this price could be quoted to government and educational establishments (prime CDC markets) but not to commercial customers.

To say breaking the law is a strong indictment, and the phrase is not chosen lightly. If one believed that IBM was operating a monopoly in law as well as in fact, then the law was being broken, because it holds quite clearly that a monopoly cannot selectively price between customers; the same product must be offered to all at the same price. Selective pricing, however, was what was being proposed.

It did not matter whether or not IBM was held to be a monopoly. The Consent Decree of 1956 stated quite clearly that IBM was not allowed to practise discriminatory pricing. IBM had signed that decree and agreed to be bound by its conditions.

Nonetheless, IBM did discriminate in prices between customers—it still does today. Two methods are employed. One is the special system, the non-list price system order bid to government and its agencies. This price is easy to justify: the rules have been set up, and IBM must play by them.

The second is the 'bleeding heart' discount, so termed by sceptical observers. It is the discount given to educational institutions. Strictly, it may be illegal, but a blind eye is usually turned to it, for it can be made to look like a philanthropic gesture. After all, does it not show a saving to the public—and private philanthropic—purse? Should it not be welcomed?

Yes, except that IBM does not engage in it for philanthropic reasons or purposes. Educational institutions having IBM computers train students to use IBM computers, which achieves two ends: users of IBM equipment, not the competition's; what is more, users who learn about computing on IBM equipment at the time when they are most impressionable, while they are learning about computing. Secondly, it ensures that there will be a supply of people with IBM skills to man user installations, users who will not have to take all their training from IBM or their employers.*

But at the heart of the IBM educational market policies pre-Series 360, lay a cheerful, polymathic and shrewd executive, Charles de Carlo. (He was the only person in IBM during the fifties to forecast with any degree of accuracy the size of the scientific market and the profits that IBM might legitimately make from it.)

I met him in 1964 when he subjected me to a brilliant *tour de force* about the future of computers in education: not what was then being done, but what might be done given that one eventually had the technology. At the time, he was very involved in the educational market allowance programme, a subject much under

---

* It was to be well put in March 1966 by the IBM executive who supervised marketing to education. 'The term educational allowance implies an intent to underwrite education. This is not our intent.' Between 1966 and 1970, IBM's contribution to education was to total $35·7 million, a good 'charitable' investment.

discussion in IBM. Four months later, in October, he put forward a detailed exposition of a possible programme, one which would reconcile the interests of IBM and the education community generally, no mean feat.

The nine-page document covers a wide territory. It discusses how IBM has had a 20% discount programme for educational institutions for ten years, a programme which allowed a further 20% discount for machines used for scientific research and a further 20% for those also used for business research. Since institutions have begun to be involved in both areas, many have thus obtained a discount as high as 60%. By 1963, this meant that IBM was allowing the educational market a discount of $40 million, or around 2·5% of the revenues of IBM's Domestic DP operations.

Then the government went and changed the rules. IBM was interested in funding the research not being funded by the government. However, in the case of the Carnegie School of Technology, the government ruled that the educational allowance was a discount, and that educational institutions, therefore, should bill U.S. government-funded research projects at the 40% rate.

Thus, in the spring of 1963, IBM in turn reduced the allowance back to 20%. De Carlo proposed a massive programme which would get around the government's objections. The programme was well thought-out. He foresaw a university computing requirements bill over ten years of $2 billion, which, given that manpower costs equalled systems costs, worked out to $400 million a year.

Obviously, he did not expect IBM to foot that bill. But why should not IBM set up a foundation on the lines of the Rockefeller and Ford Foundations? With, of course, some differences. Series 360 would soon be to hand; as a result, IBM would have a large inventory of usable but commercially obsolete equipment returned to it. What better use for it could anyone foresee?

Among the suggestions he put forward was one in which IBM still held title to the computers, while the universities established a fair billing rate for government-funded work. IBM naturally did not want to get caught in a situation where it found itself giving things away to people who might then compete with IBM at rates below those it would normally charge.

But of course, a 20% discount and the other measures

proposed may not add up to 60%. There were provisions to take care of the interim period till the new policy was established and a proposal to fund and support university R&D in programming and applications on a value received basis.

It was this last that IBM's management was to develop. And the words 'value received' were to be loosely interpreted. This was to be the case with IBM and its relationship to the 'leadership' schools, the thirty or more major American universities which the rest tried to emulate.

Those grants were to be the mechanics by which IBM was to unhook many CDC orders. IBM would bid and so would CDC. IBM would be outbid, and would promptly counter not by lowering its prices but by offering grants, in one case for the exact difference between the CDC and IBM bids.

Those value received grants were in many cases to be the climax, for the value that IBM was asking to receive was not, as one might think, for IBM systems generally, but for the development of the institutions' own systems, providing of course that they were signed up to use IBM machines.

University administrators might be skilled at extracting money from corporations, but they were not as skilled as IBM. They might welcome IBM policies, but . . . Thus, for instance, Harvard in 1965 asked for value received contracts and liaison staff costing IBM a quarter of a million dollars a year, and stated that it was willing to commit to IBM for the next several years. In 1966 Dr Herman Goldstine of IBM recommended a separate grant of $100,000 a year to Harvard's Computation Centre for five years, an extension of a grant made in 1961. He noted that the University had made estimates of its net installed monthly position.

In 1967, it would be $229,000 a month, by 1970 it would have crept up to $865,000 a month. Over the five years Harvard would pay out in rental a total of approximately $32·5 million. 'Potentially, all of this can be ours and I would like to be sure that it is,' wrote Dr Goldstine. At half a million, it would be a cheap investment. It was. By the autumn of 1968, nine out of ten of Harvard's installed/on order computers came from IBM.

Investment indeed was how IBM regarded it, and anything it gave it meant to get back. In 1966, T. V. Learson wrote to John R. Opel agreeing that the education allowance on Series 360 machines should be 10% and telling him that someone else in the corporation was also considering what further reductions could be made.*

Both sides were playing games: the problem that faced IBM was that while it could give machines away, the recipient could not charge the government for the computer time that government-funded R&D took up.

MIT, therefore, proposed to rent an ill-fated IBM 360/67 at 30% discount. 45% of its time would be spent on government-funded R&D, to be billed accordingly. But MIT would receive a $350,000-a-year value received contract.

By February 1966, IBM was offering a $1 million a year value received and joint studies contract, had recommended—and had had accepted by MIT as the head of its Computing Centre—a man whom Goldstine was to describe as 'a good friend of ours'.

Goldstine had said that IBM was 'out of patience with institutions which took IBM's money and then went competitive' and had obtained understanding and agreement from the MIT dean concerned. He, in turn, had pointed out that MIT would soon be spending $5 million a year with IBM, not counting a Model 91 IBM hoped to sell to an MIT laboratory. Furthermore, within a few years he expected IBM's business with MIT to run at $10 million a year.

At the end? IBM was supporting MIT's computation centre with grants of $1 million a year.

IBM was also giving away free machines. Not entirely free, however: there were offers of so-called gratis machines at MIT, Cal Tech, and New York University, the last a straightforward attempt at unhooking CDC's lone 6600 1965 university order. But that attempt did not work. Normally such matters in IBM were decided in IBM's own stately measure, with some semblance of dignity. In this instance, New York University, a member of the corporate staff was advised on Friday that the matter would be raised at the Management Review Committee by Learson on the following Monday. He ended his internal memo up the line with the plaintive comment: 'I believe that DP should be required to clear such items as this through corporate staff with more advance notice in the future.'

---

* It has been 10% since 1969.

IBM might be able to contain the education market with cash*
and gratis machines. It was not to have the same luck at the AEC
where it was also in competition with CDC.

At Livermore it was offering 'free' 75s and had a $3 million
value received contract to try to hold the line. At Los Alamos it
was offering machines with free rental, and at maintenance
charges only, with hardly any rental returned to IBM for two
years, and then offering to buy back the two IBM 75s at 90%, all
so that it could get an order placed for a Model 95J. At Argonne it
was offering a 75 at full rental with a second one thrown in for free
for eighteen months, both interim to a 91 scheduled to be
delivered a further eighteen months later.

These were not merely straight attempts to match the competition—they were attempts made by IBM to live up to contrac-
tual responsibilities. It had taken orders for large machines it
could not deliver the proposed performance, and it was facing
substantial penalties.

The situation was no better at NASA. In late 1965 another
plaintive memo suggested offering them three machines on free
rental for two years after delivery 'because of this boo-boo on our
part'. 'Perhaps,' continued the memo, 'this will be the direction in
which we can find salvation.'

*   *   *

It is impossible, however, to recount IBM's war on CDC
without becoming involved in Series 360 and its announcement.
Series 360, however, is also at the heart of the case of the Justice
Department versus IBM, and to introduce it here means utilising
material which would otherwise be developed elsewhere.

According to *Fortune*, on 7th April 1964 there was a certain
amount of dancing in the streets, at least in those parts of
Westchester County (and elsewhere) in which IBM plants were
located. IBM had announced Series 360. It was a grandiose con-
ception, hence the number 360—as in 360 degrees, covering all
directions.†

---

* This allows the IBM cash contribution of approximately $63 million to educational
institutions in the thirteen years 1960 through 1972 to be put into better perspective.

† Which has led to the joke concerning its successor, Series 370, that it covers all
directions plus ten degrees.

The PR line might have been more specific, and there was talk. There was to be quite a lot of such talk, because TJW Jnr had put his thoughts to paper for the benefit of advertising and public relations. 'I would like to have this new product line announcement the biggest publicity announcement we have ever made in our whole history.' The memo continued: 'I would like to make sure that we have sufficient mock-ups.'*

The main mock-up was in the gymnasium at Poughkeepsie. It illustrated very well how unready IBM was to launch Series 360, and how it had been pushed into a premature announcement by its competition, thus totally violating TWJ Jnr's own rules, and that on his own orders.

Totally? Series 360 had been under development since 1961 under IBM's contention system.† It won through against two far less ambitious systems extensions of existing practice, designated the Series 1700 and the Series 8000. 360 was (at announcement) for a series of six computers ranging in size from the 360/20 at the low end through models designated 30, 40, 50, 60, 62‡ and 70, with the promise of even more models to be added later at the top and bottom ends of the range. All the computers were to be built of similar technology and would have common interfaces, standard software to control their operations (designated OS—for Operating System—360) and common input and output devices: there were to be 44 different peripheral devices.

IBM was now going to jump computer manufacturing into the standard model mass production business eliminating the production of its seven existing computer systems and replacing them with one homogeneous series with all that would imply for the user in terms of economies of scale and so forth. Except, of course, that the announcement was premature. It seems that the only machine that critics will agree was actually ready when announced was the 360/40—and much of the guts of that were

---

* The memo from which these quotes are taken appeared in the CDC trial brief and is quoted from an article written by Robert Samuelson which appeared in the *New York Times*, Sunday 3rd June 1973. It was not in the public domain at the time of research.

† The contention system is an ancient technique in IBM. The first record of it dates back to 1915 when Mr Watson Snr had put two separate teams of engineers to 'improve' an existing machine, and then held a competition between the two developments, the winner going on to full production.

‡ The 62 was a 60 with a different memory.

developed in the U.K. The critics, however, were more charitable than Tom Watson Jnr was to be. According to another of his internal memoranda written in late 1965: '. . . by the spring of '64, our hand was forced, and we had to *with our eyes wide open* [author's italics] announce a complete line—some of our machines were 24 months early, and the total line an average of 12 months early . . .'

TJW Jnr was writing at a time when IBM was under great production and delivery pressure, when at the top end of the range, the 90 Series and in the area of time-sharing, 24 months is nothing compared to what is to come.

The years of panic were from 1964 to 1966, the years when IBM sought to bracket every possible competitive announcement. Where the 90s were aimed at the CDC 6600, the 360/70s of the new series were targeted on the CDC 3600. But the 360/70 was a computer interim to the 360/75; it was a holding operation . . .

IBM annarntly CDC was experiencing problems of its own. The IBM fears of high CDC internal competence might be confirmed by the electronic computer that CDC had built. They were not, however, in terms of the turning of that mass of inert electronics into a computer system: CDC had underestimated the complexity of the task it would have to undertake, was experiencing delays with the writing and debugging* of its CYPRESS operating system and was raiding the rest of the industry for talent. Consequently, deliveries were running late. And on the market CDC was, as we have seen, facing not only a bewildering number of competitive announcements, but also extensive price-cutting to levels lower than cost.

In the spring of 1965, IBM took stock. The 90s had done their work well. From its having been without a competitive system to offer when the CDC 6600 announcement was made, IBM had in eighteen months achieved the following: it had won 76 CPU orders from 50 customers and lost 53 from 58 accounts, a 59% success rate. Expressed in this way, the figures masked an ugly reality for CDC: four out of every five of those wins had been against it. IBM might have other products to rely on, but CDC's options were few.

---

* Debugging means exactly what it says. To call it a process would make it seem more deliberate than it normally is. To debug is to remove faults and errors through a period of checks, test runs and working runs.

It was not just the price-cutting which led to a loss of orders that CDC had to worry about: one suspects IBM's actions also had another purpose. The selling of computer systems differs substantially from the selling of most capital goods. Each installation is supposedly tailored to a customer's requirements, and the proposals therefore take considerable time to prepare, as well as being costly in skilled man hours—of men who, because of the level of skill involved, are in short supply. It is possible for a large, aggressive corporation to run a small competitor ragged simply by putting in counter proposals against anything he bids. It weakens him in two ways. It ties up his resources, and it delays the time in which that order is likely to be settled, because the would-be customer is given an alternative to consider. If, in the process, one can add cash flow problems to those one's competitor is facing . . .

Naturally enough, while all this IBM activity was going on, CDC had not sat passively by. The CDC counter took two forms: it too cut prices, and then it too went down the road of the premature announcement, of which the 6800 was an example. That had much more basis in reality than anything proposed by IBM, for at least it was based on the notion of extending a system which existed, the CDC 6600. This is not, however, the game which one would choose to play against IBM. T. V. Learson, who had not got to the top of IBM's marketing section without gall, now started to accuse CDC of creating 'paper machines'. (His gall was eventually to be carried further when, after the filing of the CDC suit, IBM counter-claimed that CDC was trying to monopolise the large machine market. Yet at the time it did so, any market measurement of machines on order would have shown that IBM had in fact more large computer systems orders than the rest of the industry put together. That IBM could not deliver . . .)

But IBM had done its work well. Its phantom computers had brought in orders, even if they could not be delivered, and the serious growth of CDC was checked.

Settling CDC's hash at the large scientific number crunching end of the market had not, however, solved all IBM's problems with CDC. It still faced two others: the first was the minor one of the CDC 3000 range, the other that of Time Sharing. Initially, before Series 360, IBM coped with the first on an interim basis, offering an upgraded and repriced 7094 Model II. This upgrade was a holding job: IBM was preparing to announce a hastily-thought-out programme for a 360/44—a computer with near 360/50 performance at 360/30 price. This was essentially a 360/40 with extra core memory added, for CDC machines were hurting 360/40 and 360/50 sales. To ensure that IBM didn't lose in the 40/50 normal market, the 44 was not compatible with the rest of 360 and its programming limited. But IBM marketing was not to be anywhere near as successful here as it had been at the larger end of the market. CDC held on to many of its sales, and IBM only sold a few 44s: the size of the market had been overestimated.

Again, however, it was not just the small size of the market which was to cause IBM problems. In May 1965 the 360/44 was still not announced, though it was being touted and was continuous more willing to adopt other almost in desperation.

One memo to A. K. Watson stated that delivery would be in 24 months if the announcement were made within two weeks, that production limitations precluded manufacture of more than three units the next year, 1966, unless something else be given up, and that 104 360/44s could be produced in 1967. Whether 104 could be sold . . .? Three weeks later a memo to T. V. Learson stated that a final evaluation of the 360/44 indicated that it was a loser in price and performance.

The area of time-sharing was a different matter. The Series 360 might in theory be all-encompassing, but it was so only so long as everybody else was content to let IBM define what all-encompassing meant.

The notion of time-sharing is of critical importance in the development of computing: it is based on the proposition that not every user of a system will require the full-time use of a computer. The requirements might be for a large machine, but many users might only need a few milliseconds of that CPU time every few minutes. With time-sharing, they can get it when they need it and do not have to settle for a time chosen by others.

The solution to the problem is obvious and easy to specify, though at the time in practice not quite that easy to achieve: create a system which can be accessed by users from their own locations via communications lines, a system which will give each the semblance of having a computer at his own unique beck and call, though it may in fact be servicing many users at any given time. To make this possible demands a host of special tricks, both hardware and software. The first were not too difficult to manage, but the second were to cause IBM horrendous problems. Many of the problems associated with the Series 90 machines had been operating system software problems: in time-sharing those problems were to be compounded.

Time-sharing began in scientific and academic communities on both sides of the Atlantic. Much of its initial use was for mathematicians' calculations. There was a CDC offering in this area, but CDC was not really challenging IBM. The danger came from GE and its 600 Series which was entrenched at the Lincoln Laboratory of the Massachusetts Institute of Technology as the core of a much-publicised time-sharing system known as Project MAC (Mac for Multi Access Computing). CDC might be tackling everybody everywhere, but GE was riding high on the back of Project MAC. The tendency of centres of excellence to follow in each other's footsteps that had been noted by Dr Piore was in fact in full swing. GE had orders or letters of intent from Bell Telephone Laboratory; the Mitre Corporation, a noted, largely government-funded think-tank; the Systems Development Corporation, the computing offshoot of the RAND Corporation; the Universities of Michigan and of Stanford; and there seemed to be many others in the pipeline. What was at issue was specified in an IBM internal memorandum in September 1964:

'There is much more at stake than these few prestige accounts. What is at stake is essentially all computing business, scientific and commercial, *except in accounts where tradition or the superiority of the IBM sales force can overcome the fact that we offer an obsolete product.*' [Italics added.]

The IBM answer was the 360/64 and 360/66, proposals for computers based on the initial models of the 360/60 and 360/62, proposals so hurriedly put together that every sale seemed unique, the differing offers being referred to as 'so and so's variation'. These were 'withdrawn' and soon followed by that major fiasco, the 360/67, discussed from April 1965 and announced in August. Initially each sale was subject to systems assurance, which meant that every time a sale was in prospect the salesman concerned had to check back with DPD HQ in White Plains before being allowed actually to put anyone's name on the contract. White Plains, however, seemed to be giving approval to almost everything.

Once again, the anti-competitive nature of the offers was to be IBM internally demonstrated; once more Finance non-concurred. And, to put the seal on it, so did both Technical Development, the one IBM department which can be trusted to know whether a computer system can or cannot be built, and Field Engineering —which will have to service the offering. 'It is our opinion that the Time Sharing Systems being marketed today are *completely unserviceable in any manner that will result in customer satisfaction.*' [Italics added.] Management might overrule those non-concurrences, but how much did they actually know?

The 360/67 programme was to show IBM at its most unattractive. The system was clearly a loss leader; indeed, more loss than leader. However, it showed the limits to which IBM would go. The system required both a technological (electronic) and software advance. For the first, IBM did provide some advances in circuitry, but it lacked the critical 'virtual' technology. (Virtual is a technique we shall meet again.) While it is possible to create such Time Sharing systems without it, it is much easier with it—and now almost all large TS systems are virtual systems. The lack was even worse in software, and that was the real problem.

There are three ways of developing software. The first is to find a genius. The second, given that geniuses are scarce, is to aim for the next best thing: a small, highly-skilled, well-led team able to think through the problems; this route had been chosen by almost every successful management, but it was not to be IBM's solution. Natural to IBM was the third alternative: break the problem down into its component parts, assigning a part to each man; the more complex the system, the more analytical and programming manpower required. The difference in these basic approaches was summarised some years later as the 'Superprogrammer versus the Mongolian Horde'.

It was a disastrous undertaking—and offered no solution whatsoever for a very long time (though the team leader, such is the way these things work, was to be awarded a software prize for his contribution, shortly before IBM scrapped it).

At one point IBM had reportedly nearly five hundred specialists tripping over each other—including a hundred or more PhD graduates—trying to write software. Unfortunately, the route chosen for them to follow was virtually guaranteed to cause the maximum confusion. They were trying to write TSS (Time Sharing Systems) software and to reconcile it with standard IBM operating system software—it was an attempt to reconcile the irreconcilable, a situation which seemingly could be seen by everybody except IBM.

At its height the progress of a nearly normal ulcer-provoking day was described by one of the participants as going roughly like this: 'You would come in in the morning and find thirty or forty memos on your desk, mostly dealing with specification changes and announcing meetings to take place later that day. You would go through your version of the specification, enter the alterations in your manual, and think about what they meant. This would lead you to see that if you changed *this*, you might well need to change *that*. Or, instead of something being wrong, for that always happened, you would find flaws, things that people had overlooked. So you would spend the rest of the morning seting up meetings for the afternoon to discuss these things, which, as everybody else seemed to be doing the same thing, was time-consuming.

'And then you would go to lunch, followed by the afternoon meetings. These would probably be over in time for you to get back to your office before the end of working hours, dictate the results of that afternoon's work and send out the appropriate memos to all concerned about the new changes that had been made.

'The next morning you would come in and there would be another pile of thirty or forty memos, for everybody else had been doing the same thing.

'And that went on week after week, with management breathing more and more down our necks and introducing more and more changes en route, more requirements that the system would have to satisfy—which would mean that you would need to make basic changes again and again and again.'

This story has all the hallmarks of the exaggeration of the exasperated: however, other sources indicate that if it is not true in all details, it is true in substance and feel: that's the way the situation was. Though IBM put on a brave face, releasing various versions of the software, the original 360/67 software development was never to succeed. Indeed, some of the versions that were to work were brought in by users without benefit of IBM; in one case, the customer, having done all the work, reputedly refused to let IBM have access to the software he had developed.

IBM needed that software, whatever its origin. Though the experience gained with the 360/67 development was to become useful particularly with Series 370, its lateness meant that IBM, sometimes for months at a time, was unable to obtain rental from systems already out with customers, because rental was due only when the software was ready, though the machine might have been—and often had been—delivered. Indeed initially it was only released to a few selected coustomers on an experimental basis and was not delivered in what IBM claimed as a fully operational version until 1969.

Eventually IBM was to release many of its customers from their order commitments, a euphemism for IBM's inability to deliver. At one time, market indications were that, IBM had taken orders for the best part of 200 360/67s and had seriously impacted the sales of both GE and CDC (for although, in an overall sense, CDC might offer little challenge in terms of the width of the market, the orders that CDC might otherwise have taken would have counted for a lot within the scale of its operation). These IBM offers had one major effect: they were effectively to set the seal on GE's computer business. GE might not leave until some future time, but IBM had made the business too resource-consuming for it to cope with.

*   *   *

What, however, was the effect on IBM of all these manoeuvres? Costs had been heavy. A Series 90 summary in the spring of 1968 indicated that the net result of IBM's efforts was that eighteen systems were to be built (eleven were eventually delivered in the U.S.A., mostly to largely government funded institutions): revenue was projected at $57·9 million, costs at $172 million, a loss of $114·1 million.

Of the Series 360 systems it had produced to fight off CDC (and GE), the Grey Book Management Summary update of 1st April 1970 (the same update seen in Chapter 1) showed the following: the 360/44 CPU had brought in $53·5 million, for the derisory profit of $1·3 million, or 2·4% (though by the time some loading had taken place on the other parts of the system, memory etc., the profit had risen to 21·3%, or $21·9 million on a total revenue of $102·8 million); the 360/67 had shown a loss of $78 million on a CPU revenue of $30·1 million*; the 360/75 CPU a loss of $19·1 million on a revenue of $43·5 million; and the 360/85 CPU showed a loss of $23 million on a revenue of $336 million.

If one totals the figures, the extent of IBM's losses on its anti-competitive CPUs looks like this. Between the Series 90, and the 360/44, 67, 75, 85 and 195 CPUs (nearly five hundred computers in all), IBM was to incur losses of nearly $235 million. Not all, however, was loss: the permutation of parts of the Series 90 and the 360/80s were eventually to result in the creation of the 360/195, whose CPU was projected to show a profit of $40·4 million. But it was not until the seventies before IBM saw any of that.

The losses on these 'scientific' computers need to be contrasted with the revenue produced by two other 360 Series CPUs, the 360/40 and the 360/50, the mainstay of IBM's commercial business. Between them these two CPUs alone eventually brought in profits of $971 million on revenues of $2,150 million, an average profit of 41·5%. Yet these were in the market around which clustered those major profit spinners—standard peripherals, printers, tape and disc drives, controls and the like—which were to bring in even more profit.

IBM was also to be challenged in these areas, and its reactions here were to lead it into further difficulties. The cause was not due to major competitors producing computers, what is known as the mainframe industry, but a new and smaller industry which IBM's inordinately high profits was to create, the plug-compatible peripherals industry: the PCMs (M standing for manufacturer) as they became collectively known. That challenge, and the IBM response to it, was to lead to the Telex case.

---

* The Justice Department in its U.S. versus IBM trial brief released in November 1974 was to claim that initially in August 1965 the 360/67 programme was projected to show a loss 'or at best show a very low profit rate' and that the final loss was in the neighbourhood of $100 million.

CHAPTER FIVE

Round 2: The Peripheral Bubble: The Telex Affair

'IDM's sales force in 1970 achieved only 50% of its selling objective. In 1971, IBM experienced the worst sales record in its history for EDP (Electronic Data Processing) equipment.'

> IBM's Counsel's submission to the court during the first round of the Telex versus IBM anti-trust suit.

'IBM world wide gross income and earnings *grew moderately to record levels.*' [Italics added.]

> IBM Annual Report for the year 1971.

'*Peripherals.*

As a percentage of total rental, peripherals have been increasing steadily. In 1956, for instance, the 650 CPU represented 80% of the rental. By 1968, the Model 30 CPU represented only 33% of the systems rental . . .

'. . . In the mid-sixties, when the major systems suppliers started producing their own peripherals, the OEM's* entered the end user market with little success. More recently, this has changed as a result of the availability of financing, expanded marketing and services, and proven products. Competitors now have price/performance advantages in terminals, tapes, disks, and memory.

---

* Original Equipment Manufacturer, a term in use for companies making equipment which they then sell to other manufacturers who put it in their product line as if it was of their own manufacture. This can lead to great economics in volume.

This occurs in part because our product line is at the end of a cycle while most OEM equipment has been announced recently ...
... There are a large number of competitors in every peripheral area ...
... In summary, the peripherals area represents a huge exposure and is our number one challenge ...
... Key to the solution of this problem is our need to ensure technical exellence throughout the peripheral product line. In addition we must understand more regarding the various pricing alternatives ...
... The MC (Management Committee) has asked that work be done ... to more precisely assess the current and future impact of competitive compatible products on our line. This includes a review of strategies, policies, and practices presently in existence to identify exposures and to recommend action programmes ...'

Extracts from IBM Management
Committee Report to the Management
Review Committee, 26th of March 1970.

To understand and keep track of what follows, the reader needs to know the following equipment numbers, placed in time sequence.

Telex	*IBM*	
Magnetic Tape Drives		
M 3000	729 ⎱	(incompatible and not
M 4000	729 ⎰	technically equivalent)
4700	729	
4800	2401	
5420	2420	
6410	3410	
6420	3420	
Disc Drives		
	1311	
5311	2311	
5314 ⎫	2314	
⎬	2319/2313	
6330 ⎭	3330	
Printers		
5403 ⎫	1403N	
⎭	3211	

On Roger Wheeler's desk in Telex's Tulsa H.Q., stands a plaque carrying Santayana's aphorism: 'Those who do not remember the past are condemned to relive it.'

Roger Wheeler has no intention of doing so. He says that IBM has achieved its objective, and asks: 'Surely this is not what the computer business is about?' Mr Wheeler's views are worthy of attention, for he is Telex's Chairman and a major shareholder. His views are also of interest in the wider context of the computer industry generally. Telex is an unusual computer-industry company in that the Wheeler fortunes are not wholly dependent upon Telex's survival. In tackling IBM, he has been playing with his own money, not earned in computing, and when one is doing that one is perhaps more circumspect than when simply dealing with other people's—the more usual computer industry situation. This made it all the more surprising to find a Telex legal challenge to IBM. It is not so surprising, however, if one knows Roger Wheeler's background. He is knowledgeable on anti-trust matters; his knowledge comes through his other interest—the fine metals industry, a notorious hunting ground for cartels and would-be monopolies. Yet he has managed to find a niche in that business without himself running foul of the trusts—though it has given him some experience of the jungle that anti-trust law tries to police. One would expect then that he might have achieved a similar position within the computer business, that his previous experience would have made him wary of becoming involved in direct fights with large monolithic corporations with dominant positions in the market: it was not to be the case.

*   *   *

What has become known as the Telex case has its origins on one side in IBM technological sloth, managerial arrogance, economic greed, and a remarkable capability for rapid organisational turn around, for over-reaction; and on the other, in the naivety of men who should have known better, who really didn't realise what they were letting themselves in for.

The Telex case deserves pride of place in any study of IBM's relations with its competitors, because it is concerned with events of the recent past, events whose effects have not yet fully worked themselves out. However, the growth of Telex and other plug compatible peripheral manufacturers, and IBM's reaction to that growth, is a tale of great complexity. There are really three stories: what actually happened in the market-place; the end that IBM willed; and how it brought that end about. All this illustrates the managerial mechanics of IBM, some of which are dealt with here and others in Chapter 9. They also illustrate the legal mishaps and tribulations which befell Telex, mishaps which tell us something about how American competition law operates, and, probably more importantly, how IBM manipulates that law.

But what brought the IBM machine down about Telex? What Telex did in the mid-sixties was to see that IBM had left a gap and try to fill it. The gap came from IBM's inordinately high peripheral equipment rentals. To understand that gap's dimensions, one needs to go further into the differences between scientific and non-scientific computing in the sixties, the days of the batch processor (the after-the-event computer)—into the profitable heart of the IBM computer business, the commercial computer and its peripherals.

To the layman who had long ago been sold the notion of a giant electronic brain soothingly and quietly chugging away like an electronic nanny, the peripherals business might seem to be relatively unimportant. Users know differently—as does the computer manufacturing industry. It is now the peripherals that matter: it was not always so. In the late fifties, before the IBM 1401 computer system, peripherals used to account for twenty per cent of the rental or sales price. Today, as that MC report shows, they can account for anything up to eighty per cent, an almost total reversal.

The prime cause of the change has been the increasing speed—and thus capacity—of the CPU. As speed has increased, so peripheral device requirements have grown, and they have accounted for more and more of total hardware costs. But why do CPU speeds increase at all? There is the need to make things happen faster, to get improved performance which has led to substantial components research development and production capability expenditure. In the latter instance, CPU components now are critically subject to the economics of volume. A recent estimate maintains that the costs of 'fourth generation' circuitry are falling by around thirty per cent every time production volume is doubled. And those volumes seem to double every year—which has its impact on CPUs.* Nobody can be found to agree with anybody else about the speed at which change is happening, but a generally held estimate among specialists would have it that the costs of electronic logic, the critical components in CPU operations, are falling by a factor of ten every four years. These changing economics cannot be entirely hidden from users.

Were this economy to be passed on to the customer simply and directly, were he to be sold equivalent power to that which he already has, the CPU manufacturing part of the industry would be committing economic suicide. This, however, is not the case and there are no signs of its becoming so. Rather, it continues to expand the market by thinking up more work that can be done with that computing power, for the industry does not so much reduce the costs of computing as try to give the user more power for the dollar, and then sell him the application programmes to make use of that power.

The programs often are not very efficient: they may consume more of the power of the CPU than they should, had they been more carefully devised and designed. But this, if you think about it, is in the manufacturer's interest, if not in the interest of the users. The more machine resources a program consumes, the more likely is the CPU manufacturer to sell the user a larger and faster CPU and memory. However, if more is to be done with the CPU power, then the user will also require more peripheral units to go with it: secondary storage, tapes and discs on which to keep the extra data, input and output devices to cope with that increased throughput, all these will become more essential.

The Plug Compatible Manufacturers business did not initially cover all IBM peripheral devices. The PCMs originally hardly touched the computer terminal business; the manufacture of input/output devices which allow users to directly query a computer. PCMs were eventually to manufacture printers, devices for dealing with output where that output is relatively bulky and a fixed copy is needed. But the IBM-compatible video-display-with-keyboard terminal business was not high on the list of PCM priorities.

The prime reason for their initial absence was the low IBM

---

* Though the growth, like everything else, is subject to the law of diminishing returns. Some experts believe that IBM for one has, in some components areas, already passed economic optimum.

volumes. Such devices are usually at the end of communications lines; they enable the user to question the computer remotely. In this area of computing IBM was a late starter, almost the last manufacturer publicly to admit that computing and communications would become indissolubly linked. In the mainstream of its commercial business in the late sixties IBM was still pushing 'batch processing', the traditional after-the-event method of using computers.

However, as IBM evolved its computer systems so that they could be used remotely, so it began to step up its terminal production and marketing. This, too, was to bring a number of companies into the IBM-compatible terminal business. The competition here started from a much stronger technological base. The terminals business had been technologically active for years. By 1971, indeed, there were more than 150 terminal manufacturers in the United States, making terminals on an OEM basis, or to enable users to buy a CPU from one manufacturer and the terminals from another.

The PCM business was also to cover a territory which the layman might not recognise as being in the peripheral field at all, the business of add-on memory. Any specific computer can often be made to behave like an apparently larger computer—and thus save a user the problems and costs involved in switching to a larger computer—simply (sic) by adding extra memory to the CPU. The business was itself made possible by IBM, which manufactures computers to which it is prepared to add extra memory. However, its memory ranges for each model are often arbitrary and not inherent in the capability of the particular model of computer. Capacity can be more than IBM (and not only IBM) states. Thus, two businesses can be seen to exist here: one, the provision of extra memory which competes directly with that offered by IBM; two, the extension of memory beyond what IBM proposes, making a smaller computer behave like a much larger computer, and thus slowing down the rate at which users will convert to larger machines.

But why was there a hole? That hole was caused by IBM's large profits, and its seeming unwillingness to change the technology of its peripheral devices at a similar rate to that at which it was changing the technology of its CPUs; this, though such changes in peripherals were not as difficult to achieve. And why should IBM change, since there was then no one around organised enough to do anything about it?

It was IBM which was to open the hole to a size where it would pay other companies to climb through and rummage for profit. The first company to do so in any serious concerted way was to be Telex.

To understand how Telex ever got into a position to mount any sort of challenge to IBM, a position where IBM could regard it as large enough—and fast-growing enough—to be a threat, one needs to go back in time to the Telex Corporation before its entry into the computer business.

*   *   *

The Telex Corporation has its origins in a hearing aid and audiometer business of the thirties, Telex was incorporated in 1940. Since then it has roamed across much of recording technology. It claimed to have produced the first wire and tape recorders for professional use (in the late forties) which would ironically give it a longer track record in the electronic recording business than IBM.

Telex grew in part by a process of amalgamation, and throughout much of the fifties and sixties was developing and marketing recording products for a wide range of home and industrial users: tape recorders, oscillographs, galvanometers and the like.

It obtained its first taste of the computer business in 1958, when it developed and delivered equipment for the recording of data, and its conversion to digital form, to Boeing Aircraft and found itself a small niche as an OEM supplier. Computer-related equipment, however, was not to be a major Telex business for some years. Between 1958 and 1967 it devised and manufactured a series of magnetic tape drives, designated the M3000, which were sold on an OEM basis. But sales during those years were few: Telex only produced two hundred. The M3000 was followed by the M4000, of which Telex delivered three hundred.

Even by the then standards of the computer industry, Telex was small fry. However, it sought change. By 1965 Telex was looking at IBM magnetic tape drive numbers and developing product to attach to IBM's Series 360. The numbers it was examining had to do with the pre-360 tape drive, the 729, essentially a ten-year-old development which had made its major impact on the market with that best-selling IBM computer system, the IBM 1401. There were tens of thousands of 729s out on the market. The majority were technologically obsolescent, and leased to users at high rentals. Considering that each was rented out at around $1,000 a month, while the 729 cost IBM only $2,400 to build, the 729 was a sitting duck (an appropriate cliché in view of what was soon to follow).

Yet the notion that there might soon be such companies as PCMs seemed not to have entered IBM's managerial mind. Telex, however, knew that its M3000 tape drive was technically competitive, that it was only costing six to seven thousand dollars to build—and that when manufactured in small quantities. What might it cost if manufactured in volume?

And if the machines were so cheap to produce? Here was a situation where IBM's equivalent units were on the market at between $800 and $1,000 a month rental—the latter for the high speed Model 5 version—and $40,000 to $50,000 purchase. If the market was that good pre-360,. surely it would be better post-360?—particularly as the 729 successor, the 2401, was simply a better package without any great increase in performance.

Telex played with the numbers for quite a time, thinking 'these are too good to be real', but almost as soon as it entered the compatible tape drive business, it found that they were indeed real. The first market move came in 1966. It was not initiated by Telex but by a would-be customer, Du Pont, one of the world's larger chemical companies. Du Pont was unhappy about the tape drive rentals it was paying IBM. It put out a RFP (a request for procurement: a term used when seeking competitive bids for a specified unit or system). The competitive product settled on was from Telex.

More sales soon followed, and from this was to stem the IBM-compatible peripherals industry: IBM-only-compatible, because at no time until around 1973–74 have there been enough computers manufactured by other companies to make it worthwhile for anyone to seriously invest in creating compatible devices to go with them and thus in turn give the customers of those manufacturers a choice.

Throughout the litigation, IBM has talked in terms of the PCM industry as parasitic. At first sight this might be true, but first sight is once again deceptive. It ignores the fact that the lack of other competing manufacturers with substantial volumes is primarily due to the strength of IBM in the market-place and the moves it has taken over the years to ensure that it obtained the majority of the business.

The computer industry is the most concentrated industry of all, ahead even of the auto manufacturing industry. Indeed, if one is to compare the two, some major differences in the degree of concentration quickly become apparent. The auto manufacturing industry has evolved a degree of standardisation not present in computer manufacture, a degree of standardisation which cuts across the various final assemblers. This has come about through time, large-volume production, and the standards that have been imposed on the industry by economics, and by society and its institutions. Hence, it is possible for the auto manufacturing industry to become much more fragmented into volume producers of differing parts and assemblies, to be put together by the final producer: it is the OEM situation on a massive scale.

But this is not the situation that exists in the computer industry. IBM is primarily an in-house operation, manufacturing computer systems which, at their most basic, are not compatible with those of most other manufacturers without special, and often complex, electronic and software changes. Some manufacturers have made their own versions of IBM systems (notably RCA), but generally there is much technical argument in the industry as to whether the IBM solutions are the right ones or not—as there has been almost from the beginning. The situation is further confused by the fact that IBM's solutions to problems are as often as not likely to be less advanced than its competitors: technologically IBM usually follows, it seldom leads.

The 1966 consequences of IBM's practices, however, were that, for its own aggrandisement and profit—and in moderation, there is nothing wrong in that—IBM had evolved Series 360, and that was theoretically compatible across the entire range. That compatibility, however, was not created solely with users' benefit in mind. IBM wanted to 'grow' its customers, it did not wish to face a competitive fight every time a user increased the scale of his computer operations by moving from a small computer system to a larger one. IBM had, however, left margins substantially wide enough for someone else with compatible products to jump in: it was merely a question of time. Naturally enough, the competitors moved in to the easiest area for them to tackle.

How was it possible for Telex to be allowed to copy IBM products? The answer is threefold: in part, much of the technology is in the public domain; in part, Telex took a licence from IBM to cover areas where there would otherwise be patent infringement—IBM was almost duty-bound by the provisions of the 1956 Consent Decree to give such a licence and initially IBM gave such licences freely; in part, as a result of its own past operations, Telex had expertise and patents of its own.

So, Telex jumped in. Telex management had calculated that IBM might allow them to survive in the market with a share of up to ten per cent. This was a miscalculation: Telex had not really taken into account the possibility that other companies might have seen the same slot and were soon going to go after it.

In 1965, Telex began a concerted programme to produce compatible peripherals. First came the equivalent to IBM's 2401 tape drive (one of the 729 replacements to go with 360 Series). This was announced in July 1967 as the Telex 4800, with initial delivery scheduled for March 1968. In 1969 it announced an IBM 2311 disc drive equivalent, the Telex 5311, and the Telex 5314, equivalent to the IBM 2314: Telex had latched on to the IBM equivalent numbers game, so that customers would be in no doubt about what they were buying.

But why not produce an entirely different and better product? Why not follow the route of that popular mythology of the competitive free-enterprise market which maintains that if you build a better mousetrap, the world will beat a path to your door?

Telex had indeed built a better mousetrap. IBM's own internal analyses, whatever IBM might say later, soon indicated that Telex products were initially superior in performance to IBM's own. However, there were two reasons why Telex could not devise an outstanding mousetrap, reasons more fundamental than any surfeit or shortage of money, skills and available time. The first reason was concerned with the task those devices were to do: they were peripheral, called up by an IBM-built CPU, and not the other way around. The throughput tolerances then were determined not by what Telex might want to produce but by the levels required by that IBM CPU. So what point was there?

The second reason was even more commercially critical. There is a class of customer, right at the heart of IBM's commercial market base (often snidely referred to by the expert as The Great Brainwashed), who do not want anything better than IBM produces; indeed, they would be suspicious of any offer of a compatible product that made too much of its claims that it promised great improvement. What they want is a 'Chinese' copy, a guarantee of a similar standard of service—and they want it all cheaper.

This can and does have peculiar effects on the market. America is replete with manufacturers with compatible products that will latch on to an IBM system. Sometimes those products exist before IBM has mass-marketed its own equivalent version. The best move that IBM can make, the one move likely to make the small manufacturer's product take off towards profit, is for IBM to announce that it will deliver an equivalent

I have been in a small IBM-compatible systems manufacturer's plant on the day that IBM did just that. Instead of gloom, the announcement was received almost with rapture. It was the finest present that IBM could make to help a small, ambitious (but not too ambitious) company and its management. It would open up a market hitherto closed because would-be customers' first questions were always the same: 'What is IBM doing about it?'

This was the broad market-place that Telex was entering. By August 1969 Telex had a thousand units out. The climb thereafter was rapid. By March 1970 the number had grown to two thousand, to three thousand by August, four thousand in November. It was to double, and peak over the next twelve months at eight thousand, falter for a time, then grow some more, but by that time the thrust was gone from Telex.

For between 1966 and 1969, Telex was to be joined in the business of marketing IBM-compatible equipment by, in the tape drive market, the Potter Instrument Company (eventually itself to sue, though the suit was withdrawn on receipt of a small contract from IBM), MAI, Ampex and Texas Instruments; and in the disc drive market, again by Potter, Memorex, and California Computer. Indeed over the five years 1966 to 1971, Telex was at one time to be joined by the best part of a hundred IBM-compatible manufacturers, making tape and disc drives, add-on memories, printers and the like.

A hundred companies (in the suit IBM claimed that at one time there were over a hundred-and-fifty), even if only a dozen or so are large enough to offer volume competition, do not enter a market unless they can see something for the taking, and at that something good. What had they seen?

What they saw was a compound of two factors. One, the late sixties are the boom years of the computer business, not just in figures but in confidence. They are the years when, as the president of Telex, Stephen Jatras, expressed it: the feeling in Telex was that the company 'was going to the moon'. Other companies' prospectuses indicated that this was pessimism—they, it seemed, were on the point of take-off for destinations outside the solar system. The American economy was buoyant and no part of it more so than the total clutch of specialities which make up the computer industry. IBM continued to grow (between 1965 and 1970 its volumes and profits doubled), which indicated that there must be a slot there. But if Telex, why not everyone else?

The second factor arose from the way some of that IBM growth had been achieved: the hole was not just in simple peripherals sold or leased directly to end users. The late sixties are the years of the rise of the leasing companies, essentially finance houses with some know-how of the economics of computers. They were to purchase Series 360 systems in large quantity (an estimated $2·6 billion) from IBM alone at list price. However, they did not necessarily purchase entire 360 systems: they bought CPUs and some peripherals which were not made by the PCMs from IBM; they bought PCM peripherals where these were cheaper and then put the lot together in what are known as multi-vendor systems. These were then leased to users, usually for a longer period of time than IBM rentals indicated that IBM expected them to be out, for the leasing companies had their own ideas about true life. Thus the rental to the user would be competitive, and the leasing company and the money behind it could still live comfortably off the percentage differences. Many people examining the sorts of figures involved just would not believe that it was this simple.

It all looked too easy: and it was. But the immediate effects on Telex were quite dramatic. In 1967, the first serious year of Telex's PCM business, the Telex Corporation's revenue was $34 million, of which computer peripherals accounted for more than $6·5 million. Its net profit was $1·2 million, of which peripherals accounted for a third. By April 1971, it was reporting total revenues of $81 million, of which those peripherals accounted for $58 million. Group profits were $5·5 million, all accounted for by compatible peripherals: the rest of the operation was running at a loss.

This is an after-the-event set of figures, for at the time Telex, like many peripheral companies, was including the full value of its leases in that year's income—though the income and profit might not occur till the next year or even later—a practice not entirely approved of by conservative accountants, and which was to lead to much adverse comment. More important, the accountancy practices board went and changed the rules in mid-stream, with a consequent effect on the Telex, other PCM, and leasing company balance sheets.

However, whatever the real figures may have been, we do not have to take Telex's word for it that its future looked reasonably bright. IBM's internal documents of the period indicated that IBM thought Telex to be in a sound position. IBM had forecast Telex's probable future, including a range of options (see page 261) based on the impact of the probable moves that IBM could take.

By the end of 1970 the U.S. market looked like this: of the magnetic tape drive units attached to IBM CPUs, IBM's market share had gone from 100% down to 87%. Of the 45,000 units installed, IBM had 39,600, the PCMs the rest. In terms of revenue, however, IBM, with rentals of $43·7 million coming in every month, had just over 90%, and the PCMs just under 10%. The PCMs then were competing both on performance and price. And half that PCM share (whether measured in units or dollars) came from Telex.

With regard to disc drives, the later entrance of the PCMs in the market meant that IBM had 94% of a 48,700 unit market. This was worth a monthly rental of $48·8 million to IBM (or because IBM prices were higher, 97% of disc drive revenues). The PCMs had the rest. Telex with more than 1,200 drives on the market had 40% of the remainder, which brought in $1·7 million a month rental.

It looked as if the Telex PCM dog was going to wag the Telex Corporate tail. In the autumn of 1970, Telex was reorganised into two groups: Telex Computer Products Inc, and everything else.

But the competition had been noticed by IBM and as early as 1968 had seemed worthy of attention. However, it was to be the late summer of 1969 before it was to be of any real concern at a senior level, and early 1970, before the problems began seriously to attract corporate management's attention.

The initial cause was a January 1970 order of the Federal Government's Bureau of the Budget which opened up the Federal market to the PCMs. In theory this had been possible as the result of a Congressional bill (the Brooks Bill) for some time. But implementation was a different matter.

IBM studies had indicated that the Telex products of the time were technologically superior to IBM's, but technology was not the main factor. That was price. In mid-1969, some of the government agencies had got together and agreed that OEM peripherals could save the government substantial sums. Now the order they were bringing out made price a determining factor and allowed for federal mixed-vendor computer installations to be created, which would in practice often mean IBM CPUs and PCM peripherals.

We can get some idea of the scale of profit that IBM was making from an IBM internal report of February 1970. This stated that the U.S. Air Force was soon to release an RFP to replace 147 IBM 729 tape drives. 'Competition will offer purchase prices of about $12,000 each. 729's with 53 mo(nths) depreciation are about $24,000 each.'

In other words, on the basis of these figures, by going PCM the U.S. Air Force could save the U.S. taxpayer around one-and-three-quarter million dollars in the example given alone.

As far as IBM was concerned, this was a serious matter. The report noted that 52% of the systems rental at the Air Force Logistics Command was made up of disc units. Moreover, even the Marine Corps, described as 'a dyed-in-the-wool IBM user', was going to buy its disc and tape drives from elsewhere.

The report ended with the following paragraph, which recalled the rationale of the attempts to fight off CDC:

'The Federal Government is a special case because the procurement of large amounts of equipment is governed and controlled by a relatively small group (GSA). However, in many ways they may be leading edge and the same thing might happen to the 100 largest commercial accounts if they set up a Corporate ADP procurement procedure.'

Shortly after, IBM corporate management designated peripherals as a Key Corporate Strategic Issue (see page 259).*

As a result of this decision, and IBM corporate initiative, in March 1970 there was set up what was to become known as 'The Cooley Task Force', under H. E. Cooley, then a Systems Development Division Vice-President. The task force was to look at both IBM's competition and what IBM might do about it. IBM had a 'survey' done by its field engineers, a polite form of saying that it did quite legal industrial espionage (see page 148). Installation records and field visits by service engineers in the normal course of their duties produced figures of the number of units out in the field. (The numbers were different from those put forward earlier, but the percentages stayed roughly the same.)

The figures to be reported to IBM corporate management in the summer of 1970 gave the PCMs 11% of the tape drive and 9% of the disc drive markets. Assuming that there were to be no drastic changes, the task force foresaw that the PCM tape drive market share would stay constant until 1976 and the PCM disc drive market share would grow to 15% in the same period.

The task force concluded that if IBM did nothing, Telex and the other PCMs would remain viable, a somewhat gratuitous conclusion, for that task force had not been set up to recommend that nothing be done. The task force made a number of recommendations to management, among them, to move the disc drive controls into the CPU. They suggested going as far as to physically integrate the peripheral devices, the ultimate in lock-out situations. They recommended a programme to enhance product performance, this on a moving basis. The programme was to be planned before the initial product announcement, and would work roughly like this: you bring out, say, a new disc drive; the product goes out on the market, the competition gears itself up to meet it; then you announce the Mark II version. The competition is now back at the starting gate; by the time it has geared itself up for Mark II, you announce Mark III; and so on. In other words, you make yourself a moving target. Customers who want to add will not take the now no-longer technically competitive alternative

---

* The KCSI designation in IBM indicates that corporate management is interested in the subject named at the strategic policy level, and no moves are to be made without reference to corporate management.

product, they will come to you. These enhancements are known as Mid-Life Kickers, kickers in that they produce boosts in capability at a small increase in price (and practically no increase in cost to the manufacturer). They thus increase orders and revenues and make life difficult for your competitors.

Such mid-life kickers can require the most trivial adjustement to substantially increase price/performance. A machine may be delivered with the ratios between two gears being two to one. A year later the manufacturer changes one gear and the ratio becomes four to one—and suddenly you have a product with twice the performance.

The task force also considered making the diagnostics proprietary. This would mean that, when calling up external devices, checking to see their status, serviceability and the like, the CPU would also be able to tell which were from IBM—and which were not: it would then recognise and call on the first but not the second. After discussions with IBM management, Mr Cooley was to refer to this one as 'a real swinger', and seek to obtain approval from IBM's legal department. If he got it, it is not recorded in the available Papers. IBM however has not yet gone quite that far on the market. The task force was to consider many proposals, among them one seeking to put the challenged peripherals on long leases. However, that was turned down since IBM Corporate thought there was seemingly no way of limiting such a plan to products where IBM was facing competition. The task force also considered across-the-board price cuts, which too were turned down. And it came up with what the Management Committee was to call an 'ingenious little item' known as Mallard, an aptly named decoy duck. (The item was to be a little too ingenious and was soon to cause a number of shuffles around of the members who had made the recommendation.)

Management accepted price cuts but only in selected products; the mid-life kickers philosophy; and Mallard. IBM was now beginning to play the numbers game and begin to shuffle both technology and prices about, as it had done in its fight with CDC.

The first challenge had been in the tape drive area, but within a couple of years that challenge had been contained: even if IBM might no longer have 100% of the market, its share ceased to fall. IBM did this by introducing some real technological enhancements to its tape drives. At first, the moves were a combination of minor improvements, new packaging and price cuts. IBM was taking off the shelf developments it already had in hand. Each drive was to be cheaper in cost/performance terms than its predecessor. What Telex could do, IBM could do also. Indeed, so quickly did it start introducing change that far from being on the market for eight or nine years, one tape drive, the 2420, was to be out for no more than a year.

IBM's track record when unchallenged might be somnolent, but it now had considerable understanding of the technology. However, understanding the technology was one thing, producing something better was something else. Thus IBM's late sixties records indicated that its commercial analysis specialists considered that the 729, 2401 and 2420 were all technologically inferior to their Telex equivalents. Real technological improvements were not to come from IBM for nearly three years, until the spring of 1973.

The real challenge to IBM was to come in the disc drive area. Here the technology was in the process of rapid change. Essentially, tape drives are sequential machines: the thrust of development had been to enable people to search that tape in a non-sequential order, to roam around it at will. But as computers got faster, so tape drive limitations became more apparent. Disc drives using multiple recording heads enabled discs (resembling plastic LPs) to be searched a lot faster: and for non-sequential operations, with much greater ease. The technology was to evolve so that discs were to be seen as the prime medium for working directly with computers, with tapes used for back-up and what is known as dumping, the removal of data in a relatively fast fashion so that the computer can be cleared for other purposes.*

The first really commercial mass market disc drive and its associated disc packs, the IBM 1311 system, had come on the market in 1963. For some years IBM was to be the only serious manufacturer of disc packs, so much so that the Learson/Cary overselling of Series 360 was to cause a minor embarrassment. IBM had held the rental of disc packs to $15 a month throughout

---

* The dumped data can then be re-sorted outside normal day-shift working hours when the demands and pressures for the services of that computer system are at their lowest. This is housekeeping, and in the larger organisations usually takes place during the evening or night shift.

the sixties, as it held down pack production. The miscalculation became apparent in 1967 when the shortage of packs became so great that independent brokers were renting out packs—at $1 a day—they had bought from IBM.

But wherever the packs came from, by the time the Cooley Task Force reported in mid-1970, there were 47,000 disc drives installed in the United States. Most of the drives at least came from IBM and were out on rental.

It was on this great soft underbelly that the PCMs were next targeted. What IBM wanted was a quick response: and that quick response was really required to tackle a group of ex-IBM employees. For Telex did not manufacture disc drives: its IBM equivalents, the 5311 and the 5314, were primarily manufactured by a company called Information Storage Systems set up by ex-IBM peripherals specialists.*

Now, though the IBM 2314 was referred to as a disc drive, it was really a disc-drive control unit; the drives themselves bearing other and near numbers, depending on how they were boxed and packaged. One drive in one box was the 2312, four drives in one, the 2313, and two in one the 2318.

How could IBM obtain more benefit from that line and produce a quick response to the challenge without making any great technological changes, for which in any case there was not much time? IBM's first move was announced in September 1970, coincident with the announcement of the 370/145 computer system. This system 370 computer was the replacement for the particular slot in the 360 range, taken by the 360/40s and 50s. Its marketplace was IBM's major commercial users, and thus the marketplace most responsive to price cuts.

The IBM move was to unveil its decoy duck, the aptly named Mallard 2319†, a 'new' disc drive unit. The 2319 really consisted of a 2313 (four drives in a box) with one spindle removed, making it three in one. But that was not all that IBM removed. The 2314

---

* ISS itself is interesting in that if IBM seriously believed that it was suffering losses as the result of the activities of ex-IBM employees taking their know-how with them (see p. 145), here was the clearest example of a company primarily based on IBM know-how, whether proprietary or not. If IBM really believed in the notion that it had rights over its product, then it was almost duty-bound to sue ISS. To this day it has made no move whatsoever to do so.

† Eventually there were to be two versions: 2319A for 360 Series machines and 2319B for 370 Series.

controller disappeared, to be replaced by a device called an Integrated File Adaptor or IFA: this exercised similar control functions, but was placed inside the computer.

And the 2319 could only be attached in this way. The package rented for $1,550 a month, as opposed to a 2314 controller with the equivalent number of existing drives which was priced at $2,875. The 2319B package then cut more than 46% off IBM rentals. That price cut was to put IBM under the PCM competition by anything from $17 to $184 a month, according to which competitor one looked at.

What IBM wanted was a lock-out situation in the 370/145 market. Either the customer would take Mallard, or the existing 2314 equivalents—in which case he would pay an extra $1,325 a month—or he went to a PCM. But PCM prices were predicated on IBM's previously higher price, and not just Mallard options.

The price conclusion now ran like this. IBM with Mallard at $1,550 a month was faced by Telex with a conventional system at $2,505, with the rest of the PCM competition in the $2,300–$2,500 bracket. There were, however, two snags. Mallard was no technological advance: Mr Cooley indeed was at one point to describe it as a 'kludge', and a kludge, as any student of the folklore of technology knows, has been defined as 'a collection of ill-fitting parts forming a distressing whole'. So IBM was still exposed to PCM-improved technology. The Telex 2314 equivalent (the 5314), for instance, gave 100% faster access to data—with the consequent effect on total system performance that one would expect.

The other snag was that the initial Mallard offering was limited to the 370/145. In the rest of the market, IBM still preferred the existing 2314 options, and that at pre-Mallard rentals. And it quickly became apparent that IBM had grievously underestimated the PCM marketing capability, and the market responsiveness. The timing of the PCM thrust was such that they were taking orders during the period when IBM was starting to market its larger Series 360 replacements, the 370/155 and 370/165, then recently announced. So the PCMs were not simply taking away existing 360 business around the end of its life: they were cutting into the new systems market base right at the start of rental life.

One of the major reasons for IBM's underestimation had little to do with whether the PCMs were producing a better product offered at a lower rental. It derived from two of IBM's own practices. The government apart, IBM abhorred doing special discount deals with large users; it fought for its list price.* Management took the view that if you started doing special discounts here and there, you would end up having to provide them right across the market. Any discounts that were to be given, IBM would prefer to give in an orderly manner. But the PCMs were discounting almost anything to anybody.

The second practice had to do with IBM's service organisation. This had always been its strength, but even in IBM there is a learning curve, a period of time when performance is not what it should be. And in the latter half of 1970, many of the engineers were on the wrong part of that curve. They were discovering System 370; true, the service organisation was so structured that no service engineer covered the 370 range in its entire complexity: CPUs, peripherals and the rest. However, it did mean that IBM was thinly spread.

The PCMs, however, had no such problem. Their product range was limited, and in the large user installation this meant that the almost permanent resident PCM service engineer could be specialised and know the product he was servicing intimately. Also, as the PCMs had little reluctance to do special deals with users of large numbers of their peripherals, they were often in a very strong position.

The reasons for the initial failure to contain the PCMs were to be extracted from Mr Cooley by IBM management, who asked him to explain how the miscalculation had occurred. His reply was that IBM had underestimated PCM manufacturing and marketing capability and that IBM's forecasts were unsound: there was no constraint to the possible penetration of the PCMs into the 2314 market.

So IBM once more set in hand means to close the gap: it created a second task force. The task force report was presented to Management, approved, and in December 1970 IBM announced its second plan. The 2319 pricing was extended to offers of drives to go with all IBM systems. This time, however, IBM did

---

* It might have abhorred doing so but where necessary, and when pushed to it, IBM would discount just like everybody else. It simply took longer—and had to be referred higher up.

not bother about putting the controls inside the CPU via the IFA: Mallard Mark Two, the 2319B was marketed to be controlled by a standard 2314. And, in a move of far-reaching importance, IBM made a breach in a very long-standing policy; with the new offer, it selectively eliminated use charges above the standard one-shift terms.

The situation now was that where IBM was facing competition, a customer could use his peripherals for more than the standard shift without being charged extra rental. Where there was no competitive equivalent, the extra charge was still applied.

It might seem at this point that this could be made out to be a standard competitive reaction. Such was not the case. What IBM had done with the 2319s was to make a price cut look like a new product, and in doing so thought it had eliminated the risk of having to make price reduction across the entire IBM line. What IBM wanted, as 'Buck' Rodgers its Director of World Wide Marketing was to testify at the trial, was to have the benefit of cutting prices without the economic impact of doing so. For the 2314 market was not a small one. IBM, as its annual report for 1970 shows, grossed that year 7\frac{1}{2}$ billion. And at the time of the initial 2319 announcement, the disc drives out on rental were bringing IBM in $512 million a year, or nearly 18% of total revenues.

It did not want to put all that revenue in jeopardy: had it cut prices across the entire 2314 range, its income would have been reduced by $120 million, almost all its profit. It was, therefore, carefully tailoring its moves so as to have the maximum impact on the PCMs with as little hurt to itself as possible.

But not carefully enough. What IBM had failed to realise was that the Mallard solution did not really provide an entirely foolproof answer to the competitive problem, for a loophole still existed. In one version, the 2319 was priced at $1,000 a month rental, $333 a spindle. However, the user was thrown back on to the 2314 for control, and the rental of that stayed the same as before, $1,480 a month.

Now, on a nine-drive system, three 2319s and a 2314 would cost between $700 and $800 a month below the PCM's equivalent nine-drive system. However, suppose that the user wished to permute it all differently? Suppose that he did not want three, six or nine drives, but four, five, seven or eight? Combining the various IBM options at standard 2314 prices with the 2319 at the lower price would still leave the PCMs competitive,* and under IBM prices.

The market reaction to the 2319 was as expected: customers still went to the PCMs for drives; however, the PCMs had to lower their prices. Over the next year Telex was to cut prices by some 35–40% in order to keep pace with IBM. For while IBM might have made a mistake on some disc drive configurations, it had not made a mistake on all: 2319 was biting.

The 2319 is an attempt by IBM to contain the PCMs by using more than what one would call mythological free enterprise methods, the better mousetrap, fairly priced: it was not to be the last. There were more major strikes to come, and some short, sharp, subsidiary brawls. They were, however, in many ways pointless, for though Telex revenues were to continue to rise during the financial year 1970/71, IBM had effectively taken care of its future as a rapidly growing PCM.

For IBM had carefully engineered its price cuts so that the PCMs involved would have to lower their prices beyond the point at which they would be viable. They would either have to take a loss, sometimes a substantial loss, on each sale, or restructure their financing and their debt. The PCM operations had become possible because the gap that IBM had left was a compound of antique technology and high profit margin. As a result, operations such as Telex were critically dependent on IBM price levels and margins: they had to have, if not an IBM-size margin, at least one wide enough to allow both Telex, and the financial companies who underwrote the leasing operation, to make a profit. The lower that IBM could force that margin down, the more time would the PCMs require to have over which to spread their debt, and the more exposed would they become to IBM's product changes. The more that happened, the less attractive would the finance houses which funded leasing operations find the proposition.

Telex's problems were now to begin. In the two years 1969/70, Telex had obtained $120 million in financing from two leasing companies, Hudson and Transamerica. After the 2319 announcement it could only raise another $30 million. At the start of 1971, however, Telex did not know this. And though IBM's manage-

---

* The mistake was to affect quite a few careers at IBM, some members of the task force concerned being shifted sideways.

ment might 'know'—in the sense that they had seen projections, the market order/delivery volumes indicated differently, for the Telex installation rates were up. That Telex was bound for trouble was a long-term forecast, what IBM still wanted was short-term results.

As an after-the-event justification for its actions, IBM was to claim that the 1970 sales quotas had nowhere near been filled. It was not to mention too loudly that T. V. Learson had set quotas unrealistically high. And IBM was also to claim that 1971 had seen the worst year for EDP sales since it had entered the business, forgetting to mention that it had been the same for almost everybody else in the mainframe industry—so why should IBM be so different?

From the spring of 1971, the running was to be made by IBM, not by the PCMs. The competition that IBM had faced in 1969/70 had primarily been for equipment which went with its 360 Series CPUs. The IBM leases were short, mostly cancellable at thirty days. However, the PCMs were now attacking the Series 370 market, and the peripherals that went with it: the new 3420 tape drives and 3330 disc drives.

The 3330, IBM claimed, had cost it $30 million to develop (if so, it did not get its money's worth): the 3420, however, was initially a warmed-up 2420. Indeed, in an injudicious phrase, IBM was to refer publicly to 3420 technology as having been 'proven' in the 2420, the basic technology of which went back many years.

Then there was the printer market. In October 1970, one of the Telex analyses that IBM had made stated that Telex had now entered the printer market, and that this market was similar in characteristics to the disc drive and tape drive market. 'IBM', was 'very strong in the market place' but continued 'to use old technologies'. By December IBM's estimate was that its 1403N printer was outclassed both technologically and in price. Technologically, in this case, meant that the Telex printer had a more than 10% throughput advantage.

IBM could not even win with its newer and much faster printer, the 2,000-line-a-minute 3211. That was technologically superior to the Telex product, but the rentals had so been set that a user could still obtain better performance by taking two IBM 1403 equivalents (the Telex 5403)—and this would still be in the user's financial interest. In February 1971 Ralph Pfeiffer (then President of IBM's Data Processing Division) was informed that the 3211 was not price/performance competitive. He in turn was to report upwards that something would have to be done, for this left IBM dependent on the 1403, described as 'a key system 360-system 370 input/output unit'. And one of the things that would have to be done would be to eliminate the charges that IBM made for extra shift working for these added 30% to the rentals paid by the user.

It might be thought that as seen by IBM the PCMs were about to destroy IBM's market entirely, but such was not the case. In the February of 1971 Mr Cooley reported to IBM corporate estimates of 17,500 printers attached to IBM CPUs by 1978, of which the PCMs were expected to obtain only 1,500. So grave was the PCM printer threat to be seen, that the IBM management were to be told that while IBM then had ten thousand printers out on the market, the PCMs had a remarkable thirty-two!

The situation was similar in the add-on memory market. IBM had begun to study the possibility that the PCMs would move into this area in 1968. By mid-1969, this too had become a KCSI. It needed to be: already one would-be competitor, Ampex, was offering plug-compatible add-on memory at a third of IBM's price. And here, as Dr Piore told management, IBM was technologically two to three years behind its competition. That competition was basing its product largely on what are known as FETs (Field Effect Transistors), an integrated circuit technology, which Dr Piore estimated could not appear on IBM machines before 1973/74. (He was to be wrong.)

In 1970, IBM's Financial Analysis Department set in hand a study of memory competition. The basic question posed was simple: what would a competitor have to charge in order to become strong and viable?

The memories IBM was concerned with were large, and measured in megabytes (mgbs).* The conclusions of this study were obvious. The key PCM dependency was seen to be the price that IBM charged. The lower the IBM price, the lower the PCM profit margin and the more time would a competitor require to get to a break-even point in his cash flow. But they went further: were

---

* Memory is measured in K's—and megabytes (mgbs)—the first standing for 1024 bytes, each byte being based on eight bits of information; the second a thousand K's.

IBM to set a monthly rental price of $9,000 per mgb, a competitor would break even in four years and go on to make 'fantastic profits'; at $7,000 per mgb break-even would come in six years, and at $5,000 per mgb, a new entrant would still be running a cash flow deficit of $10 million a year at the end of six years.

But those six years were critical: it was IBM's planning-production-new systems introduction cycle time. If IBM adopted a $5,000 monthly rental price, this would mean that a new entrant would never become financially viable, for at the end of six years, he would be faced with heavy losses which he could not recoup. For then he would be starting to feel competition from the next generation of IBM product.

The PCM's activities, the evidence that IBM was suffering a bad year for sales and the reports to Corporate management now coincided to seal the fate of Telex and the rest of the PCMs. IBM was once more to show itself at its most unattractive. The evidence convinces me that IBM Corporate management in the shape of the Management Review Committee, the company's highest court, was to take the recommendations of its task forces, add tricks of its own, and set out quite coolly, clearly and systematically to destroy PCM competition.

There had been some indications of IBM intentions in the reports and memoranda pre-1971, but the events which were to make the most impact on the market-place, and eventually on that first trial court, were now to happen: IBM was to demonstrate yet again that it was unable to live in a market-place in which there was genuine and meaningful competition.

It can be argued that IBM's management did not know what they were doing: if that is so it could also be argued that Mr Katzenbach did not deserve his legal reputation, for he was always present. But why should corporate executives at this level have put down on paper thoughts which, if thinkable, would not be regarded by any man with a due sense of caution to be recordable. There is a simple explanation, and it fits well the situation of a large corporation with monopolistic intentions. It has been best explained by Maxwell Bleecher, a noted Californian anti-trust lawyer, in a paper on anti-trust practices:

'... aside from the Supreme Court, for which the plaintiff's bar must constantly thank Heaven, the single most important fact in anti-trust life is the tendency of corporate executives ... to record their misdeeds. This tendency probably results from the fact that only by such a recordation and reporting process to their superiors can these misdeeds be rewarded.'†

*   *   *

IBM management went into calendar year 1971 much worried by PCM competition, but without a clear philosophy, clear directives or an orchestrated score to deal with them. On the market IBM drifted: but it was not drifting internally. The processes of working out how to deal with the PCMs were in progress, for as IBM's management was to be told, by 1971 the market that the PCMs had entered, and were entering, represented over 60% of IBM's installed base. It seemed that much thought would be required to work out how best to protect it.

It was the Learson–Cary axis which was pressing for action, but it was TJW Jnr who was to give the signal to move—and to wash his hands thereafter of the rationale underlying the moves that IBM were to take. The minutes of the Management Review Committee of 23rd April spelt out the Watson message and indicated that IBM's long-standing philosophy had not changed. TJW Jnr said that he wanted a clear understanding that the company would swallow whatever financial pills were required and prepare itself for the future. Over the next one or two years, IBM must be 'returned to a growth posture'. They should, therefore, operate accordingly. He went on to stress that they must 'make the hard decisions today so that the same problems do not have to be faced again and again down the road'.

This was as clear a signal to go ahead as one could possibly give. So IBM now set up another task force, this time not just any low-level task force but one composed of corporate executives of considerable rank and authority. It was referred to in IBM as The Blue Ribbon Task Force, and not without reason. Of its eight members, one—Katzenbach—was already a director, and three more were to become directors within two years (Beitzel, Opel, Rizzo). One of them also became President—Opel—while those other two became Group Executives, and had the responsibility

---

† Private Anti-trust Actions, Copyright the *New York Law Journal*, 1973.

for the Corporation's domestic operations split between them. Maxwell Bleecher, it seemed, was right.

Naturally enough, even at this level the task force was not going to get it right the first time, and there was some to-ing and fro-ing until, after a nudge from Frank Cary to follow a strategic line of long-term leasing, the task force came up with proposals. These were presented to Watson, Learson and Cary sitting as the Management Review Committee.

What went into that Committee was a set of proposals to put all the products on which IBM was experiencing competition from PCMs under long-term leases—and that was the basic policy that was to come out and to be adopted.

It took a number of days to fight it through, during which time some very peculiar documents were presented. For it was now no longer a question of allowing the PCMs to survive, but of killing them off.

One of the presentations indeed quite clearly spelt out the expected consequences on the PCMs of IBM's proposed long leases on tape and disc drives, and printers.

'Corporate Revenues Lower
   —No Funds for MFG, ENG. [manufacturing, engineering]
   —Dying Company!'

How was this to be accomplished? The package was to be called Fixed Term Plan. IBM was to slash rentals, but only where customers signed two-year leases, carrying financial penalty clauses for any who sought to get out earlier. It would eliminate all extra use charges within that lease, thus bringing IBM in on the same footing as the PCMs: the policy which had been turned down a year before as being fraught with danger was now the one adopted.

The MRC knew quite well what it was doing. For, as TJW Jnr had recommended, IBM was prepared seriously to reduce its revenue and profits through 1971 and 1972 to remove the competition and thus in the process eventually to get it all back, and more. It would cost IBM over $75 million in lost revenue and profit in 1971 and 1972. However, the prediction was made that by 1975 IBM would be making an additional $466 million *profit* [author's italics] as the result of the elimination of competition.

FTP was announced later that month. It was soon followed by PCM price cuts, but the damage had been done; there seemed little that the PCMs could do in reply. By the end of the year, their order rate had been cut by half; by the start of the next year, by two-thirds; and a year after FTP's introduction IBM management could read in a Quarterly Product Line Assessment that there had been no significant increase in the number of tape drives installed by the PCMs during the year, and little else in the PCM product range was doing any better.

But FTP was not all that the MRC approved. It is pointless having IBM peripherals if you do not have an IBM CPU for them to plug into. Yet IBM was not to put those under FTP; it was not necessary. In any case had IBM done so, it would have had to stabilise CPU prices. That was unacceptable. On the contrary, what the user had been given with one hand, was now going to be taken away from him with the other.

The page of the MRC presentation chart which contained the remarks indicating that the PCM companies could soon be dying was followed by two others. The first stated some of the terms of the FPT long-term leases (8% price reduction in the monthly rental for a 12 month lease, 16% for a 24 month lease—on printers, disc and tape drives and their controls; a 15% reduction for purchase and for maintenance on new disc and tape units). The second gave some indication of how IBM was going to recoup in part the immediate losses (increase in the price of maintenance calls, etc.). To ensure that the connection was not seen, the announcement of the two sets of measures was to be carefully separated in time. However, when it came, the second announcement went much further than minor changes in maintenance contracts and prices which the presentation envisaged. The increases now included CPUs, software products, and, to cap it all, non-PCM competitive peripherals.

The increases were to average $1\frac{1}{2}\%$ of revenues, now nicely counterbalancing what had been given away with FTP. There was, however, a slight delay, for this was the year of Nixon's price freeze, and the increases were not allowed to take effect until the following January, by which time no one but the PCMs would be likely to remember the connection between the two events.

But by that time, Telex had struck: it had filed an anti-trust suit. Whatever the financial figures might indicate, Telex had not otherwise had a good year. The PCMs were not now simply competing with IBM, they were competing also with each other. The rate of growth and the IBM measures had also had other effects on Telex: its development programme was not very satisfactory, its add-on memory programme was not progressing at all well, it had faced a strike, and it was undergoing manufacturing problems.

However, pride of place—and rightly so—was given to the IBM countermoves. Telex could see and feel what was happening on the market. There was a feeling among Telex's management, as there had been at CDC seven years before, that IBM was out to get it.

In the summer of 1971, letters were written to IBM management, and that autumn a meeting was held. They had quite a lot to talk about: Telex was also trying to renew its part in agreement with IBM, and IBM was being difficult. But, on the other hand, IBM, in the person of Mr Katzenbach, was soothing. Nobody was aiming at Telex specifically, and the press reports going around were over-estimates—FTP had not been that well received. (However well it had been received, the order book figures were already higher than those Mr Katzenbach was discussing, and if he did not know it, other people in IBM's 'management' did.)

Discussion with IBM having proved abortive, there were considerable arguments among Telex's management about what to do next. Seen from Telex headquarters in Tulsa, the damage looked considerable, and it looked as if IBM's moves were illegal. But, suing would take time, tie up resources, and cost money: was it worth it? What tipped the scales finally was a report prepared by counsel which pointed out that Telex had little option: if Telex did not sue, it might in its turn be held to be liable by its shareholders, who could conceivably bring an action on the grounds of lack of due management diligence.

Telex filed its suit in late January 1972.* The Telex complaint alleged that IBM had monopolised and/or attempted to monopolise the world-wide manufacture, distribution, sale and

---

* It is interesting to note that one of the sixteen banks financing Telex prior to the filing was the Chase Manhattan. In May 1972, Chase Manhattan dropped out.

leasing of electronic data processing equipment, *including the relevant sub-market for peripheral devices.* In the case of Telex, it was the last item which was critical. It alleged price discrimination, and a number of other similar practices. Telex sought damages of over $239 million, which, if awarded, would under normal anti-trust laws be trebled to $717 million.

That Telex suit filing might seem the right cut-off point here. However, we cannot leave Telex just yet, for suit or not, IBM was to take further measures. One might expect that IBM would be more than usually careful, but IBM was not to be, at least not yet. TJW Jnr's words had been taken to heart, and there was still unfinished business to take care of.

The independent PCMs were being bled, and there were no funds to support the development, engineering, even the marketing organisations that would be required to support future product. There would also be little future product.

IBM had over the years sought key specialist staff from other manufacturers to make up for deficiencies in some of its product development.* Telex was to do the same. But some senior executives in Telex seemed to approach this with no sense of caution. They did not simply seek know-how (the line between know-how and product has, in the computer field, always been somewhat vague)—they set out to hire engineers and specialists from IBM who would know something of IBM's future product plans, engineers who could then be put on to the job of designing a similar product for Telex, thus making the task of copying the IBM product much simpler once that product was actually announced and Telex could get its hands on it.

One set of legally most doubtful measures were being

---

* The problem of ISS has previously been raised. That is now part of Sperry Rand, and will no doubt therefore be covered by the information exchange agreements between Sperry Rand and IBM. However, there are three separate companies whose existence has long depended upon being able to duplicate IBM technology, companies whose speed of reaction to IBM new product announcements has indicated that they must have a close pipeline to IBM development: IBM must be aware of this. IBM has made no moves in their direction; yet, applying the same stockholder rationale as was applied by Telex, IBM has been duty bound to sue and that for a very long time. IBM did move, however, in the case of one company dependent on ex-IBM specialists, but that, it seemed, was due in part to its highly visible location—Poughkeepsie, a location not likely to endear itself to IBM management—not least for its effect on local IBM morale.

countered by another. Strangely enough, Telex set out on this path in early 1970, *after* its initial assualt on the IBM base had been successful, and at the same time that IBM was considering its own counter moves. But it was all eventually to be of no avail, and Telex was to be substantially penalised by the court for its practices.

However, by the time those ex-IBM specialists had done their work, it was all too late anyhow. Indeed, most of the work was never completed, due in part to the time required to do so and the drying up of funds while the re-development was in progress.

IBM had no comparable lack of funds. It had created a lock-out situation with its leases, it now had product which was technologically competitive, even if it might not always be as advanced, and it was priced appropriately. However, there was still one major loophole left open, and that in an unannounced product, the large systems of Series 370: the 158 and 168, with 'virtual' memory.

*   *   *

IBM had already been under pressure over memory and had still not caught up with its competitors. From mid-1969, F.T. Cary had been a proponent of solving the PCM memory exposure problem by price manipulation, (a view also expressed by T. V. Learson in April 1970). After all, an IBM user was one who had an IBM CPU. What he, the user, was interested in was the price of total package he would take, not the separate items, except where he could get the equivalent—or better—price/performance elsewhere. That had been the history—and the lesson—of the PCM war.

What IBM was to do was to change the pricing relationships between the CPU and memory, increasing the price of the first and lowering the second, a reversal of its approach in the early days.

Internally, there was no question that these structural alterations in the pricing of computers had been caused by the PCMs, not primarily by the needs of the end user. IBM's internal name for the project was SMASH, and that was precisely what it intended. Nobody appeared to pay much attention to what user requirements might really be: the users came last, and were only thought of in terms of 'would they wear it?'.

The 158 and 168 were announced in August 1972, and as one would expect the relationship between CPU and memory price had been changed. IBM had also changed its memory technology. IBM could now offer those *FET* memories over which Dr Piore had had doubt. (It was the lack of those memories which had made it impossible for IBM to announce the virtual systems any earlier.)

How had IBM got its FET memories? They resulted from a crash programme, and it had not been done using largely internal skills. IBM had gone on the market for specialists and had bought the skills of those who had gained their experience in other and more advanced electronics companies. It didn't steal secrets: it bought know-how; but this could only have been gained at other companies' expense.

The change in technology was the excuse to bring down memory prices, which went from $12,000 a month rental for one megabyte to $5,200; down to the levels at which previous studies had indicated the PCMs would be unable to survive.

Then IBM increased the CPU rentals. The changes were deliberate and bore little relation to the new hardware that virtual memory made necessary. Much of that hardware was already built in to the 155s and 165s—an example of a mid-life kicker—that IBM had out on the market. The additional IBM hardware requirement, a capability called dynamic-address-translation and generally referred to as a DAT box, cost little (its cost indeed was derisory), and it could be installed very quickly in the field.

However, the customer now found himself paying nearly 50% more for the 158 CPU than he had for the 155—and getting a less than 20% performance increase from it, if it worked as planned (though at the start, it seldom did). But in cash terms, this meant that the monthly rental was raised from $20,600 to $30,700: a 20% improvement for a near 50% increase in rental.

The user got a slightly better deal for the larger machine. The 165 CPU rented for $36,500 a month, the 168 was to rent for $47,600, a more than 30% increase. In this case the performance improvement was just over 20%.

Effectively, the door had been closed on the PCMs, but not entirely closed, for they are still active today. However, the growth thrust had been contained. What exactly had all this fuss been about? It had not been about IBM being driven entirely out of the market, it had not even been about IBM losing its majority of the market. It had been about executives at IBM unable to live with the proposition that anyone else should be allowed to have a realistic share.

Learson and Cary, nonetheless, had both talked in terms of IBM being driven from the market. Yet at no time had IBM studies indicated that it was likely to lose more than 25% of that peripheral market-place; that was the worst case, and a long-term case. More realistic IBM figures indicated possibilities in the 10–15% range over a period of four to six years. However, at no time did anyone foresee IBM making a loss or ceasing to grow.

Great play was to be made by IBM of the diligence and foresight with whioh it had built up its business, and no more so than in the Telex case. It was a proposition with which Judge Christensen was to agree: but in his judgement he made the following tart comment, an epitaph on the morality inherent in the skills IBM had used to achieve its ends—which is really what the war on Telex and the rest of the PCMs had been all about:

'. . . it must be recognised that its [IBM's] diligence and foresight have included the competitive studies and the anti-competitive objectives and intent heretofore found, and that particularly as applied to this case have included an attempt to substantially constrain or destroy its plug compatible peripheral competition by predatory pricing action, and by market strategy bearing no relationship to technological skill, industry, appropriate foresight or customer benefit.'

It is not a part of the judgement of which IBM is particularly fond, whatever the final outcome of the PCM versus IBM cases may be.

CHAPTER SIX

Round 3: IBM versus Justice

The case of IBM versus the Anti-Trust Division of the Justice Department is really the case of IBM versus the rest of the computer industry in all its varied forms. It takes in CDC, Telex and the rest of the PCMs, the other computer mainframe manufacturers, the bureaus, the consultancy and software industry and, for good measure, the major users. Furthermore, all of these both at home and abroad.

The compendium of complaints is, then, a large one, so much so that prior to the time of trial some had not been fully spelt out, even though the case had been under preparation for more than eight years. The case is, of course, different today from the case that Justice initially tried to build, because it has been fleshed out over the years as Justice has fought its way through the processes of legal discovery. The slowness of preparation has meant that though the case was formally filed on the last day of the Johnson Administration, the Nixon Presidency came and went without action being taken. Indeed, during that Presidency, the only signs of public action were to be found during the last days of the first term, around the time of the CDC settlement, and again later well after Watergate, during the time that the Nixon Presidency was crippled and in no position to exert any great political influence over the activities of Justice's lawyers.

The case has its origins in the unfinished business which arose from the Consent Decree between the Justice Department and IBM in 1956, so in a sense the antecedents go right back to the practices of IBM in its early years, back to the twenties and thirties. More specifically, however, the complaints which led to this particular investigation by Justice lie in the events which surround the birth of Series 360. But to understand those one must first backtrack to the 650.

Way back in the fifties, the market forecast for the 650 had been one hundred machines; eventually 1,500 were installed. It was never seriously thought of by management as having tapes—and was not really suitable for tapes—but they glued tapes on to it. Then in Germany they developed the 1401, a peripheral machine to transfer card to tape and tape to printer.

Now IBM had a basic machine really suitable for tapes. That 1401 in turn grew to the 1410, mainly because of customer pressure. 'IBM announces a machine to do this, but the customer says, hey we want to use it for this, and that is what happened.'

IBM came into the sixties with the 1400s, the 7000s—the successors to the Series 700 scientific machine —and the 650s still running. It was unsatisfactory, and IBM knew it. In 1961 IBM decided to investigate what to do next. What IBM was faced with was a technological spread, and that it wished to avoid: it set up the SPREAD Committee. Eventually, in 1962 after much infighting it was decided to create NPL, or the New Product Line, which was to reach the market as System 360: compatible computers all built of a similar technology. What IBM was intending to do was to obsolesce its entire product line and effectively to start again from scratch.

Now it came under pressure from what became known as the Liberator, the Honeywell 200, which, by clever software and pricing, began to cut into the IBM 1400 installed base.

'It really hurt: you don't have to get many 1401s returning from the field, which means negative commission for salesmen, for it to start hurting.'

That was the reason why IBM moved forward Series 360 announcement dates from September to April.* The moves that IBM now made were eventually to lead to the demise of a number of small manufacturers, the takeover of others, while the two major would-be competitors with substantial resources were to leave the general-purpose computer business entirely.

The moves on the market, of course, led to complaints. An in-

---

* Actually this is not strictly true. 360 was supposed to be announced in March—this led IBM executives to refer to the actual announcement appearing in the press on March 38th.

dustry with one large dominant supplier is an industry in imbalance, and one in which complaints of unfair competition are certain to abound, whether justified or not. However, the complaints became serious with the marketing moves that IBM made with Series 360 and reached critical proportions in 1966. As we have seen, IBM's Chief Executive T. J. Watson Jnr was eventually to admit that Series 360 was offered on the market up to two years before it was ready, and that this was the result of a conscious IBM management decision—which in practice meant a TJW Jnr decision.

Over the years there has grown up a myth of Series 360 as a multi-billion-dollar gamble (once expressed, in those *Fortune* articles of T. A. Wise, by an IBM executive as 'You bet your company'). In terms of that mythology the gamble was five billion dollars. The gamble really needs to be better understood than it has been so far, because it is the key to IBM's dominance of the industry from Series 360 onwards.

In reality, it was not really a gamble at all. Even the $5 billion comes from an after-the-event summary of the investment IBM was to make over the years 1964 through 1967. That $5 billion consists of R&D in the range of $500 million, the investment in plants to manufacture components and circuits, and Series 360. (IBM, for instance, was to build five major new plants.) It includes, too, IBM's investment in rental machines; that part, at least, should have been no gamble, since IBM in introducing Series 360 was indicating that it had obsolesced its predecessors. For practical purposes IBM was replacing its inventory and in the process extending the life of its ties to customer installations.

There was no question that IBM could market, and there was also no question that IBM could maintain its ties to its existing customer base. Even were IBM to fall flat on its face, there were few other immediate options available for them all.

The real gamble was a totally unforeseen one: could IBM produce? For a time it looked as if it could not. Instead, IBM executives still talk of the havoc that Series 360 caused. Production problems were horrendous: IBM's component plants were just not coming on stream according to IBM's required schedule. Domestic's Fishkill plant eventually had to be bailed out by IBM plants abroad, notably Essones in France, and by IBM scouring the market for components.

360 was to be of a standard technology, which required that IBM produce components in large numbers at comparatively low prices. But one does not, particularly in what was still a one-man band, bring home, and up to full production without a high rate of reject, a $200 million plant to produce components at a quarter or less of the price one's competitors will have to pay, without encountering delays and problems: not, in particular, when one has accelerated the marketing schedules and brought forward the announcement dates, without a price being paid.

As for the software complexity, that too had been grievously underestimated. The development of the operating system, OS 360, the instructions repertoires which could make that computer work in any useful fashion, ran further and further behind schedule.

In the end IBM proved unable to solve the problems involved in the creation of an operating system which could work all the 360 machines. OS 360 was to be issued only with the larger machines, the 360/50s and upwards. Down in that mass market of the 360/40 and below, IBM came up with DOS (Disc Operating System), an operating system for smaller machines which was not really initially any improvement over anyone else's product, though it had cost substantially more.*

At the height of the Series 360 slippages, when the operating system was still not working and what had seemed the answer to IBM salesmen's prayers was slipping further and further behind, TJW Jnr addressed a One Hundred Per Cent Club. (See Chapter 12.)

'That club contained a lot of angry men. "Gentlemen", said Tom Watson, "we made the decision to push back deliveries, and I know that you have had a tough time to convince those customers they will have to wait an extra year. When I leave here today, I have to go down and tell one of our largest customers he's going to have to wait a year, so I know exactly what you feel. But if we had to do it all over again, with the gamble and what it is, I would make the same decision." '

---

* Cost overruns on OS and DOS were to add substantially to 360 Series expenses. There is much myth here also, but it is safe to say that 360 operating software cost some hundreds of millions of dollars to fully develop—though estimates have been bandied about which put total 360 software development costs in the $1·5 to $2 billion range over the years the series was on offer.

IBM now found itself paying penalties. It might have struggled through to deliver hardware, but what use was it when actual performance was often way below the expected? So severe were the problems to become and so frantic the attempts to overcome them that in late 1965, eighteen months after 360's introduction, Frank Cary (now IBM's Chairman) was led to state that IBM's ability to sell on concepts was now exhausted.

That the gamble was of the order of five billion dollars was due more to IBM management incompetence than anything else. For now IBM was running out of money. One can get some idea of the problem from the last prospectus that IBM put out. In May 1966, IBM had to go to the market to raise $360 million.

It did not like doing so at all, because it had to explain why the money was needed. It had orders on hand for lease and purchase of Series 360 which would bring in the equivalent of nearly a billion dollars a year in revenues, and delivery schedules were still running at 24 months. It indicated that retained earnings for the five previous years had been of the order of $6 billion. However, acquisition and replacement of property, plant and equipment over those five years had been $3,665 million, and R&D $739 million. In those same years, employment had grown by over 55,000 (35,000 in Domestic alone), and in the last four of those five years, IBM had increased its consolidated property account by nearly $1·8 billion, or around 60%.

IBM did, in fact, get its money from the market, and within a year its troubles were effectively over. However, this should not obscure the fact that the troubles were of IBM's own making: what was in retrospect seen as that five-billion gamble only became so because of IBM's inability to deliver. IBM might have been in trouble, but in the process it had jumped through a barrier into economies of scale, volumes and income which were now to remove it altogether from the level of its competition. But in the process of getting there, IBM had effectively stunted, if not entirely crippled, the growth of all its major would-be competitors, to the point that within a further five years, the nine would-be major U.S. manufacturers of general-purpose computers (known as the mainframes)—IBM, GE,* RCA, Scientific Data Systems, Honeywell,

---

* American General Electric.

UNIVAC, NCR, Burroughs, CDC—were to be reduced to seven, while one of those seven in its turn had changed ownership, SDS having been brought by Xerox.

From nine to seven might not seem much of a change; however, the simple numeric listing covers an unpleasant reality. Of those nine companies, five literally had nowhere else to go: they were stuck with the computer business. IBM, SDS, NCR, Burroughs and CDC were essentially either companies whose major product was the computer—IBM, SDS, CDC—or whose major product line was one of which computers were an integral part—NCR and Burroughs. In two of the other four cases—Honeywell and UNIVAC—though computing was a critical element in their total business and its collapse might decimate the company, there were separate operations—defence-related electronics, instruments, control systems, electrical goods—which could survive as viable entities.

It was GE and RCA, two major corporations which could cut their losses without much effect, who chose to withdraw, between them racking up losses which over the fifteen odd years they each were in the mainframe computer business were to total nearly $700 million. They were really the only companies who had some alternative, and they took it.

GE was the first, and its departure illustrated full well the problem that faced IBM's competitors. GE's systems had filled a market niche which had enabled it to obtain between 3% and 4% of the U.S. market, but GE now had to decide what to do next. There were basically two choices: either to meet IBM head on or go out. If GE went the first route, it would need to invest an extra $500 million in a new product line. To obtain a goal of only 8% to 10% of new computer shipments, stated GE internal studies, it would have to have a price performance advantage of at least 20% to 40%. Furthermore, there was the problem of IBM's reaction, since much of that growth would have to come from what were IBM installations.

On that basis, the situation was clearly untenable. GE got out, selling its computer interest to Honeywell. The venture had lost GE between 125 and 150 million dollars.

But GE got off lightly in comparison with RCA. RCA had been a technical leader from the start, by creating systems which were compatible with IBM's but which gave better performance. It had also been a technical pioneer, particularly with virtual memory. But it was small. Thus, its own studies indicated that where IBM's share of the market in the major defined industrial groups ranged between 50% and 80%, RCA's in the same groups ranged from a maximum of 10%+ to less than 1%. Which was what one would expect: its marketing force was a tenth of the size of IBM's.

Unlike GE, however, RCA decided to go for broke: it determined to become number two, aiming for a slightly larger share than even GE—10%, the figure that everybody thought a competitor would have to hold to be properly viable. The way it was going to do it was to make its product entirely compatible with IBM, but with better price performance, aiming for something in the order of 15% of the market, the share at which it was thought the operation would be economically viable and profitable.

The weakness of RCA was to be spelt out in an internal RCA memo:

'In considering price–performance advantages, it must be remembered that manufacturing cost is approximately $\frac{1}{3}$ of selling price and that marketing, field engineering, and other expenses make up the remainder. A 15% price reduction (for the same performance) to be obtained from manufacturing costs only would require a 45% advantage in manufacturing costs, accomplished with a volume $\frac{1}{10}$ approximately of IBM's.'

It is as succinct a definition of the problem as could be penned—with one exception. The writer assumes that IBM's manufacturing costs were the equivalent of a third of its selling price, but already at the time the memo was written, IBM's manufacturing costs were much nearer a quarter than a third of that price, so that the differential against RCA was even greater.

In the third quarter of 1971, RCA had had enough. It sold its computer operation to Sperry UNIVAC and reported a loss on its computer operation before taxes of approximately $500 million, what is claimed to be the largest pre-tax write-off due to any single cause in American corporate history.

One cannot let the demise of RCA pass without a mention of one of the major reasons RCA failed. It made the fatal mistake of trying to emulate IBM, and it did so by taking on a former Vice-President of IBM, an eighteen-year man still only forty years old, who had risen to the top of IBM's Siberia, Service Bureau Corporation. However, the general impression was that Edwin L. Donegan was a rising IBM executive, and RCA was pleased to have him.

Donegan was brought in to head up marketing but within a year headed the whole computer operation. RCA began to copy not just IBM technology: it began to be run by former IBM executives. Soon three-quaters of the top two dozen RCA computer division jobs were held by them. RCA's computer operation became an attempt to duplicate IBM in every field: 'copies' of IBM personnel, marketing, administration and motivation 'policies' abounded. The only, and most important, thing that RCA could not duplicate was IBM's income.

But the problem that faced RCA was that, predicating its future on being number two to IBM, it was open to pressure from any moves that IBM might make as number one, and the decision that IBM did make (for instance, the announcement of the 370/145, which was of a lower price and a higher performance than RCA expected) were such that the volume of orders to justify the investment never came.

As for SDS, in one of the stock deals of the century ($920 million in stock at its then market valuation) it was bought at peak by Xerox, and became Xerox Data Systems.*

Abroad, the effects of IBM's dominance were just as traumatic: in France, IBM's growth crippled Compagnic Machines Bull, that was to fall first into the hands of G.E. and then Honeywell. In Germany, rather than go it alone, Siemens first allied with RCA, and then eventually with other continentals. In Britain, five general-purpose manufacturers were eventually, and thankfully, bullied into an amalgamation to become International Computers.

The effect of Series 360 was that around the year 1966 (or 1967; it depends on how the figures are interpreted) IBM was to achieve the seemingly impossible: recording more than 100% of the manufacturing industry's profits; it had not only showed all the true profit, but almost everybody else had made a loss.

What caused them to make that loss? Simply that, however fast the market grew, those other eight manufacturers were between them struggling for a share of the market which, in the

---

* By the summer of 1975, Xerox had had enough. Announcing total losses of nearly $426 million (including a computer trading loss of $25 million a year) from its computer manufacturing/marketing operations, it withdrew from the mainframe business.

twelve years between 1960 and 1972, never grew to more than a quarter of the market available.

The pre-trial brief of Justice in its case against IBM uses IBM's own categorisation of general-purpose computer systems on the market—categories C to G—to create a table which shows IBM's market share, in the terms that IBM understood it.

TABLE III.1

*IBM's Percentage Share of the Computer Systems In Categories C Through G Based on Installed Points**

1961	1962	1963	1964	1965	1966	1967	1968	1969	1970	1971	1972
80	82	80	80	84	74	75	75	75	73	73	73

IBM's dominance, indeed, and the effects of the introduction of Series 360, are very evident in another table found in that brief. The table deals with one of those key IBM determinants, the Net Product Installed Increase, the additional product that IBM has installed in any one year, after withdrawals and replacements have been taken away. Note particularly the effect of those 360 installations in 1965.

TABLE III.8

IBM's Percentage of NPII

Cat.	1962	1963	1964	1965	1966	1967	1968	1969	1970	1971	1972
C-G	89%	74%	79%	116%	53%	79%	78%	79%	56%	59%	76%
A-G	89%	74%	78%	113%	53%	77%	70%	78%	57%	58%	83%

Now the ability of a monopolist to fix its own price is well known; what is often not realised is how well the monopolist understands this and how aware he can be of the consequences. Such was the case with IBM, and the Justice brief spells it out quite clearly, quoting from an internal memorandum:

'J. R. Opel wrote to G. B. Beitzel and others on June 6, 1966, in a memorandum entitled "Lessons We Have Learned", noting: "Attached is the summary on pricing actions, which we discussed in detail at the General Managers' Meeting last Friday. After you have had an opportunity to read this, please return the summary, along with your comments, *since we do not wish to have copies in anyone's file.*" [italics added.] In the attachment,

---

* A point is equivalent to one dollar a month in rental income.

the April 7, 1964 announcement of the 360 series pricing stated:

A. *April 7, 1964 Announcement*

The prices established for 360 forecasted a return to the Company of 32·9% over the life of the program. Current analysis indicates a return of only 26·5%. The following observations are indicated:

1. The prices were established at 12–15% above competition on the low side of the line, and slightly above competition on the upper end of the line.

  .   .   .

4. *Prices*—The original pricing followed our generally historic trend of being above competition and returning our normal profit ratio. The outstanding success of the total 360 program now indicates that a higher price probably could have been supported without an adverse effect on the market.'

While IBM was aware of its power, so was everybody else. The brief instances the pricing policies of three manufacturers: GE, which set a price equivalent to IBM and tried for improved price performance; RCA, which set a price 10% below and aimed for a 10% performance improvement; and Honeywell, which set its prices on a par with IBM's and followed a special discount policy to where the only orders which were not list price discounted were those where IBM was not a competitor—and those were pitifully few.

*   *   *

Dynamic pricing or price manipulation, whichever terminology one prefers to use, is, as we have seen, a technique much used by IBM. However, nothing ever gave IBM as much strength as the practice called bundling.

We have seen (Prologue Two) how Hilary Faw viewed IBM's strengths and weaknesses, and the threat that unbundling posed to IBM's price control. We need to spend a little more time on the basics of bundling versus unbundling, because that has lain at the heart of IBM rise and growth, and has had much to do with its strength.

What made 'dumb funny company' such a powerful animal, what differentiated it from the rest, was what is called functional pricing, itself arising from the selling not of accounting machines or computers but of 'packages' which promised a solution to a problem.

That package consisted not simply of the provision of the computer and the units surrounding it, but also of what came to be called the 'IBM Iceberg': the operating system, the software to enable users to run applications on the computer, the design and consultancy services which would enable a user to have a system which fitted his needs (for hardly any one company required the same number of bits as another), the education of the users' staff to cope with computers, the training of staff to run them, literature, and—most crucial of all—the maintenance and engineering services which kept it up to standard. And, in the early days, those services particularly were often very much required.

For all this, the user paid one monthly charge, whether or not the services were needed or used.

IBM had known for a long time that bundling all the prices together was at the heart of its strength and a practice which gave a dominant company an ability to remain dominant, an ability to play with prices which could be used to keep opposition at bay.

It was the sort of practice that would not be helpful in a monopoly defence, and IBM executives and lawyers knew it. From 1962 onwards, they were severally and jointly to study bundling and what could be done to separate the various pricing elements without endangering the IBM position. The conclusion had always been that IBM should not unbundle, that there were few advantages to its doing so.

It was to be well expressed in what became known in IBM as the Maurer study of 1965:

> 'The single combined price for hardware and whatever degree of service an individual customer may require to achieve a successful installation always has been one of our greatest competitive advantages.
>
> To be successful, a competitor must overcome the combined strength of our entire offering rather than individual segments which, standing alone, might be more vulnerable.
>
> In general, to the extent that IBM unbundles its prices, the results would be as follows:

. . .

4. The areas of our line susceptable [sic] to attack by competition would be multiplied.
5. The number of hardware and service competitors would increase.

. . .

9. *Loss of business would result from higher total prices and increased competition.*' [Italics added.]

The net effect of bundling could be summarised like this: customers thought they were getting these services for free and were encouraged to go to IBM for solutions, knowing that they would not initially have to pay. But the solution they were offered in these circumstances naturally was one which fitted in with IBM plans and IBM available technology.

IBM was able to grow the market to suit itself. But this had all sorts of effects. Thus, for instance, one of the keys to IBM profits was for a long time the extra shift charge; such a charge could be maintained, however, only as long as the maintenance prices were bundled together. As long as IBM could maintain this, IBM could say, and say truthfully, that the extra shift charge was required because the system could be 'worn out' faster and its maintenance costs would be increased. Once, however, one could separate maintenance from rental, then the situation would have to change.

The effect of this total package, too, was that it raised the entry price for competitors: they, too, would have to offer bundled or free services. They could not simply come in with a computer system and charge for the rest separately, building up the business in a different fashion. The costs involved could be considerable: the Maurer study states that the costs of maintenance of rental hardware alone is substantial, at 11% of revenues.

But the one thing IBM did not want was a change, which would only encourage the creation of competitive service companies who could select what to service and where, and who could probably, competitively and selectively, and in some areas, price IBM out of the market.

Maurer was quite blunt about it.

'IBM's costs would increase.

' "Most Desirable" customers would be lost to competition.'

And that really frightened IBM, for it struck deep into the heart of IBM's control over its market, what IBM calls 'Account Control'. That account control rested, however, on one other factor, and a factor useful in the days when customers were generally the Great Unskilled. IBM would provide what would otherwise be consultancy services: in the initial stages IBM 'systems engineers' would come in for 'free' and effectively design the system.

The importance of this should not be underestimated: indeed, Justice maintains that the practice lay at the heart of account control. For systems engineering in this area does not simply consist of looking at the volumes that an organisation will have to handle and then specifying the equipment to meet it and the prices to cover it. It goes into the heart of the prospective user's business: the systems engineer/consultant may well dig deep into the organisation before recommending how work is to be done within the various departments, specifying the non-computer—as well as computer—procedures which will have to be carried out to make what the computer system produces useful, producing indeed a 'total' solution in so far as IBM can meet the needs of that would-be customer.

In large installations this can consume many hundreds of otherwise expensive man hours. And, of course, it gives IBM an unrivalled opportunity to find out how the customer's organisation functions. If IBM were to unbundle those services, then truly IBM would, according to Maurer again, 'lose contact with customers—less account coverage and control'.

Unbundling would encourage competition on a 'hardware to hardware' basis, and, as another internal memo was to put it, what bundling made possible was an ability for IBM to sell total systems 'and support weak products through great service'.

What bundling gave IBM was flexibility, and that was critical to IBM operations as then conceived. IBM was able to give the service it thought any individual account required, and that level was set, not by what the customer was willing to pay, but, given that the system was working reasonably well, by considerations set by IBM: how far could that account be grown, how prestigious and exposed to the public gaze was it, who had a friend at White Plains and Armonk, what were the relationships between IBM and the organisation concerned. It was a beautiful system: it meant that where IBM made a mistake, or where it wished to prove a new type of system, IBM could plough in the resources required, and those resources would be paid for, not directly by the customer concerned, but by all customers. It enabled IBM to grow in any direction it wanted or could make possible and yet spread the costs of the growth across all its customers, not just the ones in the sector of the business concerned. IBM could subsidise the losses from other users.

In late 1966, Justice began to take note of computer industry complaints. Justice had been investigating IBM since 1965, during Katzenbach's tenure as Attorney General, but it was not till shortly after his departure for the State Department in November* that Katzenbach's predecessor as IBM General House Counsel, Burke Marshall, also a former Justice Department lawyer, and his colleagues learnt that the investigation of IBM had now become serious.

Little happened for nearly two years. Then on 11th December 1968, CDC presented IBM with a Christmas present: its massive anti-trust suit. Shortly after Christmas, IBM learnt that it was going to be presented with a New Year's present: on New Year's Eve it was informed that the Justice Department was going to file its own suit. (Ramsey Clark, who brought the suit, was later to say that he was disappointed that the IBM case had not been brought to court a year sooner.)

There were to be a number of meetings between Justice and IBM lawyers over the next two weeks, with IBM trying to show particularly that Justice had its market figures wrong, and that there was not enough basis for them to proceed. But to no avail. For Justice was probably already aware that the lawyers who were facing it were part of the same team who had, between the initial period of investigation and the news that a suit was to be filed, advised IBM on how it should change the basis of the statistics it kept about its market share, excluding computer systems that were sold and the like, so as to arrive by a process of redefinition at market shares which looked substantially smaller than the ones everybody else knew to be fact.

Within a month of the Justice Department filing, IBM had set

---

* It is Mark Green of Nader's Raiders fame who has probably summed up Katzenbach best: 'Katzenbach had two fatal flaws in regard to anti-trust: he didn't believe in it and he was easily swayed by political considerations . . . his politicking was unrivalled in the last two decades except perhaps for Brownell [a former Postmaster General]'. Green was speaking, of course, before the full facts of the Nixon Administration came out.

up another unbundling task force, this time some hundreds strong. By early May, IBM was sufficiently sure of what its unbundling policy was to be to have counsel write to Justice, offering to make a presentation of IBM's plans for separate engineering services, educational courses and some programs.

Unbundling was announced the next month, June 23rd 1969: IBM Domestic stated that there would be a 3% price cut on all purchases and rentals to take effect from the last quarter of that year, but that from the start of the next, it would charge separately for systems engineering support, educational courses and new programs.*

As ever, there was a catch. There was an insistence by IBM that while some of the charges would not apply to existing product, they would apply to new ones, and IBM was, of course, soon to announce the obsolescence of its existing series.

IBM had been careful not to cut into its basic strength: thus leased hardware maintenance and servicing were not separated, nor did IBM intend to make charges for the critical pre-installation systems engineering and consultancy. Instead, IBM was left with a situation in which it could still decide for itself what services came under which heading. It could still provide 'free' systems engineering, as the need for that engineering could be apportioned to whatever cause IBM and the customer jointly cared to attribute it. Any customer with any clout with IBM could still get roughly what he wanted when he wanted it without extra expense.

The fun started with the computer programs. Throughout IBM's history, it had been careful to help its equipment/user associations. It had made effective use of those over the years, often taking the programs devised by one customer, working them up to suit others, and then releasing them to the market. In effect many of IBM's customers had been doing its work for it, which led to a muddled legal situation. IBM could not obviously charge for these reworked programs. Instead, it announced that it would make a charge for new programs that it developed. The

---

* Abroad, there was a hitch; an announcement that whatever IBM was going to do, it was not going to do it yet. Users had to wait another nine months, and then there was an announcement of similar changes, with some variations. But these were not to take effect for another two and a quarter years, the summer of 1972.

fact that some of those programs would be variations and up-grades of existing software was not stated. In Domestic the control programs, long a bone of contention among professionals in that IBM put them out in a form which users could tamper with only with difficulty, were now also leased for a fee. As for the former free applications programs, one can get some idea of the back to square one situation created by unbundling from a Management Committee minute of September 1972.

The programming products business is then three years old. In that time, the business is bringing in 3·3 million points world wide, only 1·1 million of which are in World Trade. IBM has 582 programs, of which 506 will be available by the year's end. And yet, all that the business is pulling in is $40 million a year.

It seems that, on its own, without the help of its customers in program devising and testing, IBM just cannot make it. Or as the minute spells out: 'The long range outlook projects that the program product business would take off during the 1975–79 period, remaining marginally profitable through 1975 as significant revenues and expenses pretty much washed out.'

What had IBM accomplished? The consensus of opinion was that IBM had raised IBM user costs, ranging from a low level of 10% to as high as 25%, depending upon whom one listened to, and there was considerable screaming in the market-place. Naturally enough, some of IBM's competitors thought that, as William Norris of CDC indicated, unbundling ranked with the transistor as one of the major landmarks in the development of the computer industry. Even more pleased were the independent software, and consultancy and education, companies which almost overnight began to think of themselves as possibly becoming an industry.

Yet the effect of unbundling on the industry was to be nearly traumatic: it led to the great financial boom in the computer services industry, and it led IBM into trouble. Between the summer of 1969 and the spring of 1971, IBM would have to absorb unbundling, the Series 370 announcement obsolescing 360 and the battles with the PCMs, and to start to absorb the changes that went with the more and more rapid handover of power to Learson and Cary. And for once, IBM's timing was wrong; it had to absorb these changes at a time when America was coming down from the high of 1967–68 into the minor recession of 1969–71.

It was just too much to ask any company to bear; indeed, the changes of 1969 to 1971 would have put most companies into total disarray. This did not happen to IBM, but even IBM could not take them without changing. The major change was in that area most difficult of all to pin down, company morale. Old hands might still refer to it as dumb funny company, with that mixture of respect and exasperation with which IBM was previously regarded; some of them still think of it in that way, but now that had more to do with history than reality.

The special character of IBM, that character which had taken fifty years to build, was effectively destroyed within a year. From now on, people were to work just for money, and money simply does not have that hold of the intangibles that built that mythical IBM family, though it should be noted that that particular myth had managed to survive through Series 360 and the dramatic expansion of IBM staff (40% in two years).

The legacy of Learson was to destroy the ethos that made IBM 'great'. 'IBM has plaques carrying phrases like respect for the individual, best service to the customer and the like . . . Prior to 1969, management used to emphasise that its assets were people . . . one of the phrases used to be respect for the individual. They don't do that anymore . . .'*

'Before 1969, IBM was a good company to work in. It was a collegiate environment, I felt as well off as any professor teaching school. Freedom of expression . . . doing your own thing.

'After 1969 they drew a hard line and IBM became more and more just like any other company out to make a buck.'

That change was also noticed externally. Many of IBM's major customers almost immediately began to view it differently, something which should have been expected but for which IBM seemed to be unprepared. The historic bundled price had meant that the relationship between IBM and its major customers had long looked as if it transcended money. Having paid their rental, the users had been assured of service. Systems engineers were at the end of a phone line, and software and education came free; IBM generally looked after its users. They were dependent on IBM, and as a result many had never built up the expertise to stand on their own.

---

* Not true, but few take it seriously anymore.

After unbundling, they were out in the cold. Suddenly these same services cost cash, and what was more the services were individually billed. It quickly became apparent that 3%, the allowance IBM had made for the separation of services from the hardware rental, did not by any means represent the true value of the services IBM had been providing: the allowance was much too small. IBM began to be viewed more coldly, and more independently. It began to be seen from the outside as it began to be seen from the inside—just another company out to make a buck.

PART TWO

I was only Following Orders

CHAPTER SEVEN

The Scale of 'Ole IBUM'*:
Nothing succeeds like excess

The business of IBM is conflict, whereas with nearly everybody else business is business. Of course, IBM dresses it up in terms of 'competition' and 'the free market economy', but this is really a fiction. Basically, the attitudes displayed by the management of IBM are not those of men engaged in the pursuits of peace, they are those of men engaged in war.

These conclusions are inescapable after a close reading of the minutes of the Management Review Committee and the Management Committee of IBM (till 1974 its two top corporate bodies), minutes in evidence in the Telex suit. They do, however, cause one difficulty for a writer: the major problem he faces in dealing with IBM, however experienced in the coverage of industry and large corporations, or however skilled in the esoterics of the techniques, sciences and technologies that make up the computer business, is that IBM is organisationally striking, unique in both ethos and performance—there is nothing quite like it in computing or any other business.

This factor has been the major cause of its growth. It is not simply that IBM is a distinct entity within its own industry; its uniqueness is also due to the products from which that growth has come. The computer industry has at its roots the notion that the low-level thinking functions of people are often easily replaceable by machines, and that with this will come order and cost savings.

---

* 'Ole IBUM' is the name given the company by B. O. Evans, for a long time President of IBM's Systems Development Division, a key figure in the creation of Series 360, and of FS, Future System (see Chapter 15 and the Epilogue).

It is also an industry (computing plus accountancy) built on the premise that the majority of people are lacking in both competence and honesty: that people will not do what is right; that they will cheat, will steal, and will fumble. This may seem a frivolous way of dealing with the industry's product, but it is in fact realistic: it is in the world of bookkeeping, financial records, and accountancy that IBM has had its major success, and which has provided the profit to make IBM's growth possible.

Within industry, IBM holds a unique position. Other companies have taken note of IBM's performance, and many have drawn conclusions from it. IBM is much envied, emulated and copied. Parts of its organisational package are found in many other corporations, particularly the parts dealing with IBM's all-embracing concern for employee welfare and morale.

But there is still only one IBM; the grafts seldom work as well elsewhere as they do for IBM, for they are only partial and incomplete. To be as effective, an organisation would have to evolve a similar ethos, that distinctive flavour so noticeable in almost all IBM executives which causes them usually to be immediately picked out at any conference or meeting.

To be like IBM, you have to be more than simply rich, you must also allocate your resources similarly. You must also structure like IBM, which means a high overhead, one out of line with the way other managements of corporations allocate and expend their capital and income. IBM, partly by design, partly by timing, by hard effort and by luck, was built for the long haul. And this was not achieved without expense. One cannot distort the pattern and expect to command, and generally obtain, the loyalty that IBM previously took as its right; it is a package and the ingredients cannot be selected to suit oneself.

Also, to be like IBM, there has to be a cohesive nature to the organisation's business: the map of the territory must be capable of clear intellectual delineation; it must hold together, and lead logically in the direction of horizontal and vertical integration. IBM saw very early, indeed it was forced to see, that it was not in the calculating machine or computer businesses, but in the business of information handling by machine, a business it called data processing, and organised itself accordingly.

And, the last factor in this vein that IBM has going for it is that the industry the Watsons went into was one which could be sold both externally and internally as being essential to the progress of civilisation and to the survival, the advancement and enhancement of all we hold most dear, and not just a means of providing employment and making a profit. Computing is in many ways a crusade, even if the banner which IBM carries should have IBM profit written large on one side and good intent lightly inscribed on the other.

There is, of course, a temptation to characterise IBM's uniqueness by drawing analogies, comparisons and parallels with better understood and more intensively studied organisations—to describe one thing that is relatively new, in terms of another that is older and generally well understood. Such comparisons have very limited utility, for in no way can such a comparison encapsulate IBM. With IBM parallels will only work if used sparingly to illuminate the behaviour of a part of the corporation or a particular level or function within it, and that only at some time, not necessarily at all times.

At one time or another IBM has been compared to the Roman Catholic Church, the Masons, the Klu Klux Klan, the Jesuits, a bank, a feudal court, the more boneheaded parts of the military, and the Third Reich.

IBM may sometimes operate as if this was 1944 and Armonk is Rastenberg, with the corporation going from one extreme to another, swinging this way one minute and that way the next as the leader changes his mind, but any IBM junior manager—leaving aside all moral issues—would consider the Third Reich to have been an incredibly disorganised shambles of a place crying out for the application of IBM's management and organisational methodology.

There are aspects of the Catholic Church to IBM; after all it, too, masquerades as truly international while being largely run by the nationals of one country who guard their power and privileges just as jealously as the College of Cardinals. And, the IBM answer to Stalin's famous question: 'How many divisions has the Pope?' would have to be a similar sort of answer, and for similar reasons.*

---

* The question was not really concerned with divisions at all: it was about the realities of the world of nation states, which precluded organisations like the Catholic Church from maintaining the means by which nation states ultimately threaten to do business with each other. In this world, IBM, of course, has even less standing or claim on ultimate loyalties.

IBM may sometimes act as a bank masquerading as a computer manufacturer, but again the parallel only holds good over fairly narrow territory. The only two analogies which are of some use are those of the feudal court and the more boneheaded parts of the military: the first is appropriate for some aspects of the world of Armonk (described in Chapter 8); the second has much to do with the organisation of IBM, particularly what one can describe as the modular independence which is a major feature of the way non-industrial and sales staff are inserted into the IBM structure and their jobs specified, and the organisation of communications, training and motivation.

But none of these descriptions hold true for the entire corporation. As for the analogy which is now fashionable, that large multinationals are states with some form of sovereignty in their own right, this, at least in the case of IBM, is fallacious. The notion may have some validity in the sense that Anthony Sampson put it forward when dealing with ITT*, but ITT is sovereign in a sense that IBM is not. ITT is widely dispersed in terms of plant and product. It is a conglomerate, and it is in the nature of conglomerates that they will seldom dominate anything anywhere. There are areas in ITT, particularly in telephones and telecommunications, where ITT has much industrial strength. But it should not be overlooked that these areas are closely policed by states, and ITT survives by playing the game that the states in which it operates will allow it to play. The difference between ITT and IBM is that IBM has a substantial share, often a dominant or near monopoly share, of the markets it operates in, and that these markets are not policed and subject to government intervention in the same way.

Of course, to state that they are not so now does not mean to imply that they will never be so policed in the future.

IBM may look like a state at war, with morale being closely related to the behaviour and performance of its fighting troop, its salesmen, and the results they obtain; and the victory being measured in dollars over and above the previous year's achievement, the resultant employee high morale when this is achieved, and the destruction of the opposition as an effective force (this being necessary as the markets IBM operates in do not grow at

---

* See *ITT: The Sovereign State,* by Anthony Sampson (Hodder & Stoughton, London, 1973).

the same rate as the IBM growth rate), so somebody or something has to give.

But one must distinguish between illusion and reality.* IBM is not, of course, a state at all. The only sense in which IBM is sovereign is that, unlike most other multinationals, IBM plays a game of its own, often simply out of ignorance of how everybody else plays. IBM behaves *anationally*, and it is able to do so because its integration on an international scale is unique.

It can only behave in the way it does as long as states are prepared to let it. What success it has had independent of and contradictory to the policies of governments has largely been due to the fact that the IBM monopoly has been hitherto relatively unimportant, and the totality of IBM is not grasped by politicians. It will exist in its present form only as long as real states cannot be bothered to decide what if anything, is to be done, and then get round to doing it. Given that multinationals such as IBM are allowed to cover their tracks, to hide their multinational operations in secrecy this could be a long time. Whether it will be, of course, is a different question, one more concerned with political pressures than the activities of the corporations themselves.

A major part of the problem lies in the difference between the reality of the IBM operation and the normal pressures of the political process. There are perhaps only a few serious political figures in Western Europe, who do not think that the existence of multinationals poses fundamental problems. But they are long-term problems: multinationals may pose a threat, but it is a nebulous threat.

The politician, however, is faced with concrete and immediate problems. So on one side he has IBM, providing wages above the norm, good working facilities, and usually at the minimum a stable labour force, normally one that is growing. It is a labour force that is cared for, and IBM's private welfare services are good. Furthermore, IBM's product does not seem to pollute the countryside. If the politician has any problems with local management, something will be done. The IBM civil service will talk to the civil service proper in the terms they both understand. IBM,

---

* Though some IBM executives do not. Thus M. Maisonrouge in an internal to IBM address has been heard to refer to 'the so-called dignitaries of the United Nations'.

except at the abstract level of control of long term aims and ambitions, is thus no problem to him—he wishes everybody else caused as few difficulties.

The politician's concerns are with the companies with labour, investment and management problems which lead to his having to plead a case somewhere or become embroiled in time consuming negotiations. Seen in this light, the existence of IBM is, say, number eighteen in the list of priorities to be dealt with, and most likely never rises any higher, for as soon as he deals with one of the seventeen above it, another comes along with problems of a similar urgency to take its place. The politician really wishes that in the day to day work of politics all other companies were as little trouble.

There is one final problem with the method of the general parallel or analogy: its usefulness depends on which IBM one is discussing. Though there may be just one external legal entity, seen internally there is more than one IBM.

There is dumb funny company, the IBM of the production line and office workers—the often paternalistic employer with, till recently, generally a good record in terms of the guarantees of security that those who have opted out of the competitive struggle would prefer to have.

There is the IBM of the 'exempts' and the professionals; the experts not involved in the line executive competitive struggle, whose job is to think about and devise technology, or advise management. This is the IBM of the cosseted and comfortable; the rich IBM where the main problems come from intellectual challenge set against the time-scale which IBM has allocated for solutions. This is the IBM of myth, except that for many thousands of people it is a real IBM. A good challenging and rewarding employer, and one about whom few questions are asked, certainly seldom any questions about the motivation and the methods that the IBM of the competitive struggle will use: about how the results, which will provide that comfortable living, are accomplished, or the costs that others involved in that competitive struggle will have to pay.

The IBM of the competitive struggle, IBM monopolist, is the third IBM, and it is the IBM with which this book is primarily concerned: competitive IBM, both internally for advancement, and externally for growth and profit; the corporation which chews up its own people, and externally tries—generally successfully—to chew up its opposition.

*   *   *

Before one can explore further what makes IBM tick, one needs to conduct another exercise: to put IBM into some sort of factual context and describe the scale of its operations, particularly in terms of money, for money is a well understood instrument of measure, not least in IBM.

A good start can be made with the IBM Annual Report for 1973, which showed that IBM grossed $10,993 million. Immediately we can see one reason why people think in terms of states, sovereign or otherwise. We are talking of a company with a then annual gross similar to the Gross National Product of Finland, near that of Indonesia and larger than New Zealand's. Indeed, only some twenty countries have a larger Gross National Product than IBM has income. This is a figure not far short of Sweden's or India's annual Central Government expenditure: the equivalent of four times the annual Swiss budget.

That same 1973 Annual Report contains a ten-year table covering the period 1964 to 1973, thus including within it most of the development costs for Series 360, and a substantial part of the total income that IBM has derived from it. That table shows the following:

Total IBM Revenues have grown from $3,339 million to $10,993 million. In 1964, IBM had a turnover in the same class as Kodak, Procter and Gamble, Union Carbide and Fiat have today.

IBM gross profits before taxes as declared in the Annual Report have also grown but more than threefold, from $897 million to $2,946 million. Put another way, the IBM profit that year is roughly equivalent to the $1400 million taxpayers' investment (at mid-1975 rates of exchange) that the British Government is scheduled to make over eight years in the newly nationalised U.K. car manufacturing industry, British Leyland.

The relationship has also roughly held for total taxes paid, from $446 million to $1,371 million. But only very roughly. In a world where corporation taxes have generally climbed as a total percentage of company revenues, almost the world over (and particularly so in the countries in which IBM has the majority of its operations), this is surprising.

Working capital, on the other hand, has nearly quadrupled from $899 million to $3,274 million, where the long-term debt ($370 to $652 million) has not even doubled. This conceals a difference in that debt between the start and end of the decade in that the foreign long-term debt now represents the majority of IBM's indebtedness. This is the reverse of the situation which existed in the fifties and early sixties. In reality, parent IBM is almost debt-free, the overseas subsidiaries are not. (So that, should anyone expropriate IBM or part of it outside the U.S.A., they will not get their hands on as many assets as would otherwise be the case?)

Parent IBM is now largely internally self-financing. (So cash loaded is it that even *Business Week* could not resist discussing IBM's cash resources early in 1974 under the caption 'IBM's $3·8 billion Cookie Jar'.)

In the same ten-year period, shareholders have grown from 226,000 to 575,000; and IBM has made five stock splits: 25, 50, $2\frac{1}{2}$, 100 and 25%.

IBM indeed was *the* growth share, one of the blue chip stocks of the fifties and sixties. In 1973 146 million shares were held by investors. In the general downturn of the stock market between 1973 and late 1974, IBM stock fell with the market from a valuation of well over $300 a share to at one point nearly $150.

In other words, there was a time where IBM was valued at more than $60 billion—a loss on paper of well over $30 billion?*

Mind-numbing figures of this order, of course, have little to do with the reality of IBM; they are, however, an indication of scale. And that scale is impressive. During that same ten-year period, IBM's total gross revenues were nearly $67 billion, and profits before tax amounted to 17\frac{1}{2}$ billion.

*   *   *

Where has all this gross and profit come from? Series 360 for one source.

IBM's accounting years are such that the six-and-a-quarter-year period of active Series 360 marketing is in fact covered by

---

* During the autumn of 1974, a rumour of a possible Arab take-over hit the market. IBM stock put on more than $2 billion within hours. The possibilities for manipulation then are immense—and no doubt tempting.

seven financial years (though Series 360 income did not seriously start coming in until 1965). However, the 1973 Annual Report shows that during those seven years, IBM grossed $37,994 million and showed pre-tax profits of $10,065 million.

The figures can be put into context another way. During those years, IBM made well over 90% of the profits of the entire digital computer manufacturing industry. And what did Series 360 contribute? In 1970, prior to the launch of Series 370, IBM's management was given a forecast of expected Series 370 revenues. That forecast included a comparison of the original Series 360 forecast and a forecast of total 360-linked revenues as of the new series announcement date.

The Series 360 forecast is reproduced here. The fact that the Series 360 profit figures are forecast to be greater than the profits for the entire IBM corporation during the period the corporation was in production is accounted for by the overlap between the cessation of production of one series and the amount of time it will be on the market, and thus earning rental, after its successor has been announced. In this situation, the production years obviously differ from the marketing years.

SYSTEM 360
DOMESTIC

($ millions)

	Rev.	Profit	%
Original announcement			
CPU	$2625	$956	36·4
Memory	410	98	23·9
I/O	3748	1175	31·3
Total	$6783	$2229	32·9
Today			
CPU	$7060	$2292	32·5
Memory	957	411	42·9
I/O	9853	3302	34·5
Total	$17600	$6005	34·1

SYSTEM 360
WORLDWIDE

($ millions)

	Rev.	Profit	%
Original announcement			
CPU	$4287	$1444	33·7
Memory	650	194	29·9
I/O	5826	1611	27·7
Total	$10763	$3249	30·2
Today			
CPU	$11272	$3928	34·8
Memory	1330	580	43·6
I/O	16003	5735	35·8
Total	$28605	$10243	35·8
		W.T.	38·5

$28+ billion revenues and $10+ billion profit are genuine figures in the sense that these are working data, as distinct from accountants' figures for the Annual Report or data produced in the course of litigation.

They have interest for a number of reasons. First there is the obvious: they are a further indication of the scale of IBM. Not so obviously, they show reality, the effects of IBM pricing manoeuvres; thus, for instance, the IBM trick of loading memory prices during the life of a series comes out quite clearly, something only possible in a situation when there is no add-on memory competition. One can, however, see what happens to IBM figures when competition is there, by comparing the two I/O (input/output service) forecasts, which deal with the majority of the products the PCM war was about.

Though the figures are for Domestic and for Worldwide (Domestic plus WTC), one does not even need to do any sums to see what has been going on. The profit percentage that IBM expects from IBM WTC is higher than that for Domestic.

A probable reason, indeed almost certainly the major reason, for the difference in the profit percentages between Domestic and

WTC, the reason that the profit increase for Domestic is lower than that for Worldwide is the existence of PCM competition during the two years before the forecasts were made. That competition was almost entirely domestic, the PCMs not yet being seriously established in the WTC market pre-1970.

This loading of prices so that the percentage return from WTC is greater than from Domestic is not something that simply happened in a fit of absence of mind. Like Topsy, it may initially have 'just growed', but it is now part of a planned, concerted strategy.* This is clearly indicated in the forecasts for Series 370.

SERIES 370

	MAC	Anc. Price	MMMC	Mpy.	Effect Mpy.	Resp.
LPU						
7/15.2	$18530	$890400	$2160	48	52 7	39
333	38750	1867600	4550	48	52·7	59
Modal Size						
Memory						
255 k	3000	132000	280	44	47·3	58
512 k	6000	264000	560	44	47·3	58
Printer	1700	51600	380	48	61	51
(Atria)						
Merlin						
Drive	1300	61100	200	47	55·5	60
Cont. Unit	2400	112800	170	47	50·6	64

* The strategy could be said to have come a little unstuck in 1974: but in all these things it depends on how the figures are interpreted. Total revenues that year were $12,675 million, of which Domestic accounted for $6,729 million and WTC $5,946 million. Profit from Domestic, however, was $918 million while from WTC profits were $919 million. Though WTC profits grew only by sixty plus million dollars, IBM took advantage of the change in the U.S. repatriation of profit rules (see p. 171) and increased its investment of undistributed earnings in WTC by more than eighty million dollars over the previous year. In fact, because of changes in 1974 currency rates, the figures over-estimate the real profit made. The German Mark, for instance, appreciated by over twenty per cent against the dollar in 1974, and IBM Germany, it should not be forgotten, has the largest revenues of any of IBM WTC company accounting for over 15 per cent of total gross. But one has to be careful here: IBM Germany's revenues include income arising from in–trading between IBM WTC companies. The processes of consolidation to show true external revenues would probably wash out quite a part of the paper gross—and the paper profit.

The forecasts are concerned with the 370/155 and 370/165, initially the larger computer systems in IBM's 370 Series. They are for the machines as originally announced, before the addition of virtual memory (the engineering changes for which are minimal and accounted for as a coda to the forecasts) will turn them into the 158 and 168: the changes do not materially affect the figures, though they are a good example of the previously noted IBM philosophy of providing mid-life kickers or enhancements, revealing features that are already there but which can only work with the addition of relatively minor (in cost to IBM) gizmos and thingamijigs.

The first point to be made is that six years after the introduction of Series 360, the initial forecast revenues for the larger end of the range are of the same order as the initial forecasts for the entire 360 Series six years earlier. Were the 370 forecast to bear the same relation to reality as the 360, then the two large machines alone should bring in about as much revenue as the 360 Series in its entirety.

However, the real profit will be far greater. The loading of Series 370 profit expectation on WTC is greater than for Series

SYSTEM 360
DOMESTIC

($ millions)

	Rev.	Profit	%
Original announcement			
CPU	$1662	$488	29·4
Memory	240	96	40·0
I/O	2078	436	21·0
Total	$3980	$1020	25·6
Today			
CPU	$4212	$1647	39·1
Memory	373	177	47·5
I/O	6150	2439	39·7
Total	$10735	$4263	39·7

360, which can be seen by comparing the expected profit percentage for Domestic with that for WTC which is shown in this table. This is predatory in the worst sense, not necessarily the sense in which it was used in the first Telex trial, since it could be argued, and IBM did so argue, that its pricing actions were a reaction to competitive situations.

That profit differential, too, is a reaction to competitive conditions, in that the competition that IBM faces abroad is adjudged to be less than that IBM will receive at home. Obviously, this is something of which we can expect IBM to take advantage.

There are no references to this sort of essential background in IBM's Annual Reports. Indeed, those Annual Reports are interesting in that they conceal rather than reveal. Not all the concealments are strictly legal. It may only be a technicality, but IBM's Annual Reports in fact break American public protection rules—they have done so for years, and have done so with impunity.

The American rules concerned are for the protection of the investor. They require that major corporations file detailed reports on divisional activities where those divisions are individual trading entities. They require, too, just as detailed reports on activities of subsidiaries both at home and overseas. IBM does not file accordingly, something which seems to have escaped the attention of that American corporate public interest policeman, the Federal Securities and Exchange Commission.

However, in the recent past IBM has had to file more comprehensive and more meaningful data outside the Annual Report with many Federal bodies, of which three are important, though only two are in the public domain.

The first filing is with the Bureau of Commerce. Unfortunately this is not in the public domain. The filings took place during the period of American government restrictions on foreign investment, which included provisions making it mandatory for companies to repatriate a substantial part of their earnings back to the United States. This hurt IBM, since the IBM policy had been as much as possible to re-invest earnings abroad. The policy too coincided with a period in which many of the governments of Europe were concerned about their balance of payments, which put IBM WTC into a dilemma; whatever it did, it would offend somebody.

We must distinguish here between repatriation of capital and profits and the payment to parent IBM for goods, services and the like. Thus, returning to the mid-sixties, one learns from a minute of the MRC of January 1968, for instance, that parent IBM had a net position in its balance of payments of 370 million dollars, a clear indication that only minimal profits were being repatriated. Yet it is interesting to note that the MRC minute also points out that this net position put IBM among the top five companies making a positive contribution to the American balance of payments. IBM has always cloaked its blance of trade/balance of payments situation in mystery.

Four years later, the Annual Report for 1972 tells us that one out of every eight jobs in IBM Domestic's plants was supported by the export trade.*

The second filing is with the U.S. Securities and Exchange Commission. The data is mainly that which will be found in the Annual Reports submitted. However, the reports (called 10Ks and 10Qs after the form on which they have to be submitted) do add a little information. The 10Q for the first half of 1972, for instance, gives data separating sales from lease and service income, for similar six-month periods in 1971 and 1972. Now 1972 was the first full year of 370 Series production and delivery; a year in which sales were expected to be high. And they were: total Worldwide sales that half year were $1,408 million where rental and services brought in $3,268 million. By contrast, sales for the comparative period in 1971 were $809 million, with rentals and service $3,003 million.

However, it is the reports to the Price Commision, reports required during the period of the Nixon wage/price freeze, which begin to give some serious indications of IBM figures. The last filing I have seen was dated May 1972. The Report covered the years 1968, 1969 and 1971.

The figures that are of interest are those for 1971: in its Annual Report for that year IBM states that its consolidated gross income was $8,273 m. and its earnings before taxes were $2,055 m.

---

* In 1974, G. E. Jones, IBM WTC Chairman, was to tell a Congressional Committee that out of every five IBM Domestic employees supported that export business.

1971   IBM (in millions of $)

	IBM Worldwide	IBM Domestic	IBM WTC*
Net Sales	8,273	4,864	3,409
Cost of Sales	3,191	1,960	1,231
Gross Profit	5,032	2,904	2,128
Other Expenses	3,108	1,931	1,177
Operating income	1,974	972	1,002

* Worldwide minus Domestic.

Only the first two columns come from the report; the third column was arrived at after subtracting column one from column two, the basis of the sum being that IBM had to report total operational figures and then state what part of them were covered by domestic operations, these being the only ones covered by the wage/price freeze rules.

These are not figures delivered to the Federal Government by low-level functionaries: the Form PC 50 has to be signed by the Chief Executive of the reporting company or other authorised officer, and in this case is signed by Frank Cary, then IBM's President.

PC 50 contains other data besides that given in the table. The 'cost of sales' figures for IBM Domestic are broken down into materials and labour costs. The figures indicate that materials and components used by Domestic during the year were 'worth' $452 million, of which imported materials accounted for a relatively trivial $32 million, while direct labour costs were $550 million.

The sum of these is roughly $1 billion, and is the 'true' manufacturing cost (in the sense that any of these figures are true). Those costs lump together computer systems, peripherals, discs, typewriters and the rest of the IBM product range. However, the result is in line with the relationships previously described: IBM's 1971 manufacturing costs were of the order of 22% of gross revenue. It is the difference between these costs and revenues which gives IBM its strength; indeed, we have here what many specialists think is the widest across-the-board margin between cost price and selling price that exists in any company in the entire field of manufacture.

It should be realised, of course, that the relationship expressed above is not really 'true' at all. The relationship would only hold were IBM to sell that entire production. In fact—set against revenues—it substantially over-estimates the costs of production, for other IBM figures available elsewhere indicate that some three-quarters of IBM's annual income will arise from activities connected with the rental/leasing of computer systems. And, as IBM at the time of these figures were reported was still on a growth trajectory, the costs incurred in that year will eventually generate more future income than the total IBM revenues for the year.

What IBM has here is a built-in advantage, however arrived at, over its competitors; a margin made possible by the economics of the total volumes generated: for it is the total volumes and cost package that counts, not necessarily the individual items.

Effectively, it means that the cost to IBM of any total computer system is around half that achieved by the best of its competitors. Were any competitor the same size as IBM and these relationships still to hold, it would mean that—in the early seventies—IBM Domestic alone would have had a cost advantage worth a billion a year.

It is this remarkable amount of slack between production costs and revenues which gives IBM its muscle—and which causes everybody else spasms.

*   *   *

So far, much of this chapter has had to be rather dry. The sums may be astronomical, but to grasp what they mean has not been the most entertaining of tasks, nor could it be. The scale of IBM's operations can be expressed more vividly. Thus IBM deals in the sorts of volumes one usually associates with the activities of monolithic states. IBM (Domestic plus WTC), for instance, is its own second largest user, being surpassed only by the U.S. Federal Government. Indeed, the resources devoted to computing are massive by any standards, and as a user of computers—wherever they may come from—IBM is surpassed only by a handful of governments.

* As this table below shows, during 1972 IBM's total expenditure on computing was running at around $320 million a year. However, as IBM costs its internal computers at 40% of the charge it would make to its customers, that same computing power, machines with men and resources, would have cost any other user $800 million a year. This internal computing employed nèarly 12,000 people, or some 5% of the total IBM work force.

Total IBM DP points installed for I/S [Information Systems] in 1972 was projected at 35M. Forecasts for 12/31/73 was 36·3M. I/S expenses and headcount for 1970 through 1973 is noted in the following table.

I/S Expense (@40% $)	USA	WTC	Total IBM
111 111 A nluial	010 8	112	309·8
1971 Actual	231·7	07·8	319·5
1972 Plan	220·3	100·0	320·3
1972 Est. Act.	219·3	100·0	319·3
1973 Target	213·0	108·4	321·4
Headcount Y/E			
1970 Actual	9150	4614	13,764
1971 Actual	7835	4972	12,897
1972 Plan	7555	5115	12,870
1972 Est. Act.	7423	5053	12,481
1973 Target	6310	5330	11,920

* IBM is the world's largest manufacturer of high-grade semi-conductors and micro-electronic circuits. Indeed in 1972, IBM actually used somewhere between 10% and 15% of the world's semi-conductor production.

* IBM is not just a large manufacturer, it is also a substantial purchaser of other supplies. In the early seventies it dealt with 33,000 suppliers, more than 200 of whom had over 25% of their work-load with IBM.

* The IBM sevicing organisation is the largest commercial user of short-wave radio in the United States. So much does IBM servicing depend on its use to keep in contact with service engineers in the field, that IBM's management—early 1974—was much incensed to discover that its heavy usage of radio was being monitored. Someone else had found that it paid to set up an organisation to listen in to those transmissions so that they could then offer a service to competitors or would-be competitors; that service would provide reports on which IBM installations were down, and what could be gleaned of the reasons why they were so.

IBM is a major supporter of the world's airline industry. A British joke (as the result of the habit of one airline of spending vast sums on its IBM computer installations, to the point where it offers extensive software for sale to other airlines) has it that if you want to get into the computer business, you should first of all get yourself an airline. It is a joke which IBM might well take seriously, for insiders talk of a total airline bill for 1973 of well over $100 million, one putting it as high as $170 million. It is a figure impossible to check short of asking IBM—and one I doubt: over $600 for every IBM employee. But considering the travel that some senior IBM executives do, it is possible. After all, $600 does not even represent the cost of a return fare across the Atlantic, and some executives will do that trip many times a year.

The telephone and communications bill, however, can be checked, at least for 1969. Then, Domestic's bill was $59 million, of which $25 million was for local telephone facilities, and $22 million for long-distance calls. On top of this the leased network facilities for data transmission cost $12 million, and IBM's WTC 'phone bill was around $20 million. The total 1969 communications expenditure then was around $80 million.

A 1971 report to the MRC, however, indicated that telecommunications that year were budgeted at $60 million for IBM Domestic alone. The document is not very clear as IBM by that time was beginning to become deeply immersed in communications-oriented computing, the likelihood of this being solely for data transmission is quite high.

U.S. Price Commission submission figures for 1970 indicate that IBM Domestic had revenues of $4·6 billion achieved with 160,000 employees. Dollars per employee $28·5 thousand, a decrease over 1969 and 1968 when the figures had been respectively $30 thousand and $32 thousand. A further Price Commission submission for the same year indicates that average employee compensation was $15·7 thousand, value added $24·7 thousand; total employee compensation, salaries, wages and benefits, was around $2·5 billion.

Throughout the early seventies, IBM's total employment has varied between 260,000 and 275,000. In that time, however, IBM gross revenues have increased from $7·2 billion to $11 billion: $40,000 per employee.

*   *   *

What do all these people do, where do they work in IBM? IBM has twelve divisions and two subsidiaries.* Though over the years, late sixties/early seventies, there has been some shifting of responsibilities and changes in marketing responsibilities and the like, the basic outline that follows gives a fair idea of the way in which IBM is organised.

The facts that illustrate what these divisions are about are not all cast in the same measure, or representative of the same period of time, for not all data required for a comprehensive breakdown seems to be present in the minutes. However, the following gives some indication of the scale and scope of IBM's major activities.

First, the subsidiaries.

*   *   *

Subsidiary number one, IBM World Trade Corporation, otherwise WTC, is dealt with in more detail in Chapter 11. Here, all we need to note are some basic facts. As of December 1972, WTC had 115,000 employees: 84,000 in sales, servicing and administration, 26,000 in manufacturing, and a claimed round-figure 5,000 in R&D. One year later, the end of 1973, personnel had increased to 122,000. IBM WTC was operating in 126 countries, grossed $5,142 million with a net profit of $852 million, and WTC had overtaken Domestic. As management put it in early 1970, WTC (DP) from '73 to '75 was 'going to undergo a serious expense reduction which would lead to increased profit, though on a lower than forecast turnover. It would then pass the DP Group on this basis and stay there'.

---

* Brought up to three in the summer of 1974 when IBM bought CML, a satellite operation, the latest addition to IBM's ranks, and the only American acquisition IBM has ever made in which it has been prepared to settle for less than 100% ownership. This is dealt with in Part Three, for satellites play a key role in the IBM of the future. (At the time of writing, whether CML would be given permission to operate was still subject to a ruling from the Federal Communications Commission.)

Subsidiary number two, in comparison, is the proverbial dust-cart. The 1971 IBM internal plans for Science Research Associates, IBM's publishing arm, indicated turnover in 1973 not much above $50 million with around 1,000 employees.

No doubt it would be easy to find out more, but it is not really worth it. IBM's internal studies in 1971 indicated that SRA ranked eleventh in size in its field, and that even with improved performance it would rank eventually no more than sixth. To get that financial performance, however, IBM would have to sacrifice the serious research that SRA should be doing through the mid-seventies.

SRA is something of a joke among serious educationalists, if a somewhat frightening joke. Its income in part derives from the creation and marketing of tests, where it also provides a marking service. The tests can be IQ, specialist application, entrance* and the like: however, SRA seems still to believe in IQ spot testing and similar necromantic nonsense. It also deals in structured educational material and courses, particularly the provision of 'fact' for the educationally handicapped: here it is a sort of corporate Enid Blyton.

The only other SRA point of interest was picked up by *Ramparts* early in 1974. They looked at an SRA Social Studies package entitled 'Our Working World'. The message, directed to six-year-olds using pre-packaged film and audio techniques, included such gems of nonsense as 'the two groups in society, those who produce and those who consume', and a suggestion for a game for children to play where one child acts as the employer, the others line up in front, and he hires the errand boy asking for the lowest weekly wage. One can see why SRA has not been uniquely successful.

It is a relief to turn from SRA to IBM proper and its twelve

---

* SRA, it is said, has had much to do with the creation of the IBM aptitude tests, tests which are used by IBM in the selection of its own employees and sold extensively elsewhere as a testing mechanism for other companies employing staff, computer and otherwise. These tests are subject to much argument, being culture dependent, and in the U.S. at least have not been taken up by many companies after advice that their use might infringe equal employment regulations. Well into the seventies in the U.K. the tests were meaningless, for IBM had not done the necessary control tests to go with them. It had been hiring partly on the basis of those tests for years; but as it had not followed through the future careers of those who had failed them, a true measure of performance was not possible.

Divisions. The internal organisation of IBM has changed over the years: it has evolved. Where once there was a simple division between marketing and manufacture, today it is not quite so simple. Some divisions exist because they serve a particular function, others because they serve specific markets. Simple or not, it makes good sense.

At the core of IBM lies the DP Group, of which the Data Processing Division is the heart. DPD is the marketing division for medium to large computer systems and their software to medium to large customers. DPD also markets and services the products of the General Systems Division (see below), where these are ancillary to the systems that DPD markets on its own account. In 1973 the DP Group grossed nearly $4½ billion.

DPD is the corporate emotional flagship. No one has ever got anywhere in IBM without having held some responsibility within or for DPD.

Behind DPD now come four linked divisions: Systems Products, General Products, Systems Development and Advanced Systems Development Division.

SPD (Systems Products Division) manufactures Series 370 and also has the responsibility for the development and manufacture of components. It was created in 1971 out of what were the Systems Manufacturing and the Components Divisions. (In 1973 the components production of SPD, if directly sold on the market, would have been worth about $2 billion, which would give it well over 50% of the U.S. components market.)

Also in 1971 IBM separated peripheral products from systems manufacturing and created the General Products Division. This is responsible for the development and manufacture of IBM peripherals, printers, and tape and disc drives. This separation was not difficult; its main plants were at San Jose near San Francisco and Boulder in Colorado. It was not difficult in another sense; San Jose has gradually evolved in its own way and the consensus of opinion among many IBM executives is that the San Jose executives are the most independent of an at times quarrelsome and would-be independent lot.

Separate, but a key part of the marketing effort, is Field Engineering which provides field maintenance for Series 370 hardware, peripherals and software, the one division which causes IBM major managerial headaches in that its main resource is people, and what is more, people out and on site, the one resource that IBM management has never seemed happy with or quite sure how to handle, though often its most effective.

Also separate since the start of 1974 is the General Systems Division. Indeed, General Systems is a good example of the methodology of IBM at work. GSD has responsibility for worldwide development and U.S. manufacturing, marketing and service of the smaller computer systems IBM produces and their supporting peripherals. When initially created in 1969, GSD's responsibility was for development, manufacturing and programming support only. It has now been allowed to evolve with the growth of the market to the point where it is a separate division in the full sense of the term, responsible for its own marketing and field engineering.

In 1973 IBM revenues from the type of product now handled by GSD were in the region of $800 million, representing over 50% of the U.S. market.

Separate, too, is the Federal Systems Division, which is concerned with systems sold to the U.S. Federal Government, whether destined for space, defence or civil uses, and which, during American involvement in Vietnam, included that country in its marketing territory. It is responsible for the servicing and maintenance of Federal Government IBM computers where they may be: thus it also operates with the U.S. forces in Europe.

Federal Systems has to face the fact that much of what it does will be subject to substantial interference from IBM management. It is in the nature of Federal Systems business that almost all major systems proposed will require bids at special prices, and that before those bids are made, IBM's management will become involved. According to the Annual Report, in 1973 it grossed over $300 million.

Driving these are three Divisions. There is Research. If DP is the emotional flagship of the old hands, Research is that of many of the new and of the brightest. And Research, of course, is the corner stone in the image that IBM tries to present to the outside world: employer of Nobel Prize winners and the division perhaps most responsible for the view that the outside world has of IBM as a corporation at the forefront of technology. At the end of 1971, Research employed nearly 500 professional staff—over three hundred of them working in basic sciences—spread over three laboratories, Yorktown Heights, N.Y., San Jose, California, and Zurich, Switzerland. It was then forecasting a budget for 1973 of $54 million.

Forecasts are one thing, but reality is another. According to IBM claims the total IBM R&D expenditure that year was $730 million. What it was spent on, who spent it, and how it was spent remain a company secret; it is not something that IBM would much like the rest of the outside world to know, for the R&D figures are shrouded in much suspicion. They are, for instance, believed to contain substantial sums which in other companies would come under the heading of market development. However, one gets some idea of IBM expenditure in the development area from some percentages brought forward by IBM Chairman Frank Cary in the 1973 Telex trial:

'. . . of the total development of applications, hardware, about 70 per cent of it is for development, engineering, and hardware, and about 30 per cent of it is for the development of programs, programming systems.'*

The bulk of that expenditure will be taken up by Systems Development Division, which has the responsibility for the creation of IBM's major systems and their operating software. This is very much a worldwide operation with development laboratories spread across the United States, Europe and Japan. SDD is the division which develops IBM's major future product lines and works very closely with the rest of the DP Group. Being naturally close to the market, for it deals with near term future product as well as the next generation of systems, there is considerable security, sometimes seemingly as much internally as externally.

There is security, too, over the work of the Advanced Systems Development Division. ASDD's work is much more closely related to user needs, to the ways in which IBM customers will actually use systems. Much of ASDD's work is closely related to projects within DPG coming to market at an early stage. Early seventies plans indicated that ASDD had a staff of 670 and an expenditure in 1972 of $22·7 million. There is a certain amount of flexibility over who does what, depending upon who has prime

---

* On that basis IBM would have spent some $360 million on engineering and hardware development, and $220 million on software development, in 1973.

responsibility for a programme, and DPD, ASDD, and SDD on some projects will work quite closely together.

Of the other three IBM divisions two have a marketing and service responsibility and one does not. The two which have such responsibility are Information Records and Office Products. The first, IRD, $105 million in 1971, with a projection of $105 million for the 'traditional' part of the business in 1972* (that traditional part taking up some 85% of its turnover, making a total turnover at that time of around $124 m.) is the successor to the general punch card and supplies business of IBM. Now it handles such items as disc packs and tapes, to go with IBM drives, as well as paper and punch cards.

Punch cards are not the business they were, at least in relation to IBM revenues in the seventies. Still, $35 to $40 million a year in special purpose punch cards would not be turned down by any other manufacturer. However, there is one clear sign that the punch card monopoly has been broken: the elder Mr Watson would not even have considered a business which brought in as little as 8% before taxes, even if it produced over 40 billion punch cards a year.

As for Office Products, manufacturer and marketeer of typewriters, dictating equipment and copiers, we can get a notion of the scale of OPD (Domestic) by noting that in 1970 it had 45,000 typewriters out on lease, and that the dictating equipment business was running at 55 million, which it foresaw growing to 118 million by 1978.

There is, in fact, a great difference between the two businesses: the first is immensely profitable, the second is not. IBM has struggled for years with dictating equipment, but the profit figures are thought to be small; it is a business that IBM has never really managed to make take off.

Typewriters are a different proposition. Leasing is a U.S. operation. In WTC the policy is to sell, and thus it's a good immediate cash generator. Perhaps more important in IBM's future plans, Office Products are a major operation which gives IBM access to all those thousands of little companies and organisations which might one day take to computing. It's a

---

* In 1973 the Information Records Division probably grossed worldwide over $250 million.

source of 'drag along' business, the nearest thing IBM has to a direct market interface with the public.

A major operation? Office Products in 1973 brought in the best part of $1·3 billion worldwide.

Real Estate and Construction brings up the rear. It may have a small operating budget—only a few hundred staff—and have almost everything subject to senior management approval; even so, in four years it managed to create by building from scratch, leasing, or extension of existing premises, an additional 19 million square feet of IBM facilities. It is worth recording, however, that much of that new space is due to IBM having the wrong facilities in the wrong place for the production and marketing facilities it foresees itself needing. While this growth has been taking place, a report indicated that the result of the manpower reductions taking place in the DP Group meant that in 1971 there was excess space of around 2 million square feet.

* * *

The scale of IBM, however, is best understood in terms of its forecasts, for this gives some indication of the way management thinks. The figures used in these forecasts need to be treated with caution (apart from the fact that they are all out of date, for the IBM iterative methodology means that plans are regularly evaluated, revised and rethought). However, the following exhibits give some idea of that scale, even if the real (and later) world variations should sometimes be substantial.

It should be noted, too, that there is a difference even in IBM between a target, something to be aimed at, and a plan, something more concrete, of shorter term, and which, if not kept to, can cause management to become concerned.

The first three tables show targets as seen in 1971; they project a gross of nearly $24 billion and before-tax profits of $7·3 billion by the end of 1977; were they to be achieved IBM would then be among the world's big three engineering product–service companies: ranking after AT&T and General Motors.

OPD PLANNING TARGETS
1971–1977

	Gross Income $M	NBT $M	NBT Margin %
1971	651	98	15·0
1972	770	119	15·5
1973	910	159	17·5
1974	1070	198	18·5
1975	1260	246	19·5
1976	1480	303	20·5
1977	1750	376	21·5

DPG PLANNING TARGETS
1972–77

	Gross Income $M	NBT $M	NBT Margin %	Assumptions Installed Inventory (Net)	
				Lease Mpts.	Purchase Mpts.
1972	5618	1580	28·0	329	186
1973	6462	1844	28·5	382	209
1974	7489	2220	29·6	450	233
1975	8805	2559	29·1	534	259
1976	10336	2988	28·9	632	288
1977	12214	3698	30·3	744	319

WTC PLANNING TARGETS
1972–77

	Gross Income $M	NBT $M	NBT Margin %	Assumptions DP Customer Invent	
				Lease Pt. M	Purchase Pt. M
1972	4497	1439	32·0	242·2	67·6
1973	5228	1681	32·1	287·2	86·2
1974	6061	1940	32·0	341·3	105·7
1975	7182	2328	32·4	408·8	123·1
1976	8510	2688	31·6	487·9	153·6
1977	10030	3301	32·9	578·0	181·7

IBM is, of course, unlikely now to achieve this: the forecasting methodology on this long-term basis assumes the possibility of 20% either way. Detailed planning is done on a more realistic shorter term basis. Thus at the end of 1971, the Management Committee sees a presentation of the highlights of a much gloomier DPG short-term plan.

	1971	*1972*	*1973*
Gross Income	$3774	$3943	$3898
NEBT	850	776	645
Margin %	22·5	19·4	16·5

Operating Unit expense and manpower was projected as follows:

	1971		*1972*		*1973*	
	Expense	*Man-power*	*Expense*	*Man-power*	*Expense*	*Man-power*
DPG Total	$1,973 m	105,708	$2,136 m	102,000	$2,196 m	98,500

Those plans are for what is virtually the worst of contingencies. In July 1972 planning forecasts extend the Domestic DP and WTC gross through to 1976. They project a take-off for WTC in which it will overtake Domestic. And a take-off is what happened even if not exactly the one predicted (see pages 187–8).

The 1973 figures here should be read against reality. IBM's Domestic Gross at $5,851 million is better than plan, even allowing for all the other divisions which this plan covers. Profits at $723 million however are down over expectations, substantially down. The situation is similar with WTC. Gross is up at $5,142 million, but profits are down below plan at $990 million.

The reasons for all this are of course complex; however, the charts give something of the flavour of expectations—as opposed to targets—over the longer haul.

TARGETS

Year	Revenue ($M)	Net Before Tax Profits ($M)	Margin (%)
1973	4859	1060	21·8
1974	5561	1309	23·5
1975	6631	1753	26·4
1976	7835	2163	27·6
1977	9332	2635	28·2
1978	11180	3166	28·4

BUSINESS VOLUME ASSUMPTIONS
(Installed Inventory after Purchase Removal)

	1973	1974	1975	1976	1977	1978
Lease	315·0	370·0	438·9	523·1	626·0	741·4
Purchase	192·3	204·5	218·4	232·0	248·0	270·6
Total	507·3	574·5	657·3	755·1	874·0	1012·0

This, then, is the scale of IBM. It is important to reiterate at this point that the fact and projections recorded here are used for one purpose only: to give some idea of the dimensions and complexity of IBM, the size of IBM and the frame of reference within which management must operate.

What must never be forgotten is that the challenge of IBM is unique: because IBM is the world's largest corporation based on income primarily raised from sales to business and industry. One has to go way down the size scale to companies with half IBM's turnover before one comes to any corporation whose prime markets lie outside the field of general consumer sales, whether done directly or inderectly (as in the case of 'phones provided through the telephone company).

So how is it done, and who does it? How are these figures arrived at? What is it that makes men still behave with IBM as they did when it was a one or two billion dollar a year corporation; behave as if it's all going down the tubes tomorrow unless they perform with greater efficiency, obtain a better return?

DP COMPLEX 1972–76 PLAN

	1971 Actual	1972	% Inc.	1973	% Inc.	1974	% Inc.	1975	% Inc.	1976	% Inc.	CGR 71–76
Gross Income (millions)	3742	3892	4·0	3886	—	4159	7·0	4339	6·9	4805	10·7	5·1
Gross Profit	2872	2966	3·3	2930	-1·2	3157	7·7	3324	5·3	3673	10·5	5·0
%	76·8	76·2		75·4		75·9		76·6		76·5		
Expense Apport.	2025	2145	5·9	2211	3·1	2278	3·)	2407	5·7	2558	6·3	4·8
NEBT	847	821	-3·1	719	-12·2	879	22·2	917	4·3	1115	21·6	5·7
%	22·6	21·1		18·5		21·1		21·1		23·2		
Manpower	106·1	101·6	-4·2	97·6	-3·9	95·4	-2·3	94·4	-1·0	93·6	-·8	-2·5

NOTE: The DP Complex plan assumes that IBM can increase DP gross income by 28% over five years, yet reducing staff involved by 12·5 thousand. On this basis, income 'produced' per employee would have risen to over $50 thousand, and NEBT to nearly $12 thousand per employee.

WORLD TRADE 1972–76 PLAN

	1971 Actual	1972	% Inc.	1973	% Inc.	1974	% Inc.	1975	% Inc.	1976	% Inc.	CGR 71–76
Gross Income (millions)	3409·3	4081·1	19·7	4551·9	11·5	5170·4	13·6	5835·8	12·9	6539·1	12·1	13·9
Gross Profit %	2178·2 63·9	2580·4 63·2	18·5	2843·8 62·5	10·2	3122·6 60·4	9·8	3489·9 59·8	11·8	4143·2 63·4	18·7	13·7
[Operating and other expense]	1098·6	1309·1	19·1	1472·4	12·4	1647·2	11·9	1895·1	15·0	2137·5	12·8	14·2
NEBT %	1079·6 31·7	1271·3 31·2	17·7	1371·4 30·1	7·9	1475·4 28·5	7·6	1594·8 27·3	8·1	2005·7 30·7	25·8	13·2
Manpower	116·6	115·7	−0·8	117·2	1·3	121·2	3·4	126·0	4·0	127·8	1·4	1·8

NOTE: The World Trade Plan assumes that WTC can increase gross income by 90+% over five years. This will involve a staff increase of 11·2 thousand. On this basis, income 'produced' per employee would have risen to $57 thousand, and NEBT to nearly $16 thousand per employee.

Our starting point in that enquiry needs to be the men who run IBM, the successors to Mr Watson Snr, the men who have taken itty bitty company from a turnover of three hundred and twenty million dollars in 1952, the first year of IBM production of computers on a commercial scale, from a ranking of around fifty on the *Fortune* 500 list to over $10 billion today and well within the top ten. The men who could foreseeably end up, before the eighties are out, running the most profitable commercial operation on the planet, not just measured against turnover, for among the major corporations it is that already, but overall.

CHAPTER EIGHT

I decide, you manage, he executes

Real power in IBM, the power to make decisions—the only power that counts—resides in the Corporate Office. That office is at the apex of a hierarchy so carefully defined that it would delight the senses of any protocol-conscious United Nations bureaucrat. The men who man that office are the highest paid,* best served,

---

* The IBM system has much in common with that of the Russians: there is no trace of egalitarianism at the top, and no nonsense of a graduated salary slope, gentle or otherwise. Instead there are sharp steps in salary and compensation between those with real power and responsibility and those without.

The sixty directors and officers whose position or IBM income levels are such that their earnings must be reported, between them received $6,902,497 in 1973. Of this, the top seven executive directors: The Chairman, Vice-Chairman, three Senior Vice-Presidents, the Chairman of the Executive Committee of the Board, and the IBM General House Counsel were paid nearly 30%: $1,995,200, or an average of over $280,000 each, with IBM Chairman Frank T. Cary receiving $446,900 or nearly 6½%, and the Vice-Chairman Gilbert E. Jones and the then Senior Vice-President John R. Opel picking up 9% between them, $334,100 and $297,700 respectively. The 37 other executive officers in that top sixty income group averaged $125 to $130 thousand each.

The 16 external directors were each paid directors fees of $10,000 plus committee chairmanship fees where appropriate, and a near nominal attendance fee for committee meetings. It is unlikely that those external directors between them collected much more than 5% of the total payments to the group.

Part of the income of the 44 executive officers in the top 60 group comes from what is called Variable Compensation. This is based on the corporation's performance and net earnings after taxes in any year. In 1973, those executives between them received $2,182,292 of which the top six got $885,200 or over 40%, an average of $147,500 each (IBM's Chairman Frank T. Cary at $246,900, more than 10%).

The average for the 37 executives outside the top seven was of the order of $30,000+ each. That differential is a good incentive to those below to set up those at the top and to those on top to perform to stay there.

The 7 top executives owned stock then worth $55 million, of which former IBM Chairman TJW Jnr's holdings (including family trusts) accounted for nearly $50 million.

and most powerful men in the computer and electronics industries, some would say in any industry. As important, the administrative machine has been so devised that it will support and not hinder them, elsewhere more normally the case.

They share their power with few people—either externally or internally. It is possible to be near the top and hold a seemingly very senior position within IBM for ten to fifteen years; to have a list of 'responsibilities' almost grandiose in extent; to be a Vice-President with line 'responsibility' for a division employing tens of thousands of people, and with a turnover running into hundreds of millions, if not into billions of dollars; to be listened to by the outside world, and respected, even feared by many of the more than 260,000 IBM employees hierarchically ranked below; and yet to have no real power at all. For it is possible, indeed it is normal, within IBM for men to be in such positions, yet also to know that the final decisions which will determine the major— often even the most minor—activities of their division will not be made by them. The decisions will be made within that Corporate Office, with the divisional president being one, and not necessarily the most important one, of those supplying input to enable the Corporate Officers to arrive at what is to be done. The IBM Vice-President may be president of this, that or the other division; in terms of Corporate he is often of little more account than the staff of Corporate HQ.

The power of the Corporate Office is absolute and almost unfettered by what happens elsewhere within IBM, the advice that is given, the procedures gone through within the rest of the Corporation, or the decisions taken at the Annual General Meeting. To get to a position of power within that office, and thus within the Corporation, demands more than ability or the capacity to perform. That one has the first and can manage the second is in many ways taken for granted. It begins early: what you have to do to succeed in IBM is to pick the right master—you hitch your career to someone else's. This has been almost a *leitmotif* running through the many conversations I have had with existing and former IBM executives, which contain many unprompted references to 'your career being dependent upon . . .', 'it was his misfortune that he was chosen by . . .', and the like.

As in all organisations led by a strong and independent chief executive, some will achieve positions near the top through their own efforts, but more usually those who acquire real power will be 'The Chosen', and to achieve that status will require more than ability. If ability was all, then there are many many more just as good (or bad, it depends on one's viewpoint) within IBM's ranks; lots of them. They all might make it to the top, but whether they do so or not ...

These are somewhat different thoughts to those I originally had when I started to think about the way in which IBM was run and managed. At first it seemed that there were many parallels between IBM and the military. If these held across the board, they would, I thought, do so right up to and including the top. IBM's leader would be supported by a committee of chiefs of staff or some similar institution, on which all the key functions were represented: headquarters, force, theatre, fighting troops, supply and the rest. Below would come chiefs of staff committees, and each function, theatre or divisional leader would be supported by the appropriate organisation also modelled on the military. Military style titles would abound, as would the military differentiations in rank, clear and sharp.

IBM was organised by function, and the IBM equivalents to the military titles were there: Chairman and Chief Executive, Corporate President, Corporate Vice-President and Group Executives with responsibility for theatres of action, Division Presidents with seeming line responsibility for an operational arm, such as Data Processing or Systems Development. There were also corporate officers with staff responsibilities for corporate functions, legal, financial, and scientific advisers and the like.

It soon, however, became apparent that in terms of power, the parallels did not hold. The line officers, for instance, had almost no tactical power; almost all decisions were referred upwards before they were made, which meant they were no longer decisions made at the line level. At the top was a situation which was much more interesting and far older in form than the organisation of the modern military. It was a twentieth-century version of the feudal court. In the past, power resided mostly with one autocrat, but gradually his role had been taken over by a troika, almost as if IBM was entering an interregnum and waiting for the natural successor to 'emerge'. That, however, would not happen till the previous autocrats had finally handed on all the power they wielded—and their prestige. But the organisation and ethos almost cried out for the single autocrat of the past.

The only power held by the IBM executive outside the Corporate Office is the power not to make mistakes; to execute, not to initiate. It is an illusory power, for if they do not get it right, they will soon discover—if they did not know it already—where power really resides.

A journalist and fellow IBM-watcher delights in recounting the following scene:*

Former IBM Chairman T. V. Learson, sitting in his office, feet on the desk, cleaning his nails.

Enter Manager in charge of sales of System . . ., Model . . ., to make a presentation.

The presentation was lengthy. Buried in the middle was the ɪɪ ws ɪɪ[ɪ ɪʰʊʊɪɪɪɪ̈ȯ ɪ̈ɪ̈ tho luʌt quɑɪ teɪʲs suɪes.

At this point Leai son stopped cleaning his nails and looked at the presenter over the top of his glasses.

'Did you say sales were down, boy?'

'Er, yes, sir.'

'And how long have you been with us, boy?'

'Er, fifteen years, sir.'

'I think,' said Learson, 'that you had better go out and fix it.'

He went back to cleaning his nails.

(End of presentation.)

'Fix it,' said Learson. Fixing it is the duty of IBM management outside the world of the troika and its supporting staff. The role of the IBM executive is to execute, as the word's origins imply. He is there to act, not to think except within carefully delineated parameters, and even then he cannot take action without referral. His role is to carry out his given orders in an orderly and disciplined manner, orders which are usually well and clearly specified, as are the rules in the books he will have to refer to, books

---

* This story is a rarity among those that follow, in that it is not a view from the inside. The majority of the quotations in this chapter (and in this book) share one thing in common—they are mainly views from current or ex-insiders, sometimes very senior insiders. Almost all have spent some time at Corporate; perhaps some are still there.

which set his guidelines and parameters.

There is a little more flexibility at the senior Group and Divisional level, but not much. At this level, the role played is that of the executant of strategic decisions, giving them the appropriate form for lesser mortals to carry out.

Most of IBM's management, indeed, goes through the motions, if management is meant to imply that the decisions taken are of any real importance to IBM's survival or direction. Looking back through the sixties, it soon becomes apparent that the list of those going through the motions of management, without actually having or practising any of the substance, has been appallingly long. It includes the presidents of most of the divisions, including Data Processing and IBM World Trade Corporation, or WTC. It includes, too, most of the executives of the Corporate HQ.

As for the Board of Directors, it also soon became apparent that little internal power has resided there: it was occupied devising schemes for executive compensation and the like. The Board of IBM was like the nuclear deterrent: it was a force whose reality lay only in the threat of use. If it were used, everybody would notice, with unforeseeable effects to be avoided at almost—if not quite—any cost.

Due to special circumstances that situation has now changed. It is, however, unlikely that the change is a permanent one. For to be on top of IBM demands full-time commitment and the appropriate staff support. The change is linked to the past history, personality and former positions of some of the current Board members. It will not, one suspects, survive them. The Board will probably revert to its traditional role, the ratification of what has been decided elsewhere, to approve or to modify or delay what is to be done, not to change or alter it in any basic way.

In the past, to make sure that the full force of the Board was never exercised the key positions have always been filled by executive officers who man the Corporate Office. The Board as such was of itself singularly powerless. Of course, in terms of protocol there always was—and is—much genuflexion in its direction. It was, and is, listened to with great politeness and on some issues, particularly the political or economic, the part-time members were heard with great attention. The men who really run IBM were never thought, and are not now thought, to be stupid, and ratification of executive-initiated policies apart, politics and money are that

Board's major function. Otherwise the Board *qua* Board was and is there to affix a stamp to decisions made elsewhere.

Here, then, was a situation in which, as in all feudalisms, the chief executive could normally function by whim, as if divine right existed. When that power was challengeable, an uneasy peace existed—as it does today.

Looked at in this way, a way thrust upon one by the evidence, the successes and failures of IBM are not quite as widely attributable to anonymous management or passing cadres of highly-paid executives. They are the result of the activities of a handful of men, and that handful must take the credit—and the blame—for the events that have taken place. They cannot have the one without the other (though no doubt they would like—and have often tried—to behave accordingly).

The rest—with the exception of a handful of specialists without whom IBM could not have survived as effectively—were largely well-paid, expensively-accoutred froth and fancy. The judgement may seem extreme, but there is nothing in the evidence to lead one to any other conclusion or to make one think that it does not also apply to the present situation.

Who are these men? One must delay the answer to make two further points. First, the talk of associates and present/past IBM executives, discussions within the industry, and the process of research has turned up much information about IBM's decision-makers. What follows seldom includes such things as whether they are kind to women, animals and children; how they live their private lives; their marital state; whether they play clean, play dirty, or just play (although on all these subjects quite a lot is often known), except where it can be proved, or at the least strongly inferred from the evidence, that it has affected the way decisions are made and thus the way IBM corporately acts.

Secondly, I have thus far made no genuflexions in the direction of equality between the sexes. This is no accident: IBM is male-run almost without exception. There is (at the time of writing) just one woman director, and though she would no doubt regard the charge as hackneyed, it would not be unfair to call her the near ultimate in token minority appointments. She is Patricia Harris, former U.S. Ambassador to Luxemburg, Chair Person of the Credentials Committee at the 1972 Democratic Convention, a lawyer and a partner in that prestigious and highly political

Washington law firm, Fried, Frank, Harris, Shriver and Kampelman. And she is black.

There is just one woman Vice-President, June Cahill, in charge of the ubiquitous and euphemistically entitled 'Communications Department', more jocularly known among some IBM executives as 'The Thought Police', which amply summarises its role. For a time in the early seventies, June Cahill seemed headed for the top. She was (September 1970) Executive Assistant to Tom Watson Jnr and appeared on the list of members of the Management Review Committee. However, she appears and then disappears during the transition of power, for her position was closely linked to TJW Jnr's and went with his retirement.

One can infer from other IBM evidence that short of a total up-heaval at IBM, neither lady is likely to be going anywhere important. For the ethos of IBM is quintessentially male. It has in the past occasionally flirted with the proposition that women should be given real positions of power within the corporation. For a business which prides itself on doing what is publicly and visibly 'right', the lack of female talent in the higher executive ranks is embarrassing, but it is an embarrassment IBM is willing to suffer; to flirt with the proposition is all that Corporate has done.

Running IBM is a full-time job; that is the nature of the system as it has been set up. In such a system there is always resistance to the notion of change in persona: the successors are expected to come from the same mould as those whom they succeed. Thus, how can women move up when marketing has till fairly recently been largely closed to women, yet marketing experience is essential for corporate climbing, for self-advancement?

The people we need to consider, then, are men, and very few at that. From 1960 to 1974, IBM was run by less than ten people. Between them, those happy few have made all the critical decisions and many thousands that were not critical at all. Mr Watson Snr was a born meddler, a talent he exercised in IBM for over forty years. He left behind him a corporation attuned to that meddling and expecting that those at the top would continue to do so. This has been a temptation not so much hard to resist as one whose existence as a temptation has not even been acknowledged: they still meddle.

The people we need to consider held all the key positions in IBM during those fourteen years: three Chairmanships—Tom

Watson Jnr, T. V. Learson, and Frank T. Cary, the present incumbent; five Presidencies—Tom Watson Jnr, A. L. Williams, T. V. Learson, Frank T. Cary and (1974) John R. Opel; and the Vice-Chairmanship of IBM, Arthur K. 'Dick' Watson, TJW Jnr's younger brother who was also for much of the fifties and sixties Chairman of IBM World Trade, the last a post taken over in 1970 by Gilbert E. Jones, now Vice-Chairman and a member of the Corporate Office.

On the way up, some of these men have also held the second-level posts in IBM: the Senior Group Vice-Presidencies and head of the Data Processing Group Division.

On the periphery of real power have been the two present Senior Group Executives: George ('Spike') Beitzel, a man with responsibilities in 1974 for everything except Data Processing, and Paul Rizzo, the successor to A. L. Williams as IBM's 'money man' and now the other Senior Group Executive. Also on the periphery have been men such as B. O. ('Bo') Evans, whose responsibilities for systems development cover both Series 360 and much of Series 370. And, of course, Nicholas de Belleville Katzenbach, Chief Legal Officer during the spate of anti-trust problems that have beset IBM since the late sixties.

*   *   *

It became apparent a long time ago that in writing about the men who run IBM, pride of place would have to go not to a Watson, but to Thomas Vincent Learson, its first non-Watson Chairman. For the computing years at IBM are really the Learson years—if they are anybody's. It was Learson's marketing drive and his ability to motivate the sales force which made the growth of IBM possible. His executive career spans the years of the computer, from the introduction of the IBM 701 through to System 370 and beyond. During the critical years of the launching of Series 360, he was in the key executive marketing seat.

He is a large man. 'Vin Learson? Physically a sort of corporate John Wayne in a business suit.'

He is generally referred to in the industry as 'Vin' Learson, though few people in IBM call him that to his face without some prior indication of the way he feels about them or the mood he is in. He was held in great respect in IBM, but it was the respect due to force of personality, not to the nature of the man.

He had few known friends in IBM. 'Which is perhaps fitting as he gave the impression that he didn't think he had any equals.' For friendship after all presupposes equality in some department of life.

'Oh sure, he had the gift of making you feel equal. But it was localised. He switched it on at his own time, and you should not presume on it just because that had been the way he had behaved with you at some time in the past.'

The start of T. V. Learson's rise to power was to be noted by Tom Watson Jnr in his McKinsey Foundation Lecture series. It appears in the passage which follows that concerned with Remington Rand and UNIVAC as being 'off to the races'.

'The loss of our business in the Census Bureau struck home. [See page 32.] We began to act. We took one of our best operating executives, a man with a reputation for getting things done, and put him in charge of everything which had to do with the introduction of an IBM large-scale computer—all the way from design and development through to marketing and servicing. He was so successful that within a short time we were on our way.'

Vin Learson is a Bostonian born in 1912, who went to Harvard and, if some of his latterday remarks are to be believed, began to distrust intellectualism and 'education' very early. The formal Learson career can be run through quite quickly, and who better to do it than Mr Learson himself? This version comes from his deposition in the suit of the Justice Department versus IBM:

'I joined IBM ... October 1, 1935, as a student in Endicott, New York ... I was up there about six months, finally got on the payroll and went to Boston as a junior salesman ... In '37 I became a senior salesman, stayed in Boston until January of '42, was assigned to the Washington office from '42 to ... some time in '46 ... Then I went to New York and became an industrial manager, special representative we called them in those days, for the retail field. Ultimately the wholesale field was added ... Sometime in '47 I went to Philadelphia; around June of '49 I went to become a district manager, located in Detroit. In September of '49 I was made sales manager of what was then known as the

EAM (Electric Accounting Machines) Division. I was this for two or three years . . . sent to Poughkeepsie in '54 with a title of Director of EDPM (Electronic Data Processing Machines) in charge of our engineering and manufacturing and sales of the equipment of that day. I would guess I became a vice-president later that year . . . ultimately I became vice-president in charge of sales.'

In 1961, he was made a director.

'. . . at some point I was made a Group Executive . . . That is in the early '60s . . .'

What was the significance of 'Group Executive'? He had responsibility for 'most of the affairs of the business except . . . [the] EAM divisions and research divisions . . . the World Trading Company [World Trade Corporation] and of course the Corporate Staff. I had whatever was left.

'. . . Sometime in '65 I was made a Senior Vice-President and the company was split in two pieces. A. K. Watson had half: I had the other half . . . I had the Sales Divisions.'

He was appointed President in 1966, and Chairman and Chief Executive in 1971, posts he held till his premature retirement in December 1972. IBM now has a mandatory retirement age of sixty; however, that age was fixed at a time when there were intercorporate battles in progress about the future of IBM, battles which Learson lost. Part of the result was to accelerate a policy decision settling the full-time senior executive retirement age at sixty, and Learson was one of the first senior executive casualties.*

Learson, however, is still on the board of IBM. He sits on its Finance and Executive committees, on which he is joined by Tom Watson Jnr, and, until his death in the summer of 1974, by A. K. Watson, both of whom had also retired from full-time executive positions. This now ensures that for the first time in its history, IBM is not entirely controlled by its Chief Executive, Frank T. Cary, and that the troika who man the Corporate Office, while in theory still pre-eminent, can no longer run IBM exactly as they like—as their predecessors had done. No newish Chief Executive is going to run counter to the wishes of those predecessors, par-

---

* The MRC minutes make clear that as late as April 1971 the retirement age discussion was progressing on the lines that the age should be fixed at 65.

ticularly when they took their prestige with them and control the critical committees of his board, committees they themselves have created.

'Learson? Brilliant man, sharp guy. Binary. Yes or no. It's "no playing games". No indecision. No politics. It's—"That's lousy. I won't accept it. Get it out of my office".'

'. . . This was very refreshing, because there were a great many senior executives carrying those flip charts around, making a career out of them . . .'

'Like the Army?' I asked. 'If you want to stay out of trouble, pick up a file and wander around looking busy?'

'That's right,' he replied, 'just like the Army. They make careers out of presenting these great programmes which aren't going anywhere, and ten per cent of them—if that—ever do anything sensible for that company.'

'Learson? He's the guy who says that instead of going the slow methodical way, *do it.* Or this is atrocious, *get rid of it,* whatever it is.'

*   *   *

'Vin Learson? He really enjoyed socking it to them. Not in a real sadistic way: he didn't gloat over it. He figured it was a part of business managing, and it was a part he really rather liked, as he liked winning yacht races. He didn't sail for the pleasure of the wind in his hair, he sailed to win, and that's how he ran IBM. Even after he had won he was still willing to crash his bows into the opposition just for the sheer pleasure of hearing the sound of the crunch. I think a guy like this is enormously useful in some companies, but he wasn't really needed in IBM.'

*   *   *

'One day he was in a bad mood, and someone gave him a presentation. He wasn't turned on at the time. The guy had a lot of things being presented on Learson's desk. And Learson swept his arm across the desk and swept it all on the floor!

'This guy had a little more guts than most. And he said to T.V.: Okay, I presume that you prefer I continue my presentation from the floor. And that's exactly what he did.'

*   *   *

'T. V. Learson? He would never refer to you by name. If he ever said to you, Mr Malik, that's the day you were on your way out.'

* * *

'He was not called Attila the Hun for nothing. It was Learson who decided to get tough. The thing was thought out and fought out. Learson's team won. If Watson then had stayed on, it might have turned out differently.'

* * *

'I fear for that company. Learson is so driven to surpass TJW Jnr that he is liable to do something foolish.'

* * *

'I think Watson's heart attack was caused by Learson's decision to "get tough" [the P.C.M. reaction policies]. You will notice that Watson [TJW Jnr] had his heart attack [November 1970] just two months before the new pricing policy was announced [January 1971]. To understand IBM, you have to get your timing right. Something happens in Corporate two to three months before it hits the streets.'

* * *

If the first part of this last comment is true, there is once again irony here. For it was TJW Jnr who initially willed the end, though it was to be Learson who carried the responsibility for execution. As to the second part, this has been so historically for many years and was still true in 1974; for instance, the decision to make IBM's first ever non-one-hundred-per-cent ownership acquisition (CML, a satellite operation; see page 444): this was made in March 1974, though not announced till June.

So why *did* Learson go?

'He [Learson] made some classic unbelievable decisions that legally have got to haunt them. And I think Tom said, "Oh my God, look at this guy Learson. He just will not realise that one of our biggest fundamental problems is this anti-trust thing." '

The former executive was discussing the events which led to both the settlement of the CDC case and the battle with the PCMs. Though these two sets of events are separated in time, they have one connection. The chief mover in both was Vin Learson.

The savageness of the reprisals on the PCMs was primarily due to Learson. Though TJW Jnr might have willed the end, he did not, it seems, fully understand the means and their consequences. In some ways the problem was of his and IBM's own making. It was IBM which had decided that its growth should be roughly constant at twelve to fifteen per cent a year; it was IBM which had given the financial markets the expectation that this would continue, and the share price was predicated and discounted accordingly. The accounting of IBM may be conservative, but it can still have elements of creativity to it, and the means that had been adopted to keep up the gross financial volumes in the late sixties did not necessarily represent an increase in IBM's market share. That huge increase in sales due to the activities of the leasing companies might have been welcomed by IBM at the time as adding to volume profits and thus allowing targets to be more than met; but it was a one-off situation. The basic IBM problem was that it just was not growing the total market fast and consistently enough to enable it to maintain corporate growth, except by resorting to one-off situations.

In April 1970, the DP Group reported to the MRC (via the Management Committee) on its outlook for 1970: customer purchasing was reduced, down $254 million as compared with 1969, and the DP Group's profit forecast was down from $740 million to $544 million. The unnaturally high business levels just were not holding up. Nor had unbundling helped—rather the reverse: sales had been steadily decreasing for three quarterly periods.

The Watson-inspired, Learson-boosted and Cary-executed IBM reactions were eventually to have many results, but a major one was the Telex suit which was to cause IBM's management to stop and think. The timing was wrong for Learson; it was becoming obvious to IBM that it would have to settle with CDC. Learson's strategy might be working, but it was bringing problems with it.

'So he's bringing the morale back. But one of the ways of

bringing that morale back is that he is saying things that we have eventually got to retract.* And boy, I had better get back into this company awfully fast.'

'And I think Learson said, "Fine Tom. If you want to run it, I'll go and sail my boat." And he did.'

This last comment is perhaps a somewhat poetic version of what might have happened. There is another way of looking at it which makes just as much sense and arrives at a similar conclusion. Given IBM's preoccupation with image, one could not keep Learson in that post. As it has been expressed by another source:

'Tom Watson would probably deny that they unloaded Learson because of his impact on the image of IBM, but I suspect it's partly true. You have to realise that Tom always took that very seriously, he felt it in his guts. And the measures that Learson took would have hurt him more than the effect on the competition. He would say to you if you asked him that no doubt Vin was pretty anxious to retire. If the joint was bugged, you could never prove that he meant anything differently. But then Tom Watson can be quite transparent...'

'Norris (CDC's Chairman) and Learson did not like each other very much', said one who has known them both. 'Norris thought that Learson was the one really responsible for CDC's troubles. He wanted Learson's head, and he was going to have it. He knew quite well that to tab a senior IBM executive with a failure of that magnitude is to destroy him.

'It became apparent as the case progressed that Norris was in a position to take IBM all the way and intended to do so. The IBM position was untenable.

'Learson on his part did not like Norris. It was quite clear that Norris was as clever as Learson, and as tough, possibly even tougher. Such people had posed no threat in IBM. However, the tactics used there could not work on those outside who owed nothing to Learson's favour.'

And Norris got him. There is poetry in executive games at this level, at least for the spectator.

'You will not find any trace of it in the public record,' said one source, 'but Learson was sent to come to an agreement with

---

* Learson was not the only one: Frank T. Cary has publicly stated—in a reference to the market and competition: 'We want 100%.'

Norris. It might not have been put as crudely as this, but it was made quite clear that it had better happen.' The IBM version of the incidents, of course, differs: Learson did not want to leave a thing like this behind him to be dealt with by his successors; they should have a clean and clear start.

Learson was succeeded by Frank T. Cary (of whom more from p. 219), at first sight a contradiction if a change of image was sought.

'Cary? Learson's man. Learson played bridge like poker, and he always picked Cary for a partner. They'd be up in that company plane with Learson losing, and he would keep that plane circling around twenty minutes or more until the losing stopped.'

'Cary? A totally functional being devoid of any ideology.'*

'That's dangerous,' I said.

'Right.'

Cary was to be the chosen instrument of Learson's destruction. Learson, Cary and their henchmen had, as we shall shortly see, set Dick Watson up: Cary was now to set up Learson. Cary's career had been dependent on Learson (as Learson's had been on TJW Jnr) but he was still his own man and was now to prove it. One sees signs of Cary shedding Learson very early. Learson is not yet even Chairman, but Cary is covering. The Management Review Committee Minutes of 2nd July 1970, Tom Watson, Learson and Cary present, give an indication:

'FTC [Frank T. Cary] . . . reviewed the results of his analysis of the reasons for missing on the 1970 plan. He concluded that the clues were seen reasonably early in the year, but that the Group had unrealistically held on to their high targets 90 days after these clues were available. He stated as the big mistake in judgement misreading of the economy. TVL stated that he had forced NSRI [Net Sale Revenue Increase, the key IBM measure] quota up another 10% in 1969. FTC pointed out that our whole planning system and philosophy was upside oriented and focussed on stretching rather than attainability. TVL agreed on NSRI but stated that other factors should have more balanced judgements.'

It is an opening salvo: Frank Cary is making quite sure that the responsibility for the failure to reach the sales quota is pinned on

---

* Strangely, that remark was to be made independently and in almost identical terms by three unconnected people.

Learson. It is fitting that it should be Cary who was to be the instrument by which Learson was brought down, and it was in pattern for IBM, where executive knifing is a way of life.* But . . .

'It shook Vin up, you know. Cary of all people pulling that on Learson. He never thought that someone would do it to him.'

All this implies much corporate in-fighting, and there is. The system is, after all, feudal; the stakes are high, and the more so since it became apparent that there was no automatic succession to the Watsons. 'You should see some of the games that get played. There's always someone in IBM intent on nailing the other guy with failure.'

'Corporate in-fighting. It's brutal: it's constant, subtle and long-term. And it's very dangerous, because you have this continual situation of people trying to set up each other and getting them into a position where this guy's going to fail and the other guy is going to succeed. So it's an ongoing thing. It's not as if you go in and look for an overt act which indicates that someone is going to do something. For instance, Learson set up A. K. Watson to get him knocked off at the time when the 360s were coming along. Learson knew goddam well that A. K. Watson couldn't handle the manufacturing and engineering problems; that there was nobody in the world who could do it. What he did was to jump out of the manufacturing boat, said, "OK, AK, you handle it, I'll take care of the marketing and the installing." He knew he had plenty of time: Frank Cary did the same thing.

'What happened was that marketing sat there holding their cards, engineering sat there holding theirs, manufacturing sat there holding theirs, and the program people sat there holding theirs. And everybody said, "Don't worry, we'll meet the due date, don't worry, we'll meet the due date." Cary was the smartest of the whole bunch because he knew that if he went out and sold like hell he'd create such a backlog of activity that the whole thing would break down before he would ever be responsible for installing it all. He had no capability whatsoever of installing the 360 load in 1965 when it was supposed to come along. And so

---

* He was to do it again in the Telex trial, after TVL had retired. Floyd Walker for Telex was cross-questioning Frank T. Cary about the meaning of an embarrassing T. V. Learson memo concerned with memory price manipulation and eventually elicited a reply of which the following is part: 'The Witness: I think Mr Learson was a bit over his head in the subject of pricing that he didn't fully understand.'

what he did was to bet his whole career on the ability to force either programming, engineering or manufacturing to blow the boat. Then he could sit there and buy another couple of years of time to get his system engineering boys in place. And what happened? Sure enough ... the programming group go down in smoke 'cos they can't make it, engineering ... can't make it, and manufacturing are in real trouble.

'And when the dust clears, Dick's back to his World Trade Corporation and the coast is clear.'

* * *

'Oh, sure, the way that Learson and Cary fixed Dick Watson was a classic. They boosted his ego, got him to look after manufacturing. Here was a problem worthy of a man of his talents. And then kapow ... They oversold. And there was just no way Dick could produce enough. And they knew it.'

* * *

And what of TJW Jnr? The word is charisma, a word now very much abused: yet it is something that Tom Watson Jnr has, and it is not solely accounted for by his height, manner, or silver-grey locks. Perhaps part of his inheritance? If so, it is a triumph of genetics over environment, for by all the rules of the game, given the elder Mr Watson as a father, he should have been swamped.

That charisma is now fading. What is not is the public face, that of the man accustomed to being at the top, to having his wishes and whims respected and acted on; almost, if you will, the face of the ex-emperor, the face of a man who learnt early that acting was part of his survival kit.

His career was the sort one would expect from Mr Watson's eldest son and namesake: the career of both father and sons, indeed, was to illustrate how little control shareholders have over the affairs of a successful corporation; how a strong chairman can demolish even the notion of the possibility of shareholder control. And nothing was to make more nonsense of it than the way in which the power of the elder Watson was transferred to his sons.

Tom Watson Jnr was brought up in feudal fashion to inherit IBM, and to inherit it in his father's image. A private education and considerable foreign—mainly European—travel might broaden the mind but did not necessarily make a scholar or an intellectual: and neither did his university education. After graduating from Brown University in the late thirties he went into IBM. Almost immediately, he was at the top of his salesman's training course. (Whether he achieved that on his own merits it is impossible to determine, and it is doubtful if even Tom Watson Jnr himself really knows. For these were the real megalomaniac years at IBM, and no one was going to allow a situation to be created which was likely to bring down Mr Watson's wrath, whether on Tom Jnr or themselves.)

TJW Jnr spent the war years flying in the U.S. Army Air Force, rising to the rank of Lieutenant Colonel. When he returned to IBM, however, his rise was even more rapid. He was given a sales territory in New York, became a director in 1946, and by 1947 was well on the way up. By then, IBM was already running a 'Tribute i amplylit to Lincoln, Vice-President Thomas Watson Jnr', and one source still has the pencil embossed with the above slogan to prove it.

In 1952, his father made him President. By the time his father died in 1956 he was the obvious choice to become Chief Executive: he was already running the company anyway, and the post-war promotions were mainly his men.

However, that fast rise made nonsense of IBM's pretensions that a man should be rewarded according to his performance and merits. He was after all thirty-two years old when he came back from the war, thirty-three by the time he moved to the Executive Vice-Presidency, and when he became President he still had less than a ten year service record with IBM.

He was never publicly embarrassed by this, however. The most effective method of defence being attack, he himself was to tell some of the best stories about his rise, no doubt in the hope of defusing any possible animosity there might be, though this was only necessary while his father was alive. There was the story about the old hand who said: 'Tom, you and I have both gone about as far as we can go with this company.' And there was his attribution of his rise in IBM to the fact that 'he had a friend'.

However, the company did change. Much of the time he was busy proving that he was Tom Watson *Jnr* and not his father. He surrounded himself with his own friends: different friends. Till recently IBM was littered with them: fellow ex-officers from the

Air Force and the like, who, while they might not be going places, were what are colloquially known as 'trusties', people who could be relied on to do their benefactor's bidding. (Most of that generation, however, is now not far short of retirement.)

Of course, he was reacting to events. IBM post-war was a different and larger company, its products covering a much wider technological—and market—territory. IBM management, too, was intellectually much more capable, and emotionally more independent, particularly its new members. They were not, for instance, prepared—at least in private—to put up with the old man's nonsense about drinking. Officially, of course, IBM 'headquarters' (Corporate is an invention of the 1958 Williamsburg senior executive conference called by TJW Jnr, the occasion on which he set his own stamp on IBM by massively reorganising it) was dry, at least in public and upstairs. But downstairs, behind the shades, the liquor sometimes flowed freely and TJW Jnr was occasionally down there with the others, bringing beer by the case to IBM Country Club, Endicott, the 'Hundred Per Cent Club' meetings and the like.

But all that was before his total ascendency. Afterwards, his drinking with the IBM 'boys' seemed to stop.

Being your own man, of course, demands that you make your own moves. He scrapped much of the fun and games: the annual 'family' get-togethers, fireworks and the rest. IBM was now simply too big for them to be fun. However, he did initially try to maintain the patriarchal family atmosphere, larger though that family might now be.

What was not changed was the business style of IBM; that was difficult to do in the short term without destroying the ethos that had built the company. It is doubtful, in any case, if he had any deep desire to change it at all. The organisation of IBM was such that he was protected from the more ugly facts of Corporate life, exactly as his father had been. Since TJW Jnr's temper was as rough as his father's, though colder and more biting, nobody was going to cross that if they could help it. In public, that temper was usually under control. But in private: 'Tom had a butt—Whizz Miller, who used to head up OP [Office Products]. When Tom got mad, he used to take Whizz into his office and for all practical purposes kick him around for half an hour, till he [TJW Jnr] had cooled down.'

A man does not sit at the top of a corporation for twenty years without leaving a mark, particularly not a corporation like IBM. Tom Watson Jnr left more than just a mark. However, his real years of undisputed power are not many. Up till 1956, there was his father to contend with. After 1966–67 and the success of Series 360, there was a triumphant Vin Learson.

Between them were the years of unchallenged inheritance, unchallenged by anyone that is except the Justice Department and competing manufacturers, but these were something that IBM was well equipped to cope with. These were the years when Tom Watson Jnr ran the place with the classic iron fist: there was seldom any attempt at justification to subordinates. Rather, 'That's the way I feel.' Or, 'It just does not ring right, so I have cancelled it.'

Thus, the announcement of the 360/85 was cancelled by TW Jnr on the morning it was due to be made, simply because he said it didn't feel right, though the preparations for that day's launch (let alone the design and production) had cost over a quarter of a million dollars.

Yet it is from these years of uninterrupted power that the best of the Tom Watson Jnr stories spring.

'One day Tom started his speech by saying that he had learned that some of the salesmen were drinking vodka because you can't smell it. He cautioned the sales managers to have their salesmen drink other than vodka at lunch because if they then called on clients, at least the clients would know they were drunk and not just stupid.

'It brought down the house.'

Part of the myth of IBM is the Wild Duck story, of which almost everybody in IBM it seems has a different version. (It is recorded in the previously quoted McKinsey Lectures.) The moral to be made is drawn from a story by Kierkegaard of ducks flying south in winter, till someone took pity on them and put out food on a lake the ducks overflew. Some ducks continued to fly south, others didn't. After a time, those who stayed found difficulty in even flying at all. The moral was, 'You can make wild ducks tame, but you can never make tame ducks wild again.'

Watson then continued:

'One might add also that the duck who is tamed will never go anywhere any more. We are convinced that any business needs its wild ducks. And in IBM we try not to tame them.'

'Tom really believed this, you know. He had this great capacity for self-deception. He said this at a Hundred Per Cent Club, and followed it with: "I just wish somebody would stick his head in my office and say, 'Tom, you're wrong!' I really would like to hear that. I don't want yes-men around me." '

The Wild Duck story immediately gave rise to anecdotes, including the obvious: 'But even wild ducks fly in formation'.

Much better was: 'Watson says he wants us to stick our heads into his office and say, "Tom, you're wrong": you should see the collection of heads he has.'

He was also deeply impressed by the Presidency of John Kennedy, and that was to do IBM no harm. A few months after Kennedy was inaugurated, TJW Jnr made a eulogistic half-hour speech—again at a Hundred Per Cent Club—which was all about Kennedy. Some of the salesmen who didn't share his enthusiasm were a little uncomfortable. When he heard about it, he promptly wrote a letter of apology, saying: 'I'm sorry. I had no right to take your time at a company business meeting to express my personal political beliefs.'

He was more sensitive to people's feelings than Dick, but then he could afford to be. And in any case, he was only sensitive to people's feelings when he chose to be.'

* * *

'You have to realise that there is a strong (emotional) relationship between the two Watsons. There has been this intense sibling rivalry between them, so intense that you know quite well that it is going to mean that when one is under serious external challenge, the other will come running to his defence.'

The speaker is a man who worked closely with Dick Watson. He is indulging in amateur psychology, but there is sense to it. Dick Watson was a man who had been brought up under immense pressure from his father, simply for not being Tom; the result and effects on his personality were to have much to do with the way that IBM World Trade grew and was managed.

Yet there was even less pretence with Dick Watson than there had been with brother Tom. Dick was five years younger, coming into IBM only after World War II. He spent that war in the Pacific, returned afterwards to Yale, and eventually (1947) he too came into the fold. The evidence indicates that he did not particularly want to join the company, for he spent much time thinking up excuses to avoid working in IBM. And when he did join, he spent just as much time thinking up more excuses not to get involved.

All this was to no avail. Father was going to leave his sons well provided for, and the price of that provision included carrying on the good work at IBM. Dick Watson's rise in the company was nearly as rapid as Tom's, though obviously it could not be to the same heights. Nonetheless, after less than five years, he found himself (1952) appointed Vice-President and General Manager of recently formed IBM World Trade Corporation, a move made by IBM to consolidate its overseas interests.

These titles were not really meaningful and were to change as the overseas operations grew, were organised and reorganised, and WTC's importance to the parent company became more pronounced. So Dick became President of World Trade Corporation in 1954, Chairman in 1963, Vice-Chairman of IBM in 1966. What was important, however, was that Dick Watson had been given his own fiefdom. Like the medieval Popes before him, his father had decreed that Tom should have one part of the world, in this case the United States territory and Dick should have everything else, though everything else did not originally add up to much.

'It was the only way it could be done, but I suspect that the old man also recognised the difference in talents. Temperamentally Dick is what in our (American) corporate world passes for an intellectual; he reads books that have no connection with business, goes in for the traditional fashionable things, art, opera—and incidentally has a feeling for them. And he speaks languages.'*

Besides, it was the best solution between them. It gave them a chance to be apart. 'There's always been this intense thing between them, they can drive each other to apoplexy.' They

---

* The interviews from which these excerpts were taken were done before Dick Watson's death in the summer of 1974, hence the use of the present tense. However, as he is no longer alive, the material on Dick Watson has been extensively cut. To be funny or critical about a man, where justified, and within the limits of the context, is perfectly proper while he is alive; he has after all a chance to answer back. However, that situation changes on his death: there ought to be a decent interval. So, regretfully, only the really important incidents and judgements have been retained, those which help to explain, or lead to an understanding of, major events in IBM.

would have separate bases to which they could retreat and be as far apart from each other as was compatible, while still being at the top of the same company.

Dick Watson took over, though in a comparatively small way, one side of his father's activities—the collection of memberships and honours. He picked up membership in the International Chamber of Commerce, and some of the appropriate decorations, though now that IBM was really an international reality not everybody was quite as forthcoming as they had been before. He had to be content with recognition from eleven countries, only four of them Latin American.

We cannot yet leave either of the elder Mr Watson's sons, for events will not let us. But, on a lighter note, it has to be recorded that they saved their executives from one purgatory: Corporate golf. IBM was never a golfing corporation, in which success depended as much on one's performance on the golf course as in the executive suites. It was never necessary, for the Watson's social life was not organised round the corporation and round friendship with their executives.

The sporting pastimes were more solitary. Initially, Tom's passion, however, was sailing. Sailing was also Learson's passion, if passion can describe it. That Learson once beat his boss in a race which the boss had been trying to win for years is a story trotted out any time sport and IBM are mentioned together: '. . . Learson was always the more interested of the two in results.'

This comment was made by an early user of IBM magnetic tape systems, a user with tape wear problems so serious that he had to put his own men to work on seeking a solution. 'They came up with a graphite-type substance as tape coating. This provided lubrication and the wear ceased. But this left another question to which we had no answer—would this graphite-like lubricate get into the relays of the tape transport and foul up the contacts?'

IBM was asked whether or not the user should use the lubricate. After some time elapsed without answer, a visit was paid to IBM's tape engineers. Nothing had been done about the application of the lubricate to tape problems, but Vin Learson had supposedly had it tested on a boat hull in the MIT model basin. If it would reduce friction in one area . . .

Both Watsons were skiers, and sport was to play a substantial part in their lives. After the mid-sixties, however, IBM became intensely political: company political as the jockeying for the succession began, and internationally political as governments began to take an interest in the computer industry. 'And that,' said one of the participants, 'led Dick Watson to begin to withdraw.'

'The problem was that everybody knew Dick was not really fundamentally interested, he was doing what was expected of him, often just going through the motions. Oh sure, being in charge of World Trade gave him a position and for the first few years, before the interlocking [integration] of production on an international scale was an accomplished fact . . . it was fun. But it did not stay fun for long.'

He withdrew back to IBM World Trade. Then in 1970, he withdrew altogether to become American Ambassador to France. This was, of course, the year when IBM's troubles were beginning. It had been tough, it was getting tougher, Learson was President and seemed bound for the Chairmanship.

'It must have been a relief for Dick Watson to end up buying the Paris Embassy.'

'It was a relief to get him out. He had been blocking that [World Trade] position for years. He used it as a retreat after intra-corporate defeats.'

It is not a particularly kind judgement, but a fair one with important consequences. The problem was that IBM World Trade was for a long time—from the mid-sixties onwards—really managed by Dick Watson's subordinates, in particular Gil Jones, who, precisely because they were subordinates, carried little weight in Armonk. So, effectively, World Trade was for all practical purposes run from Armonk, via World Trade Headquarters in New York. This was particularly true after the rise of Learson, when for years almost all efforts to make WTC more independent of its parent came to naught.

Publicity following a drinking incident on a Pan American trans-Atlantic flight eventually led to Dick Watson's resignation as Ambassador. (There was not as much publicity as there might have been: by the time the story was told in Jack Anderson's column, the flight crew had already been told by Pan Am not to talk.) Shortly afterwards Dick Watson reappeared in IBM. He was back on the Board and had been appointed a member of the Executive Committee.

And it was not too long before, as one former executive put it,

'. . . they offered Cary the company. Of course, nobody put it as crudely as that . . .' The effect was the same, Learson announced his retirement to take effect from the end of 1972.

Of course, there would be a price to pay all round. The corporation would still be run by its chief executive. But from the beginning the new one would have to look more closely over his shoulder at the Board: the people who had put him into the Chairman's seat were not going to allow him the independence that Learson had been allowed after TJW Jnr's illness.

Indeed, not long before Dick Watson's return to IBM and its Board, the minutes of the MC had carried a cryptic comment: 'Hubner* was asked to develop an IBM statement relative AKW's return to IBM in case it was required in the future'. It was the kind of comment that executives were not going to be allowed to make again on paper for some time to come, at least until the transition from the Watson generation was fully complete, and that time had not yet come.

Even before Dick Watson had become Ambassador to France, there were indications that Tom Watson Jnr was unhappy with the composition of the Board, that he wanted more Watsons and their relatives around. The truth was that there were not many who were old enough or with the right qualifications to pass muster. One was to be found in a Watson brother-in-law, John Irwin II, a lawyer—one of the team of lawyers who had signed the 1956 Consent Decree on IBM's behalf, and State Department official.

John Irwin was duly appointed a director in 1970. Irony, however, often surrounds and envelops the Watson family: he was initially only with IBM for nine months and was to succeed Dick Watson in Paris, saving, as one writer put it, the necessity of the Watson clan's having to change the family pictures. Later, upon his leaving the Paris post, he was to return to the IBM Board.

In the end, the method that was finally chosen was to bring on to the Board politically well-connected friends of the family (see Chapter 13). Indeed, in 1973, in New York it was rumoured that a seat on the Board had been offered to Senator Ted Kennedy.

*   *   *

---

* Robert W. Hubner, now a Senior Vice-President.

Mention the name A. L. Williams almost anywhere in IBM today and the answer is Al Who?—almost as if the name were Agnew and the time early 1968. Yet without Al Williams there would probably not be an IBM Corporation as we now know it. It was Al Williams who stopped the elder Mr Watson from 'blowing it'—an ex-executive's description—indeed, old hands say that the relationship that Al Williams built up with the elder Watson was much more than between son and father, with Williams being that impossibility—the complementary filial character: cool where Mr Watson was hot, and sympathetic when sympathy was needed. Whatever one could write about the two Watson sons, complementary to their father would not be in the description—they were both too much like him.

Much myth surrounds the Williams career. He kept in the background and did not compete for the limelight; indeed, in the five years he was to be IBM's President, he was to be the most publicly self-effacing President of any major American company, probably of all time.

Yet, next to Tom Watson Jnr, he is the IBM Board's longest serving member, having been elected in 1951, in the days when Mr Watson's word was still absolute, the days before the Presidency was handed over to his eldest son. That timing was no accident. 'It was purposefully done: Mr Watson might want his sons to take over, but he had doubts that they could hack it on their own.'

The Watsons apart, Williams has had the most meteoric of IBM careers. He joined IBM as a salesman in 1936, one year after Learson, yet was to be on the Board ten years before him. By background he is an accountant, which led him to the post of Controller in 1942. By 1947 he was Treasurer, and by 1948 a Vice-President. He moved up to Executive Vice-President in 1954, and became President in 1961.

If anyone cultivated the Eastern financial establishment, it was Williams. Indeed, the importance of Williams was recognised by Mr Watson Snr in an unusual way. For years Williams was the only executive in IBM who had a company car: everybody else had to settle for a rented one (though it was, in fact, used by Mr Watson more than by Williams. Still, it allowed Watson to boast that he did not have a company car).

It was Williams who oversaw IBM's financial dealings, particularly in the mid-fifties to early sixties, when IBM was turning itself into the dominant force in computing that it is today.

Until he became President.

'No IBM President was ever so anonymous as Al . . . he's an accountant . . . a money man, at home and happy with bankers. That was his forte and he was good at it.'

*   *   *

'He was not a very good President. But then it is doubtful if with the Watsons around and Learson breathing down his neck anyone else would have been a good President either.'

'You know about the famous incident of the return of the $160 million loan in 1963? (IBM repaid a long-term loan to an insurance company borrowed at low rates of interest, and then, because of the difficulties with the creation of the Series 360, shortly afterwards had to go out to the market and borrow it back again, this time, however, paying substantially more.)

'Williams usually gets the blame. If you are to understand IBM, you have to realise that every failure has to have a name tabbed to it. Someone is responsible, and if they are not, there will be plenty of people around to make sure that somebody will get stuck.'

*   *   *

'. . . he was responsible. After all, he was President, and he was the hot shot financial guy.'

It is the only *public* blot on the Williams' copy book.

*   *   *

'He's got this friendly image: a courtly gentleman, and he is. But over the anti-competitive moves against CDC and the rest, he was in bed with the rest of them. Indeed, some of the best ploys are his.'

*   *   *

'Tom Watson [TJW Jnr] and Al Williams had large files on everybody they had ever met, everybody they had ever corresponded with, so that if at any time these people came up to them again, they would get their assistants to look through the files to find out from any previous correspondence what they had met them at, or what they had corresponded about, so that it would appear that they had an infallible memory. They had a superb research organisation working for them on these things. The Watson one was never as well done as the Williams . . .'

* * *

'Watson and Williams were really entities in themselves. They would have two or three secretaries each. Tom Watson had a male secretary all the time. They had two or three female secretaries. Up to three or four administrative assistants and an executive assistant in addition to that. They really moved, they were large power houses there to support the boss.'

* * *

'You can criticise him all you like. But there's one thing for which he should take the credit. The rest might babble on about supporting science and the rest of it. But he had a better feel. Without him, it would have been the same games the old man was playing.'

* * *

'He gave Piore the money and he supported him. You must remember that the public think of IBM now as a company out at the far frontiers of technology . . . But it was not always like that. Without Williams indeed it would have been nothing.'

* * *

A. L. Williams was a Watson man, initially the father's if not the sons'. But he was also a Nixon man and was to serve as Chairman of the President's Commission on International Trade.

George Beitzel was a TJW Jnr man through and through, and though he has not been Chairman or President, this is one reason why he precedes others who have.

'Spike Beitzel?' (Nobody thinks of him as anything but Spike.) 'He comes from a very wealthy Philadelphia Main-Line family. There are certain guys anointed at an early stage: he was one of them.'

'Spike's the only assistant Tom Watson ever had that he accepted socially. They owned a plane together, all this stuff.'*

He joined the company, after an outside career, in 1955, and became a Vice-President ten years later. Today, after progressing primarily through Data Processing till he became General Manager of the DP Group in 1969, he has his reward. He was brought on to the Board in 1972, during the in-fighting that led to Learson's retirement, and has since, in a reversal of the situation that existed between Dick Watson and Learson in 1964–66, been made Group Executive in charge of everything except mainstream commercial computing: Science Research Associates, IBM's educational publishing arm; Office Products, that lucrative typewriter and allied kit producer; and sales to the Federal Government, all come under him, the last being something which suits his diplomatic talents. He has never really been at home with the circus routines that IBM senior executives must practise with the DP sales force.

'I can remember an IBM director telling me back in the late sixties that the two coming men were Beitzel and Opel, and that one would eventually end up running the company.'

*   *   *

'IBM's been very lucky. They needed Tom Watson Snr to form the company. When he was starting to be a negative influence, he faded out of the picture and Tom Jnr took over. And he started to decentralise, just at the right time, the Williamsburg Conference and all that junk. When he was starting to lose, Learson was there to give it just the right shot in the arm: now they have turned it over to two hand-groomed guys.'

---

* They also jointly own Madonna Mountain, an American skiing resort.

Frank Cary has had the classic IBM career. He is a product of sales and marketing all the way through.

'But he's not the classic IBM salesman. You have to realise that he was an exceedingly thorough sales administrator even by IBM standards, and that made him. Even in IBM, salesmen are not generally that well organised.'

He owes his rapid rise not simply to performance but to an internal process of executive selection in the late fifties, when IBM started to search its own ranks looking for those suitable to be groomed for promotion.

'Oh, sure, the guy is capable. But he's anonymous. Take away the trappings and you could enter a room full of people and not realise that he is there.'

It is a hard but not an unfair judgement. One can understand *Rolling Stone* getting the spelling of Mr Cary's name wrong. But *Business Week*? It managed twice to spell it wrongly as late as July 1974, putting 'Carey'* both on the front cover and the list of contents.

A capable, anonymous administrator? I kept describing him during the interviews for this book as 'the best civil servant at the head of the most effective civil service in the world'. It was a counterpart to the view of IBM as the most organised corporation ... It was a viewpoint with which I could find no dissentients, monotonously so, so I kept trying. At one point in Frank Cary's deposition in the Telex case, indeed, there occur the sort of words likely to be emblazoned somewhere on any good bureaucrat's office wall, or even on his anatomy: 'I do not have any understanding independent of the document.'

Cary has degrees from UCLA (BSc) and Stanford (MBA), joined IBM in 1948, and also followed the career path which in IBM is regarded as the route to success: salesman, assistant branch manager, branch manager, district manager (1959), and then the test, the Presidency of the Service Bureau Corporation.

'Absolutely no charisma. He's a very solid unimaginative guy. They gave him the job of running the Service Bureau ... the Siberia of IBM. He did a yeoman's job with it: any job given to

---

* Anonymity was to be strengthened by the Appeal Court judges in the Telex suit: they made the same error in passing their judgement.

him the guy does. He's solid, he's unflappable, you just don't shake him up.'

The parallel with the military may have only limited application, but it does surface in the language that both use. In this context, Cary is no exception. In that same Telex deposition he described a part of his career thus: 'In March of 1961, I was made Assistant Director of the IBM Corporate staff. I returned to the *line operations* [italics added] in the Data Processing Division in September of 1962 as Vice-President of Field Operations.'

His rise thereafter was rapid: President of the Data Processing Division in 1964, Corporate Vice-President and General Manager of the Data Processing Group from 1966, Senior Vice-President and a Member of the Management Review Committee in October 1969, Executive Vice-President of the IBM corporation in March 1971, President in June 1971, and from January 1973 Chairman of the Board, President and Chief Executive Officer, until the reorganisation in 1974 when John R. Opel became President.

Yet he remains anonymous. A speech he made in 1974 was recently described by an IBM executive: 'It's the first time I have heard a speech written by a computer also spoken by a computer.'

*　　*　　*

'You have to realise the guy is a bureaucrat—', disparagingly, '—and he's re-creating the corporation in his own image. The bureaucracy increases almost daily.'

*　　*　　*

'I never thought he had a sense of humour. But someone in his family must have. His brother's name's Grant Cary.'

*　　*　　*

'You will have heard that he has no sense of humour. That does not mean that he does not go through the motions. He has favourite anecdotes he tells over a couple of drinks, and you can read what you like into them.'

'In the early sixties, they had a Hundred Per Cent Club out West. And everything was Wild West, everybody was in cowboy costumes instead of dark business suits for the banquet. And they had a whole lot of guys on horseback to meet Tom Watson and his plane.

'And they had all the cattle grazing around the hotel, real Western motif. Watson lands and he's just not in the mood for that. Word flashes back. Hey, kill the cowboys. Everybody's sent back to their rooms to change into their dark business suits, get the sheep and cattle off the lawns, there was just one big panic.'

Throughout all this, cattle and all, has climbed John Roberts Opel, now President of IBM. It has taken him twenty-five years effort, years in which he has not always managed to conceal the internally much-discussed Opel temper. The number of times he is supposed to have threatened to resign grows with each telling, but it is ㅤㅤㅤ ㅤㅤㅤ ㅤㅤ ㅤㅤㅤ.

'Learson, Cary and Opel were always very much in synch.'

'Opel did things that Learson would never have done at the same level. Learson managed to control himself much more closely till he was really well established.'

*   *   *

'Opel? He was respected by Learson. He was his Chief of Staff.'

*   *   *

'His reputation was always that of an extremely brilliant, logical, cool young man who speaks his piece and who belongs in the big league.'

Opel came out of the same internal selection process which produced Frank T. Cary, and, as one would expect, was a product of marketing, ten years of it. Like Beitzel, he too was one of the chosen and even more than Cary has been at the heart of the decision-making process in IBM, having served both as administrative assistant to Tom Watson Jnr, and as assistant to Vin Learson. He was in and out of Series 360 production as director of product programmes within four months, and went back to marketing, steadily moving up through the mid-sixties until, in

1970, he became Chairman of the Management Committee. In January 1972 he took charge of the DP Product Group, and finally made it to the Board of IBM, September 5 of the same year.

Opel is interesting as we shall see because the IBM of tomorrow is Opel's IBM, the product of tomorrow is Opel's product. He and Cary, of course, face the same problems that were originally faced by the Watsons. 'It took years to make IBM seem respectable to the banks, and it needed the mix of Mr Watson Snr, A. L. Williams—and many more—to do it. It rubbed off on Tom. But who are Cary and Opel, even with that Board behind them? All they have for IBM is performance.' But this time, as we shall see, it is a problem that has been taken care of.

'The company always has a Mr Inside and a Mr Outside. You've always got the guy who can run that shop; financial strategy, do this, do that. And then you've got the outside image guy, outside being to the world and to the troops. Tom always had that. Learson was a Mr Outside. With Opel you have the smartest, sharpest Mr Inside type of operator you could ever imagine.'

The company, of course, no longer has a Mr Outside. Whether the times have changed and it does not need one is still moot. It would be a different IBM if it did not, and there is little evidence that it is that much different.

This, however, does not seem to faze Opel.

*   *   *

The present Corporate Office currently consists of three serving full-time executives, one Chairman who must keep a watchful eye on his Board, one President without many of the normal Corporate presidential responsibilities, for John Opel's life is currently bound up in an attempt to change the whole basis of IBM's business, and, at long last, the Chairman of IBM World Trade.

'. . . Both Cary and Opel got where they are without any World Trade experience. And I don't think that if IBM stays anything remotely like the way it is that will happen again: they are going to look for a man who has had World Trade experience. But if you look around today, there are not many people at the top who have . . .'

Which is the reason why Gilbert 'Gil' E. Jones is there. 'Jones and Learson were competitors.' Gil Jones has two unusual distinctions, not normally found in classic IBM sales careers. He is the reverse of Spike Beitzel, the first example of an IBM executive triumphing over the unspoken rule that some are more equal than others. And he is also the first example of another part of the IBM myth working out in practice: that an executive tabbed for failure and accordingly demoted can work his way back up. In reality, hardly anyone demoted ever really works his way back up. Before him, no one has ever fallen from so high and then worked his way back, up to the Board and the Corporate Office.

IBM is littered with former Presidents of this, that or the other division who are now stuck in back rooms ranking number three or four to men who used to be their assistants.

It is one of IBM's strengths that it encourages its executives to take a chance. If they fail, they are demoted and sent to the 'penalty box', (A favourite place in the Federal Systems Division.) It is, however, also one of IDM's strengths that while one's being sent to the penalty box does indeed mean demotion, it does not necessarily mean a cut in salary. In the early seventies FSD was littered with low-level but highly paid executives, some earning more than their immediate superiors. IBM's attitude is that they took their chances on behalf of the corporation. Having failed, it is right that their careers should suffer, but that suffering should not be financially inflicted on their families.

Few make it back up the ladder.* Many, in fact, just leave and go on to something else. But it is surprising the number who will stay, even if often the demotion has been for no better reason than the fact that at IBM a failure must have someone's name attached to it. Conversely, so must each success, and this in the past has led to some questionable promotions: there are still some executives who owe their promotion, often to quite senior levels, to no better reason than the fact that they were the nominal heads of whatever it was that had succeeded.

Gil Jones was President of the Data Processing Division in 1959 and then disappeared: out in the cold, tucked away in a little office. He worked his way back, however, collecting the titles of Vice-President of IBM, Group Executive, and President of IBM

---

* This is one thing that IBM shares with the U.S. military, though failure in the military does lead to demotion and to the corresponding level of salary.

World Trade in 1963, and eventually became Chairman of IBM WTC in 1970.

'He's a bit of a masochist in a way. He came back and talked quite openly of the time this [demotion] happened to him, and how good it was for his soul and so on.'

'He's the most effective executive IBM ever had. A sharp mind. Very tough. Regarded as inhuman.'

'Management by fear. He had somehow the ability to frighten people. He has said that management by fear is a technique you can employ on a man only for a short time. After that, it is not going to work. But during . . . you can get quite a lot out of a man that way. And he uses that technique quite coldly.'

*　　*　　*

But what of the pressures on these men?

'The only one who doesn't exhibit any sign of the pressure is John Opel, though some must be there. But Opel swings along in public with that boyish image now on his more than $300,000 a year, briefcase in one hand, raincoat in the other. He's the only character I can ever remember seeing in a crumpled suit. Oh, except Bo Evans, of course, who lumbers around those corridors with his shirt tails hanging out, and whose language can be appalling even by locker room standards.'

Bob Overton ('My name is Bo; if you want to be formal, please call me Bob') Evans, though he is not at the time of writing on the Board of IBM, has been critical to the development of IBM throughout the sixties and early seventies. An engineer by training, he is the architect of much of IBM's technology. With the exception of two intervals—one, when he too was sent to the penalty box, and that because of the disagreements over the future of IBM's software; the other, when he bacame President of the Federal Systems Division—he has effectively presided over the development of the major products that IBM brought to the market since before Series 360. Since 1970 he has been President of the Systems Development Division.

It is probably 'Bo' Evans' manner and language which will preclude him from further promotion, however. And—the fact that in a corporate world in which senior executives take great pride in being and acting tough, 'Bo' Evans really is, in addition to being hardworking and a fierce pacesetter. He is, however, no respecter of IBM's rules of business dress, which jeopardises his further advancement; but his really critical disadvantage is the fact that, though he may have been one of the key figures in the creation of the product that IBM salesmen try to shift, he himself has not formally commanded IBM line troops.

* * *

A psychiatrist, many of whose patients had come from the electronics and computer industry, talked about the pressures.

'No, I have not seen any of the top ones, and if I had I wouldn't talk to you like this. I have seen some of their competitors' executives. It has turned me into an IBM watcher, which I gather is a large industry in itself.

'Pressure? Oh, sure, even without seeing them you can pick out some of the signs. There is for a start this obsessive neatness . . .

'They are faced with problems which really set up strains. One, they have set a faster pace than anyone else around. Their own actions lead them to obsolesce technology at a relatively rapid rate, they have to obsolesce product, and that is pressure enough, for if they get it wrong, they are in trouble.

'Two, they have that rate of growth to keep up. It is unprecedented, they are measured by it externally, and they measure themselves by it internally. The whole shooting match stands or falls on it.'

And then he proceeded to answer the question I had not asked: 'To cope, they have to over-react. They have no option. When you think of it, that's the only way you are going to get a colossus of that kind to move.'

CHAPTER NINE

Armonk: The View from the Bunker

Armonk, IBM's Corporate HQ, epitomises the conditions in which the men who run the large corporations of the latter part of the twentieth century like to be found. Armonk (which someone has pointed out is an anagram of Monark) was built in the early sixties when it was becoming fashionable for large corporations to move their headquarters out of New York City (IBM was one of the first) and to surround themselves with the beauties of nature, though nature unassisted was never quite like that. This is nature as seen through the filters of no-expense-spared architects and landscape designers. Indeed, the immediate IBM joke when the executives finally moved in was that Armonk was the sort of place that God would have created if he'd had the Watsons' money, a phrase originally used by George S. Kaufman to describe the Rockefeller Pocantico Hills Estate, not many miles away.

Armonk lies in New York State, slightly to the north west of the Kensico Reservoir. Across the water lies, appropriately enough, the community of Valhalla.

Corporate HQ sits snugly on a hilltop, surrounded by the carefully tended and cultivated remains of an orchard; the era of the motor car has meant extensive provision for car parking, but this has been generally sited so as not to interfere with the corporate view.

From Corporate one can see that much more tax-favourable state, Connecticut, where IBM originally would have dearly loved to be able to move; TJW Jnr, however, thought it was politically the wrong thing to do. This consideration did not affect private life, and most of the senior ranks of IBM do live across the state boundary.

Not far away from Corporate, lest any IBM executive should become anxious, lies the complex of IBM sites around White Plains, Data Processing Division headquarters and some of its satellites: thus, the driving forces behind IBM's growth and profits are almost all within sight of each other.

Armonk looks at its best in the late spring: it is the product of the boom years of corporate capitalism, the days of rich corporate living, of onward ever onward almost exponential growth.

It is quite easy to find, though there are few signs to direct one. A small 'IBM' on a metal plate supported by a short staff stuck into the ground—almost like a medieval battleflag—marks the turn off into corporate country, and even from there one cannot see the corporate HQ. The heyday of the brand of capitalism that IBM best represents was yesterday. Today it is concerned with keeping a low profile, in case dangerous radicals can read: a bomb in Armonk would not be good for the corporate image. (Bomb threats, of course, arc not uncommon. The Papers indicate thirty of these threats in 1969, though the one that seemed to exercise management the most was July 1972 when Frank T. Cary reported receiving an anonymous letter threatening to place bombs in several unknown IBM and/or customer facilities—whether Armonk was one of the sites is not reported—unless IBM agreed to hand over a substantial amount of money. Instead, IBM turned the matter over to the FBI, who recommended going along but using a 'plant'. What happened is uncerain from the documents, but it seems not to have ended too well. There was, however a 'dangerous radical' slight explosion the next year at one of the New York offices.)

Armonk was primarily created to bring the corporate staff together on one site. 'In 1965, the staff was scattered. There were some temporarily at the Yorktown labs, there were some in New York, modestly called World Headquarters. And then we all moved into Armonk. Watson was appalled at the size of the corporate staff. He had never seen it all in one place before. So a big study was put under way, and we reduced the size of the corporate staff by ten per cent.'

That was years ago. At the end of 1972, the corporate Division Plan indicated that the corporate staff, from senior executives to

janitors, numbered 2,071, and that the cost of supporting them
and corporate HQ was $77 million. The MRC minutes also men-
tion that those staff numbers indicated a reduction of 15% in corporate manpower over the previous year, and that cuts had been
made in all departments—except legal, where employment had
increased by 7%.

*   *   *

When one looks at the world of Corporate, particularly as seen
through the IBM Papers, the force of the feudal and military
analogies become apparent: feudal, in that it is a world in which
effective power is held in very few hands, and that the light in
which those few in power regard one is absolutely critical to one's
advancement, thus the jockeying for position is intense;
militaristic, in that there are sharply delineated boundaries to the
duties and responsibilities that an executive will carry, the whole is
carefully ranked in a rigid hierarchy, and any action undertaken
likely to change the strategic picture one iota has first to be
cleared upwards: it is not an atmosphere to encourage independent decision-making.

At the apex of Corporate and IBM is the Corporate Office, the
setting in which most of the men described and discussed in the
previous chapter operate. Long an appendage of the Watsons',
the Office really goes with the job of Chief Executive, and contains also the other members of the present troika and their
associates, including an Executive Vice-President, there to make
sure that their whims, wishes and thoughts are transferred into
action.

During the period covered by The Papers, the Office exercised
power through the Management Review Committee. According
to the organisation manual this was the formal mechanism
through which the members of the Corporate Office collectively
consider and act upon key Corporate policy, planning and
operational matters. In other words, as one ex-member of Corporate expressed it: if it moves, the MRC want to know about it.

These policy decisions flow down to the organisation on paper.
Everything in IBM is noted and filed. (Since the Telex case,
however, the output of paper has drastically declined: requests for
more recent records by parties suing IBM have more and more

been met with the response that IBM no longer keeps 'this' sort of record; 'this', covering a wide territory.)

The MRC is supported by the Management Committee; the one fact on which there is agreement by all parties is that the MC belies its name: it does not manage. Vin Learson in his Telex deposition stated it succinctly: 'The Management Committee has no responsibility.'

The MC is an extension of the MRC, an appendage and channel through which it can make its wishes known. It is a monitor and a lower-level contention resolver, passing on to the MRC those recommendations and plans which carry some semblance of lower-level agreement, and acting as a report producer, gutting to essentials the material presented to it and then passing them up in the form of reports.

The route to the MRC is formally through the MC, no is the route from membership in the MRC. It is as obligatory to serve on it as to have been in a senior marketing position in DP Division. (In this sense IBM is much like air forces the world over: all officers have equal prospects except that it's usually pilots who tend to be promoted.)

The minutes of these two committees were in evidence and provide much of the information about how IBM formally works. The MRC Minutes cover most of 1968 through to the end of 1972: those of the MC, again from through 1968 to August 1972.

There are substantial deletions—on legal grounds—but in all more than 3,000 pages are in evidence, more than enough to show the concerns of IBM management.

'The minutes? They existed long before, but they really are pure Cary. The guy even used to read them . . . [Learson]. Most of the time he couldn't be bothered with all that crap.'

If Cary could read the minutes, so could I. They make for rewarding reading, even if the typed versions should be the minutes 'for the record' and not a verbatim transcript of what was said or the sometimes Nixonian language in which it was spoken.

Some overall impressions* stand out: the total dedication to

---

* Among them the remarkable lack of discussion about unions. It is odd: parent IBM hates unions—yet IBM looks like a company with a seeming immunity to union pressures.

IBM's profit, an absence of any concern for the affairs of the rest of humanity except in so far as they concern IBM, and certainly no humour or wit. The manner is overwhelmingly earnest, grinding over details endlessly (the very mechanics which make the IBM machine so effective). Moreover, they are totally IBM-centred.

But should one expect anything different? Is not all big business like this? The answer is no. That there should be such a total dedication to a corporation has been found surprising by executives in other major industries with whom this has been discussed. Some find this eerie.

There is, of course, drama, but always concerned with money. Indeed, the Corporate ethos is well and succinctly captured in an MC Minute of December 1970: 'The MC stated that the Plan is sacred in terms of profit and that if new news is bad enough to affect the installed position, dramatic actions must be taken to achieve the committed profit.'

That is the running theme.

'The MC wants to realise the bulk of the savings without the proposed costs.' An MC summation of a discussion on the reorganisation of trucking.

'Rizzo' (Paul J. Rizzo, then Vice-President, Finance and Planning, now Senior Vice-President, a Director and Group Executive DP Group) 'pointed out that if the copier programme isn't successful to the degree planned, then we are spending too many development dollars.'

Occasionally, of course, even IBM cannot help but record something which outsiders will find funny, but it is unprompted, no doubt unwanted, and internally unlikely to be recognised as such. (If it were, it would probably be deleted.) For even IBM cannot evade exhibiting touches of Parkinson. Thus, on May 22nd 1972, the MRC Minutes, under the heading 'Significant Items', discussed a proposed IBM Board meeting to be held in London:

'Thomas Watson queried the decision to supply directors with $10 for incidental expenses since no apparent requirement. All agreed nothing should be done at this meeting.'

At which point one can see why the MC does not manage. And not just the MC. It has been the contention throughout that IBM is run by no more than four or five people at any one time, the opposite of the public face that IBM puts forward.* For more than fifty years it was run by only two, Mr Watson and his eldest son. However, IBM has many officially designated managers; in fact, IBM has more managers going through the motions than the majority of companies have employees. At the end of 1971, Domestic alone had classified 17,542 of its employees as 'managers' (the Minutes noted that the traditional IBM management-to-employee ratio of one in eight, around 12%, had been exceeded by several divisions).

However, all that the figures really indicate is that there were 17,000 people carrying managerial titles. Vin Learson, in his CDC deposition, stated that all that the managerial titles meant is that people need to be given some sort of status; this does not mean that they engage in management. Sometimes even promotion serves little more purpose than to give a man an increase in salary; it may indeed just be a feudal reflex, the reward for good service. This has been summed up by Henry E. Cooley, the head of the first Peripherals Task Force, the results of whose work were partly responsible for bringing on the Telex suit. In his deposition, he summarised his move from Director of General Systems for the System Development Division to be Vice-President, Development, Systems Development Division, like this:

'The title change was not indicative of the change in position in the hierarchy. That just meant I was in good graces at the time.'

Mr Cooley is acknowledging that the figures do not reflect reality. Vin Learson goes further, saying that there were seventeen-plus thousand people in IBM Domestic going through the motions. What is more, twelve thousand of those were managers who had been led to expect further promotion. They

---

* Question: '... How many decisions do you think come before you or the Management Review Committee in a given year that increase or decrease IBM's revenue by $10 million or more?'
Answer: '15 to 20.'

(Frank T. Cary, during redirect examination by IBM lead Counsel, Thomas Barr, during the Telex trial.)

*   *   *

'Corporate bullshit maintains that only a handful of decisions are made at Armonk. That the job of corporate management is to give advice and counsel and to ratify ... It is all done by you guys out in the divisions and in the field. It just is not true.'

(Former Corporate Executive)

had been so led by one of IBM's promotion mechanisms known as Advice and Counselling. IBM employees have their performance annually graded on a one-to-five scale; one and two being the grades of those who can expect promotion. 68% of the managerial force had been so graded at the end of 1971: IBM's ratios, indeed, had got totally out of line, for 'managers' are given clear-cut guide lines, staff percentage limits for the top grades.

The situation had arisen, however, during the fat years: those A&Cs involve a face-to-face confrontation with the employee's immediate superior who must review his performance with him, and show him his grading.

What happens in good times, of course, is that the standard slips, and so it did in IBM. If one relates a man's performance to that of the previous year, if sales, revenues and profits are booming and his contribution to them is measurable and worthwhile, one certainly does not hold him back. But now one has raised his expectations . . . What does one do when the bad times return? Bring down the grading? Do that, however, and at the first opportunity a good man might be lost.

It is a problem with which the A&C system is not particularly well suited to cope, and naturally enough many managers take the easy way out. Of course, such is the nature of the system that some people manage to be away at A&C time. And, of course, they do not believe in A&Cs at Corporate; that would be too much—it's too near the seat of power.

So titles proliferate in IBM.

*   *   *

It begins at the top. There are twenty-four directors, of whom six are full-time serving executives, including the Chairman and Chief Executive, the Vice-Chairman and the President. Twenty of these directors also man the four Board Committees. Next comes an advisory board consisting of old hands, including the protractor himself, Bruce Bromley.

But this is only a formal order of precedence. Below them and the Corporate officers and their Corporate office come the Group Executives, who are also Senior Corporate Vice-Presidents. Then follow some thirty Corporate Vice-Presidents, Treasurers, Controllers and Assistant Controllers, who between them hold all but four of the thirteen divisional or subsidiary Presidencies. So add four more Presidents without Corporate Vice-Presidential title. This is only the beginning. Each division also has a clutch of Vice-Presidents of its own: thus according to the organisation chart, in the second quarter of 1971, the President of DPD at that time was supported by twelve of them. They, too, are supported. A divisional Vice-President may also be a General Manager. Below him will come Assistant General Managers, or Directors, followed by Manager of (function), and (function) Manager.

The twelve DP Division Vice-Presidents of 1971 were supported by six Directors and five Managers all told. Each of course had his own clutch of supporting and reporting managerial grade staff, but they were not important enough to get on to the chart. (Nor are those key sales executives on which the show depends, the more than 700 branch managers.)

DPD, of course, is part of the DP Group, which contains other divisions with similar forms of organisation, though none are quite as large. DP Group has its own set of senior executives, two Assistant General Managers, eleven directors of this and that, plus Group Counsel.

IBM World Trade Corporation had till recently its own nineteen-man-strong board of directors, one of whom was on the IBM main board and eleven were full-time IBM executives, some of them key corporate executives, so that IBM WTC policy should be IBM Corporation executive policy. Below them came a WTC organisation based on a New York HQ, regional organisations, and country subsidiaries. Each country had a General Manager, President or Managing Director all theoretically responsible to a local board of directors, for most of the subsidiaries were also incorporated in the countries in which they operated.

This was formally changed in 1974, when IBM created IBM World Trade Americas/Far East Corporation and IBM World Trade Europe/Middle East/Africa Corporation, both subsidiaries of IBM World Trade Corporation.

The national operating companies in WTC are now subsidiaries of the two regional corporations. In practice what IBM has done is to eliminate the New York HQ stage and to substitute a stage much closer to Armonk. This has naturally enough meant some devolution of powers to the new corporations, but in practice Armonk powers remain absolute. To make certain of that, the first of the corporations has twelve directors, eight of whom are full-time IBM executives, six of them parent IBM corporate executives, while the second has thirteen directors, eight of them IBM executives, three of them corporate. As befits their history, the second has more independence than the first, but that independence is still nominal.

We are some hundreds of executives into the organisation, and we have not yet left the land once so aptly characterised by an IBM secretary as 'playing office'. This does not mean that people are not serious about it. They work hard, particularly in Corporate. It is the one characteristic that seems to stick in all memories, the Protestant ethic carried to its ultimate.

'They have learnt from the earliest Watson days to behave as if the company was going to collapse tomorrow unless they sell that next machine, however big or small, or if they don't win that next law suit or react to whatever it is that is put before them. The fact that the company is not going to go down the tubes whatever they do . . .'

They take great pride in their ability to work. One ex-Corporate executive summarises it like this:

'It was almost a disgrace not to work ten to twelve hours a day . . . To have a heart attack . . . was like a badge of honour for working. But if you had a heart attack, that was the last of your opportunities, it penalised you, you never went any further. Even Mr Watson himself . . . Of course the company would look after you . . .'

It is a pattern still largely in existence today—and naturally people try to cover it up.

Of course, Corporate management is aware of it, many of the heart attacks and other stress ailments that senior IBM executives are prone to have been very noticeable. So what is IBM to do? What it has done is not so much to change the basic system which causes people to work so hard, but to change its appearance. IBM demands the same standard of results as ever: but should an executive work late in the evenings or come in at weekends, he will hear about it.

For a lot of senior IBM-ers can see Corporate from their homes, and if any of those lights are on at night, the late worker can be sure that someone the next morning will be checking up to see who stayed behind and wanting to know why they did so. So, the executive works in the office, during normal hours, at home, or when away or travelling to attend an IBM meeting some place else. And as IBM executives are always going to attend meetings some place else . . .

The IBM system which leads to that overwork is a highly structured one, in which there is a date for everything, a time limit in which work has to be completed, and that time limit is set by the next meeting, presentation, report. Of course, there is just never enough time . . .

Except at the very top, there will be few occasions in which anyone (outside Research) can pick the time that he feels he requires to come to a decision; the decision will be forced upon him. Whatever that decision is, it will not really be much better for all. Outside the Corporate office what moves IBM is group think; the results will be the result of group think, and those results will be no results in that another group somewhere else will have to ratify them—or not.

It is a system that in its turn can produce effects, but at a cost. It eats up resources, and it eats up people. So why do people endure it? In part fear, for the world of IBM is a very comfortable world; in part career, for IBM has always sought those with drive and ambition. That most will fall by the wayside . . .

But it is, strangely, a world without one of the key business satisfactions, and that lack tells you a lot about IBM. The satisfaction that is missing is that of personal achievement (and personal failure). There are no entrepreneurs in IBM, and no one will make a fortune as the direct result of his own decisions—until he reaches the very top.

The system works, but it can lead to a considerable dissatisfaction, which also can reach quite near the top.

There were days in the late sixties, the days of the mad price earnings ratios, when one could still stand at the bottom of Lower Wall Street and shout 'computers' and be half trampled to death in the rush of people trying to make you take their money. Those days, however, it should be noted, were when IBM was making even more of the profits of the computer industry than it is today.

Naturally this dissatisfaction had been noticed, and IBM executives were in great demand elsewhere. The head hunters were busy, and IBM senior executives were being taken on everywhere. One competitor, one of the aptly named Seven Dwarfs, decided that if his firm could not beat IBM, they should join it. And what better way of doing so than to take on a senior IBM executive to run their show?

It took little research to find the man they thought they needed and wanted. He was approached: the reception was favourable. A number of meetings followed in which the IBM executive and his future boss circled each other warily, talked terms, discussed the thoses and wherefores, and finally the IBM executive was asked the key question. Why should he, a heartbeat away from the Board, want to leave IBM for what was, in IBM's terms, a minor scale operation? He had his answer ready: 'Because unless I make a break soon, I shall never know whether I can do it myself. And I would like the chance to find out.'

He never did take the job: and now, sitting on the Board of IBM, he will never know.

A former lower-level IBM executive, Lester Gottlieb, now President of a small company, Data Dimensions, in Greenwich, Connecticut, put it even more pungently to Laton McCartney for *Dun's Review:*

'I know of no major decision I made in thirteen years at IBM that did not require six months of staff work. In my own business, no decision takes more than two days.

'I had a bizarre vision one night when I was thinking about my tombstone. It read "When he joined IBM it was a struggling $500 million company. When he got his gold watch, it was a $40 billion corporation. We think he helped, but we're not sure".'

* * *

Any discussion of IBM's performance will almost inevitably contain references to IBM's superb management, the sort of claptrap to which even the most respectable of management and business jounals are prone. If one looks at the standard external indices, IBM *is* superbly managed. But this tells one little of the philosophy of management or the specific set of tricks which make it so corporately effective.*

'It's the organisation that makes the men effective rather than the men themselves. The entrepreneur is not there . . . It's a well-oiled machine. In many ways, it reminds me of many German-type companies, disciplined, precise, exacting.'

'The decision in the Telex case seems to me an unemotional one. They are willing to go to court, they are willing to take the risks. Go right ahead and do it. It doesn't matter whether it impacts these people or those people. Well, take care of that by spending so much money over there. They operate almost as if they are guided by a computer . . .'

'IBM long ago mastered the tricks of being able to reorganise to meet different opportunities and in the us quite quickly if not painlessly. It's something which most other organisations have never achieved.'

With IBM reorganisation is a way of life.

'Of course, IBM pays a price for it. Its reaction time can be very slow. If management is not seriously involved or committed . . . But as everybody else is usually slower . . .'

It was not always like this. Before the ascendancy of TJW Jnr IBM was still a patriarchal family. In terms of IBM of the seventies pre-1956 IBM lacked many things that are today taken for granted. The corporation that TJW Jnr inherited had been organised around his father.

'He [Mr Watson Snr] kept the company profits in a desk drawer, there was no real budget, no real financial control whatsoever. Of course people watched him to make sure that they could put out a financial report, and they had to have figures to pay taxes on. But all that was a recording of his actions rather than financial operations as more normally conceived. When you wanted to start a new machine project in IBM, you went and

---

* While doing the research for this book, I was discussing IBM with the editor of an American journal for whose judgement I have considerable respect. I was talking in shorthand, hyperbole, and with considerable enthusiasm of IBM as the most efficient corporation I had seen, which a moment's reflection would have shown me to be untrue.

He stopped me. 'Perhaps the best organised,' he said, 'certainly the most effective among the majors, but the most efficient: No.'

And of course, he is right.

asked Mr Watson. It was as simple as that. And he would say, All right, you can have a million dollars, or how much do you need, or something of that sort. Someone made a record of it so that the books would be kept straight. But he made a decision, a decision right then and there. The decision-making process was to sit outside his door until you were admitted and were permitted to ask him. If you weren't high up enough in the structure to be able to sit outside his door you never got a result. There was no answer possible because he was the only one that had any answers.'

The first attempt at formal organisation not linked to the office of Chief Executive and the temperament of the man who ran it occurred at what has become known as the Williamsburg Conference. It was one of the first moves made by Tom Watson Jnr to set his own stamp on the corporation. Pre-1956, IBM had been a patriarchal family: afterwards it was to start to look much different.

IBM came out of Williamsburg with three organisations: Data Processing, Office Products, and Military Products.

'If they had not organised, at best they would have been a General Motors: At worst? Something much worse.'

It is with Williamsburg that the bureaucracy begins to grow. However, some things had not changed. Between 1956 and the middle 1960s, IBM had almost formalised Mr Watson Snr's desk drawer for his successor. At the top, management controls consisted of: 'Finance on one side, and all those other guys on the other. Whatever they—the other guys—did, Finance would stick its own numbers on it and that was that.'

Finance, of course, was Al Williams, and thus effectively TJW Jnr. Another ex-Corporate member put it this way:

'Up until 1965, IBM had no idea what its profits were by product type. It couldn't tell you whether it was making or losing on any particular product line. Nobody knew over any period of time whether a 1410 or a 7000 Series computer was making money or losing money. Nobody really cared, all they were interested in was the total company: Were they making money? They did not try to analyse the particular segments of any product line: all they cared about was that the total company was making profits at a certain rate. So you had half a dozen winners and losers.

'Some of those products were losing money hand over fist. It was in 1964 that John Powers was given the task (by Ted Papes,* at the request of A. L. Williams) to come up with a method whereby they could start analysing the products by product line, and that is where the Grey Books came from. They became the output of this process of trying to determine profitability by product line.

'It is only in the last ten years that the company has been using and getting high-grade management techniques, particularly in trying to measure what is happening to the business and why. It was in 1965 that they began to make major strides in that area, up till that time they couldn't even tell you whether they were making money on spare parts . . .'

Before 1965, one could still have situations on the top Corporate committee in which a presentation for a new product was made and prices put forward for management approval, to be met by Tom Watson Jnr saying: 'My father said you should never charge more than X for this,' X being well below the rental proposed (and getting called stupid for one's sins by the executive concerned, who threw a cup of coffee at him).

In 1965, Finance, which seemed to be responsible for all kinds of management information including the state of the market and the economy, began to lose some of its reponsibilities. IBM set up a separate management information systems group; then it brought in an economist and also took economic forecasting away. So now Finance, had three sides: true finance, management information systems, and economic forecasting and modelling. From this the reputation for skilled management—and for bureaucracy—stem.

The new set-up was to begin to bite in the late sixties, when the famous THINK signs began to have a different connotation. (The sign on ex-IBM executive Sullivan Campbell's desk read 'DECIDE'. 'Why "DECIDE"?' I asked. 'Why not "THINK"?' 'Ah,' said Campbell, 'All that really means is *procrastinate*.') It might lead to bureaucracy at the bottom, but at the top it was this mapping out and separating of responsibilities, the treating of men as if they were only modularly independent, which was to blossom in the methodology which was such a marked feature of the war on Telex and the other PCMs.

---

* Theodore C. Papes, then Vice-President on the Corporate staff, now a Corporate Vice-President.

'Ted [Papes] was the key active instigator and probably in the end was the one who caused them as many of the problems they have today as anybody. It is the result of Papes and Learson. Ted's the great analyst. He's the one who got all those flip charts. Nobody would ever have thought of analysing the competition to the extent that you created a model, seeking to discover what actions could be created and at what point they would cause that competition's demise. Ted Papes is a tyrant for all kinds of analytical detail. He wants it all six ways. All this stuff you see in the documents, none of it would ever have existed without Papes.

'In many ways, during the late sixties, Papes was probably even more influential than Opel. He was operating closely at the right hand of Frank Cary. Opel was at Corporate, and he was pushing for things there. Cary [then General Manager of the Data Processing Group] was the great civil servant who would only execute what he was told, but Papes was feeding Cary constantly with programmes, activities, and undertakings which gave Cary the semblance of being able to create something within the DP Group and of being able to answer or respond to what was happening at Corporate, at least as far as putting the pressure on the opposition.'

*   *   *

'They decided that they couldn't depend on Minnesota Mining as the sole source of magnetic tape. They were really worried: "Gee, what happens if we get into a bind?" So they shopped around, they really shopped around. They finally found this guy in Poughkeepsie as a separate source of magnetic tape. The price was much higher, but it was worth it to have two vendors. For years they bought this tape at a higher price from this second source until they found out this guy was buying from Minnesota Mining and just marking it up.'

'You have to realise that IBM's forte is not in the recognition of business opportunity.'

'IBM's forte,' I said, 'is in getting things done?'

'Yes ... You see, IBM in the past has been late every time. Battele came to IBM and said: "Here is an office copier" and IBM looked at it, the engineers came in and said: "Yes, that's very good, but we are sure we can make a much better one." So Battele took what they had and it became the Xerox Company. And sure, IBM came out with . . . a copier, but look how much later.*

'You know of course that they were also offered what became Polaroid—and they turned it down?'

And then there was Science Research Associates, that first acquisition since before World War II. It began with a conviction of Tom Watson Jnr's that IBM had better get into the education business. It was a line he had been sold and an enthusiasm which would not be content till something had been done about it.

'So, we had better get into the education business. So we bought SRA. Lyle Spencer was the President, a fabulous salesman, he could sell you seawater.'†

SRA's forte was the repackaging of ideas obtained from educators.

'Watson got taken on SRA. I think his friends moved round and said: Boy did you get taken on that stock deal. You paid too much. So Watson turned round to Learson and said: "Hey, you make this thing work." It reported directly to him (Learson) this ittsy bitsy 500 employee thing. And it used to take an inordinate amount of his time.'

Most of the mistakes, of course, are not as highly visible. Indeed, IBM senior executives can make mistakes which, in many other companies, would result in their dismissal; and yet, in IBM, they survive. A significant factor concerns security at IBM: decisions were made privately, few outsiders had access to the inner workings of IBM, executives simply did not talk shop externally. Thus, adverse decisions never surfaced publicly, even at Annual General Meetings. What better way to maintain secrecy than to retain the individuals involved.

Yet the losses that IBM can incur—and withstand—can be in-

---

* The original IBM dry copier was a Heath Robinsonish device which took up sizeable room and explored some of the same technology on which Xerox was to base its fortunes. It was actually working within IBM, at Endicott, before 1950. IBM, however, missed its true potential—looking at it in terms of an output device for IBM machines, not as a straightforward office copier..

† He certainly sold TJW Jnr. In the year prior to its purchase by IBM, SRA's revenues were nearly $14 million. IBM bought SRA for IBM stock, then worth around $70 million, of which Spencer's share was nearly half. The highest market value ever put on SRA was $64 million.

credibly high. Thus, for instance, over a period of two days in 1971 the MRC was to be told of miscalculations leading to lost revenues and profit of staggering proportions.

It began on the morning of April 15th with a report on the IBM installations in San Francisco's Bay Area Rapid Transit System, a new urban passenger railway. The system IBM provided was one in which the BART passenger purchases a season-ticket 'card' and then presents it to a machine which calculates the amount of fare to be debited every time he rides.

Senior Vice-President R. W. Hubner, in making his report to the MC, talked of environment testing, the testing requirements being meetable, and following the normal IBM test procedures. One hopes that he was right. A major problem for IBM is that the system was to be handled directly by the public and not cosseted by specialists: it was an environment in which IBM has had little experience. Non-specialists are as likely as not to goo up the holes with chewing gum for the hell of it.

Also, IBM did not have the experience of bidding in such an environment, and Mr Hubner talked of an 'obvious exposure'. IBM in error bid $5.3 million, for a system costing it $25–$27 million to build. 'TJW Jnr comments that the exposure of bidding to 1/5th of ultimate cost could only be done by a large company.'

The loss does not amount to much, just two weeks of that year's domestic net profit, and the experience IBM gained will probably eventually allow it to recoup that loss from the creation of systems in other areas where similar problems are faced.

At 10 a.m. the next day, however, first the MRC was told that the competitive market estimates for the 360/195 large machine programme had been slashed by more than half, and that the nearly $500 million in revenues and $80 million net profit that IBM expected to make have been cut similarly. (If anybody said that this washed out the system's profitability, and that the 360/195 has been turned into a loss, it is not recorded. But that is the case.)

It may not have been in the end a total disaster, nor was the next item (time, 11.25 a.m.). This was concerned with inventory write-offs, a loss of $44 million in 1970, an exposure of $50·5 million in 1971. What had gone wrong is called bureaucracy: it took an inordinately long time for the news that the inventory needed cutting back to reach those actually taking in the parts. The comment, again from TJW Jnr, was that changes were needed and that those changes must be such that responsibility was not put so far down the line that IBM had lost control.

It would take a long time to go through the various calculations which led to the figure, but on that second day the MRC had been told of losses, real in that they are past, and projected, amounting to over $300 million in revenues, and the equivalent of something in the order of well over $200 million in profit: in less than two days, the MRC had been told of the disappearance of something like the equivalent of three months of IBM Domestic's then annual pre-tax profit.

*   *   *

Even by IBM standards, it was a lively twenty-four hours. But ιιιιιιι ji ιѕ ιιιιι ιlιг ιιιljι MΓΓR ιιгιιιιιjιᴦιιlιιι ᴧѕ ιιιι ιιιιιιιιι expect, management hao a number of subjects in which it is seriously interested and which appear with regularity: state of order book, pricing, future product plans, internal divisional budgets set against expectations, internal resources available, and employees—number, compensation, morale—dominate the Minutes.

However, the MRC/MC do not confine their attentions to the broad strategic direction of the business. In IBM, management discusses and takes part in what it considers of interest, whatever it may be. And its interests are wide: the MRC and MC roam wherever their curiosity and interest take them: product, pricing, publicity, relations with the media and with Washington, retirement dinners, bomb threats, disposal of IBM art collection, real estate purchases and discussion of new neighbours, dress, executive compensation, plant closures, abuse of executive parking lot privileges (TJW Jnr), reorganisation of trucking, promotions, pay, pensions, are lumped in with tea for retiring employees, time off to accept a *Business Week* award, a fifteen-minute break to celebrate Learson's birthday and frequent homilies from the Chairman and Chief Executive on whatever may be on his mind.

But primarily the job of the MRC/MC and the supporting Corporate staff is the despatch of business: outside the MRC, Armonk is a filter, sorting information at a rapid rate to enable decisions to be taken. And people are sacrificed to get it: that's what Corporate is there for, and if one is any good in Corporate, one has to keep running. What interests the MRC is results, and those it expects as a matter of course. Reference upon reference finds the MRC expecting something done within a week which elsewhere would take a month. Formulate a plan, discuss, clear with legal and finance, talk to DPD, and get back to the MRC with a presentation within a week! In Corporate, this is normal. Moreover, crises are handled in a shorter time period.

Opportunities for fudging are slight. The MRC spends much of its time reviewing against existing paper, comparing this period's results with an equivalent past period and with plan. And not just with one plan—two, three or more parts of IBM are quite likely to be working with the same data and putting in their forecasts. Here, for instance, is a typical comparison presented to the MRC at the end of 1971. It compares 1971 estimates with a number made for 1972, all in millions of points:

Gross-to-net spread—Phypers* reviewed the 1972 gross-to-net hardware spread (excluding program products) associated with the 29D Plan.

	1971 Estimate	29D	Most Likely	DPD	Corp.	DPD Request
Gross Orders	160	190	180	180	179	182·5
Net Orders	89	121	113	114·1	—	117
Other Displace	50	66	69	68·2	—	67
Discontinuances	40	39	38	37·5	38	37·8
NSRI	−1	16	6	8·4	10	12
P/Y Yield	44%	45%	39%	40%	—	42%

The plans are serious: what will happen if they are not met? The minutes are littered with comments on that, too. The monitoring is close, and if for instance DPG does not run to plan, Armonk will slash expenses to try to keep profit up. That budgets have been cut is a constant tale of IBM divisional woe.

Thus, in April 1970, that worst sales year in IBM history, when projections indicated a substantial drop in earnings before tax, because of tight running controls, Armonk was able to estimate very early on what this would do to plan and to cut accordingly. 'Spike (Beitzel) talked about expense reduction resulting from Mr Learson's edict to transfer $35 million of sundry to the net

---

* Dean Phypers, now Corporate Vice-President, Finance and Planning.

earnings before tax line. In essence, Spike has $41 million of exposures that he does not know how to meet, so he has gone back to his divisions and cut their expenses by roughly $30 million.'

Of course, only a large corporation can find $35 million in sundries to cut. But then IBM is only interested in large sums and large markets; it has long recognised that often not so obvious truth of modern corporate managerial life: it takes little more management effort to cope with a major market than it does with a minor one.

Nowhere do you get a feel for IBM's approach to markets better than when the MCR comes to consider diversification. A summary of a Diversification Report presented in September 1972 brings out the following points:

A new product which addresses a totally new market is diversification.

An existing IBM product which addresses a new market is market development.

Successful diversification (according to a study done by Stanford Research Institute) indicated that it normally takes ten or more years to achieve 25% profitability from products arising from diversification.

What IBM considers desirable in a new diversification product programme is potential size ten years after inception of $500–$1,000 million a year.

IBM has long been interested in diversification, but it has in the past been on an *ad hoc* basis, as the result of somebody's whim or idea—as in the case of SRA. Till fairly recently it was never approached with any regularity or consistency. The traditional IBM concerns have been profit, man performance, quality of service and people policies: the corporate family beloved of Mr Watson Snr.

*   *   *

Though IBM has always been strong on people policies, those of the late sixties and early seventies show a shift in emphasis. That shift arises from the large numbers of personnel taken on during the boom of the 360 Series, and the first recession in the computer era, a recession which began in 1969 and coincided with unbundling, for the three quarterly reports after that indicated a marked fall-off in orders.

And so the committee, not without discomfort, begins the serious study of IBM manpower and the working out of methods to reduce it. IBM goes into 'attrit' mode, and the MRC begins to discuss how to get rid of people.

'Prior to 1969, management used to emphasise that its assets were people, the whole business of respect for the individual . . .'

That ceases: instead—

'Top management put pressure on lower level management. What they said is, "We want to start getting rid of people. We want to see a lot more unsatisfactories in evaluations." And at first, interestingly enough, lower level management said, "Hey, wait a minute, we were very careful in our hiring practices and all of our people are very competent and therefore very few people are unsatisfactory."

'And top management came back very strongly, and said: "Look, we want a normal distribution, and at the lower end of that are those people who are unsatisfactory. And that's the way we want to see it." '

By the start of 1972, the wriggling had become intense. The Watson successors did not come from the same mould as their predecessors, one could not expect that. Mr Watson Snr had faced the depression by cutting down on hiring, building for stock, and a barrage of methods to milk existing customers. But generally, IBM had not resorted to firing people.

IBM had no experience of firing, and did not know how to behave or act. So now it was not simply the Nuremberg Defence that was inverted. Armonk was not going to carry the opprobrium for firing people if it could possibly help it: the MRC/Corporate wanted to make the pleasant decisions itself and to have the unpleasant ones executed elsewhere.

The MRC minutes are explicit on this point:

'The highest priority task is to improve communications downward to first level management and to crack down on managers who put tough personnel decisions off on Corporate management.'

Since then the discomfort has become even more intense. There have been reports of a corporate policy to the effect of yes, IBM still guarantees that it will not fire, but the exigencies of changing technology and the market place are such that it may be necessary to move people about. You may keep your job, but only if you are prepared to move, say from New York to California, or vice versa. If not, then the corporation will consider that it has honoured its basic commitment and you will have to leave ...

This policy is thought to operate particularly in the now overstaffed area of manufacturing, as it has been since the late sixties. Furthermore, as Large Scale Integration (LSI) techniques advance, so more and more employees become economically 'surplus to requirement'. IBM's problem is how to get them to leave. That has led to further internal broadcasts in which IBM's Chairman has effectively said that some of you longer serving employees would be doing your organisation a favour if you left by if you retired. Whatever one may feel about the elder Mr Watson, it would never have happened in his day.

*   *   *

But the world of Armonk is not simply concerned with traditional and general business-type problems, particularly in its people policies... Corporate has always been aware of the difference between the ethos of IBM and the rest of the American corporate world and aware, too, that in this ethos has lain much of IBM's strength.

To have a corporate ethos there must be corporate loyalty, and that in turn requires the many ties that bind and, at that, uniquely bind, of which 'no fire' was of cardinal importance. For to bind in this sense means to separate, something which has in the past been understood by all organisations which seek to attach people's loyalties to themselves, from the Communist Party to the Masons. It has long been so in IBM.

The web of ties that separate and bind to make up dumb funny company is composed of many things: an obsessive concern with the way employees look, behave and dress; language; propriety; songs; personnel policies which run through the gamut of stock options, retention programmes for the able and key executives and specialists, retirement benefits, equal opportunity programmes and the like. The policies have, in some cases, been developed over many years and run from the general annual increment and performance bonuses to making sure that as a matter of course an employee's wife receives flowers when she goes into hospital.

One policy that has not yet entirely changed, yet one with which middle rank executives have never really been happy, is that of the Open Door, the feudal right of any IBM employee to directly approach his ultimate masters—the Chairman and directors—with a complaint.

Open door reports pop up occasionally in the MRC minutes; a favourite illustration being from an April 1971 meeting:

"*Newbolt Open Door*—S. L. Reed, W. T. Russell. JPC. Individual was with us 9 years as customer engineer. Telegrammed TJW, Jnr. and other directors concerned that IBM is dedicated to the selling and promotion of inefficient use of computers and that we do this as a conscious business practice. TJW, Jnr. will see him before the annual meeting and Hume to handle."

Of course, it must be remembered that this occurred before Cary. Those were the days when Dick Watson, for instance, once came to the U.K., addressed IBM U.K. executives in an insulting manner, saying that half a dozen of his American salesmen could do better than the U.K. organisation in its entirety, then flew back to the United States. One of the British executives concerned wrote to TJW Jnr, stating that this was undeserved treatment. Dick Watson was sent back across the Atlantic to apologise.

Today, Corporate would prefer not to hear Open Door complaints. It would rather pass them on to a new institution known as the Resident Manager, a member of the Corporate Staff, of whom there are a dozen out in the field. In theory they are there to support line management on personnel matters and to make sure that corporate policy and policy out in the field are in line. In practice, of course, it is both an extension of the Open Door system in that line management now has a resident Peeping Tom to worry about, and a downgrading on the new principle that Open Door complaints should be directly addressed to Armonk. It is the kind of solution that goes well with the new executive-run IBM.

The language used in that new style IBM is somewhat different to the plain speech of old Mr Watson or even his sons. The language, particularly when dealing with issues that management are emotionally unhappy with or find contentious, issues which run counter to the declared public policy of IBM, is a private language, often euphemistic and elliptical, sometimes barbaric and reminiscent of Aldous Huxley's Newspeak. It is a language which tries hard to avoid calling a spade a spade and would never go as far as to publicly call it a bloody shovel. IBM management may love conclusions, but it still sometimes would like the unpleasant ones suitably gift wrapped.

Nowhere is this more apparent than in the euphemisms used within IBM when it comes to dismissing people. Nobody is ever fired by IBM; instead they are 'released from the business' or 'involuntarily separated'. And MIS does not, as with everybody else, stand for Management Information System, but rather for Management Initiated Separation. Nor does IBM prepare plans to dismiss its employees, or even enforce lay offs; instead IBM goes into 'attrit mode' (mode is a modish suffix in IDM. Cynical insiders talk of the quite frequent rapid one-hundred-and-eighty degree policy turns as IBM in 'panic mode').

Even in IBM, of course, words go in and out of fashion: two other IBM barbarisms popular in 1974, concerned with IBM's policies towards its employees, were 'injecting technical vitality', a reference to the constant internal education programmes that a changing technology makes necessary, and 'retreading', a term much applied in the technical re-education of many of IBM's older engineers.

Non-concurrence, of course, we have met before, and means 'I do not agree'. However, to non-concur is only one of three formalised degrees of dissent possible, and at that not the most powerful, though the most public. At the bottom comes 'concern', and, as one IBM sceptic put it, those whose only powers are to be concerned or not concerned are usually candidates for retreading. At the top end of the scale comes dissent itself. Dissent, however, is a senior executive form of disagreement, and there are very few who are, in practice, sufficiently in a position of power to do so.

To non-concur, however, is much more dreaded, in that it is that much more widely known within IBM. It is a word much used, for instance, in the formulation of policy to deal with situations in which user installations have become 'contaminated', an IBM word meaning that somebody else has sold equipment to a user previously entirely equipped by IBM.

Anyone in IBM with the right to non-concur is on the way to

the power of dissent. For a non-concurrence means that a project or programme cuts across the rules laid down, and that the person with responsibility for their enforcement in any particular area is not going to sign off as approved until they have been absolved of the responsibility by senior management: for non-concurrences that are held to have to be cleared right at the top.

At its funniest the language is a product of those frequent changes of mind, of technical policy course alterations which mean that IBM may take up a particular line of development, drop it, and then execute an about turn. This can be described in the language of IBM as first IBM commits, then it decommits, then it undecommits.

Then there is 'exposure'. IBM is exposed when, as in the case of the 2314, the calculations made still leave IBM open to competitive moves, or when data appears in public which IBM management would prefer to keep private. Exposure is what happens when policy and reality differ, when in the eyes of IBM management, something has not been properly taken care of.

And then there are songs. The songs were largely an American IBM phenomenon. They have been a joke for many years, one in which many of IBM's employees share, and Corporate IBM is now somewhat shamefaced about them. Officially, today they are below its dignity.

But the songs should not be underestimated. They were one of the first things to make IBM noticed, particularly as they differed greatly from company songs as sung, say, in Japan, or even Europe. There the songs were strictly company songs. In IBM, however, they usually contained a tribute to the grand old megalomaniac himself.

These are five lines, each taken from a different IBM song:

'The name of T. J. Watson means a courage none can stem'
'With Mr Watson leading . . .'
'With T. J. Watson guiding us, we lead throughout the world'
'Of T. J. Watson proudly sing'
'We thank you T. J. Watson, the leader of our team'

The songs may be disowned, but the fact remains that some were still being sung in the seventies. I know people who have heard them at Poughkeepsie, coming from the sales training school buildings early on a Monday morning as late as the summer of 1973.

What they probably heard was an update of one of the two songs below, as the others are too sycophantic for modern tastes, even IBM tastes.

MARCH ON WITH IBM

Words by Fred W. Tappe   Music by Vittorio Giannini
The fame of IBM
　Spreads across the seven seas;
Our standards fly aloft,
　Proudly waving in the breeze,
With T. J. Watson guiding us, we lead throughout the world,
For peace and trade our banners are unfurled, unfurled.

1. March on with IBM. We lead the way!
　Onward we'll ever go, in strong array;
　Our thousands to the fore, nothing can stem,
　Our march forever more, with IBM.

2. March on with IBM. Work hand in hand,
　Stout hearted men go forth, in ev'ry land;
　Our flags on ev'ry shore, we march with them,
　On high forever more, for IBM.

IBM SCHOOL SONG

First Verse
Working with the men in the Lab.,
Backing up the men in the field,
Behind each one in the factory,
To a peer we'll never yield!

Chorus
In every phase of IBM
Our record stands for all to see
The Alma Mater of the men
Who serve the world's best company.
To every one who's enter'd here,
A memory will long remain—
We build, we work together
To a world acclaim!

Second Verse
Customer and Field Engineer
Men who build and those who sell,
Inspired by pioneers,
We will ever serve you well!

Third Verse
With our sights on bigger records
With the training we receive,
With service as our watchword
Success we will achieve.

Fourth Verse
With Mr. Watson leading,
To greater heights we'll rise
And keep our IBM
Respected in all eyes.

Fifth Verse
Trained to make the finest tools
With the best machines in the world
Our apprentices are exceeding
Every challenge that is hurled!

As for clothes and appearance, IBM's past, the IBM image, and the expectations on the market-place that IBM employees will be distinguishable by their neatness and dress, mean that IBM continues to be that 'dumb funny company': the obsessive IBM concern with the way its employees look and behave publicly remains.

*   *   *

The short hair, dark blue suit, white shirt, black polished shoes, sober tie and always sober employee, days may be over: one could not, after all, keep the old classic rig for ever. But IBM is still concerned with the way its employees personally present the IBM image.

Back in the sixties, TJW Jnr was heard to remark that were he to turn up in a coloured shirt, it would be construed as a signal within IBM. Well, the day came: he turned up in what was then thought of as a television-blue shirt and sports shoes, the first making sense as he was going to be televised. And in next to no time, IBM was a symphony of colours.

However, these things are carefully graded at IBM. At the bottom end of the pyramid, the initial change seemed to be shirts carrying thin stripes. But as one progressed into middle management, one-shade ensembles become the rage: men would turn up dressed entirely in matching colours, browns and similar or matching shades, but still, of course, neat and kempt.

The riot of colours, of course, was limited. And, up at the top, they still seemed to dress like New York bankers or Watergate conspirators. Of course, out in the labs almost anything was possible, though even there the neatness seemed obsessive.

The labs, of course, did allow for some exceptions. Beards were not and are not now uncommon. Cotton beards were also allowed elsewhere; for instance, IBM U.K. had at least one, but he was the resident film director.

In the ranks of the sales force, of course, no such allowances are made. Whatever else is missing, neatness has to be present. Even less allowance is made for sales trainees. Even in the seventies such trainees have been bawled out for hair that is too long or have been sent home to change their coloured or patterned shirts for white ones, exactly as if they were in boot camp.

However, out in the field, the IBM rule seems to be that you should dress as much as possible like your customers, the theory being that you will then merge into the background. Of course, they don't always get that right. Would-be users and customers in the City of London still talk of the IBM financial salesmen who turned up wearing new bowler hats and carrying all the brand-new traditional appurtenances, and were promptly dubbed by all concerned 'the bookies' runners'.

Memos concerned with dress crop up at least once a year. They originate at the MRC level, where they are also discussed. Thus, in May 1971, TJW Jnr was found talking of the press coverage of what is called 'the white shirt briefing' and the seemingly mixed opinion that the briefing had received in the company. Frank Cary mentioned concern at research but thought this was not a problem.

These same memos are a standard joke among executives. I have a copy of one which originates from WTC HQ in the

autumn of 1974, which reads: 'World Trade Requires that
Jackets and Ties be worn in their Cafeterias'. Over it have been
scribbled such comments as 'Why?', and 'Wild Ducks must be
kept in formation'.

These rules of dress have become an even better joke within the
rest of the industry, leading to such outbursts in print as adver-
tisements in the trade press which read: 'At so-and-so's, we don't
really care how you dress. If you are qualified, we would like to
talk to you.'

*   *   *

Whatever the private behaviour of its upper levels, IBM
proscriptions on drink still remain. Back in 1969, the MRC made
it quite clear that a business meeting would not include the serving
of liquor, and that business meetings included the so-called social
Family Dinners to which IBM employees bring wives, and now
husbands.

Abroad, of course, it is different. IBM follows the custom of the
country, though it took a long time for it to do so. Thus one can
always distinguish Americans in IBM from their European
counterparts: for instance, at lunch at Maxim's in Paris with
senior IBM people the Europeans drank a glass of wine, while
their American colleagues took half a glass which remained un-
touched throughout lunch, except for the ritualistic touching of
the lips during toasts. (It is, of course, different in IBM France's
factories; the French drink with meals and it is a habit that even
working for IBM will not change. The IBM canteens carry wine.)

Maxim's is one thing. The Playboy Clubs are another: again,
back in 1969, MRC took the position that business meetings are
not to be held within them, they are 'inappropriate'.*

Which leads naturally to Corporate's concern with private
behaviour. It is an IBM rule that one does not sleep around in the
company, particularly not with one's secretary. It is a rule that is
enforced, at least outside Corporate. At least one middle-ranking
manager was, according to a good source, fired in 1973 for dis-
obeying it.

---

*Inappropriate, too, is any hint of sex at an official IBM function. One WTC regional
manager was demoted not many years ago for having brought on dancing girls as the
entertainment at a Hundred Per Cent Club.

But, as ever, some are more equal than others. Not long ago a senior Corporate staffer was sleeping around the company; he, however, was an assistant to one of the executive directors. Everybody knew he was doing so, but no one was going to do anything about it which, while it might at worst get him fired, was more likely to annoy his boss, create enmity, and possibly put someone else's head on the chopping block: for the executive director concerned was unlikely to forget it.

The problem was solved in a typical IBM way. He was told that if it happened again, the secretary concerned would be shifted. There is, however, only one way for secretaries in that situation to be shifted, not downwards, that's too dangerous; it has to be up and out of reach. The result of that manoeuvre was that he later went around saying: 'Hey, you sleep with me. It's a sure way of being promoted in this company.' As a result the word spread, and there was a period when that seemed to work almost everywhere.

Actually, that privileged assistant was an unusual case. Whatever may happen in the rest of the corporation, there is generally little sex in Armonk outside the marital bed, though there might be some away from base. There is, indeed, as little sex as there is sport, for both are something one does in one's spare time, and in Corporate one should not have any of that. One should go home, play with one's children in the little time one has available, and then fall into bed to be ready and able to come fresh-eyed and bushy-tailed back to IBM the next morning. Life revolves around the corporation: life belongs to the corporation—they pay enough for it.

For the real mystique of IBM needs to be distinguished from the trimmings, no loud clothes, no sex, no liquor habits, no drinking on the premises, 'dumb funny company'. All these may embellish the stories, they may be buttresses, but they are not the things that give IBM its real strength or the real mystique.

Mr Watson Snr's major strength was that he could issue challenges to able people, and this got things accomplished. When he wanted something done, it was done. This naturally produces real phenomena. It made it possible for IBM to get where it was initially without being organised.

Today, IBM is organised.

CHAPTER TEN

The System: Run Proud,
Run Scared, but Run

Ted Papes may be a tyrant for detail and want it all six different ways, but in the late sixties Papes on his own would not have been enough to influence events. For the analyses which were to cause IBM its legal problems are the result of the deployment of extensive resources, and resources in IBM are not deployed in any substantial way without clear management approval: for Papes to have been able to operate, he had to find a receptive climate.

The IBM climate was as receptive to Papes as it had been to those before him who could suggest ways in which any possible competition could be contained. This is the natural state of any monopoly or would-be monopoly; competition or the threat of it represents an inroad into a market that is already held. Nevertheless, in IBM, there is an almost obsessive concern with the competition. Certainly, when Frank Cary can state in court—as he did in the Telex trial—that the reason IBM took the sort of measures that were put in hand against the PCMs was because it thought that IBM would be driven out of the business (. . . the tapes and disks. These were under very severe technical competition, very severe price competition. We obviously had to reduce our prices on them or go out of that business . . .') when the IBM forecasts indicated that IBM stood to lose around a sixth of a market growing roughly in the same proportion each year, this is obsession. (This is not to infer that anyone in IBM is in a state of mental imbalance, rather that this is the more interesting situation where a person can hold two contradictory opinions at the same time without recognising indications of irrationality.)

But if one understands IBM, the obsession is a rational one. To

the men at the top, the threat is mortal. The reason for it is not
hard to find. Those men have grown to managerial maturity in an
atmosphere in which, except for a short period in the early fifties,
IBM has generally been technologically outclassed by most of its
would-be competition; that, after all, was often the only way in
which IBM could be attacked. IBM's management knows this,
and the jibe that IBM is usually technologically backward is one
they feel: they do not forget—or forgive—it. What is more, they
lack external managerial experience; indeed, in the American corporate world they are unique. And they pride themselves on it.
Executives have been told 'You are lucky you work in IBM. We
are never going to bring in people from outside to replace you'. It
is almost impossible to go through any of the other major corporations and find senior executive ranks so inbred: IBM is a
world of its own, a family in the IBM's sense of the word. The
atmosphere, then, was prepared for Papes; the family seemed to
be under challenge, and IBM had access to funds, resources and a
basic methodology capable of development to enable it to formulate plans to contain the competitive challenge.

In its component parts, much of the methodology is not unique
to IBM. The IBM uniqueness comes from the totality of the
package and the shaping of the organisation to enable that
methodology to be fully used. To be like IBM one must do more
than take up a modish management technique or two, one has to
go much deeper: the IBM methodology is systemic, not simply
systematic.

So what does one have to do to operate like IBM? First, a
methodology cannot be entirely separated from the people who
will have to put it into effect: one must have the skills and the
experience available, and if one does not one must set out to
obtain them. Supposing one has both, however—one still has not
accomplished anything. To emulate IBM requires specific personnel policies: tight job specification and a strictly controlled,
carefully detailed reporting and monitoring system. In IBM lines
of responsibility are rigidly laid down, as are lines of communication. As the market changes, so IBM will change the organisation
as well as the lines of responsibility and communication. Almost
everybody would accept that this makes obvious sense; few companies, however, ever make the changes quite as thoroughly.
Tight job specification has, in its turn, two effects: first—given

that one has the resources—in the process of tightly specifying what a man is to do, one is necessarily in part specifying what those around him will be doing; one can build up a matrix of people to cover any particular area of interest and ensure that all territories are properly covered.

But, in the process, one is also creating something else, and that is unusual. IBM-er after IBM-er will say that he enjoys working in IBM because he is given freedom. And he is. He may only have the freedom of the cage, but at least he usually has a cage to himself. It is an exercise in tunnel vision, and tunnel vision has both advantages and disadvantages. It allows concentration on specifics: a specialised and localised expertise to be built up. The disadvantage of structuring a labour force in this way is that after a time the work may well become boring. It seldom gets boring in IBM due to movement and re-organisation. Both are a way of life at IBM. The first leads to the old joke that the initials 'IBM' stand for 'I've Been Moved'. The second is a result of changes in the product that IBM is to market. But here, too, there is a further reason, harkening back to the feudal analogy: nobody is allowed to build any sort of power base which is independent of Corporate, and the easiest way of ensuring that is to keep people on the move.

'I've Been Moved' serves, of course, another purpose; it allows the corporation to give its manpower experience; if you are on the move in IBM you are on the move upwards. You have to do a lot of moving, for, because of the restrictions of the tight job specification, a man needs to try on a large number of hats to get the required experience to fit him for promotion and higher office. The result is that what one has in IBM is modular independence, and once one has that, reorganisation is not as difficult as it might at first seem; one can just move the pieces around to make new patterns.*

That short description of the bases of IBM executive managerial life does not do justice to the quality of the results that IBM

---

* Of course, it makes it a quite simple matter to ease someone out, a peripheral bonus for IBM's controllers. One can shift him around the board, one can take away his functions and break up his subject territory.

'There's nothing crude about the process of being on the way out in IBM. And this applies right up into Corporate. Everybody there knows as soon as a guy's got Corporate halitosis. The joint just dries up on him.'

will obtain from treating men as building blocks. On these bases
IBM has built its managerial organisation. Much of it is conventional in a large stratified and centralised company, and we can
take it as read—with one exception. The methodology seems to
work in committee country. IBM has committees where other
companies have individual managers. IBM executive ranks are
anthill, group-think country.

If this were all, it might be special, but it would not be unique
What has made IBM has been its willingness to change its
managerial mechanics side by side with growth; as IBM has
grown, so the methodology has been extended, and some specific
notions have been added, polished and brought to effectiveness.

*   *   *

The most important of these are the Key Corporate Strategic
Issue and the Task Force. The KCSI concept was originally established in 1969 as part of the IBM planning system which formalised some *ad hoc* practices of the early sixties. The rolling
processes of senior management—seven-year plans regularly updated and monitored, regular reviews of divisional performance, a
close watch on sales and returns and the like—are bound to throw
up problems requiring extra attention. These may be concerned
with existing product, with future product, in fact almost anything
can become a KCSI if senior management can be convinced that
it deserves its attention, and that attention requires a special in-
depth look at whatever-it-may-be. Thus the start of the war on the
PCMs came with designation of peripherals as a KCSI.

As one of the documents states it, the KCSI Concept 'provides
a structured approach for the identification and treatment of planning related strategic issues, problems and challenges which
require the attention of the Management Committee as well as
DPG general management'.

Specification is one thing, getting an answer is another. Most
KCSI's will require the setting up of a task force.

The task force is an IBM way of life. 'An offhand comment
by Watson or Learson would send a task force off for six
months studying things, proving that the comment was not valid
or whatever. Learson was a great one for going off to family
dinners and talking to salesmen. He had this great knack of being

one of them. Then he would return to headquarters, where what he had heard would be taken up, and there would be upheaval. People would scurry off zoom zoom in eight different directions to try to prove or disprove what had been said.'

It is the essence of the task force approach that it should call on whatever talents the matter to be studied should require, wherever in IBM those talents are to be found. The job of the task force is to be as factually objective as possible and, having been so, to come up with conclusions and recommendations for courses of action. What management is interested in is the truth, and the truth may be uncomfortable. But arriving at the truth can be a great resource consumer. Thus, a Systems Development Division HQ list of the work to be done by one task force prior to management action against the PCMs listed sixteen detailed projects, some of considerable complexity, which covered everything from trying to forecast OEM activity, to devising specific IBM actions to counter the PCMs.

*   *   *

The Telex analyses are particularly interesting in that they show IBM mechanics in operation at their most effective and indicate why IBM fought so hard to restrict their circulation, for they raise many questions. There are two major and critical analyses, separated by nearly three months. The first lists many of its sources, which include the work of IBM analysts, planners and engineers, Wall Street financial reports, merger prospectuses and the like.

The second, a flip-chart presentation (see facing page), is much more interesting. Here there are no source listings except for references in the body of the presentation to special surveys and to COMSTAT (see page 444) reports—monthly figures are given for three consecutive months—which list the numbers of Telex peripherals installed and on order. After going through some fairly standard material which again seems to come from annual reports and from the public domain, and statements of Telex on the market-place, it then gives a Telex customer profile and a breakdown of where the then more than 1,200 Telex tape drives on the market are installed. There are 92 customers; immediately one can see why IBM should be worried. Between them, six users have more than 400 Telex drives. And they are major customers:

Lockheed, Boeing, McDonald Douglas, Continental Assurance, Humble Oil and International Harvester. Financial analyses of Telex product and financial strategy follow. And then there appears The Model. The Model is a general competition model which was adapted to deal with Telex. The Model is computerised, which can be ascertained from number-referenced data lines.

From it are developed the Telex installed inventory forecasts up to 1976 and the Telex cash flows by product. From it are developed the forecasts of individual machine sales for each product also up to 1976.

However, to run a model you must have data; some of that data raises the question of how it was obtained. One former Telex executive has maintained that though there is no proof, there was a spy in the camp, because, if the estimating of Telex costs was simply an estimate, it is a surprisingly accurate one.

TELEX MODEL

Selling Cost

—4 Dist. Mer. at $40,000/Year
—Salesmen at $32,000 Salary & Com.
               6,000 Trg.-Ovh. Trav.
—Office Space:
    —15→18 Offices at 3,000 sq. ft.
    —Cost, with Utilities & Maint.= $10/sq. ft.
—Secretaries & Ovhd.
    —1 per D.M.   ⎫ $15,000 Girl
    —4 Salesmen = 1 Girl ⎭
—Advertising: $100,000 + 10% Year

Administrative Cost

—HQ Executives: 6→8   at $50,000
—HQ Staff: 5 per Exec.   at $14,000
—HQ sq. ft. 8,000— + 15% Year   at $10/sq. ft.
—Other: CPA–Legal: $100,000 + 5% Year

Engineering

—DE's = 25 Men + 15% Year ⎫
  PE's = 10→20 Men   ⎬ $28,000
—Tech. = 35 Men + 10% Year $16,000
—Lab. Space: 15,000 sq. ft + 10% Year at $12/sq. ft.

Nearly a year later, the MRC heard a presentation dealing with IBM's Fixed Term Plan, the long-term leasing operation which was the final market strategy which drove Telex to sue. It would not be IBM if the consequences of IBM actions were not spelt out (proving once more that Max Bleecher was right). The clincher, and it is one with which Telex is to play havoc, comes on Page 8 of the Exhibit and has been quoted before: three lines which deal with the effect of the proposed IBM actions on the PCMs:

'But, PCM Corporate Revenues lower.'

'No funds for mfg, eng.' (Manufacturing, engineering)

'Dying Company.'

It may be a damaging conclusion, but it is at least a conclusion. IBM's strength is that it loves conclusions, even if they should be the obvious. Sometimes it will go to great lengths to arrive at them. Thus, in September 1971, Frank T. Cary reported to the MRC that the DP Group had broken the market-place down into 2,500 levels of customer types, and was trying to establish specific applications which have potential. 'The work,' stated FTC., 'reinforces the conviction that the market will move towards remote computing and that non-CPU equipment will be a continually increasing portion of the business.' It is a conclusion to which everybody else in the lower echelons of IBM came to at least five years before.

*   *   *

Which leads naturally to computers: the use that IBM makes of those hundreds of millions of dollars worth of its own systems and technology. IBM, of course, does all the standard things that corporations do with computers, it would be poor advertising if it did not. Furthermore, it often does them long before other companies get around to it—IBM is used as a test bed. Thus, in August 1971, the Management Committee was being told that CMIS, a logistics system to control the manufacturing of parts and assemblies, was going to cost IBM Domestic over $200 million, that this system would involve 1100 programs, that the software was good, and that there already was activity within IBM to try to bring some of those programs out on the market as products. (It is interesting to note, however, that IBM finds it just as difficult to quantify cost savings and benefits as anyone else does. The committee minute carries the note '. . . pointed out, and all agreed, that cost savings will be difficult to prove.')

CMIS is the Domestic version of a system later installed in World Trade, whose major systems also link in to Armonk. The many systems installed make it possible to connect sales offices with production, via the various HQ, which enables management to be kept informed of what is in progress. Those same systems can be used for communications and, of course, are used to disseminate engineering changes. When one runs production on a totally integrated basis, it is essential that all the plants are kept informed of any changes made. At the plants themselves, IBM has computers where other corporations have people. It uses its systems for everything from the production of engineering drawings and circuit diagrams, to personnel files, accounts, and the control of plant heating and lighting, something out of which considerable capital (and savings) can be made in the energy conscious days of the mid-seventies.

It is, however, Armonk which has the best toys. The world wide networks allow corporate management to monitor on a regular and routine basis what is happening in the field, another way of keeping check on what is loosely termed 'management' out in the field and what it is doing.

Inside Armonk IBM operates a large information retrieval system, which allows managers to examine hosts of files and data, to browse, search, select and sort out information held, as well as communicate with each other. That system has surfaced on the market in STAIRS (Storage and Information Retrieval System). The more advanced IBM Armonk version is an on-line and called AQUARIUS, 'A Query and Retrieval Interactive Utility System' (see Chapter 14).

AQUARIUS, of course, is no more than a logical extension of the technology. It would not, however, be IBM if it had not thought up ways to make use of computers which, if not necessarily unique, are a little unusual. Thus the same modelling techniques used in the breakdown of the market and the study of its interactions, or in the PCM studies, can have other applications. One of them uses the techniques at the most trivial of levels, but one which fits IBM's profit pre-occupations very nicely. It has long been a standard joke within IBM that the more organised it has become, the longer it takes to pay; the less likelihood there is of anybody's obtaining his payments on time (apart from salary cheques—that would never do). Today, however, IBM often gives the appearance of prompt payment without the reality. IBM has devised a system which will allow the best of both worlds: this pays accounts on the basis of the maximum clearing time possible. It has been so devised that wherever you may be, IBM will draw a cheque on one of its accounts (180 banks throughout the United States) which is as far from you in clearing time as the banking system mechanics will allow. Thus IBM is able to add a week at least to the time it will retain the cash in its own account; that week of course represents extra income in that the cash can stay out earning interest on the market much longer. This is but one aspect of a computerised money management system in which computers play a substantial part. They need to, for IBM has substantial liquid assets, mostly out on the short term money markets earning interest (nearly $340 million in 1974).

The money is not simply that which arises from trading profit: there is also substantial cash which arises from one of its major holds over its employees, its ability to sell them a dollar for eighty-five cents (though that is predicated upon the stock market, at worst remaining steady, at best continuing to grow).* What IBM does is to offer employees shares in the corporation (up to ten per cent of their salary) at 85% of the market price on the 1st of July each year. This has been an effective way of bringing in cash: in 1973, IBM's employees bought more than $300 million worth of

---

* When it does not, problems can arise. Thus, in 1974, reports kept on coming through of IBM insiders selling their IBM stock. Among them were a clutch of Vice-Presidents and other officers, including the Corporation Treasurer, Corporation Secretary, and the President of Field Engineering. It was noticeable that while the reports monotonously indicated that they were selling, nobody in IBM was buying. One could well ask 'what did they know' and leave suspicion hanging in the air. The reason for the selling is probably much more mundane. Many of the executives are believed to have borrowed to purchase their stock, figuring that the differential between the interest rate they would have to pay and the appreciation due to a rising market would more than cover the difference. But that was on a rising market: and the market was doing anything but that in late 1974, falling at one time as much as 40% from the high of the same year.

85 cents on the dollar stock, which no doubt went to swell IBM's hefty liquid assets.

*   *   *

One of the outcomes of the use of the business school techniques/computer processes are the Grey Books. The Grey Book programmes have been running since 1966, and nothing is quite so illustrative of the differences between IBM's methodology and everybody else's than the way they have evolved.

In any normal bureaucracy a format once fixed is usually adhered to at least for more than five minutes. It is not so within IBM—what IBM seeks is as complete and relevant information as is available and useful, and if the Grey Book format and procedure has to be stretched to accommodate it, stretched it will be, thus the Series 370, 155, 165, 145 and 135 Grey Books differ, the last being much more thorough, clear and revealing than the others—reflecting the fact that they are separated in time.

The basic Grey Book format contains three sections. One puts the product in the context of IBM's existing product and includes the all-important Blue Letter which is the release of product information to marketing; the claim of what the product will do and the terms on which it is to be offered. Section Two contains the forecast and deals with how the product compares to that offered by competition. With Section Three one reaches the full flower of IBM mechanics, the analyses of costs, forecasts of profit—there is no loss forecast, however, for products nowadays just would not get to the Grey Book stage unless a profit can be seen to exist, however the profit may be arrived at. This section also carries a summary of pricing and how the price was calculated. (Much of all this, of course, was computer generated.)

At the real core of the Grey Books lies the IBM answer to the problem of migration: how IBM is to shift an existing user from his present model to the larger and faster one with which IBM will seek to replace it. It is not a question of the user indicating a need: if IBM were to wait for that, little would happen.

The problem is put at its starkest in the 370/145 Grey Book, where the migration of a 360/40 user to a 370/145 is discussed as follows: 'If however the customer wanted the same capacity as he previously had with his [360] Model 40, he would get it for an increase of 10% in rental.'

So much for the notion that the costs of computing are falling.

It is in the Grey Books that one finds part of the answer: the 'mid-life kickers', pre-planned enhancements to a new product line to be announced at a later time, enhancements which do so much to destroy IBM's competition and to keep the user off balance. Thus the 135 Grey Book gives four separate dates on which new 135 linked product will be announced, indicates first customer shipment dates, and designates both announcement and first customer shipment dates for the 135's successor, the first four years ahead, the second five years.

What gives the Grey Books their strength, as the excerpts which follow show, is their clarity.

M135 ANNOUNCEMENT P&L's

Domestic Summary ($ in millions)

	Revenue	Profit	Per cent
PRICING LIFE			
[48 months]			
CPU & Memory	$1202	$332	27·7
Features	452	139	30·8
Sub-total	1654	471	28·5
DASD [Direct Access			
Storage Devices]	$ 633	$201	31·7
Tape	372	76	20·4
Printer	288	98	34·1
Card	169	42	24·9
Commun[ications]	23	6	26·9
Sub-total	1485	423	28·5
Total System	$3139	$894	28·5

COST ANALYSIS

A cost breakdown of the Pricing Life P&L [Profit and Loss] for the M135 CPU and memory gives the reader a fairly

M135 ANNOUNCEMENT FORECAST

	1972	1973	1974	1975	1976	1977	1978	1979	1980	1981	1982
Lease Accepts	607	1141	786	526	492	466	199				
Purchase Accepts	144	248	158	84	44	19					
TOTAL ACCEPTS	751	1389	944	610	536	485	199				
REMOVALS	0	29	157	325	442	489	861	679	535	434	266
Lease Inventory	607	1719	2348	2549	2599	2576	1914	1235	700	266	0
Purchase Inventory	144	392	550	634	678	697	697	697	697	697	697
TOTAL INVENTORY	751	2111	2898	3183	3277	3273	2611	1932	1397	963	697

good idea of what the major cost areas are and where the key profit levers reside.

	Dollars	% of Revenue
Manufacturing	$222 M	18·5
Reconditioning	5	·5
Engineering	14	1·1
CE [Customer Engineering]	87	7·2
Scrap & Rework	4	·3
Other Direct	8	·7
Apportionments	465	38·7
Profit Contingency	65	5·4

MANUFACTURING

Although Manufacturing is easily the largest single area of directly estimated expense in the M135 program, responsibility for approximately 75% of this cost rests with CD [Components Division] and not SMD [Systems Manufacturing Division]. The memory technology, Phase 21, absorbs about 50% of each new build cost, while the MST-2 logic cost accounts for another 25%. Both technologies are cost sensitive to quantity variations and yield percentages. The performances of East Fiskhill, Burlington, and Endicott CPM are, therefore, as vital to the financial success of the M135 as the effectiveness of Kingston in providing the power and the assembly and test functions.

FIELD ENGINEERING

For every *$2.50 spent to build* an M135, *$1.00* will be expended over *48* months to maintain it in the field. The cost of this Field Engineering effort can be sub-divided into five elements. Shown as per cents of CPU and memory revenue, they break down as follows:

Hardware Labor	1·5%
Software Labor	3·4
Installation & Removal	1·0
Training	·7
Parts	·6
TOTAL	7·2

From all indications, the M135 should prove to be a marketing and financial success for IBM. It is aimed at the midsection of the market where IBM has a very large base and where considerable growth in compute power and applications is expected. Those customers that need or desire more function will find that the M135 can provide plenty of it *without imposing that much of a price increase over their present equipment* [italics added]. Enthusiastic reports from the sales force and the very high order rate following announcement were viewed as confirmation that a good price/performer was indeed being offered to the M25 [360/25] and M30 [360/30] marketplace.

Financially, the M135 should also perform well. On a worldwide systems basis, it was expected to generate $5.5 billion of revenue over its *Pricing Life and earn $1.6 billion in pro tax profits* [italics added]. The program has the potential of earning considerably more for the Corporation if its life can be extended beyond 48 months per build. The likelihood of this occurring is good based on the *Forecast's life per build of 70 months* [italics added].

The Grey Books may not make the lightest of reading but they are relatively digestible. They arose as the result of a long process of work, one which usually begins with something much simpler: a flip chart. The flip chart is as critical to the IBM method of working as any of the complex mechanisms so far mentioned.*

How can something so simple as flip charts be turned into a subject which cannot be disposed of in two sentences? Though in abstract the flip chart may be as dull at IBM as anywhere else, the IBM reality is a different story. Flip charts at IBM are yet another way of life; not just one flip chart but flip charts in tens of thousands, for they are IBM's basic presentation medium. The flip chart has one major advantage: flip chart presentation forces material into a structure. It requires order, and order and structuring are key elements in IBM's success.

The flip charts have been developed out of the simple presenta-

---

*There was a point where this book was almost flippantly titled: 'At the Sign of the Crossed Flip Charts'.

tion routines that Mr Watson Snr used to give in the company's early days, the days when blackboards served as the medium that today is a flip chart, and carried basic slogans—short, easy-to-understand messages to an often poorly educated, follow-my-leader audience, the days when Mr Watson Snr used to write on the blackboard: 'THINK. THINK IN BIG FIGURES. Study. Learn. Teach. Learn the things not to do, Don't guess—know. A man is known by the company he keeps, a company by the men it keeps. All men should be judged on their records', and the like. Today, all salesmen, systems engineering and programming staff, and almost everybody within IBM's managerial ranks, are at home with the flip chart, and there will be provision for a flip chart presentation in almost all working offices.

IBM's flip charts no longer carry just idiot reinforcement messages for the IBM masses. Now they are a much wider-ranging medium, used for the presentation of the most complex data, from sales pitches to future system studies. They are more likely to carry the visual shorthand of the accountant, engineer, programmer and analyst, mathematician, planner and manager: flow charts, bar graphs, scatter diagrams, comparative analyses, time/investment dollars, investment/sales and other ratios. Indeed, many of the IBM internal analyses of the competition, as in the war on the PCMs, were presented to management on flip charts.

Flip charts, then, have evolved. They have not only evolved in these dimensions but have also evolved in another. The flip chart has become the IBM executive version of Peanuts' blanket, a necessary prop without which little can be done.

It was then to be expected that such an essential aid to executive happiness, effectiveness and stability would not be allowed to remain simple and unassuming: that would be too much to ask. As in all other essential corporate toys the world over, the IBM flip chart has become irretrievably linked with status, and there is now a flip chart/status mythology. At the bottom of the ladder the frame on which the chart is placed will continue to be the straight and simple blackboard type construction, complete with two hooks on which the presenter can hang his chart and a bar across them to make sure that everything doesn't fall down as the sheets are flipped over.

As you progress, and as the data becomes more commercially

sensitive, so that simple easel becomes more complex—complete with wooden covers which can be closed and locked round the charts at night. However, security in IBM, like anything else, depends on status. Some easels have covers which will only extend across the front. (If you care to stand on a chair, said a former executive, you can often pull the charts out one by one, read them, then one by one slide them back in again.)

At the top, such a possibility has been guarded against. There, the flip chart presentation mechanism can be even more complex: built into the wall, it can be pulled out for a presentation and then pushed back again when the presentation is over, and its doors securely locked.

There is, of course, provision for the carrying of flip charts. The Corporate staff often have them—cases made of the best leather, which have become a status symbol and now also tend to be presented as prizes at Hundred Per Cent Clubs. Behind all this comes computer aided flip chart production, and such Ole buzz phrases as 'What this corporation needs is a flip chart data bank'.

It is obvious that one cannot have thousands of flip charts without some element of standardisation. The crucial element is the standardisation of the width between the hooks, so that any IBM chart can be hung on any IBM hooks in any IBM location or office.

But this was not always the case. Not so long ago, there was one set of non-standard width separation hooks in IBM. They belonged to Vin Learson: and for that there was a reason. Learson might disapprove of other people playing games, but that disapproval did not, naturally enough, extend to himself. The non-standard hooks had an object, to keep other people away from Learson's own flip charts. They created a problem for those who came in prepared to give Learson a presentation, one prepared on charts with standard hook separations—a part of the continual one-upmanship wars that IBM executives play with each other. 'What Learson wanted to see was how someone who had not been warned would respond, what would he do'.

The snag with flip charts is that they are often large, bulky things. There came the time when IBM was going through its annual security panic, and someone—reputedly Frank Cary—made the brilliant deduction that if you were to go round Armonk looking at all the flip charts in the offices, 'you would find a pile of stuff on them, and that on semi-public display. There would be the five-year plan, and the three-year plan in the greatest detail'.

Thus, one Saturday, one of the executives went in to see for himself. Sure enough, there it all was, every detail about every strategy, every product. He took all the flip charts away and locked them in a conference room. The following Monday, when the massed ranks of Corporate turned up, the flip charts were gone. What made them notice was described by one of those present: 'Whenever anyone came in with almost any broad query, you would go to your flip charts for the answer. And when you noticed its absence and set a search in motion, you soon discovered that they had been locked away, and you would have to go and get them.

'The message came over loud and clear'.

Today, one can tell those who have worked in Armonk, they have the same concern for security as any good intelligence worker. Within the computer business, ex-IBM/Armonk executives can often be identified simply by the lack of paper they have on display and their habit of checking to see if all paper has been put away and locked up before they leave the office at night.

The IBM passion for security makes itself apparent in other ways. The papers are full of product referenced simply by numbers/letters or code names, some twenty of the former and ninety of the latter, and those names feature heavily in correspondence. Why code names? Shorthand, and need to know.

The code names range from the trivial: Vanilla, Apricot, Eric, through genuine acronyms, 'Raid' for Rapid Automatic Inscribing Device, to the mythological and Wagnerian: Apollo, Faust, Galaxy, Hydra, Midas, Olympus, Zeus. There is only one piece of humour, and no doubt because of American–British cultural differences, the humour is unconscious: Data entry equipment, code-named Poke (it would be as if an American used the code name Knockup).*

*   *   *

---

* These Anglo-American differences also featured in the code names for a set of units which made up one financial system. The American units were code named using the names of the signers of the American Declaration of Independence. The lone British built unit in the system was named by its IBM U.K. creators 'Burgoyne'.

It would be possible to continue with this topic, to become involved in the detail of the routines that Armonk makes IBM executives perform, the constant involvement of management in the organisation of IBM, the seemingly endless analyses of the world, whether it be the state of the economy everywhere, of the industry, of specific competitors, or of the emotional state of IBM's employees, what are white–black attitudes to each other and is there anything that need be done about it? how did the employees take to the attrition programme? And on and on.

But to continue would be pointless. For IBM does little that is not done somewhere by some other organisation or corporation. It simply does more—to cover as many organisational options as its management can conceive of, to do it all, and to do it as well as possible.

If there is a trick to IBM, it lies in its belief in structure and its ability, almost reflex, to allot one man or however many men are required to look after any task at hand and to do so quickly once management has so decided. Once the men have been allotted, IBM's managerial mechanics are organised to deal with the results of their work. The machine will filter these reports, will refine, and if necessary send it back down the line six times until all conceivable options are covered and management are sure that they have it right. From there on the corporate machine has the ability to synthesise and to extract what is relevant, and again, almost as a reflex it issues orders, sets courses of action in motion and has action taken. The system is so organised that once the orders have been given, the actions that should be taken, are taken; management has the lines of communication so established that it is connected to the real world of IBM; signals do flow up and down, events do happen.

It is, of course, a system which can only be run by a rich, high-mark-up company, for it is, by anyone else's standards, a wasteful and expensive system. But it works. Yet after a time any close observer cannot but help feel ambivalent about its nature. On one side is a machine which can act quite ruthlessly in the defence of the ends of IBM without much reference to the needs of the societies in which that machine operates: a machine seemingly dedicated solely to the aggrandisement and profit of those involved.

On the other side one has a system which cossets many if not most of those within it, one which has all the appearance of knowing where it is headed, which seems to have a sense of purpose and with all the appurtenances of a safe haven for those within it in an uncertain and unsafe world.

Of course it may not be very efficient in the abstract, the organisational solutions chosen may not be the optimum, but this is not necessary to consider. All that is demanded of the IBM machine is that it should work more effectively than those it encounters, than those with which it has to deal. And up till now it has certainly done that.

As for its effects on people: Papes and his colleagues have done no more than add a hefty load of refinements to an organisation which was already paper-bound, one in which rampant individualism was not very welcome. What resulted is a heavily layered and structured world, a unique world, in which any tendencies anyone may have to make any meaningful decisions on their own are carefully curtailed.

It is best put in the words of a former, very senior, corporate staffer who naturally enough had come up through marketing. It is as good a summary of the differences between the world that Armonk has created and the rest of commercial country as one could wish for:

'Leaving IBM? . . . It took me months to settle down . . . some never make it . . . Soon, I had to sack some hundreds of people. Now I knew how to hide from union people, I knew how to manage through them, but I had never seriously had to deal with them before.

'Suddenly, I saw dimensions of business I had never seen before; contracts, financing, stock options. In IBM you are so buffered . . . You open up your mail in the morning, and out in the field here's this Blue Letter, here's this product, and here's what you do. Here's this guy and this manual, and behind you there's this other guy. Fill out the forms, look at the index. We like wild ducks, you know, but let's keep them within the constraints of how we like our wild ducks to fly. I had reached the point where I said, I know how to manage within the context of IBM. I know how the pyramid goes up there. I know the tremendous resources and the smart people they have, but do I know how to *manage*? It turned out that I did, but I was lucky.'

He was very lucky. For IBM has long known that its pretence

that the corporation is not run by a handful of people is a managerial fiction. There is an element of this in all companies—only IBM would carry it to the absurd limits of total denial.

IBM has long known . . . In fact, IBM has to be run by a handful of people. All companies go through phases, fads in which jogging, or T Groups, or business school techniques are seen as likely to lead to salvation and better performance. It has also been so in IBM. Not so long ago the particular route to salvation was thought of as the external executive computer and management course, in which IBM executives would meet directly with executives from other companies and compete with them in the usual end of course, 'now let us see what you have learnt', competition. IBM did not continue sending people on those courses for long, for it soon became obvious that IBM executives were being outperformed by the others. The conclusion drawn was simple: IBM executives had had little experience of making real decisions.

CHAPTER ELEVEN

Troops & Battlefield: We have ways of making you conform

In T. V. Learson's deposition in the CDC case, counsel for CDC Elmer Trousdale and T. V. Learson discuss IBM's organisational manual, impeded, as is his wont, by counsel for IBM.

As Learson looked at it, there occurred the following exchange:

Learson: 'Let me answer it. These are beautiful words. "Excellence must be a way of life." I can hang any man, or promote any man on that saying.'

Counsel for CDC: 'And have you done so?'

Learson: 'I've hung them, and I've promoted them.'

'There are few, if any, organisations anywhere in the world as completely dedicated to excellence. This philosophy has important practical consequences because, among other things, IBM people do "try harder" and the widespread knowledge that this is a way of life in IBM helps in recruiting the best people who work for the company, including many people who would otherwise pursue careers in education or government because short-run profit objectives in other businesses necessarily inhibit the creativity which far-sightedness and the quest for excellence compels'.

—Excerpt from an IBM internal document.

* * *

'I have always said IBM doesn't know how to make computers,

276

they don't know how to program at all, but what they really know how to do is sell. The genius of IBM is in marketing. Everything else, I can name six companies who can do it better.'
—Herb Grosch.

'... You know what IBM's theory is? If something doesn't work, spend more money marketing it.'
—former IBM executive.

IBM really spends money on marketing. The table below shows IBM marketing expenditure as a percentage of IBM's gross from 1956 through 1968:

1956	14·3%
1957	15·5%
1958	13%
1959	13·7%
1960	15·9%
1961	16%
1962	16%
1963	17·2%
1964	17·6%
1965	18·6%
1966	18·7%
1967	17%
1968	16·4%

These figures appeared in an internal IBM unbundling study. To get some idea of what this means in terms of cash, consider the five years of Series 360 marketing effort which this covers. If one were to take out all non-computer related marketing effort, this would still have meant an IBM marketing expenditure of well over $3,500 million. [Pre-unbundling, it should be noted, IBM considered that its Systems Engineering service (software) was part of the marketing effort, and it was accordingly covered within the marketing expenses.]

*   *   *

As the record has shown, promotion to the top of IBM depends on the right career path: it is essential to have come through the ranks of the fighting troops and to have commanded such troops.

The only IBM briefcases which contain the hopes of advancing to senior status and the power to make people jump, a six-figure dollar income, and access to the full range of executive toys are those of the men of marketing.

What kind of people are they? In terms of service the gap between top and bottom in IBM may be of the order of fifteen to twenty-five years' IBM service, but at the bottom they are still largely men, ensuring that IBM will continue to be male-dominated well into the future. Of the more than two hundred DP branch managers in the U.S.A., the key command of fighting troop positions from which the promotion selections are made, less than ten are women (the end of 1973)—and these are the product of the climate of the early seventies and IBM's reaction to it.

Generally, the men of marketing are nominally Protestant Christians. (The quota concerning Catholics—and Jews—particularly went overboard a long time ago. In the early fifties the place seemed to be full of the smoother offspring of the Boston Irish. There was no quota on blacks or women, the question of employing them in managerial, professional or marketing positions simply did not arise.) But with minor blurring at the edges, IBM remains what it generally was, male, white and essentially middle-American.

A distinction, however, must be made between IBM sales and field forces, and those of manufacturing and administration, between the IBM troops that the customer will see and those he will not. The 'rules' apply to the first group much more than the second. No exception to the rule ever arrived in the field force without clear senior management involvement. IBM management shapes that force according to what it thinks the sector of the market will expect from IBM, and thus there will always be some minority representation in accounts where minorities are in preponderance or in control.

That marketing force—4,000 salesmen in American IBM DPD and 4,200 systems engineers as of the middle of 1971—is generally much younger than the rest of IBM. Particularly in the marketing area, IBM tries to hire only the young. It is not alone in this practice, but it is one of the worst offenders. The cult of youth and the equation between youth, dynamism and growth is a regular and public IBM management preoccupation, one which comes up at one AGM after another.

However, like discrimination on grounds of sex, religion and colour, this is not something to which IBM wishes to have attention pointed. Age discrimination, too, conflicts with fair employment practice laws in force in America and does little to enhance the desired public image of IBM as a socially responsible employer. However, IBM does discriminate, and not just on grounds of age. The MRC minutes contain references to minority employment percentages which should not be exceeded within periods stated—though the theoretical norms should be higher. Whatever justice and the law may require, IBM management persists in treating these issues as if they should be under IBM control, not under society's control. This is so whether the discussion concerns colour, ethnic origin or sex.

'The blacks and women? [Management] play the numbers game, and they will promote enough blacks and enough women and put them in enough places to stay a step ahead of the game. But I guarantee it is a contrived game, it's not a natural thing at all.'

In this area, then, IBM sails as close to the wind as ingenuity and the bureaucratic procedures of the policing agencies it will deal with allow, which gives it considerable leeway.

In marketing, the result is a force which generally has the pre-requisites for promotion noted above. But these are not the only pre-requisites.

Where IBM really differs from the rest of the American corporate world is in the thoroughness with which it has settled on a particular type as befitting the needs of the corporation and its management. To ask the question, what sort of men man marketing, is to presuppose that there is a relatively clear cut answer, and that alone would be unusual: the answer *is* generally clear.

IBM, once these basics are out of the way, tries to match its would-be employees against personality profiles. The mechanism is a culture-loaded standard test, tests much under challenge as they load in favour of the factors outlined above and cannot therefore be entirely justified in terms of ability to do the job, whatever it may be.

One does not have to rely on those tests, even were the results in the public domain, to obtain an idea of the types that IBM actively seeks: all that is required is that one know enough IBM salesmen of both the past and the present.

The personality profile of an IBM salesman would probably look like this. By background, IBM salesmen are generally Solid Middle-America, or its equivalent elsewhere; the Beitzels of this world are the exception rather than the rule. They are unlikely to have gone to the better universities and colleges or to have been high level academic performers, because, with the exception of its professional ranks, IBM distrusts these. Where they have gone to the more prestigious institutions, the courses they had taken are unlikely to have been for anything as old-fashioned or esoteric as education for education's sake; those who end up in IBM went to college to obtain qualifications which would equip them for a job in corporate country, and the education will have been such that all one could initially do with it would be to get a job in that country.

It will probably have been a very formal education in the sense that one man teaches and the others listen, a methodology with which IBM feels happy, for it uses it in its own training schools. It is the authoritarian method, which tells one much about IBM.

The IBM entrant will have been a worker, who has had to apply himself to make his grades. IBM wants those with a proven capability for fitting into the system. That point is best summed up in a view of the University of Chicago found in TJW Jnr's files. After noting that the University was predominantly IBM-oriented and that its President was in close association with top IBM executives, as were other members of the university's administrative and academic staff (it is typical of IBM to list them in that order), the memo contained this sentence: 'However, there are also many free thinking individuals'.

IBM is not fond of those. Nor is it fond of university political activists, ex-Presidents of the Student Union, members of the university drama club, writers for the university paper and the like.

One of the key figures in British television, a man with just such a background, tells of the time he came down from Oxford, wondering what to do and thinking that he might like to give IBM a try. He applied for a job: after the interviews he was told that they thought his blend of talents might be more suited to television. So he tried there and has not regretted it since.

Those same IBM tests contain questions about sport: IBM

likes sportsmen, but not all sportsmen. It prefers those who have played team sports, preferably the rougher, body contact sports. 'The place is full of former second-rate college quarterbacks.'

A former executive put it more politely: 'IBM just tries to hire winners. Aggressive young guys who are ambitious ... and the fact that you may have been a quarterback on an Ivy League football team won't hurt you.'

Here IBM is team think, group think, there's little trace of any individualism (outside the field of research, and there IBM is buying already proven talent, and if that is the price that has to be paid, IBM is prepared to pay it. In the labs, it will put up with eccentrics who treat the walls as a practice rockface during their lunch hours: it will not put up with them anywhere else).

Sports, in the sense that IBM understands them, are team sports of the each-man-does-his-bit kind, the whole is greater than the sum of the individual parts, in which to achieve success the individual will have to subordinate himself. It follows that he will have a proper respect, innate or instilled, for leadership and authority.

'IBM management frequently make comparisons between their salesmen and professional teams. Vince Lombardi [the American football coach] is their idol. Win at all costs; there's no room for the second place.'

'IBM marketing is very much patterned and structured on the military, and goes in for the same kind of crap. You know that thing that the boxer Tunney said? "It's the fourteenth round and you've got to go one more round, you're bleeding, and you can hardly pick up your arms. But you pick them up and you get out there." '

'IBM constantly motivates using the techniques of the Marines, the professional athlete. If you are not a rah-rah boy, you are pegged to go out'.

This is a picture of the IBM salesman essentially as a doer, not a thinker; a sheep, not a goat. It is a case of tunnel vision by inclination; of the selection of people whose psychological profiles will be such that they need and are responsive to authority, which provides the atmosphere in which they perform best. IBM does not obtain the individual talents by which the West was won, or seek to do so: it wants those by which the West was settled.

What IBM wants and what IBM has set out to get are modularly independent people, IBM will build the group, so that there will be no confusion over loyalty. And there is no such confusion. Almost as a matter of course, IBM really, truly and sincerely believes that IBM is good for you, and where it can be proved that it is not, IBM's employees are absolved from the responsibility because they were only following orders. The strength of IBM is to be found here: it is precisely because IBM is so carefully structured with every decision having to be made according to guidelines set from above, orders for which those above take the responsibility, that IBM is so effective. The strength of IBM, then, is to be found in the very bureaucratic processes which clearly delimit duties and responsibilities. Nowhere is this more the case than in marketing.

To build the group, IBM would prefer and has so organised itself that it starts with the inexperienced. The would-be IBM salesman may not have come to IBM straight from school or university, but IBM generally prefers him not to have been a salesman. Today, he will often arrive in IBM in answer to an advertisement of the you-can-have-your-cake-and-eat-it-too variety: come and solve industry's problems and get well paid into the bargain. IBM will seldom take on anybody over thirty to thirty-five years of age, except where a sudden management panic shows that IBM lacks the skills and the particular expertise in its sales force, and that the new product, whatever it may be, requires that such expertise be on display.

Generally, a salesman will spend up to eighteen months being trained, six months of it in classroom work, and twelve months out in the field doing field training, much of which consists of training by doing, acting as back-up man: making calls, helping to write proposals and similar tasks. IBM prides itself on being able to weed out those it considers unsuitable within six months, so that when examination time comes, what the examination determines is really what one will do in IBM, not whether one will stay with the corporation or not.

Thus salesmen leave the nursery, moulded into the desired image. An elite force, a dynamic force, a young force: it had better be, for if the image IBM wishes to present to the customer is that technological change is its servant, it does not wish to have its front-line troops look as if they would be more at home with yesterday's technology (even if they are).

That the sales force is the elite is also recognised within IBM by the ambitious who may have followed a different career path. During the managerial wriggling which led to the end of IBM's traditional no-firing policy, IBM decided to boost its sales force by allowing other employees to opt for sales. Hundreds almost immediately changed over, many—though not all—under no pressure.

The basic skills and techniques of marketing as they would be found in any major corporation are standard practice in IBM; they are a matter of a well-organised routine. IBM trains, teaches the techniques of selling, provides back-up, and will send its men running at the first slight indication that an order is coming its way. IBM has a clutch of sales motivating tricks which it deploys, and management gives every indication to its salesmen that it cares about what they do; it does all this expensively and effectively. But this is routine. What distinguishes IBM from the rest of the computer world lies in two areas, management support of marketing, and organisational support. First, marketing is the prime consideration of management—and why should it not be, IBM is almost entirely run by men who have come up through marketing. The marketing ethos reaches way up to the top and is not confined to the sales organisation. Corporate management is not solely concerned with targets and plans, whether or not they have been achieved, and with after-the-event recording and—where necessary—correction. Corporate management plays a much more active role, going further than the fixing of prices to be bid on major contracts or reserving to itself the decisions on whether or not IBM will bid on a request for procurement from a possible competitor (as in the case of a request from Xerox).

Senior management at both DP and Corporate levels are kept informed of the progress of competitive bids made by IBM and are often able to track through progress before the order is won or lost. It is part of the job of senior IBM executives to help in sales, to think up ways in which possibles can be turned into definites. They also see win and loss reports, which list the significant gains and losses and the reasons for both. Reports of this kind in evidence in the CDC case showed a circulation list which included the then IBM President T. V. Learson, Corporate Marketing and the senior executives of the DP Group. The reports were full of phrases like 'excellent account coverage', 'excellent rapport with the customer', 'close coverage and complete account control', and 'executive coverage', the last pertaining to a Federal Reserve Bank installation in Kansas City where IBM won over Burroughs, with the bank paying nearly $50,000 a year more than it would have had IBM not been successful. Those phrases concern instances where IBM has won. They differ in cases where IBM has lost and can become thunderous when the loss is an existing large IBM installation. Thus, the loss of $52,000 a month in rental can be accompanied by 'Reasons: Loss of account control—ineffective IBM sales effort. (Disciplinary action taken.)'

That account control, in some cases, has almost been formalised. At the end of 1973, THINK covered the creation of twenty-eight management posts and inferred that more were on the way. These were the Account Executives, special coordinators assigned to large customers. Those customers included Eastman Kodak, U.S. Steel, Goodyear Tire and Rubber, AT&T Long Lines, Texaco, and the U.S. Postal Service.

Nothing sums up account control better than the description of the job of the account executive with Goodyear. 'When he joined IBM in 1961, he was assigned to Goodyear, and has since served as a systems engineer, marketing rep, and later senior marketing manager on the account. When he was appointed account executive in March 1973, *he was about as familiar with his client's systems, needs and long-range objectives as anyone in Goodyear itself.*' [Italics added.]

IBM does not need to go this far in order to subject the customer to pressure. These executives are on accounts where IBM fears no competition; but where it does, where there is a possibility that IBM might lose a major installation replacement order to a competitor, senior executives are often found running to try to talk the would-be offender round, sometimes when that 'offender' insists on not talking to them. At that point IBM is not averse to using any methods to hand: money man will talk to money man, and the customer can receive a phone call—'Hey, you had better see these guys.' For example, when Digital Equipment Corporation decided to try to enter the general-purpose market with its DEC10, a highly, competitive version of a previous DEC system, it ran into just this sort of problem.

DEC's marketing force is thinly spread. The local force often consists of one salesman. He called on the customer extolling DEC's wares, and as far as DEC was concerned, that was often all that happened. The IBM reaction went something like this: 'Within a week IBM had fixed up to come into the would-be customer. They sent senior men around, teams of them. The IBM Vice-President would take the user's chairman out to play golf, the regional manager would take the company president out to lunch, and the local managers would take the company's DP manager out and beat him to death.'

The involvement of senior management in marketing has led to the second set of reasons why IBM's marketing is so skilful, the additional set of tricks that IBM performs which make that marketing so effective. The managerial specialities of IBM, the KCSI and task force mechanisms, the forecasting, the company information systems, these are complemented by a group of techniques whose first aim is the support of marketing. Thus, they need to be looked at in the sales context, though their impact is felt throughout the corporation: the requirements of marketing will pervade every major decision, from the research that is to be done to the location of plants, offices and facilities that are to be built.

Prime among these specially devised tricks is COMSTAT. It used to be the proud boast of IBM that its marketing, sales and service organisation was second to none: IBM employees were never off duty. This was an image carefully fostered as it had been by AT&T and its associated 'phone companies, and it was just as true.*

It may still be true, but they are not there simply to render assistance: your friendly local IBM salesman, the local systems engineer (software service) and the local field engineer (hardware service) are also your friendly local-neighbourhood IBM spies.

Among the IBM documents put into court by Telex was a memorandum and attached script dated October 1968, which came out of the White Plains office of the then DP Division President, F. C. 'Buck' Rodgers. The memo and the script are headed 'Why COMSTAT?', COMSTAT being an acronym for Com-

---

*In 1974 . . . IBM customer engineers responded to a malfunctioning machine within one hour in 81·5 percent of emergency calls and within two hours in 92·2 percent of such calls.' (IBM Justice suit trial brief.)

petitive Statistics, an IBM internal service controlled by DP Division's Commercial Analysis Department.

COMSTAT is an important internal service,* because it is the basic raw data intelligence gathering system around which much of IBM's intelligence analysis activities are organised. The memo states that the taped sound track/linked slide presentation (typically it begins with music) is designed primarily for sales personnel, systems engineers and members of (DP) branch administration, and is to be viewed during a regularly scheduled sales meeting.

The presentation begins by discussing why the COMSTAT system is essential and then proceeds to impress on the listeners that the information they gather reaches the attention of IBM management, and that the input is used by them in the creation of marketing policies.

The presentation recounts COMSTAT's workings. The salesman completes an entry form for any competitive situation which he has not previously reported, a form also used when reporting a win or a loss. The win–loss report is given express treatment within IBM to appraise DP HQ, and where a loss occurs that review report must be completed within ten days. In return, the branch is provided with regular COMSTAT territory listings which are updated monthly, and which, the presentation states, 'is a prospect list for you'.

The presentation stresses that COMSTAT is used outside the direct sales situation, and that information obtained from it plays a part in the preparation of many different competitive reports, including manufacturer/industry revenue summaries and exception reports highlighting unusual conditions. These are for use by management: indeed, the presentation stresses that the reports go to Corporate, Group staff, Systems Development Division HQ and plant locations. The COMSTAT file resides on the DP Division management information system computers, and there are (at time of presentation) over a thousand terminals installed in

* It is a service whose importance IBM management has tried to devalue. The IBM trial brief in the Justice suit is full of comments about how little attention management pays to it and how inefficient it is. It became IBM's interest once COMSTAT became widely known to publicly downgrade it as much as possible. If IBM could not disown it, IBM could try to show that it did not pay much attention to the results. This was not the case in the late sixties, much the reverse: COMSTAT was treated as the script maintains.

regional and Divisional locations which have access to it.

One might still be thinking that what interests IBM is its own equipment: such is not the case. Slide 24 and the associated commentary spell it out:

'All the reports which are distributed are built up from the individual product entries which are submitted to COMSTAT. When a competitive manufacturer announces a new system, we generally hear conflicting reports about the sales activity of this equipment. To completely evaluate its impact precise and factual information from each salesman who is affected must be available.'

The presentation continues: 'It is true that we are often able to recognise market trends and requirements for new products by other means than COMSTAT, but the evidence to support a judgement frequently comes from your competitive reporting.'

COMSTAT forms go into considerable detail. The salesman is expected to list competitors' equipment by product type, and each form has a competitor's status code.

'The status code describes whether the hardware is being proposed, is on order, is installed, or is installed but scheduled for displacement. We are trying to track each product through its life cycle and the status code identifies its stage of life. Since our objective is to track equipment [through] its entire life cycle, it becomes important to report the existence of competition as early in this cycle as possible, ideally before an order is placed.'

To ensure that the troops understand how to cope with doubtful situations, they are told to report any situation when the competition has a 20% or greater chance of winning: it eliminates chance taking.

The terminology used is that of market research, in fact, towards the end of the presentation, the system is referred to as 'this comprehensive market research system'. However, even the language cannot camouflage the fact that it is primarily an intelligence operation, encompassing all those who enter users' premises as a matter of course in the execution of their IBM duties. This is spelt out as clearly as such a sensitive topic would ever be during a presentation: 'Systems engineers and field engineers should also be alert to the presence of competition, and must keep the salesman informed. COMSTAT needs everyone's cooperation to be successful.'

COMSTAT, however, is only one form of business intelligence, and at that perhaps the most innocuous. Some are uglier. Management is provided with regular lists of suppliers to IBM, changes in existing relationships and new relationships. Those engaged in business that is competitive will cease to be suppliers to IBM at the first available opportunity, those who are not already users of IBM equipment can expect to be called on to become so. One major European supplier, a user of competitive equipment, has been on the IBM list for years, and IBM has devoted considerable resources to try to make him switch. The chairman has been brought to the local IBM headquarters and has been much flattered by the amount of interest IBM shows in the supplies of his company. Nobody is so tactless or crude as to say directly: 'Hey, Jack, what about making it a two-way business?', but the inference is there all the same. (Thus far he has been either remarkably shrewd or remarkably obtuse. It had still not become a two-way business in 1974.)

But even this technique could be said to be legitimate. Other methods, however, cross the borderline, and what is more they are standard IBM practice. IBM sales branches keep individual dossiers on the companies they deal with, including who their key people are and their attitudes to IBM. In the case of major companies, dossiers are also kept at the level above the branch, the district, particularly in the case of large prestige accounts—the banks, insurance companies, oil companies, aerospace companies and the airlines.

The dossiers are used: IBM plays a strong hand in the hiring and firing of managers in companies in which it is interested. Thus, another IBM user and watcher:

'They over-emphasise the capability of the new generation [of computers] and over-emphasise complexity. By making it sound complex, they develop a breed of manager that cannot relate to the managers of the company but instead relate to IBM. If they simplified the language, IBM would be in big trouble. They control that DP manager, and by doing so create a rift between him and his company, a rift where there is no communication. And therefore that man has got to communicate with somebody, and that somebody is IBM. They talk of the strategy of the new generation, but you never hear them talk of saying that DP manager reports to me for all intents and purposes and therefore I control what he gets and not the company that's paying the bills.'

The effort is not solely concentrated in the sales branches. Because of the nature of the product, IBM executives and salesmen will always be talking at senior levels in other companies. They can suggest, and often do, that there are other and better ways of getting things done than the man currently running the DP installation on non-IBM equipment is using. It is in the nature of the computer business after all that almost any installation is obsolete.

Of course, nobody actually says that. It is phrased more like this: 'We have a guy who can come in and resolve this.' Indeed, cases have been known of IBM managers saying to prospective customers: 'If this guy worked for me, I'd fire him.' All this is usually discussed within the sales branch. 'Thus if some DP Manager is anti-IBM, it is not unusual for an IBM manager to say, get him fired, get rid of him.'

What IBM wants is not just the installation of its product: it wants some form of guarantee that its installation will continue. The best possible guarantee is influence with the man in charge, or the one intent on being in charge. From him IBM wants dependency.

Naturally a price has to be paid. The man becomes known in IBM as the internal salesman, usually well known within the local branch office, which if the account is large enough, will pull all the stops out to help him.

'The internal salesman? There's almost no limit. There's the usual lunching routine, the small giveaways. But they'll help him out with his technical problems. They'll help him write his reports so that he can go into the office in the morning and dictate them to his secretary. They'll put a presentation together and write it up for him so that he can present it and make it look like his own work.'

But the process does not stop there. IBM branches run a placement service: every branch has its little placement bureau, and career resumes are circulated and exchanged between branches. The only surprise about this dubious practice is the lack of security surrounding it. At least up till the start of 1973, the files in some branches were kept in the offices and often quite openly circulated. The system is documented to the branch and district level, whether or not management at even higher levels officially washes its hands of it.

'Even incompetent people who are pro-IBM will get every benefit of the doubt. They'll find him a place. But if you are anti-IBM, then as far as being involved with IBM installations in customer premises is concerned, the guy will get nowhere—at least if IBM local salesmen know about it.'

Naturally, the kind of atmosphere which this breeds will encourage people to take chances. The rule book may state that there will be no unhooking and that IBM will behave with a due regard for ethics; reality much of the time is different.

'Unhooking? When somebody has sold to an account, theoretically the IBM salesman is not supposed to go and talk to that account until it's been installed. [It is a provision included in their Consent Decree and was noted earlier in Thomas Watson's 1961 remarks.] From the time of order to the time of delivery that's a stay out period. However, if the customer should invite the IBM salesman by written letter or similar means to come in and talk ... The salesman can always call the customer and ask him to do that, and it is not an infrequent event for a salesman to do so.'

'In the fifties and early sixties there was no such thing as losing an account. That was unheard of: it wasn't acceptable. You didn't lose. A lot of harm was done because customers decided to go another way. IBM would go all the way up to the top. I call it pissing on the ashes. It's all over, but you still have to try everything. And in going up to the President, you may have hurt IBM's chances for the next fifteen years, but you've got to do it. Because every battle was like the end of the world. Every sale you couldn't lose.'

That the rules are breached is no secret to IBM or the rest of the industry. What is argued over externally is whether the rule breaking is done with the blessing and encouragement of IBM senior management or not. The pattern of attempts to influence purchasers, however, would indicate that it can only be done with the cooperation, silent or otherwise, of senior management.

'IBM is like that TV programme "Mission Impossible". You give the guy this tape which will self destruct. And he's told: Now, should you get caught, we will naturally disallow any connection with you.'

Nowhere is this more evident than in the area of public procurement at the U.S. state and local administration levels.

Rows over computer procurement, in which IBM has used the most blatant of pressure tactics to reverse decisions which have gone against them, are common: 'You are finished in this state' against the individual with the responsibility for authorising procurement; disparaging the equipment selected in place of IBM's; and using political pressure in getting IBM's local political friends to kick up a fuss in the legislature or council chamber. All these were tactics used in 1973 in such states as Delaware, Nebraska, Rhode Island and California, and in such cities as Framingham and Springfield, Massachusetts, Oakland, California, and Warwick, Rhode Island.*

Why should salesmen behave in this way? The reason is that they are under pressure. Often there is nothing else they can do if IBM management's wishes are to be achieved.

'You have to be a manager in the field. If you're promoted from salesman to headquarters, you've had it. Nobody listens to you unless you've been a field manager. Were you there, were you in combat. It's like combat infantry status. You have to be a field manager or you'll never make it to the top.

'Management? When you see them you can be pretty certain that you are in a good successful branch. Generally speaking, they only speak to the branches that are top performers; if a branch is mediocre or below, you won't grab the top people.

'They have good ways of taking care of those who are successful, and correspondingly have good ways of taking care of those who are not. You get sent to Siberia. You don't go to any of the Clubs, you don't get to the parties, etc. Naturally these people are going to exceed the bounds of fair play when necessary.'

IBM management knows it. 'The simple rule is "Don't get caught". Management know of many infractions on many occasions. They even promote people, many of whom have done things which were unscrupulous and unethical but they didn't get caught.'

However, if they do get caught, IBM will not hesitate to fire them on the spot. 'Up to branch managers, they are expendable,

---

* These are not by any means new tactics; I have a copy of an IBM letter in my files illustrating the use of similar tactics in Britain back in 1966.

though that's not to say that they like to see a branch manager go. But up at district level, they are protected.'*

What about those down below who are not protected? Someone whose face, for instance, doesn't fit, or who doesn't perform according to the level that is expected of him. The techniques used here are simple and standard. As managers have said: 'A salesman can be made to look as good or as bad as we wish. For you can play with the territory he is given, or the type of customer he is asked to serve.'

The IBM salesman is expendable. 'If they sell and perform, their future is guaranteed. But if they don't ... they are eliminated.' The ex-salesmen is being melodramatic.

One would not expect in IBM anything quite so crude or abrupt as an instant decision without its first going through a managerial gavotte, causing the offender first to run through a set procedure: there must be a decent formality in these things.

'They have steps they put offenders through. The first stage is specific performance. Instead of letting the salesman be on his own, they pretty much dictate what they expect him to do and the time by which they expect him to have it accomplished. They write him a letter and say this is what you have to accomplish and the date by which you have to do it, and you and I—the salesman, the manager—will sit down and evaluate them together.'

The next step is the improvement programme:

'You have a certain amount of time in which they meet with you periodically, and they advise you and evaluate you, and your actions are even more circumspect.'

'Really, they make you jump through hoops. People really have to do something very extraordinary to get out of this trap.'

As Gil Jones pointed out, there is a limit to motivation by fear, particularly the fear of losing one's job. There is another and more publicised side, motivation through greed.

'They would hire young guys, work them hard, pay them well and get their earnings up quickly. Look at the Hundred Percent Club, where do you go? Florida, the West Coast†, what have you,

---

*Not all are protected. It has much to do with whether one's face fits. One or two persons in the seventies have been fired for the most trivial of reasons.

† San Francisco is a favourite.

you live in the nicest hotels. The first time it's usually a revelation. He wants to take his wife there, so he goes back and runs harder.

'He makes the Hundred Percent Club and thinks how great he is. Then they parade all the winners before him, and he thinks, gosh, I'm nothing, let me go back next year, I'm going to be in that winner circle.

'I remember I had a sales contest. I had the salesmen come in early, and I brought in coffee. My wife put gold ribbons around certain cups and black ribbons around others. I handed out black ribboned cups to those who hadn't qualified and gold ribboned cups to those who had. And they sat there, the gold ribboned cup holders just sipping, the black ribboned cup holders drinking as fast as possible, anything to get rid of that cup.

'My wife said, what are you running there, a kindergarten? I said, no, it's motivation. Salesmen can be motivated by money, but after they've been on money motivation for eight or ten years, they lose it. The wife has the mink coat, they have the Cadillac, and the kids are in college, so why are they going to run?

'It's the status game,' I said.

'Right.'

The Hundred Percent Club has surfaced time and again throughout these pages. Hundred Percent Clubs are an IBM institution, and much money and time are lavished on them. The key to the Hundred Percent Club is 'the quota'. However careful the team selection and organised the back-up, IBM still needs to be able to shift iron on a consistent basis. The quota is the salesman's horizon. It is doubtful if the men who built up IBM had read Pavlov, but IBM's marketing force behaves as if they have done so.

IBM motivates by both 'Here's the good news', and 'Now here's the bad news'. The size of the quota is dependent upon the type of territory and the equipment that the salesman is dealing with. The quota works on the points principle, varying between 10 and 20 thousand points per salesman per year. Thus a salesman on the bottom end of the scale would be expected to bring in a net 10,000 points or rental income of $120,000 a year if he were to make quota.

However, expressing it this way understates its long-term worth to IBM. As all IBM equipment rentals are priced on a multiplier varying between the mid-forties up to eighty, with an average in the late forties, this being the IBM expectation of the length of time that the equipment will stay out on rental, even the salesman at the bottom end of the range will have placed equipment eventually worth at least half a million dollars of revenue to IBM. This figure excludes returns, or retirements as they are known in the trade, which in the early seventies were running at below 50%, as they should be if the salesman is not for ever going to be chasing his own tail.

[However, much of the time the salesman now is chasing his own tail. For the quota is above unscheduled returns (and these, since the start of the PCM onslaught, have sometimes been high). More important, a large part of IBM's business should come from add-on sales/rentals. In times of cost savings, these may not be as likely to go IBM's way. IBM instalations are not 'growing' at the rate that IBM management thinks they should.]

There are always quotas.

'There's always quotas. It's like the traffic cop on the beat . . . The Federal Systems Division salesmen may not officially have quotas, and IBM would officially deny that there is one. But what happens if he falls below the average for the month or the accounting period? "What the hell are you doing out there?"

'The field is unable to think objectively. They just live from day to day. Always the unannounced equipment is the panacea that's going to solve all their problems. There's always a tremendous amount of pressure from the field for an announcement. On the other side there's the engineers who never want to announce anything until it's completely finished. The irony of it is that if you didn't set an announcement date you would never finish it. IBM's toughest years were when engineering was moved out from under marketing and then you really had a battle.'

The quota system at IBM may be the salesman's horizon. It is, however, an imposed horizon and one subject to management initiated change. Rewards are structured, based on a salary and attainment of quota, having gone from a sixty salary/forty attainment-of-quota percentage split in their income in the sixties, to 90% plus 10% split. Within this management has played with various schemes, linking the accomplishments of territory objectives with a bonus plan, adding special bonuses for outright sales, but striving all the time to find acceptable structuring of salesman's income plans with NSRI (Net Sales Return on Inventory) objectives. What IBM wants is that its salesmen shift iron on a lease basis: outright sales are regarded as a moveable feast, something to concentrate on at times prior to equipment being obsolesced, or when the financial forecasts indicate that IBM would like the money this year and not next. So IBM manipulates the structuring of the quota accordingly, rewarding sales more than leasing or the reverse as necessary.

This is no better illustrated than in an MC Report to the MRC for the 1970 outlook for the DP Group:

'Spike Beitzel reviewed with us the DP Group outlook for 1970. The net of the problem is that New Earnings before tax dropped $196 million to $544 and the margin has dropped from 27% to 23·6%.

'The first cause, as you know, is reduced purchase. The Group is now forecasting $254 million long purchase in 1970. This reflects substantial reduction in both leasing company and regular customer activity. The Group is looking at several possible actions such as a fire sale on older tape drives and on the /44. However, it is obvious that we have missed on outright purchase for 1970. *Since a high proportion of these dollars go directly to the profit line, there is no hope that it (plan) can be achieved.*' [Italics added.]

(Purchase, by August 1972, according to an MC minute, had put approximately $6 B of IBM equipment in the purchase market and S/360 equipment is available at ½ price'.)

Purchase helps to keep IBM viable. It is not, however, IBM's main strength. There has been much argument within IBM about the origins of that strength, and that is reflected in IBM management discussions.

There are many ways of looking at the IBM markets that IBM operates in. There is the traditional way: how much of the market for computers do we have by industrial sector; how many of the computer users in any sector use IBM equipment. That was answered by IBM during the Telex case (Exhibit 123) with the following table, which records market shares held by IBM in specific industries in the U.S.A. as of 1968:

Segment	IBM Market Share %
Public Utility	80·7
Federal	55·5
Transportation	83·3
Finance	76·3
Insurance	88·5
State/Local Government	80·8
Distribution	86·1
Education	83·4
Printing and Publishing	79·2
Process	81·9
Manufacturing	81·5
Medical	82·1
Business and Management Service	73·6

That vast measure of market power is awesome. But how true is it? In the sense that IBM has or had these percentages among the companies using computers in those industries, it was as accurate as any figures available. In the sense of IBM having obtained those percentages of the total number of possible computer users in those industries, there is no relationship at all. One might therefore think that the possibilities for IBM and for everybody else were, if not endless, at least large enough to provide enough to fill IBM's and everybody else's ambitions.

Unfortunately, this is not the case, and this in the end has much to do with the pressures that IBM salesmen are subjected to. The major users of computers are the world's largest companies: these are the ones which have been IBM's major growth base. They have also, at times of financial stringency, been a major cause of IBM setback, for they can cut back, switch to PCMs and operate on the basis of price. Generally, however, they have served IBM well.

They are its best customers. We can quantify it this way: consider any industry, whether it be manufacturing, distributive, service, utility or financial, and go through its top twenty companies. In each case, whether on an American or European basis, IBM will have more than 50% of the computer installations within the top twenty companies in that sector. Or, considering companies by their size alone, for example the *Fortune* top twenty or, in the U.K., *The Times* top twenty, again IBM will have well over 50% of the installations. In fact, in the one market in which IBM is held to have fallen below 50% generally—that of the U.K.—fourteen of the top twenty companies have some IBM equipment, and of those fourteen ten are predominantly IBM users.

We can put some flesh on these figures. At a minimum, one expects that a major American corporation will probably spend around $20 million for every billion of annual turnover on running its computer installations, and that it will have installed kit worth twice that: a five billion corporation will be spending probably $80–$100 million a year for computing and have around $150 to $200 million's worth of computing equipment.

The fifty top U.S. companies in 1972 grossed around $250 billion. On the above basis, they would probably have spent $5 billion on computing and had installed something of the order of $7·5 to $10 billion of equipment, well over half of which will have come from IBM.

Is this relevant? Do not large corporations rise and fall? In fact, no. As Galbraith pointed out a long time ago, among the majors there are few collapses. The RCAs and GEs of this world can swallow losses of cash, skill, pride, and market, which, had the loss been proportionately the same, would have destroyed smaller companies.

But more important than that conclusion is the following: there is a notion that a small company, say the mousetrap company, can originate a product and over the years grow with it until it becomes the mousetrap corporation, a multi-billion-dollar giant. It may have worked like this in the past, but it has not worked like that for quite some time. The Xeroxes are the exception rather than the rule.

What happens is that the small corporation that wishes to grow does so by being taken over, by amalgamation. Of the nine companies discussed earlier which form the computer mainframe industry, IBM and the dwarfs by which it is surrounded, seven were large companies before the computer came along. The two new entrants both grew, but, SDS ended up being taken over by Xerox, and CDC itself took over a large finance company, from which much of its strength now comes.

This, for all the strains and stresses that face IBM's marketing, is the environment in which its field forces work, one in which the majority of the rich, large and powerful are committed to IBM, for a change in method of working would prove just as difficult for them to achieve. For all the worrying that IBM management may do, IBM is not all going to fail tomorrow: at least in America nobody as yet can afford it.

CHAPTER 12

IBM World Trade: Puppet on a String

'Our business is translated foreign currencies into dollars.'
—Gilbert E. Jones, Chairman, IBM WTC, 1st March 1973

* * *

'The lowest form of life in IBM was the Supplies Division. After that came the Service Bureau [Corporation] followed by World Trade. It was tough to try to make a re-entry into IBM proper after you had been sent to World Trade.'

* * *

The former senior executive was reminiscing about life in IBM in the mid-sixties. Though it was never put to him directly, he would perhaps agree with the proposition that, the protestations of those legally held responsible—in that their names are on the books as directors—to the contrary, IBM World Trade Corporation does not as yet really exist. Which, given the size of IBM's overseas operations, may seem more than odd. How can properly constituted and registered subsidiaries—operating in almost all the countries in which any form of white-collar class and employment are found—*not* exist? How can the IBM World Trade organisation—with some form of representation in more than 120 countries, employing in 1974 around 170,000 people, with a turnover measured in billions of dollars, showing a greater profit with its subsidiaries than IBM Domestic—*not* be real?

Of course, IBM World Trade, otherwise WTC, has a physical existence. It has plants, laboratories, offices, machines, personnel; it consumes, utilises services, pays taxes, sells to governments, and has speeches made on its behalf about its place in the community and the friendly nature of IBM as the local good employer, the contributor to the common welfare, and the bringer of the delights of advanced technology to relieve humdrum toil.

But having written that, it is nearly all that needs to be stated. For the above activities are largely concerned with managerial fiction—not a living, breathing organisation at all. Though WTC may look alive to the outside world, in reality it lacks any internal dynamic of its own: it is a zombie; a puppet, wherever the strings may end, they all start at and are pulled from Armonk.

If any part of IBM really deserves to come under the general rubric which heads this section, it is WTC, for IBM Domestic in comparison is a model of free-thinking and free-wheeling independence. Whether its employees know it or not, it is the case that in WTC 'I was only following orders'. While this may not matter too much near the bottom, where the employee is usually doing just that, it can have consequences at the top.

Internally, IBM propaganda focuses on the 'One World of IBM'. And it is one world, in which, irrespective of the extent of nations involved, all the critical decisions are made by nationals of one country, having first in mind the interests of the parent corporation in that country and not the interests of the countries in which WTC operates. If the situation were otherwise, foreigners would be high enough in the executive ranks of IBM to have been given both power and the status that goes with it: seats on the main IBM Board.

Instead? The cosmetic treatment.

'TJW Jnr decided that you couldn't have a guy named Charlie Smith as President of IBM World Trade. So Charlie Smith left, and Watson got him a job at Bankers Trust'.

Eventually, IBM World Trade got Jacques Maisonrouge —who had been groomed by Dick Watson. But IBM retained the basic parent IBM stock, 94% of which in 1972 was owned by Americans. If one wishes to buy into IBM, one buys a piece of the totality: one stock is retained because it enables parent IBM to maintain control.

This was put quite clearly in the minutes of the Management

Review Committee, July 15th 1971. The MRC was listening to a presentation on World Trade ownership, the results of the work of a committee set up specifically to consider what moves, if any, IBM should make to change the existing situation.

The MRC was told that: 'From IBM standpoint total ownership is desirable in order to:

'Maintain freedom for unified and optimised management decisions. Key items are product sourcing, R&D missions and expenditures, product pricing and dividend payments.

'Assure control of basic policies. Key are salary and personnel practices and business ethics.

'Obtain favorable inter-company pricing structure in order to minimise financing requirement, pay realistic duties, and pay taxes as revenue earned'.

One hour and fifteen minutes later, the session ended with the MRC, agreeing with the general conclusions, which were essentially that the only changes to be made should be of emphasis, not of substance.

The IBM Organisational Manual spells out that control in a little more detail. The section dealing with WTC and entitled 'powers reserved to the IBM Corporation as they relate to WTC' is unfortunately even older than the MRC minute, three years older. However, it does spell out the control that the MRC was discussing. As for the years since, though WTC like the rest of IBM has gone through some reorganisation, the data made public, including that in an IBM WTC press campaign in the summer of 1974, indicates that the only changes made are essentially those of reporting lines: they are not basic changes in control. The critical decisions, as ever, are made at Armonk. Thus the position described in the quote from the Organisational Manual can be said still to be generally valid:

'The responsibility for ensuring continuous optimum performance of the Corporation as a whole is retained at the corporate level. The principal method of delineating and describing the scope of these responsibilities and authorities is to reserve selected powers or authorities to the Corporation.

'These powers ... are reserved ... through the Chairman of the Board as the Chief Executive Officer, unless specifically delegated'.

The opening paragraphs of the section proceed to state that

General Executives and General Managers of operating units will act autonomously in all matters not reserved to the IBM Corporation and have the right to recommend to Corporate that the powers be eliminated or revised: it does not state that Corporate must take any notice, or that the powers reserved are so wide that local managers will have a hard task to find a meaningful decision they can make unaided.

The powers are grouped into two areas, general and specific. Under the heading of general come objectives, policies, management practices, organisational structure, title usage (pure IBM bureaucracy), and the mission and business scope of WTC. This group also covers approval of all strategic and operating plans, operating budgets and cash budgets, and concurrence with major capital expenditures. It includes establishment of standards and of uniform practices to ensure that there will be consistency in IBM Worldwide operations.

All these, one might think, reduce the freedom of action of so-called WTC management to infinitesimally low proportions. However, when one turns to specific, it is reduced even further. It lists the responsibilities delegated by IBM's Chairman among the Corporate staff and includes approval of senior management appointments and salaries and approval of employee benefit plans in WTC (where these provide benefits in excess of those in IBM Domestic). Both are the responsibility of the Vice-President, Personnel.

Naturally enough, almost all outside appointments at any level of seniority—consultants, accountants, architects, outside counsel—are subject to a Corporate veto, as are most external image matters including press relations and the release of any financial information to the public.

Indeed, in the area of relationships with outsiders, there seems to be no trust at all. The list of activities which are subject to direction from the Corporate Vice-President, Commercial Development, includes contacts with other companies operating in IBM's field of interest (excluding normal sales), purchasing or sub-contracting contacts, negotiation or approval or working relationships or know-how agreements, and engagement in new business ventures. Control over acquisition or sale of companies or divisions or any of their assets should be expected, but what is one to make of control over the establishment and co-ordination of overall IBM relationships with trade and professional associations?

Patent activity direction, of course, is a reserved matter, as are WTC's activities in America, but those were to be expected, as is the administration of corporate procurement and international buying activities and the negotiation of corporate supply contracts—against which the operating divisions may issue purchasing orders. After all, if one can obtain supplies at a more economic rate by negotiating for the corporation as a whole, then it makes sense to do so.

However, all these together put a decided crimp into the decision-making power of IBM WTC management, wherever sited, whether at international or national level. But this is nothing compared to what is to come: much of managerial life in the subsidiaries has about as much freedom of choice as the battery hen.

This is so whether one is discussing the major working sinews of IBM life, special situations such as the 1969 unbundling programme (though timed differently for WTC, the programme was carried out strictly to the letter as laid down by Armonk, and no deviation was allowed once the plan had been finalised) or more normal and regular events such as the introduction of leasing plans and price increases throughout the early seventies.

So far, control has only been discussed in terms of abstractions, reserved powers. But to have control, one must have effective reporting procedures and properly organised lines of communication. IBM has tried to make sure that it has both and that the troops in the far foreign field will react to the orders that Armonk originates, though, by the time those orders get to them, their origin will have been suitably camouflaged and translated into a more locally palatable form.

At the top still lies Armonk, which is supported closely by ... *Armonk*, for it is there that the Chairman of IBM WTC has his office—though officially WTC headquarters still remains in New York.* At the side of Armonk is IBM Domestic with direct lines of communication to the parts of the WTC empire. Till recently, the next step to New York would have been Paris and what was

---

*New headquarters are currently being built at Tarrytown, New York. The building is designed in the shape of a W, as is the lake in front of it.

effectively the WTC tactical HQ outside America, for that European part of WTC did the majority of the business and still does two-thirds of it.

There were always two sides to IBM's foreign operations: those which were thought to be the province of WTC, primarily Europe, and the rest, the Latin American countries and the Far East, really a euphemism for Japan, long an area of concern to IBM management. However, in the late sixties/early seventies there began to be substantial growth outside Europe, particularly in Latin America. This has been recognised in the creation of the two previously mentioned new corporations—in reality, IBM WTC operating divisions: IBM Europe/Middle East/Africa, and IBM Americas/Far East. Today these theoretically control the national subsidiaries in their areas; however, the control is just as national as it was in the days of WTC, for the same familiar faces and figures turn up in the new IBM organisation and in parent IBM.

Below come the national operating subsidiaries. At this ex-American level, there is a rough match between the organisation of WTC and each of the national subsidiaries, rough because not all will require such a match. Some are simply sales agencies; others are so small that it makes more sense to compound the divisional organisation of the larger subsidiaries into something more fitting commercial reality. But basically, the major subsidiaries will each have seven divisions: Data Processing, Office Products, General Systems, Finance, Research, Personnel/Communications, and Manufacturing.

At the top of these, at the head of each national subsidiary and leading the local troops, there will be a General Manager, the IBM terminology for Managing Director/President.* He will have the appropriate number of local divisional managers, the key slot, as in IBM Domestic, being held by the head of the equivalent of DPD. Generally the local DPD will include the Sales and Field Engineering organisations.

There are two classes of division within subsidiaries: the sales

---

*He will often have been picked not according to seniority or experience, but for his ability to execute orders. Thus, the Managing Director of one of the major European subsidiaries was not even on the initial short list of twelve names drawn up, who were all judged to be too independent.

oriented and quota-ridden divisions, over which the General Manager will have some control since it is his job to see that quota is met and plans are achieved; and the rest, divisions which differ quite fundamentally.

The General Manager will pay the most attention to Data Processing, primarily because what little power he has will depend on its performance. He will pay attention too to Office Products and General Systems, no doubt in proportion to their revenue-earning potential, for these are also sales organisations. And he will pay attention to Finance, since that is primarily devoted to the support of profitable sales.

He will not pay so much attention to the rest: if one is to map on to the local organisation the powers reserved to Corporate, these, while they affect the sales divisions, at least give the GM some leeway. He has little leeway over other matters, in which other primarily indirectly affect his control.

Research is only nominally under his direction. There are two kinds of research facility in WTC: those under the administrative direction of WTC but whose research direction is set by IBM Domestic's System Development Division; and the much smaller national laboratories, usually working in a highly visible area which has some direct relevance to problems encountered in their own countries—such as Italian IBM's laboratory in Venice, which researches and models the properties of lagoon waters and the like, an obvious mission.

These small national laboratories will be paid for out of the local company's budget, but even this will not necessarily give the GM extra powers. The field of research in which the national laboratory is engaged will not have been decided solely by the local company, for that could lead to world-wide duplication. The laboratory's main working links will be with other IBM laboratories and with local research 'partners', universities and the like, not primarily with the local company.

The larger labs work in much broader fields; though the work will generally be carried out by nationals of WTC countries, the links are to Domestic. Here IBM makes use of national skills and preoccupations. Thus, Hursley in Britain has done much machine design and has worked extensively in software, its main claim to fame being the development of the IBM software language, PL1. Le Gaude in France is deeply committed to communications, having done much of the work which led to the development of IBM's computerised telephone exchange which can handle both voice and digital data, the overpriced 3750. (The computer 'power' inside that exchange is trivial. It is based on that old, reliable, small IBM work-horse, the 1130.)

The one-world philosophy of IBM, however, has an unfortunate effect which causes resentment among some IBM researchers. The general public in America and abroad believe that all product research/development is done in the United States, an assumption which IBM does little to correct. IBM's work on voice response originates out of its Zurich laboratory; however, when it surfaced publicly, it came out of San Jose, and no mention of Zurich was made. Insofar, then, as Research reports to anyone in WTC, it does so more as an official courtesy and for informational purposes than for any serious reason.

The links between Personnel and Communications are more mixed. As that Reserved-to-Corporate listing makes clear, the powers of the General Manager in this area are much circumscribed. Yet he will be much involved in the day-to-day work of these areas, for they are a constant source of problems and complaints.

That personnel should not be under the nearly sole control of the local GM and his management might seem odd, but there is a reason for it. The level of staffing is a key IBM determinant and a good way of keeping a squeeze on local management. IBM operates a pressure-cooker system, for staff employed are a proportion of revenue, not of sales, which means that employment is always below what should be required to sustain the current level of activity.

It is when one turns to manufacturing, however, that the limitations on the local GM's powers become most apparent. Personnel/Communications, with their strong links to Corporate and their formal reporting to local management, may tear that management two ways; however, when he turns to manufacturing, it is surprising that the local GM is not driven mad.

Manufacturing plants are allotted according to total Corporate needs: 'We feel there are some items such as manufacturing planning which should continue to reside in the United States' (MC Report to MRC, July 1971). However, that does not mean that the location of a manufacturing facility is made solely by Armonk thrusting the plant on an unwilling subsidiary. Much the reverse: to obtain a manufacturing facility in its country, the local management will have to put up a case and to fight for its acceptance. Everybody fights: the spectacle of IBM country managements fighting with each other to obtain a plant is not, says one who has taken part, a particularly edifying one.

In the end, there is seldom any single reason why a plant should be sited, say, in the U.K. rather than Holland. Availability of skills will play a part but so will the local political situation. IBM will take into account the local balance of payments, size and profitability of market, strength of the local capital market, political stability—and attitudes to IBM, particularly among politicians.

This last concern is particularly important. It was one of the key reasons why the U.K. obtained its 2701/1401 manufacturing plant. The situation was made clear to IBM that if it wanted to maintain any sort of stake in the British government-controlled market (which includes central government, local government and the nationalised industries) a small plant at Greenock in Scotland, producing peripheral equipment, was not enough.

Why do the national managements fight among themselves? The new manufacturing capability will represent a substantial increase in turnover and profit to the local company, because it will take its place in the integrated manufacturing system and can end up supplying many countries. It will not, of course, increase the profit as a percentage of revenue but, because of the commitment, will strengthen the position of the local management within WTC and thus enhance career prospects.

But having got his plant, after the headaches of setting it up, getting it staffed and running, the GM will then find that he has almost no control over its plans, including the critical manufacturing plan. Moreover, a country GM may not even know in detail the manufacturing plans of any plants for which he is theoretically responsible.

The reason for this is to be found in IBM's international manufacturing integration. There can be no national production independence: all product changes have to be made on the basis that they will probably affect something being produced elsewhere. So, for all practical purposes, WTC manufacturing is fully integrated with IBM Domestic.*

This interlocking of production can have interesting consequences. Not many years ago Britain's Cambridge Mathematical Laboratory bought a 370/158. When the order was finally placed, they were presented with a set of colour cards. (IBM does allow some leeway, particularly when one is spending over a million pounds.) The cards were considered and then the Cambridge men said yes, these are pleasant colours, but would it not be possible to have a system in Cambridge blue? Unfortunately not, replied IBM. It would require the mixing of special paint, and that mixture would have to be sent to all the plants and countries where the various units which would eventually become the Cambridge system were made—and this was not practicable.

The GM, as we have seen, retains some responsibility for Data Processing, Office Products, General Systems and Finance. That responsibility is primarily a marketing one: he will be responsible for seeing to it that the plans are achieved and that quota is reached and within budget, both of which will have to be first cleared through WTC with Armonk before they can become 'policy'.

However, even within these confines there are further restrictions. DP has both sales and Field/Customer engineering organisations. Field Engineering provides a good example of Armonk control at work, of the limitations placed on independent managerial action.

The FE organisation can be fairly substantial. It is structured into districts which map fairly closely onto the sales organisation,

---

*The same integrated product by plant policy which is now creating political problems for IBM looked very different when IBM began. The IBM subsidiaries in Europe had picked themselves up after WWII largely by their own efforts and were often trying to go their own ways. IBM saw early that the future would bring into existence something of the order of a free trade area or common market and began to try to organise itself accordingly. Independent thinking had to be stifled, and stifled it was. In the fifties it seriously began to plan its product by plant organisation and to start setting up within Europe. This was not, of course, quite as simple as it sounds and was further complicated by Dick Watson's habit of visiting countries where IBM did not have a plant and talking to bodies like the Chambers of Commerce about IBM's supposed intention of setting up a plant or laboratory there. (In this way Sweden originally got its IBM plant.) He would send a note back to WTC HQ in New York afterwards, asking them to determine what to do next. Finally the confusion caused his assistants to try arranging his European visit schedules to send him elsewhere than to countries in which IBM did not already have a facility.

with the addition of an education facility, spares and service back-up, and a field support organisation. So far, all this is pretty conventional—what is not conventional are the limitations on the actions of its management.

Management planning here is of the pre-set variety. The FE budget will be set in relation to marketing's success, for FE obtains a fixed percentage of the income from machines on rental, and FE will be informed of what it needs to know about the products it is to service, product by product.

'Be informed' ... It is called the IWI, the International Workload Index, a comprehensive method of work control used within both Domestic and WTC. The IWI system indicates to the FE manager the average number of service hours that any product should require, at any part of its life. It will also give him clear indications of how much training his FE force will need to learn enough about new products to be able to go out and service them; the costs of that learning exercise eventually come from the maintenance charges users will pay.

The instructions he will receive on training, time, and part expectations geared to product life, will drastically limit any managerial initiative. Limit? It is possible to take the number of machines that are field engineering's responsibility and correlate them with the amount of service that the literature will tell the manager each will require, tot up the number of hours involved, and quickly arrive at figures which can be translated into manpower strength. Now tie in market forecasts and orders received, using in the case of new products the lag between order and delivery as time to train field engineers ...

There is little slack in the system. The year after introduction of the product to the market the machine IWI will be reduced, as the bugs should have been reduced. Conversely, as the men become experienced and the learning curve takes effect, the IWI per head will increase. The system is a giant international factory, in which the country FE managers are little more than foremen.

What does that make the FE manager's boss, the General Manager? He is responsible for the smooth running of the subsidiary, for the levels of service and the like, only when and where things go wrong. He is a resolver of conflict, not really a manager in any traditional sense of the word, for he exerts little guidance over the direction of the subsidiary's affairs. He is really a sort of human Maxwell's Demon, a nearly automatic governor. The consequences are that, if one wanted him to run the business or someone else's business, there is little in his IBM training or career to indicate that he would be able to do so.

Nowhere is the difference between a manager in the traditional sense, and one in the IBM sense, more apparent than when one considers the process of financial management. The traditional method of financial management as practised, say, in ITT, would have the division of a subsidiary preparing its financial plan and, at annual budget approval time, presenting a plan which contains profit expectation, cash needs and the production and other evidence necessary to support them. Time to approval? One week: at the outside, one month.

Approval is by no means the end of it. No senior management of any competence will allow subsidiaries to go then through the rest of the year without some monitoring, in some cases on a monthly basis, in others quarterly. More often than not the best managements operate by exceptions—they are only interested in any departure from the forecast norm.

The situation in an IBM subsidiary is totally different: that annual budgeting exercise will more usually take the best part of four months. In IBM, planning is a rolling process, partially dependent on the IBM situation at the time and where the overall corporate plans indicate IBM should be—up to seven years ahead. IBM's four months are in large measure due to the reconciliation of lots of local actuality with broad IBM WTC targets and with the approval, or not, of the result by Armonk. Once the plan has been approved, however, there is now no question of the General Manager being left to get on with the job. WTC will require monthly results set against plan, and that quite quickly—the previous month's results go into the communications system at the start of the next. Cash flow control is tight: Armonk wants to know total revenue and total expenses so that it can assess the difference. In WTC this operates on a weekly basis. The books are balanced, and what cash is not immediately required is lent out on the short-term market. (In the U.S. this is done on a daily basis and the money is lent out overnight.)

Should IBM Corporate needs require major alterations to the current plan, they are liable to be thrust on to the subsidiary at a moment's notice. Quotas will be raised, pressure applied and budgets slashed so that profit expectations for the year can be met and prices altered without so much as a by-your-leave.

This is but an outline of the limited world of the country General Manager and his executives. Let us now go up that pyramid to consider some of the IBM rationale for treating WTC in this way, and some of the practical consequences and effects.

In the summer of 1974, WTC introduced a lease plan differing in one critical respect from that of IBM Domestic. Where Domestic exercised a fixed price over four years, WTC reserved the right to increase rental charges by up to 10% a year. No sooner had enough customers signed up than IBM gave notice that it would take advantage of that provision from the autumn of the following year. It did so within three months.

IBM would prefer that we all live in a world in which there is no inflation or balance of payment problems, whether or not caused by ever-rising oil prices; and so would everybody else. However, the spread of IBM, its methodology and executive skills, enable it to turn what are problems for other people into global benefits for itself. IBM will agree with almost any government which makes an issue of it, and where of course the local market is large enough, to try to keep the local payments at least in balance. Naturally considerable pressure will be required; that has happened in the U.K., Australia and Japan, among other countries. But the larger the local market, or the more growth potential it has, the more IBM will go out of its way to accommodate that government's wishes. Thus those who are in surplus are those countries in which IBM has the largest manufacturing facility, the countries where IBM has the largest commitment. The results are predictable: the richest are in the strongest position to complain; and the poorest, those who can least afford a foreign trade deficit, will end up with one to which IBM makes a contribution.

It should not be assumed, however, that the rich are always necessarily the strongest. IBM knows how to turn the skills of the advanced countries against themselves. The international interlocking of production can be turned to IBM's advantage, and it is. As a general practice, customs authorities the world over treat computing equipment on the basis of the price at which it will sell or rent. However, what is an item of computing equipment? Is it just an electronic electrical assembly, or is it something to which much human ingenuity and instructions need to be applied, before it can become valuable. This is something to which IBM has devoted much time, arguing the latter. It is, after all, in IBM's interest to make its import valuation as low as possible, and it does.

The general conclusion of experts in the field is that IBM has achieved probably the lowest average customs valuations of any computer manufacturer anywhere and that it has done so on a world-wide basis. This is a good way to turn IBM's comparatively low manufacturing costs and its high marketing, service-providing costs into an even stronger asset. IBM effectively has argued a case which states that, since it costs more for IBM to turn a computer into a working system than it costs its competitors, the value put on the electronic item before these additions should be lower than that put on a competitor's.

Nothing in IBM, however, is quite that straightforward. There is no standard valuation made by all customs authorities everywhere nor will an item made by IBM in one country necessarily cross a frontier at the same price as if the same item were made by IBM in another country. Nor, indeed, will there be a straightforward relationship between differently-rated machines of the same classes, units and peripherals.

For IBM, export/import is not trade in which a second party lies at the other end: IBM trades between its own various national companies, which then take the item on to their books and deal with the local would-be user.

This makes it possible for IBM to play that basic export/import game of fluctuating prices depending on origins and destination. It tries to export from high tax and high duty countries at low prices, thus reducing the local turnover and profits, and to export from low tax, low duty countries at high prices, thus increasing the profits that the consolidated group is able to return after taxes.*

The words used at the Corporate instruction level were that IBM should pay realistic duties—what is realistic evidently being left to IBM to determine.

It has long been the IBM doctrine that its international integration of production gives cost and price benefits which would not be present were production to be organised in more traditional ways, with plants in each of the major markets each manufac-

---

*This fact is still much disputed among former IBM executives. What little evidence is available tends to indicate that it is indeed so.

turing the broad range of requirements for that market. This is true; however, what IBM does not state is that the chief beneficiary is IBM, not the user.

For IBM's prices are no lower than anybody else's; indeed, much the reverse. This fact, when one thinks about it, is strange, since IBM's production costs are generally much lower than any of its competitors. This is not just due to the economics of volume—it is also in part due to the low cost of IBM capital.

As we have seen, IBM is now largely internally self-financing. So far, in the seventies, Armonk has been able to ignore what happens to the share price and its effect on the capital market.

In any case, the DP Group Financial Procedures manual shows how notional IBM capital-raising costs are: the specialists entrusted with pricing are told to calculate the costs of that capital at 1.5% internal sources indicate that this has since been increased; however, when this instruction was issued, the best external market rates were of the order of 6%–7%.

IBM, however, has had to raise capital abroad. The meeting between Maurice Stans and Dick Watson (see page 362) was set to discuss possible alleviation of an American Treasury ruling (in force from the late sixties to early '74 and enforced by the Office of Foreign Direct Investment of the U.S. Department of Commerce) which restricted American companies from investing more than 40% of the net profit of their foreign subsidiaries in the country in which they had been earned: the rest had to be repatriated. These profits, royalties from WTC companies, and WTC payments for IBM Domestic's products, caused IBM to repatriate $800 million in 1972. As a result, IBM had to borrow abroad to finance investment programmes. In early 1974, IBM's long term debt—repayable from 1975 to 1991—was $518 million, of which $154+ million had been borrowed abroad. It required no public issue and no prospectus.

We get some idea of the scale of IBM's annual borrowing for repatriation purposes from a 1971 MRC minute, which reported WTC borrowing $228·6 million, $154·2 million of that for repatriation. It also reported that the net cost of that $154·2 million capital–raising exercise was $543 thousand, or as the minute stated it, 'equates to effective $\frac{1}{4}$% interest'. Those profits were not repatriated with any rider that IBM invest them in its American business: the profits simply had to be transferred to

America. All that IBM probably did was to put them in its cookie jar and invest them on the short-term market (investments which, in 1974, were yielding 7·8%).

The same 1971 minute indicated that IBM's foreign borrowings were scheduled to be $305 million in 1971, $191 million of it for the same repatriation purposes; cost $1·97 million, effective interest rate $\frac{1}{2}$%. However, it should be noted that what IBM repatriated was net after taxes in the country earned, which, under the no–double–taxation arrangements normally held between most countries, meant that the only tax payable thereafter would be the U.S. dividend distribution type. However, unsubstantiated reports maintain that, where possible, IBM charged the interest paid on the local market against taxes in that country, where allowed. If this is so, the situation seems peculiar: the effect of the borrowing was to strengthen the net position of the local companies in the countries in which funds were raised (France, Canada, Belgium, the Netherlands and Switzerland among them).

One cannot label this tax evasion, rather prudent management. IBM does not need to cheat on its taxes; its organisation is now such that the tax base is almost superfluous, as are any restrictions a country may care to place on the repatriation of profits or transference of funds from one country to another. The beauty of a multinational organisation is that one can apportion expenses in any way one chooses. Thus, one standard way during the sixties was, where possible, to make use of the annual Hundred Percent Clubs.

The idea of a Hundred Percent Club as a way to avoid currency control regulations may sound ludicrous, but few people outside IBM realise the real scale on which these clubs operate. The Hundred Percent Club is both an opportunity to reward effort—to 'parade the winners' and commend them with applause, gifts and cash—and an opportunity for managers to try to build a base, to make a reputation.

Presentations and speeches are especially well rehearsed, for slip-ups will not help anyone's career. Sometimes they are so crucial to the advancement of the career that the executive speaker will go to the length of making sure that all the staff attending and connected with the affair are his own. The regular slide machine operator will be supplanted by his own assistant, and members of the 'audience' will be carefully primed to laugh in the right places.

A WTC Hundred Percent Club occasion is serious and officially celibate, though not as much as an IBM Domestic Hundred Percent Club meeting. Entertainment is of high standard, with name stars, and in part 'uplifting', e.g. the Rome, Paris or Covent Garden Opera. It is not unusual for a thousand salesmen and their managers to attend, and though IBM in the U.S.A. is sometimes quite casual now about how they travel, even using chartered aircraft, in IBM WTC in the sixties it was unheard of for a country's contingent to all get on the same aircraft. IBM had strict rules concerned with the numbers of IBM salesmen and executives allowed on the same plane. Suppose there were an accident?

The clubs take a long time to organise. An executive will be assigned for a time and will be involved with nothing else for a year but preparation and organisation.

It is an expensive institution. One of the two European IBM Hundred Percent Club meetings held in 1974—in the West Indies—for instance cost over three quarters of a million dollars.

And where did they go in the sixties? Spain was a preference. Since Spain had restrictions on capital transfers, it was a good way of making use of the cash. IBM Spain picked up the tab, and no doubt IBM corporately made notional book transfers. But effectively IBM had got some of its cash out of the country without benefit of national rules and regulations.

This, however, is a digression from a discussion of the strangeness of the situation where IBM's prices on the market are generally higher than anybody else's. One reason concerns the origin of production. The majority of IBM's competitors are American; however, unlike IBM generally, their production facilities outside the United States are fairly limited so that the systems they sell abroad have a high percentage of American components and American costs built into them. IBM has no such difficulty. The majority of its systems sold abroad, particularly in the industrialised countries, are built abroad—and in countries which have far lower labour costs than America. The only competitors with the same labour cost levels are the local manufacturers, who are not large enough as yet to cause IBM any serious worries. With the exception of Britain, IBM is the largest computer manufacturer by far in Europe, just as it is the largest in the U.S.A. Elsewhere only in Japan is IBM outclassed.

One would expect that the economics of volume would operate in IBM's favour even on the local WTC scene. There are few figures available. However, talks with other manufacturers and IBM data for IBM Domestic give us some idea of the range of variation between IBM production costs and everybody else's. Expressed as a percentage of sales price, IBM Domestic's average hovers within a per cent or two either side of 20%. The other companies vary between near 30% and 40–45%. In Europe the IBM figures are, with a hiccup in the early seventies, lower than Domestic—while the competition's costs can be as high as 50% on the same unbundled basis. Thus one would expect that IBM WTC product would be on the market at lower prices than Domestic's.

But it is not; in fact, much the reverse. If we are to price out a typical large IBM system's configuration—a 370/158 with 2 mgbs of main store, 16 disc drives, 16 tape drives and a clutch of controls, line printers, terminals and the like—the following table gives a comparison between what the rental users will pay in three European countries and that paid in the U.S.A. as of spring, 1974:

	Rent	*Purchase*
U.S.A.	$ 85,767	$3,727,900
U.K.	$ 99,110	$4,253,904
France	$111,705	$4,199,743
West Germany	$103,450	$4,390,629

These differences between U.S. prices and European prices are no accident. An unrepresentative system or configuration has not been selected in order to make a case against IBM. There are MRC documents which make the point still more effectively and forcefully. In approving some WTC System 370 price changes early in 1972, the MRC was shown the following:

S/370 PRICE COMPARISON

	CPU		*Other*	
	*MAC	*Purch.*	*MAC*	*Purch.*
U.S.	95–98	95–98	95–100	95–100
WT Base	100	100	100	100
Japan	112	116	112	116
Germany	104–108	103	111	110

*Rental: Monthly Availability Charge.

The chart gives some indication of the relationship between Domestic and WTC prices and shows how WTC prices are kept higher than Domestic's as a matter of Corporate policy. What is worth pointing out is that, in the instance chosen, the figures are the result of price alterations due to changes in currency rates.

These changes in currency rates can bring bonuses: where the rate goes in favour of the dollar, IBM increases prices to keep up the dollar income. Where the rate goes against it, however, as in late 1971, IBM does not necessarily reduce prices in turn. Thus, early in 1972, when the MRC was discussing the 1972–73 plans, the minutes state: 'Revaluation assumption was that $355 M additional revenue would accrue, of which approximately $45 M would be returned via selected price reductions.'

However, parent IBM does not simply rely on the vagaries of international currency fluctuations in its milking of WTC above and beyond costs fairly apportioned and profit however earned.

The summation of data in the Form PC 50 quoted earlier indicates that where for every $100 of sales in the U.S.A. IBM ended with profits of $20, for every $100 of sales abroad, it obtained $30. This is somewhat different from the situation shown in the Annual Reports, in which the differentials are substantially smaller. What IBM wishes to do is to understate true WTC profits and to push up IBM Domestic's; to reduce the disparity between the two by transferring what would otherwise be WTC profit to Domestic above and beyond the profit that parent IBM earns from WTC's normal operations.

This has another effect. WTC pays the statutory taxes in the country of origin, transfers the taxed profit to WTC, and consolidates: this is the reporting procedure. In the ten years 1963–1972, the profit that was remitted and the costs of WTC imports from parent meant that there was a positive contribution to the American balance of payments of $4·44 billion. In that same period, IBM WTC's subsidiaries paid about $3·1 billion in taxes to non-American governments.

However, the effect of the financial manoeuvres, legitimate though they might be, is to inflate WTC costs, for these are borne by the countries and not by parent IBM. That inflation of WTC costs, of course, has the effect of reducing the tax bill that is paid. If taxes are to be incurred, IBM would much prefer to pay them to the U.S. Government, where, in any case, rates are generally lower than those of, for instance, Europe. IBM would no doubt explain all this away by its need to have headquarters and corporate functions somewhere, and that these and the R&D costs need to be paid. But this argument is not adequate: the internal-to-IBM pricing instruction documents make it quite clear, as Mr Katzenbach pointed out in the Telex case, that IBM uses full cost recovery techniques, which in turn implies full cost apportionment techniques. And the documents, long comprehensive cover-all-options instructions, show it to be so.

On top of this, IBM charges WTC an average 3·68% royalty, as a contribution to IBM's R&D budget, a know-how payment wherever the equipment is manufactured. Again, in 1973 that amounted to $200 million. Further, IBM Domestic shipments carry a charge above and beyond the full cost apportionment: IBM adds cost and service charges for machines and parts shipped from Domestic to WTC companies: 33·5% for machines, 26·5% for parts. (There is a service charge in reverse, from WTC to Domestic, but in that case it runs at 25% for completed machines and 15% for parts.)

This adds to the value of exports both ways, Domestic to WTC, and WTC to Domestic. However, since in 1972, Domestic exports were $485 million while its imports were $180 million, this system does substantially more to boost Domestic's profits than those of WTC subsidiaries. The net result of these practices is further to increase WTC costs to the benefit of Domestic.

As will have become apparent, this is a concerted policy, above and beyond the normal meddling of Armonk. That meddling in the case of WTC assumes extra dimensions. The problem is standard for IBM: Armonk wants WTC to be more aggressive in seeking out opportunities; however, it doesn't really want WTC to do anything that is not done by Domestic. And it certainly does not want WTC to become aggressive without first obtaining approval from Armonk, a recipe guaranteed to lead to clash.

Thus, there is a constant struggle between Corporate and those theoretically in charge of WTC. The struggle can operate at the most trivial levels. For instance, in 1972 the MRC rejected proposals to give individual countries some powers over the way they organise their working time. The system at issue was one in which, at its most basic, employees would work a set number of hours a day but, within limits, would be able to pick the hours that they did so.

The MRC turned down a request to mount a trial in IBM Sweden: Corporate Personnel's conclusion was that there should be no further expansion 'until the optimum U.S. system is identified and a judgement made on our leadership versus followers role'. In its turn the MRC agreed that no one was to do anything new without its review and approval.

The rule, indeed, seems to be that anyone in IBM will be allowed to do anything, provided that first it has MRC approval and second that it has already been done in Domestic. For there is a chauvinistic streak in the way that Armonk runs WTC in which the NIH—not invented here—syndrome plays a strong part.

IBM, for instance, does not play the property market, though in WTC it has been urged by M. Maisonrouge to do so. The proposals he put forward (in October 1971) to go into the property business (a joint venture with outside interests) indicated a 'market' in projected IBM facilities of $400 million by 1977 and a market of similar sum in outside real estate projects.

The MRC was not having any. After all, it will not even let WTC decide what to build and where. Still, in 1971, WTC decided to build a manufacturing plant on land owned by IBM in Hanover. Hanover agreed to find the right site for IBM and tore down a race track on the basis of an IBM commitment to build a plant which would provide jobs for 4,000–5,000 people. The planning method can go haywire. After the expenditure of some $10 million, the MRC rejected the proposition and suggested giving the property back to the city.

Why? '. . . Plant capacity is not needed, personnel to occupy the plant are not needed, the situation will become much worse in the future, and the entire proposition makes no financial sense'.

One does not need to have a crystal ball, just some hindsight, to know that in this case the MRC was right. But more important, this incident illustrates full well the dilemma which faces WTC. It cannot, on the present basis, manage its own affairs: it is not competent to do so, not because it lacks competence, but primarily because it lacks plan data. IBM is run as a total ship and cannot be run any other way unless it be restructured.

Nor will Armonk let WTC start looking around for diversification opportunities, though M. Maisonrouge has been urged to do so. Thus, still in 1971, M. Maisonrouge and a representative of bankers Morgan Stanley got together to discuss the potential acquisition of Sweden's L. M. Ericson, one of the largest of Europe's telecommunications manufacturers. No contact had been made with the company. The MRC questioned Maisonrouge's authority huffily and quickly pulled back—or, in the IBM jargon: 'MRC also asked that no further contact on this subject be initiated in World Trade, either internally or externally, until a more formal corporate diversification strategy can be developed'.

It has become more and more evident that the global IBM concept is under strain. These strains and stresses get stronger rather than weaker and are a major problem with which Armonk more and more has to struggle. The problem is to retain control without appearing to do so. It is the classic problem of industrial folklore: 'how to keep all the big tits to oneself while fobbing off the little tats on to the other fellow'.

Perhaps the best example of the strains of running IBM as if the U.S.A. were in front and everybody else should wait was also a 1971 problem. IBM was then developing a terminal for the banking market. WTC wanted the development speeded up. The terminal was scheduled for announcement in the first quarter of 1973, but IBM Japan wanted an announcement in July 1972 and IBM U.K. the following October.

The problem was to reconcile that six to nine month mismatch, because the sale of some 18,000 terminals was open to question; in both Japan and the U.K. some of the major banks were intending to make their equipment decisions in 1972.* IBM was just not ready—it would not even have the cost and price data before the first quarter of 1973. So at stake were some ten million points, or rental of $120 million a year. The MRC

---

*There are times, of course, when IBM just cannot win, and the banks are a case in point. IBM set out to recover as much bank business as possible. Among the equipment it eventually sold to major banks in the U.K. were cash dispensers. These had been devised in part on the back of the direct public interface experience that IBM had gained with the BART system (the loss mentioned in Chapter 9).

Some of the first dispensers to be installed were put in by Lloyds Bank in the U.K.—which had a lot of trouble with them, much to the bank's dissatisfaction. As if that were not enough (according to Washington sources) IBM almost immediately found itself in trouble with the Federal Government's National Security Agency in Washington. One of NSA's concerns is cryptography, the breaking of codes. IBM had created and sold a system before NSA had cracked it; what was worse they had sold it abroad, and NSA objected, much to the glee of those who had devised the system.

wriggled, but, primarily due to the way IBM is organised and structured, there was little that could be done.

A global market which is not increasing in size in a nice orderly progression disturbs IBM management. It much prefers one that can be controlled in traditional ways. Thus, an MC report to the MRC discussed the business of Information Records Division in WTC countries and the strategy to be adopted. The tapes, cards and consumables business in WTC was running at $100 million a year and projected to grow to $130 million during the plan period.

The report was based on the conclusions of a task force which concluded that IRD supports the DP business, costs little 'and enhances the small country image because of the multiple plant locations, particularly in Europe'.

One gets the feeling that the MC was happy—it was a business that it understood, it behaved itself. Nowhere was this more clearly put than in the sentence: 'Although revenue and profit will increase over the plan period, volume in both tapes and cards will be down, i.e., the revenue increase results from pricing actions.'

This is the context in which the IBM WTC companies operate, a world in which the mechanics of IBM may allow for some self-fulfilment if one has little ambition and little liking for real responsibility—in other words for those 90+% of employees in most companies—but which can be stifling to those who wish to run a show of their own and are not content to rest happily within the private, highly-paid welfare state that IBM has created.

It should not, however, be thought that that is so wide a world. Corporate public relations may talk of a world of IBM of nearly 130 countries. In fact, in most of those countries IBM maintains a profile: the glossy modern building which is often the local office may be all the substance there is. IBM WTC has real industrial weight in few countries, four or five in the area of IBM Europe/Middle East/Asia, and three in IBM Americas/Far East.

*   *   *

At the heart of WTC lies France. The relationship between Armonk and France is the kind that would also call for the services of a corporate psychiatrist. France is the country which has provided M. Maisonrouge. It is the country in which whatever little management IBM had abroad was long found. For years it acted effectively as European headquarters since, as Europe provided most of WTC's business, Paris was the natural stopping-off point and was provided with a WTC form of headquarters.

From that HQ, IBM could look around at a situation in the early seventies in which its four main European subsidiaries—France, Germany, the U.K. and Sweden—were the largest computer manufacturers around and, set against all companies, were often very high in terms of profit expressed as percentage of revenue; number one in Germany or number two, in the U.K. and Sweden.

IBM France has, in the seventies, become a billion-dollar corporation: manufacturer of the 370/158, components and some peripherals equipment. Emotionally, France is the flagship, and people within IBM WTC still refer to it in these terms.

It was largely France which got IBM out of many of its components problems during the Series 360 crisis when the components plant at Corbeille Essones was for a time the only plant that parent IBM could rely on, the rejection rate of Fishkill being so high that it caused a lot of the Series 360 delays. And it was IBM France which, French sources indicate, General de Gaulle threatened to nationalise. The occasion was a row between the General and Washington over the supply of computers for the French nuclear programme and the equipment of the French Armed Forces: it was a row which the General won—no contest—and the result could not have been anything else. French Defence has a large number of Series 360 machines, particularly 360/50s. As for the nuclear programme, though in part the work is done on CDC machines, much of French nuclear weapon design has been executed on a 360/85 just outside Paris.

IBM France is, say those who have worked in and with many IBM companies, the most intellectually stimulating of them all, technologically one of the most innovative—the one company which can, more often than not, manage to do what it wants.

One perhaps can best summarise the relationship between IBM France and IBM parent with an anecdote from the mid-sixties. With other journalists I had gone to look at IBM Essones. It was the end of the afternoon and I was walking down the central staircase to the entrance hall where M. Maisonrouge was due to give us a champagne reception. In front of me were two American

IBM executives who had obviously spent the afternoon in meetings. One of them was quietly letting off steam. 'Oh, these fucking Gaullists,' he said.

* * *

No one would ever say anything similar about IBM Germany. Germany, indeed, is the one subsidiary in which many American IBM executives feel most at home; the one in which the IBM methodology is accepted almost without question. Even by IBM standards—which are high—the company is orderly, its premises clean and functional, and its employees punctilious, organised and tidy; above all organised.

IBM Germany's main strength has much to do with its post-war origins: it is largely based in the Stuttgart area, in what was the American zone of occupation. Today it is a more than one-and a half billion dollar a year corporation, the manufacturers of most IBM systems up to the 370/145 and of those large profit-earners—disc and tape drives. It is essentially IBM's main European manufacturing shop, at the heart of its commercial business. It profits also from the post-war situation when West Germany had to do without a number of defence sensitive industries long enough for IBM to become well established. For a long time IBM had a larger share of the German market than it had of the American market, whichever way that market was measured.

* * *

The two most profitable—in relation to turnover—IBM Europa companies are those of the U.K. and Switzerland; largely because much of IBM's business in both counties is with the financial community, there is a tendency in that community in both countries to go heavily for purchase, not for lease.

IBM U.K. is in the $600–700 million a year range: split roughly 60% DP, 30% exports and 10% Office Products. In 1972 it had 13,000 employees, of whom 6,000 were associated with manufacturing and internal services, 5,000 in DP marketing and associated services and around 1,000 in Finance and Research. Its responsibilities in the field of manufacture were then primarily for small systems, data entry equipment and the 370/168, which it part manufactures.

IBM U.K. is a creation of the fifties. Before that IBM products were made in the U.K. by a licensee, which after many vicissitudes has gone on to become Britain's International Computers Ltd. If it did not exist, then the British government would have to find another local manufacturer to support against IBM—there is no other large or well organised enough. ICL worries IBM U.K. The problem that faces IBM U.K. is that ICL has, in fact, a larger part of the market, in part due to government market restrictions which have reserved most of it to companies other than IBM.

(So, in the late sixties, IBM set out to deliberately weaken ICL, putting together a marketing group targeted on major ICL accounts. It was called Project Knock Off.)

Next to France and Japan, IBM U.K. is one of three IBM companies which feel product restrictions the most, largely because it operates in about the most skilled software climate in the world, in which criticism of IBM product is often on a higher technical level than IBM's own local resources are competent to cope with. IBM WTC is not much in favour of its local companies doing market research—their job is to take the product that is offered. IBM U.K. specialists know as well as anybody how deficient their product often is. Much of it has been initiated in the U.K. before being taken over by parent IBM, Americanised and then brought back to the U.K. market.

Paris may be the emotional home of IBM WTC; the U.K. seems often the one with which Armonk feels happiest, in which, for instance, they have the least worries about security. London is the centre which IBM has chosen in which to house the legal team charged with keeping an eye on any possible moves that the EEC might make in the field of anti-trust. The 370/158 plant also contains the headquarters of RESPOND, the IBM service company which operates the international computer services and links which provide that key information for IBM/WTC manufacturing plants, the state of the order book, engineering changes, and the management information that Armonk wants to enable it to keep a check on WTC activities.

* * *

IBM Sweden is another example of a company owing much of its existence to the wishes of local politicians to support a local computer industry. Thus IBM Sweden, a company in the $200–300 million turnover range, is IBM's European printer manufacturer, a highly visible addition to the Swedish economy, and by design. Jarfalla, the IBM plant near Stockholm, is probably the largest of all air conditioned plants in Sweden, has one of the biggest open-plan offices in the country, and not so long ago a Swedish newspaper judged that it ran the best company cafeteria in Sweden.

*　　*　　*

Between these countries, we have accounted for more than half of WTC's employment, and Japan apart, the guts of WTC manufacturing. Indeed, Germany, France, the U.K. and Sweden between them could probably stand on their own without any substantial restructuring or additions. This is evident from the make up of a large 370/168 Installation. The CPU will have been part manufactured and assembled in Britain, and part built from components coming from France and the U.S.A. From Germany will have come the power supplies for the entire system, and Germany too will have provided the 3330 disc units. The 3420 magnetic tape units will have come from France, the printers from Sweden, and the communications control equipment from Scotland, though Scotland will have obtained the electronic guts of that unit from elsewhere. From the United States will have come the 2305 disc storage device which makes virtual memory possible and the 2835 storage control unit. Both, however, could easily be made elsewhere; in fact, equivalent units are made in Europe by other manufacturers.

WTC has few problems in Europe, apart from the rising nationalistic trend which, while it may not go so far as nationalisation, may well lead in the direction of more and more local preference based on a differentiation between those who manufacture as offshoots of a foreign-owned and controlled corporation and those in which control is seen to rest effectively in local hands. As one MRC minute summarising a WTC task force report on ownership put it: 'Impact could come through market discrimination, restrictions on financing, exchange limitations and import restrictions.'

Also at issue is the balance of payments situation. The same minute noted: 'Projections for the 1970–77 period for the industrialised countries indicate that increasing trade deficits, royalty payments, and dividend payments to the parent company will cause *steadily increasing total deficits for those countries'*. [Italics added.]

The ownership question exacerbated by those balance of payments deficits has cropped up elsewhere. IBM operates in India on a very restricted basis, largely because of the Indian Government's insistence that foreign companies create companies which are in part locally owned. The problem has even come up in Africa, where in Nigeria IBM had to get special dispensation from the Nigerian Government to be able to continue to operate on its present basis. IBM faces similar problems in much of Latin America and the rest of the underdeveloped world. Up till now, IBM has held the line, refusing to operate on any serious basis where 100% IBM ownership is not possible (where it is not, of course, IBM is not averse to operating through agents).

These questions come up, however, primarily in the WTC area which is now the province of IBM Americas/Far East, which also has its 'big three': Japan, Brazil and Canada.

*   *   *

It once was believed by many Europeans that towards the end of WWII many American servicemen were nothing more but American salesmen in uniform, or else spying out the land for American plants. It would not be unfair to say that this happened more to Japan than to Europe (other than West Germany). This was IBM's Japanese beginnings, from the post-war days when American subsidiaries were protected against Japanese competition by occupation fiat. The result was that when the Japanese were strong enough to bring in their own policies, one of those they initiated was the closing of the computer market to foreign companies. IBM managed to ride that tidal wave, partly by threatening to pull out of Japan entirely. But it never did so, and in 1974 IBM Japan was a $650+ million turnover company. It was a company with close Japanese allies, among them the President of Sony who is now on the board of IBM Americas/Far East Corporation.*

---

*There is much suspicion about IBM's Japanese interests, it being said, for instance that IBM and Sony are part interlinked through share ownership. But if true this does not show up in the public record.

IBM Japan, of course, provides some of the best anecdotes, among them the one about the course for Japanese punch card operators in the fifties. IBM actually failed one, who, having been publicly disgraced, promptly went out and committed Hari Kari. IBM has not made that mistake since, though it has made others, notably over its copier, which, when first announced, turned out to be totally unsuited for Japanese paper sizes, which are larger than those used by occidentals (mainly because of Japanese caligraphy).

*   *   *

Brazil is the only Latin American country in which IBM has any sizeable stake. It is the boom market of Latin America. IBM has a System 3 manufacturing plant and works it intensively making sure that IBM is a net exporter. For the Brazilian market has in fact other characteristics: it is really a large systems market, one in which IBM has become entrenched and in which it has an even larger share than it has of the American domestic market. For instance, by the end of 1973 IBM had installed over 200 370/165s in Brazil—more than, it is said, it had installed at that time in Europe. IBM makes quite sure, however, that not much work of any criticality is done in Brazil: it has little faith in the stability of any of the Latin American regimes, and, in Brazil as in all the rest, tries to operate a sales policy, not one of rental.

*   *   *

Canada is probably the world's most advanced industrialised country dedicated to the proposition that as much of local industry as possible, particularly in the advanced technology industries, should end up being controlled by nationals. Canadian IBM, then, would be a considerable source of problems arising from growing nationalism for IBM management were it not for the fact that up till the mid-seventies the various branches of the Canadian Government responsible for the 'Canada First' policy were pulling against instead of with each other. At the federal level, the Treasury Board and the Supply and Services Department, which is responsible for authorising computer purchases, are much softer with IBM—having been extensively cultivated—than are the departments of Trade and Industry responsible for the 'Canada First' policy. Since much of industrial policy is, in any case, formulated by the provincial governments (who under the Canadian Constitution have considerable reserve powers) and since the provinces (particularly Ontario, in which most of IBM's Canadian investment and employment are concentrated) are more concerned with short-term interests, IBM ends up dealing with the situation it knows best how to exploit—divided responsibilities and differing aims.

Until the recent paper organisational shuffle, IBM Canada differed from the other WTC companies in that it was dealt with directly by Domestic, with only minimal reporting responsibilities to WTC. For all practical purposes, of course, it still does, for while IBM Europe is nominally headquartered in Paris, there is no such pretence with IBM Americas. That is run from New York.

The relationship between IBM Canada and IBM Domestic is closer than that. For all practical purposes its production facilities are integrated with Domestics', and it provides the majority of IBM's imports to the U.S.A. This is unfortunate, for IBM Canada's main manufacturing capability is Office Products, unfortunate, too, because many senior IBM people have long regarded IBM Canada as the best of the IBM companies, and its labour force is probably the best educated within IBM.

IBM in Canada tries to maintain a low profile, as low as is conceivable with 12,000 employees and a nearly $700 million turnover. It is content to stay away from the scientific market in which, in any case, there is a strong drift away from IBM. However, it does make use of the Canadian operation as a test bed. It may have sold SBC in the U.S.A., but in Canada SBC is a large operation and fully integrated, which means that when the IBM/CDC agreement runs out in 1978 and IBM can once more enter the service bureau business in the U.S.A., it will be able to quickly bring in a tried and tested service and mount an operation without any difficulty.

The problem that faces IBM Canada and keeps it from being quite as low in profile as it would wish has much to do with Armonk's habit of thinking of Canada as really an extension of the greater North American market. Thus IBM Canada got into difficulties in early 1975 when Armonk blocked the $2 million sale of IBM typewriters to Cuba. This was unconvincingly denied by

IBM Canada at the time, though no one was talking about the need to get permission from the State Department in Washington (American subsidiaries are forbidden to trade with Cuba under the American Trading with the Enemy Act).

*   *   *

IBM cannot help but get involved in international politics. IBM South Africa has found IBM management being questioned by American shareholders, mostly churches (who did not seem to quibble much over the hefty profits IBM made out of Vietnam) at one annual general meeting after another over the position that IBM takes on apartheid. There IBM lives within the law and custom, however distasteful it may be, but has within that context done much to increase black employment and wages. Corporate management has made special trips out to South Africa to study the issue at first hand and found the problems so complex and wearing that it could not help but record in one MRC minute: 'It was decided that the MRC is not to get overly involved in details of individual country operations.'

There are, of course, some operations Armonk has no wish to know much about. It may not wish to trade with American 'enemies', but this does not stop it trading with other people's enemies.

*   *   *

IBM has managed what is generally thought to be difficult: it has successfully broken the Arab boycott on trading with Israel. It is a major supplier to Israel, and also a major supplier to Saudi Arabia, most of whose computers are IBM machines.

IBM's involvement in the Middle East has always seemed to be fraught with difficulty successfully overcome. In the early sixties, for instance, it managed to sell its then largest system, the 7094, to an Iranian company. The salesman concerned was promptly sent back to America to receive the ultimate in IBM salesmen's accolades: the Thomas J. Watson Award, for it was IBM's first major sale in the area. There was a certain amount of consternation on his return to Teheran when it was soon discovered that the computer system was no longer with the customer. Nobody, it seemed, had thought about the reason why the company wanted the machine. They wanted to ship it to Russia, which they had done. No doubt it is still there, Strategic Embargo list notwithstanding.

One cannot leave WTC, without discussing an aspect of IBM's business which seldom gets mentioned at AGMs: IBM's dealings with the Socialist countries. In 1970, a quarter of a century after his wartime experiences,* TJW Jnr returned to Moscow, this time to see if IBM could do business. He made it quite clear that IBM would do a cash-on-the-nail sale, subject to Washington clearances, the same conditions that applied to IBM's dealing with Eastern Europe (with the exception of Yugoslavia), but that he had no interest in joint ventures or plant building.

The report of the MRC on his return featured one of the very few philosophic discussions ever to appear in the minutes, certainly the longest. Individuals were requested to make a formal statement for the record about what they wanted to do. Cary hedged his bet, Opel plumped for it, as did F. C. Rodgers and Jones, the latter having been faced with little option as he got called the culprit in the minutes for the lack of previous IBM Russian activity. As for T. V. Learson, his comment is worth noting in full: 'Does not want to do business with Mother Russia. Does not feel it is appropriate for the IBM company. Sees difference between the Eastern Bloc and Russian. Maybe several years from now would feel differently, but right now does not want our company to be doing business there.'

Of course, what goaded IBM into the Russian market was not simply the fact that it was there. Throughout 1973, it faced the galling prospect that if one was to look out of the Kremlin, the modern computing power of the State was largely provided by a competitor, and not even an American competitor at that. The biggest and most advanced civil computing installation in Russia came from ICL, and many of the crucial Russian Ministries were using System 4s, the ICL version of the system with which RCA tried to challenge IBM. To cap it all, ICL became the first foreign computer manufacturer to be given permission to have an office in Moscow.

From TJW Jnr's visit onwards, IBM's Eastern countries ven-

---

*TJW Jnr spent part of WWII based in Moscow.

tures were regularly to feature at MRC meetings, as the committee grappled with the complexities of trying to do business with Russia. The problem was basically simple: what IBM wanted to sell was old technology. The Russians, whose joint COMECON country-developed computer series, the RJAD, is based partly on IBM 360 architicture, technology and software ideas, were not satisfied. They have some IBM computers, a few bought directly from IBM. What they want, however, is new technology and easy access to the full range of IBM software.

The IBM Eastern European business is run from Vienna, the Regional Office Europe Central and East, or ROECE, which also covers Yugoslavia, Bulgaria, Czechoslovakia, East Germany, Hungary, Poland and Rumania. ROECE employs the best part of 300 staff who, in 1974, were brought under the umbrella of a new IBM company. One doubts that it made any difference: the direction of the effort is very much under the control of Armonk.

But they have not done badly. In 1969, $19 million gross, profit $6 million. In 1970 $30+ million gross with a profit margin up on the previous year, more than $12 million or just over 40%.

However, it did not, thereafter, build up as fast as IBM would like. Many of the deals that IBM was doing were for equipment where those countries have been charged with manufacturing similar units for COMECON's RJAD Series.

The unshiftable company has met the immovable object. Today, IBM has its Moscow office; it does a fairly good business in Eastern Europe, but while it has exhibited in Moscow and Leningrad, it has not pulled out the plums it wanted to. Late in 1974, for instance, it still had not been able to deliver its first major Russian installation, a 370/158, to Intourist.

The unshiftable company? One has to admire one thing: quietly, while no one has been looking, IBM has sold well over 200 computer systems through ROECE. Also, quietly, without any fuss, it is the seventies before the local IBM companies in Hungary and Bulgaria are handed over to their respective governments. IBM has managed to survive, a lonely outpost of capitalism, in two Socialist economies for twenty-odd years after all its fellow capitalists have left.

That time should not be taken as an augury of the future before the rest of the world obtains satisfaction. However, it does lead us to Part Three: the IBM interface with the outside world, and the problems and challenges that the skilled routines and management techniques of IBM pose for the computer industry, its users, and the governments of the countries in which it is a major operator.

PART THREE

And Tomorrow . . . The World?

CHAPTER THIRTEEN

Mirror, Mirror, on the Wall . . .

IBM is the only major case I know of in the Western world of a massive corporate inferiority complex. All the classic signs are evident. There is the absolute bar on IBM employees talking to the press without the presence of a member of what some senior IBM executives jocularly refer to as 'The Thought Police', or the utterance of anything remotely connected with IBM without first obtaining an IBM clearance. (Often, in highly technical coversations the Thought Police will be superfluous, not understanding the subject under discussion.) And there is the portentous answer that public criticism may conjure up, an answer often so internally emasculated before surfacing as to be meaningless.

This is no joke: in late 1973, while writing an article on equal opportunity and IBM, the author asked for some guidance as to IBM's policy. It took the IBM U.K. press office two weeks—and some nudging—to issue the following statement:

EQUAL OPPORTUNITY FOR WOMEN

It is the policy of IBM United Kingdom Limited to ensure equal opportunity in the conduct of all its business activities without regard to Race, Colour, Religion, National Origin or Sex.

These activities include Advertising, Recruiting, Interviewing, Testing, Employment, Training, Transfer, Compensation, Promotion, Termination, Employee Benefits and Social Programmes.

There is also the outraged reaction—'But it's from our Managing Director'—when a paper will not print statements better run up the flagpole. Above all, there is the hurt response which trickles down through the industry that is journalism when a reporter writes something that IBM disapproves of. No one in IBM will ever contact the writer directly: IBM does not work that way, though it continues to be puzzled that not everything it does is loved by all journalists who come into contact with it.

For IBM seriously and sincerely wishes to be loved: and what IBM wants, it tries to achieve. What IBM seeks is compliance in the media. Compliance, as interpreted by IBM, means that the only items the press should cover are those initiated by IBM and that they should preferably be handled IBM's way. There is nothing essentially wrong in this stance; the view that this is the function of press–public relations departments is perfectly tenable. The mechanics internally devised by IBM to achieve it are a thorough set of check lists concerning what is to be said and by whom (a mechanism which ensures that any question asked which does not fit the prepared script will be lost in IBM bureaucracy) and an emasculation of any statement which will commit IBM to anything short of agreeing to the fact that yes, IBM does exist.

There is a snag, however, which has become more and more apparent. It is in the nature of news that its form, content and timing cannot usually be foreseen. And, over the last ten or more years, IBM—by reason of size, law suits, technology, achievements and the like—has become news. This means that life for IBM's euphemistically entitled Communications Department is no longer as quiet and peaceful as it was in earlier days. The effect on the members of that department is now marked. They are either the young and inexperienced, low enough down the ladder to make the usual answer to a journalist's phoned query: 'I'll call you back' necessary as well as obligatory; or they are too often old, running scared and broken,* due to never-ending pressures. The exceptions in the middle are very few.

A large part of the job, said a former member of the Thought Police, consists of spending one's time internally agreeing that yes, that press comment was unfair, but no we should not do

---

* This opinion is not solely the author's; it has been expressed in private by IBM executives on both sides of the Atlantic.

anything about it—it is better to ignore it. Whether the comment is unfair is totally immaterial.

'They can do little right. If the press doesn't get them, IBM management will.'

The IBM approach to the media has much in common with its approach to the loss of IBM accounts. If the criticism is serious, sustained and appears in any publication carrying any degree of weight, a clutch of IBM executives are likely to descend on senior editorial staff and, if necessary, on the editor. This will happen either before or after the offending piece is published—though IBM prefers to move beforehand. At some time or other the descending vice-president senior executive routines have been tried on many journalists and papers, among them Jack Anderson and his 'Washington Merry Go Round' column, and *The New York Times* (in the latter once at least twice) Prior to publication IBM invested considerable time and energy to discover what *Newsweek* intended to print about the initial Telex judgement.

The procedure doesn't stop at this point. The paper's chairman (or anyone else on the board to whom IBM senior executives have access) is likely to receive a communication, an IBM objection. Trade publications in particular are subjected to this kind of pressure.*

In some cases the publisher can be approached, informally and indirectly, by senior IBM subsidiary directors and told quietly in passing: 'I should not print that if I were you', instancing an appropriate reason.†

Suppose that a publication is in the computer field, as in the case of *Computer World*. The wrong editorial appointment—as that of Dr Herbert Grosch as editorial director—will lead to a call to the publisher from the office of IBM's Chairman to come and visit him, and to be asked when he does so: 'Where have we gone wrong?'

It should not be thought, however, that all external contacts,

---

*In one case a phone call came out of IBM asking 'Why do you employ Malik?'

† On this autobiographical note, another little story is worth recording, which indicates the limits to which IBM will go. Early in 1974 I wrote a series dealing with some of the material in the IBM Papers for the French computer weekly, *O1 Informatique*. IBM found this so embarrassing that it promptly had the articles translated and telexed to New York. What no one, it seems, in IBM WTC in Paris realised was that the material was initially written in English, which *O1 Informatique* had had translated. Had they known and had the wit to ask, they could have had the originals.

the results of which are liable to end up in print, are directly handled by Communications, even with the help of Corporate. In some matters, it is important that those who will oversee it understand exactly what it is that they are saying: and those matters are financial. Security analysts will deal directly with IBM Finance. And that, reflecting the changing times, if not much more open than it was in the boom years of the sixties is now much more eager to respond, to put on a show. At least during 1973/74 almost any reputable New York analyst could get an eager 'In what way can I help you' answer to his queries.

The fact that these games generally are seen through is confronted by the arrogance of innocence. It never seems to have occurred to anyone in IBM that anyone else could consider what is stated on IBM's behalf will be taken as less than the objective truth. But no one in IBM would ever ask such a question.

This is not, in any case, the IBM way of doing things. No one in the corporation seems to have asked whether the problem as seen from Armonk or the local HQ is the one that really exists, that has to be faced. For IBM management see the world through filters. As seen from Corporate heights external criticism gets blamed on many things. (Thus, when M. Maisonrouge remarked that the reason IBM is not liked in Europe is that 'we are too big and successful and people don't like that in Europe', he missed the point. The objection is not made to IBM's size or success, but to the means by which its success was achieved.)

Part of the problem that faces IBM externally is that it is unprepared to be treated just like anybody else, and for that there is a reason. Prior to the late sixties, IBM was still a rapidly expanding company, one in which the talented generally thought there would be a future. However, partially because of IBM's success and partially because of the growth of the computer industry, the late sixties saw a new phenomenon: the former IBM executive striking out on his own, or who, because of the success of IBM, was thought to be worth substantial sums to other companies. (Hundreds left, so many indeed that they have since formed an IBM alumni association, sometimes referred to as the Ex-IBM Corporation [though it should be pointed out that there are as many more who are now rabid non-joiners as the result of their IBM experience].)

The former executive brought with him to the outside the

experience of the closed world of IBM. He often might not have had much power, but because of the strangling paper mountain that is IBM, the brave new bureaucracy, he would have had access to data and information—he knew how IBM worked. This has meant that the internal mechanics of IBM are no longer so secure.

They began to come on the scene at the right time. IBM executives in the past might have stated, as did IBM Vice-President Dean R. MacKay in the mid-sixties, that nothing could be written about IBM without its co-operation. This is no longer true.

Yet there is another reason, however, why IBM no longer always receives uncritical treatment, and that has much to do with changes in journalism. By the late sixties, the computer was beginning to energise the minds of politicians, and computing had become a major industry. Both were likely to lead to an increase of interest on the part of the press.

That IBM had previously been consistently under-reported reflected little credit on journalism, but this too could be accounted for. Probably the major reason why IBM eluded the press for so long was that the corporation had three major defences. The first was simply that IBM sales generally are made to other businesses, and other businesses are more often than not regarded by the public at large as fair game. Had those sales been directly to the general public and subject to the sort of scrutiny this involves, which can include highly visable contacts between constituents and their legislators with the attendant perils of publicity, it is doubtful if the IBM of today would exist. The start of the public querying of the computer industry and its works really began with the growth of public involvement with the data that users put into computers —with credit ratings, security clearances and the processes of computerised accounts. Those, insofar as the person involved was concerned, had one characteristic: what was being held on the computer system was subject to error, sufficiently so to make someone scream. It was only when there was enough noise that politicians and the like became seriously interested.

The second IBM defence against too much public interest was the single American stock. Outside America the growth in the business–financial press is a phenomenon of the sixties, but that press was and still too often is largely concerned with and covers local companies, and primarily companies into which the local investing public can buy directly. As long as IBM stock is in the total corporation, and primarily held by Americans, IBM is reasonably safe from close inspection.

The third defence was much more general and has to do with the practices of journalism. It is a truism of the trade that science and technology and the industries in which they play a large part are expendable. In terms of allocation of resources, editorial staff, space and editorial money, they come near the bottom of the totem pole. For few papers even today are driven by editors with any feel or ability for sorting out what is and what is not important in science and technology. While many have some notion that the subject matter is complex, that complexity is used too often as an excuse for the lack of coverage.

One should not have expected anything different. Few editors in the western world, and surprisingly even fewer editors of business sections, have any sort of background which would lead them in any other direction. This is particularly so in the U.K., United States, Germany and France. This has its consequences —the criteria applied to the selection of technologically oriented news to cover too often demands the 'sensational'. Journalists are sent off to cover moonshots and other assorted spectaculars; little money or space is left for anything else. Whereas the rise of computing has changed much of the economic landscape, a reader of almost any of the mass circulation papers in the western countries would have been almost unaware that, space exploration apart, anything except foolishness—'another computer gets another utility bill wrong'—was happening.

The result has been that technological–economic journalism, particularly that touching on computing, has become of the make-it-up-as-you-go-along variety; there has been little editorial direction or body of precept or practice to guide.

If editorial budgets have not been picking up the bills for travel and education, somebody else has. The mid-to-late sixties and early seventies are the great days of the technological boom and the technological junket, usually paid for by a company which had some economic axe to grind, an interest in the results.

That junket could take a European journalist to America and an American to Europe, and both to almost anywhere on the planet outside the Communist world at some company's expense.

IBM did its share and made its contribution to journalists' education. This posed a problem: what was a journalist to do—to refuse because someone was trying to sell him something? Everybody was trying to sell him something. The technological journalist's problem was further compounded by the fact that IBM was a changing, expanding company which gave the appearance of advancing technology on a broad front, something of which most technological journalists approved. And why should they not? Such change represents news value as understood by any news editor. Much more important was that this change and its effects were probably what had often attracted them to such journalism in the first place.

Yet, were they not to approve of companies such as IBM, they stood some chance of cutting themselves off from much that was going on.

Here one comes to the hub of the matter, the events which enabled IBM to exercise so much effective control over its own coverage: the building of a committed press corps with some understanding of computing has taken a long time and is really a late sixties to seventies process. For, as one would expect, a field which gets so little support from its own masters became a transient house for those bound for other—and more lucrative —areas of journalism. The result has been that much of the coverage of the computer industry generally, and IBM in particular, has been conditioned by strains and stresses not usually found, say, in the coverage of politics.

On top of this lay some special IBM factors. It has always been impossible for any journalist with independence of mind to establish the sort of rapport with IBM management that would exist, say, between a journalist and a politician, in which the relationship that exists will generally transcend the immediate report: IBM does not establish such relationships.

First of all, a distinction must be made. There are journalists working for papers who must be answered come what may—here the relationship is not really with the journalist but with the paper he writes for; he is merely considered a necessary evil. This apart, journalists are not viewed in terms of whether they are honest or not but whether they are malleable. The degree of malleability has a lot to do with the newness of the correspondent to the field and to the IBM company. One can observe correspondents gradually becoming more and more wary of IBM as their experience increases.

How, then, does IBM handle the press? To begin, one must distinguish between the United States and the rest of the world. IBM keeps files on every journalist who comes into contact with it. In Europe, the system early in 1974 was still a manual one, whereas in America it was computerised,* enabling IBM to 'remember' what any journalist had previously asked. In part this was due to the simple fact that IBM had not got round to this system in WTC; it was also due to publishing differences between the U.S.A. and the rest of the world. The American press corps is widely dispersed, and there is little of the involvement and camaraderie that distinguishes, say, the French and British press, nor the same involvement due to the majority of journalists being in Paris or London, where almost every journalist in the field will know everyone else and be known to IBM's PROs.

The lists, whether computerised or not, are thought to be graded by category, which (whatever the nomenclature used) cover a range from those who will write as they are told through the generally malleable—i.e. those who after having asked their slight rude question to demonstrate their independence will then write as they are told—to the thoroughly independent or hostile—i.e. who, in anybody else's terms, would be classed simply as journalists.

They will be treated accordingly. The latter will seldom be approached by IBM, whereas the former will. The independent will have to initiate the contact (no journalist should object to that). They will not be entirely cut off from all contact with IBM, but the contacts more than most will be regulated and reduced to a slow pace. Embarrassing questions will simply not get answered, and the independent journalist will be insulated as much as possible from any real IBM news that may be around.

To ensure that he goes away, IBM will practise its famous delaying tactics. It is a fact of journalistic life that all copy is written at the last minute before the deadline. IBM seldom says 'no comment' (except Press Officers, making jokes with known journalists). However, what one gets is the run-around: 'You

---

* Some key European journalists are said to be on these files.

know it's not something I can answer myself'; 'it has to go up'; even 'what do you expect in this vast bureaucracy'.

It has been necessary to discuss this at length to account for some of the reasons why so much that has been written about IBM has been so inadequate. There is one further point. In a situation where there is Corporate secrecy and corresponding product, market and country complexity—where few journalists have the time or inclination to dig hard enough to uncover, and put into context, fact and news—the usual vacuum-filling rules apply.

Much of the news about IBM is IBM-generated, partially by press release and by carefully stage-managed visits, press conferences and interviews in which the visitor will be shown only as much as IBM wishes to show him.*

A company making special press-visit arrangements obviously has a purpose in mind: it has something to show or discuss that it wishes the press to report, and obviously it wishes the press to go away satisfied with what has been shown and to report accordingly. There ensues a tussle, usually unstated, but nevertheless often colouring the press visit—we, the corporation, wish you would write about this from this point of view; we the journalists know that there is bound to be a snag. The situation is usually understood by both sides. Usually, but not always, because the reasons for press visits to IBM can sometimes be quite complex.

Once again, Ted Papes surfaces. A Justice suit exhibit of a Papes memo written in September 1967 tells us more about the rationale behind some press visits. The memo is entitled 'Purchase Brainstorming'. It concerns the problem of leasing company containment: what IBM wished to do was to switch customers away from outright purchase and back to rental and leasing from IBM. What Papes suggested was a war of nerves in which the press were cast to play a part. Of the seven items put forward, only three need concern us.

'PSYCHOLOGICAL FACTORS

1. Publicise a new technology through trade papers and discussions with user groups.

---

*There can be traces, too, of paranoia at this level: thus, some years ago, shortly after interviewing a noted IBM thinker, I was phoned up by a friend who asked whether I was dangerous or something. Communications, it seemed, had taken a close look at the IBM-er's office before I came in, making sure that anything funny or embarrassing was not on public display.

2. Have the press tour IBM's research facilities with the emphasis on our development of new technologies. The approach would be to talk about the technology and not about the product itself.
3. Send information to the investment banking community that would cast doubt upon the future of the leasing company industry.'

Whether the first two items were acted on is not indicated in that Justice Department brief, though, if so, it would account for some of the visits—and known subsequent copy—of the late sixties.* It indicated that IBM's motives in organising press conferences are not always quite the open, above-board ones of informing the press and thus the public.

Over the years press conferences have been held as the result of press reports concerned with a product, its price and performance. What happens is this: journalist X discovers that a particular product is not what it is claimed to be and reports accordingly. Unfortunately for IBM, he happens to write for a paper likely to be read by would-be users' managements. Some prospective customers do read it, which is immediately reported to management by IBM salesmen. The problem then is to obscure that report—what better way than to call a press conference to show the press the product at the first opportunity. With careful stage management, it is possible to make many journalists write something about it which contradicts journalist X; they have, after all, to justify their visit. This provides, of course, the salesmen with a

---

*That third item is included because it marks the start of a new Justice Department train of enquiry into IBM's relations with investment analysts and the information they have obtained from IBM as well as their relationship to it. Thus one noted analyst, Gideon Gartner, whose name keeps on trailing across the Telex case, has been a strong supporter of IBM, as one would expect from a former IBM market information manager. He has also been generally negative about IBM's competitors; for instance, one issue of the Computer Industry Letter produced by Gartner for his firm Oppenheimer & Co., seemed to have a lot to do with the rumours that swept New York market in late 1974 that Honeywell was considering leaving the computer business, rumours which were angrily denied by Honeywell President Edson Spenser when they were put to him.

Gartner is not the only one likely to be called on to testify. What Justice was looking for essentially was to see if the third item were acted on, and if so, whether any investment analysts were knowledgeable parties to it. Certainly it can be stated that Wall Street analysts are not normally as nearly unanimous about the future of an industry as they have been about the computer industry apart from IBM.

reply for their prospective clients: Yes, but did you see such-and-such a report?

When one looks at news initiated totally by IBM, the chances are that because the source is IBM, at least some of the material will be printed. Thus, in the case of all the law suits, IBM has been quick to make use of the legal procedures, the statements that get on to the public record as suits and appeals progress, putting out versions that ignore matters unfavourable to IBM but stress the favourable aspects, which, due to the undoubted effectiveness of IBM's press machine, usually obtain world-wide coverage. This situation was particularly noticeable in the Telex case and no doubt also will be evident throughout the cases to come.

IBM does not simply try to put out its own selective view; it would like to stop other people presenting theirs, particularly where litigation is concerned. In the Greyhound trial (see Chapter 14), in which IBM obtained a directed verdict in its favour before having to present its case, it managed to have the evidence accumulated by Greyhound sequestered by the court, so that—among other things—it could not be used by the media.

In the Telex case, IBM went to great lengths to try to stop the IBM Papers from entering the public record, but there, after a number of diversions, it was eventually defeated by a perceptive judge with a different view of the public interest. However, it was in the Justice suit that IBM scored its biggest news suppression success. As the result of some explanatory comment by the Justice Department to the press, IBM Counsel 'Fritz' Schwartz went before Judge Edelstein and obtained Order Number 4, which, for some time, was to be construed as restricting almost everybody within the computer industry from comment on the case and its probable outcome. What is interesting about this order was that no one besides Justice and IBM were represented at the time the order was sought and granted. It was not till one of the trade associations protested that a clarification was issued, which indicated that the only organisations so restricted were IBM and the Justice Department.

It eventually transpired that one of the comments which had prompted IBM to seek the court order had been on the numbers of documents being sought in pre-trial discovery, and that comment was based on data itself issued by IBM, which was not realised till the order had been issued.

Justice was scrupulous in adhering to the order. Not—whether by accident or design—IBM. In October 1972, Vin Learson, speaking in public, answered a question by saying that the break-up of IBM would never happen. The Judge would not accept this and suggested that he wished to see him. Cary, Learson and Katzenbach went off to court, where Katzenback had to get up and explain: there was no discourtesy intended, Mr Learson acted consistently with the advice given to him ... if that advice was not, in its turn, consistent with the order, then he—Katzenbach—should be corrected.

The Judge, in his turn, said the situation was perplexing and ironic, for he was being faced with an alleged breach by IBM of an order which had been initiated by IBM.

After the necessary amount of grovelling by Katzenbach, the court elected to do nothing. However, after the revocation of the more restrictive parts of the order, IBM was able to use it as a basis for not answering any questions. Effectively what the order had done was to give IBM a way out—'we can't answer that because it could be construed as comment and therefore controversial'—a weapon which it could use in its attempts to manage the news.

This technique had not been entirely successful, but it has had one effect. Much of journalism is unfortunately too dependent upon searching through the clippings in the library, paging through what has appeared before. This helped to ensure that what was uncovered was not quite as unflattering to IBM as might otherwise have been the case. However, in the long term it was of little help, for after the CDC case and settlement, the Telex suit, the further rounds in the Justice suit and the fall in the IBM share price, those clippings have not always appeared as friendly. True, the unfavourable references are heavily outnumbered by the favourable, but that any of the former should exist at all indicates that times have changed.

Today there are few if any reputable journalists on IBM's side of the fence, although there are several fence-straddlers (as Lyndon Johnson once observed, all that happens to fence-straddlers is that their asses get tired).

One would not expect that IBM's relations with the outside world through the media would be allowed to take place at a low formal level. Communications is not a reserved matter simply to keep Corporate informed, and senior executives do not descend on the press simply because it seems like a good idea at the time. Corporate worries about IBM's image.

Press relations surface in the MRC minutes at frequent intervals and involve Corporate management at the highest level, sometimes in almost nit-picking detail. Some of the comment is cryptic and obscure, but some is not:

December 1968:
'The *Fortune* article on LTV's raid was discussed. It was concluded that we should take no action at this time.'

April 1970:
'McKay reported that the WSJ [*Wall Street Journal*] will probably publish a story regarding IBM's entry into the copier business in tomorrow's edition. Any action we might take will have to await a review of the article.'

February 1971:
'TVL covers letter to editor in NY *Daily News* on clerical salaries in New York City. Our NYC posture not good, personnel had forecasted to get to $1\frac{1}{2}$% by end of year—TVL directed them to get to 5% right away. He is going to follow and report back to MCR . . .'

July 1971:
'One problem relative to System 3 pricing was brought to MRC's attention for first time. In March 1971 purchase prices were reduced on 2 of the 6 System 3 models. The proposed 6% increase would move purchase prices approximately back to previous level. The original pricing action received inordinate coverage in the press. Press reports stated our rationale for reduction was to bring prices in line with our costs. *This rationale was erroneously given out in response to a press enquiry.*' [Italics added.]

July 1971:
'System 3 purchase increase . . . Press coverage of the March action was called for and reviewed in detail.'

October 1971:
'Cahill, O'Connell, McKay, Katzenbach and Hubner enter to review suggested response to a press inquiry from CBS

News–Washington Burea relative to IBM contracts with the construction firm owned by Winston Blount, present Postmaster General ... After reviewing background FTC approved suggested response and emphasised that our position must be entirely open and above board on the issues.'

Those managerial worries can influence corporate policy to an amazing degree. Thus, in a report on the relocation of WTC headquarters, the minutes carry the following:

MRC: October 1971
'They (WTC) were also asked to consider the advisability of a total move out of New York City in light of the possible advantages for an international organisation in maintaining a headquarters facility there *and in minimising public relations exposure.*' [Italics added.]

The concern sometimes extends to seemingly trivial matters:

MC: January 1972
'Hubner [a senior IBM Vice-President] updated the Committee regarding a forthcoming *New York Times* article on IBM's industry position, Cary reported that he and Katzenbach will meet with the author next week.'

The follow-ups which devolve on IBM management apart, the MRC also reviews most commercially critical press releases, and the Questions and Answers which go with them.

The Q&A system is an attempt by a press department to prepare beforehand for any eventuality—any question that the press might raise at the press conference called by IBM to discuss particular and specific topics of which the corporation has forewarning, the only kind of press conferences that IBM ever holds.

Thus, in the projected price increase Q&As of Spring 1971, one question is phrased as follows:

Was this price increase designed to accelerate the movement of your customers from older equipment to System 370?

To which the answer is no; though that of course had played some part in management discussion. (If one is going to spout terminological inexactitudes, at least one must make sure that everybody is agreed on what they are to be.)

In the final Q&A for the Fixed Term Plan announcement there occurred the following:

Q. Why are the fixed-term leases limited to tapes, files and printers? Why not CPUs, memories, terminals, program products?

A. Each product area has certain market characteristics. For the present, we think the right business decision is to offer fixed-term leases for the equipment specified. (Decline to speculate about any future plans.)

This, though the plans to recoup through other products were already being laid and IBM was preparing itself to recover with the other hand what it was giving away with this one.

One must not, however, blame IBM for trying to be prepared. The MRC, in the guise of press overseer, is not simply trying to oversee IBM's relations with the press; what it is overseeing is its own external image presentation—as it oversees any image projections.

The processes involved in image management can, however, often create a situation which will come back to haunt one. A good example is to be found in the Honeywell/Sperry Rand patents case, specifically in the patent exchange agreement between Sperry Rand and IBM which followed the Consent Decree of 1956.

That IBM and SR had signed an agreement was known to *Fortune*, but SR was assured by IBM that *Fortune* would not publish the details. This, however, caused a problem: the protagonists would have to say something. They therefore issued a joint press release indicating that a 'non-exclusive license' agreement was now in existence, though the reverse was the case.

In August 1956, TJW Jnr sent round a memo with a script in question-and-answer form attached, telling executives how to answer questions concerning the agreement: but the script itself was designed to disclose none of the details. (In September 1956, however, SR executives were told by their management that the privileges of the deal with IBM—including the know-how exchange—were not available to other industry members.)

Eventually, when copies were produced in the Honeywell suit, as the result of legal demand, both SR and IBM were in turn to demand that they be treated as 'confidential' and covered by a court Protective Order.

Once, of course, one begins to go down this sort of route, one never knows what is going to lie at the end of it. The ramifications which arose out of IBM's knowledge that the ENIAC patents were barred both by time, and by prior derivation from Atasanoff were to be bizarre.

Naturally, no one ever told the shareholders that the agreement between the two companies was exclusive, or what it was that IBM knew. IBM had to behave as if the position generally held to in public were the true position; as if the patents would stand up. This, of course, involved the maintenance of that—also generally accepted—American view of the history of computation.

There is a much-quoted book designed by the office of Charles and Ray Eames for IBM called *A Computer Perspective*, based on an exhibition of the same name which had been on display in the early 1970s in IBM's Madison Avenue, New York premises. As a work purporting to be serious, if 'pop', history, it has been given the seal of respectability by Harvard University, who owns the copyright. It carries the acknowledgement: 'The assistance of IBM employees in the development of the exhibition and this book is especially acknowledged'.

It is all pictures and captions, a book designed for the television age. What does one find when one turns to the pages dealing with the ENIAC? Sole attribution to Eckert and Mauchly as its two inventors.

Yet in the patent suit, in overthrowing the ENIAC, one also finds that when IBM renewed its previously filed petition against the ENIAC (1959) on the grounds of prior public use, it did not then bring out into the open all the information that it had which led it to believe that there was derivation from Atasanoff.

Now one does not have to agree with the court that there is derivation from Atasanoff. One has simply to accept that IBM believed and thought it could prove that this was so: that IBM accordingly so informed SR, and that this was a factor in the conclusion of the 1956 joint agreement between the companies.

The punch line is almost superfluous: there is no mention of Atasanoff in the Eames book, certainly not in my copy which was bought in Washington in 1974.

*   *   *

The MRC also oversees advertising. That advertising 'control', however, often consists of generalised negative reactions, best seen in the context of one campaign reviewed in February 1971: 'we ended up generating ads but not of the calibre of excellence that the IBM company is capable of . . . the agency plays a role in this but by and large the problem is in our own house.'

Image manipulation in the advertising field involves placing ads where none are normally placed. It is not unusual for IBM, when it hears that an article about itself is forthcoming, and when that article cannot be sloughed off, to take a spread in the journal concerned, even though IBM ads may not have appeared there for years, if ever.

These are old, tried ways. One would expect the use of more skilful methods in influencing public opinion. For instance, while Judge Christensen was deciding on Telex v. IBM, IBM sponsored the film of the year shown on American television: *A Man for All Seasons*, the kind of film that would and could only be shown by a rich respectable company—a film, too, which has much to do with the struggle over conscience.

However, except for sponsorship, IBM seems to detest television reportage. It will do as little as it can to co-operate with television journalists. Fortunately for IBM, television poses few problems. Most of the 'copy' that IBM generates has too high a technological context for the television media: as for anything else, IBM just will not co-operate, using the same delaying tactics that it uses on prac- tioners in the typeset media.

It is not, however, simply the media that IBM tries to spindle and manipulate. Unwanted exposure to the outside world can come through other ways. There is that general slow leakage of in- formation through contacts with the organs of society, whether private or public, the data that a company normally expects to exchange with others, data which will allow it to measure progress against the outside world and which will also allow others to measure their progress against it.

One might think that, with the general tendency of IBM to pay a carefully measured slightly above the odds salary, IBM would be happy to let everbody know. This is not the case. IBM dislikes having to give away labour cost data. IBM Domestic hates unions. (Most WTC companies, being generally much nearer to their own local culture, have seldom been so paranoid about unions: they, the U.K., Sweden, France, have a much better feel for the reality of the outside world, so much so that in France particularly, the few unions involved seem even stauncher defenders of the IBM status quo than IBM management.) That hate colours American IBM attitudes to the information that it will make available. It will spend good money above and beyond the sums already expended to collect it, to make sure that the data is concealed from the public generally and unions in particular, for those unions too often have friends on the Hill.

Thus, one MRC minute discussed the containment of a 'security exposure' of pay rate information, extra cost of containment $106,000 a year. What worries the MRC is that the U.S. National Labour Relations Board procedures are such that they could conceivably force IBM to exchange information with other companies and with unions—unless IBM changes its data gathering procedures. This is a prospect the MRC does not relish. The IBM solution is to use the Bureau of Labour Statistics surveys, carried out of course with due regard for the anonymity of the company surveyed; the data then ceases to be identifiable, and IBM's data no longer becomes accessible to outsiders, wherever they may be. (IBM, of course, will still be able to obtain data from companies who have not taken such extensive measures to camouflage their activities, but that, in IBM eyes, is a bonus.)

What IBM seeks is a situation in which it discloses as little as possible but takes in as much of whatever might be relevant and useful to IBM: the question of fair exchange does not come into it. Thus, the corporation is represented at almost everything which could conceivably have any relevance to its business: it is a member or a subscriber to almost every association to which it could possibly belong, reputedly some two thousand associations and association publications in the United States alone. In some cases—for instance, the Computer Industry Association, to whose monthly journal IBM subscribes (though it publicly regards it as an anti-IBM association)—the contact goes little beyond the payment of the journal subscription. But in others, the large international conferences—such as the Second International Conference on Computer Communications held at Stockholm in the summer of 1974—IBM will put up funds, facilities and support, there will be a multitude of senior IBM technical specialists presenting papers, providing the audience and generally button-holing everybody in sight who could be useful.

This procedure is legitimate. What is perhaps more surprising is the absence of IBM from some conferences and discussions dealing with technologies. For instance, a network communications technique known as packet switching has excited interest among computer communications specialists and has been the subject of endless conferences since the end of the sixties, conference at which IBM has been almost totally absent—until 1973. Why? IBM had nothing to contribute. Packet switching was against IBM technical policy, and though everybody else was busy joining in communal experiments, IBM was conspicuous by its absence. It could not face a situation in which it was outclassed and in which its people would be seen to be technologically backward. The research 'grapevine' also indicated that management were not prepared to join in experiments requiring that IBM have network interface computers—made by others—installed on IBM premises.

But IBM's attempts to 'manipulate' everbody who can be 'manipulated' are not confined to technological and external matters. It is almost constantly sampling the internal emotional temperature, seeking to discover what employees think of their corporation and its policies. It spends heavily on house journals, from the births, marriages and deaths type to such journals as the house journal proper, IBM Domestic's THINK, whose printing bill in 1972 was $2·5 million.

The mechanics of THINK would justify the worst fears of Chairman Mao. THINK is organised to allow the cult of the personality to flower; the changing of the guard, for instance, is signalled and marked, and attempts are made to allay any fears that the troops may have about that change.

A study of THINK can provide much amusement in a sickening sort of way. THINK clearly marks the rise and fall of

IBM executives without humour or restraint—though there is some attempt at subtlety.

Nothing ever appears in THINK without an ulterior purpose, and, as with top salaries, all traces of egalitarianism are absent. It is a careful grading mechanism, a filter between management and the internal world. Thus, an early 1974 issue carried seven smiling pictures of Frank T. Cary, smiling because the Chairman of IBM must be seen to be exuding confidence, whatever IBM's sales figures may imply.

The grading mechanism can be found at its most effective in marking the successions: thus, the last issue of 1972 when Chairman Learson was handing over to Chairman Cary, showed a nice balance, four pictures of each man. Tucked away in the middle pages was a picture of former Chairman TJW Jnr. All except Watson have looks on their faces suggesting an unbounded faith in IBM's future. TJW Jnr, by contrast, having 'retired', was allowed to look visionary and pensive.

But image projection is not simply a matter of dealing with the mass public through the media; the financial public and IBM's shareholders through the technological economic press and the appropriate sections of the major newspapers; or IBM's own employees through THINK and whatever other means are available. There has also to be projection to those who matter, to those in a position to influence public policy directly.

For many years it has been the proud boast of IBM and its supporters that IBM does not indulge in politics: that no taint of the lobbyist hangs over the corporation. The linking of the two, as if the processes of lobbying covered all political activity, is a typical example of IBM at its most delphic and elliptical.

The notion that a large company working in an area which has political and defence sensitivity—one in which that corporation's relations with the outside world are bound to be of interest to the administrations of the countries in which it operates—that this has no connections with politics, need not even in principle be seriously entertained. If IBM were able to exist without having involvement with politicians, it would have discovered what many businessmen would consider the ultimate talisman. The truth is that IBM is deeply involved in politics and always has been: where IBM differs from almost everybody else is in its ability generally to conceal it.

How, then, has IBM managed to avoid more than minimal public criticism by politicians (even that minimal criticism of recent origin and having much to do with the American political climate post-Watergate)? The answer is as mundane as the truth so often is: 'The Establishment', something which IBM has cultivated world wide almost as a matter of Corporate policy. It is true that IBM does little conventional lobbying, but then lobbying as defined and regulated in America is a fairly restricted pastime. Year after year, the law which requires that corporations register their lobbyists and their expenditure on the lobbying of Federal legislators has IBM showing a nil return. (The same returns also showed that for the first nine months of 1973 IT&T also reported a nil expenditure, while expenditure by AT&T was $216 and by Mobil $312.)

Indeed, the nil returns themselves pose a question: how does ᴵ ᴮᴹ ᵐᵃⁿᵃᵍᵉ ᶰᵒᵗ ᵗᵒ ᵇᵉ ᶜᵒⁿᵗⁱⁿᵘᵃˡˡʸ ⁱⁿ Wᵃˢʰⁱⁿᵍᵗᵒⁿ ʷʰᵉⁿ ᵃᵗ ᵃⁿʸ time there may well be anything from one to twenty bills going through in whose outcome IBM will have some sort of interest?

The answer is in part to be found in IBM's very careful use of the law. The law does not require that IBM or any other corporation report its attempts to influence public opinion through advertising and public relations, or through the use of skilled legal counsel, whether or not that advice has overtones which could in their broadest sense be considered political.

IBM has in the past made use of both. For what can one make of the following? The July 1971 minutes concerned with 370 pricing also contain:

'TVL (Learson) asks for general opinions on any problems our current action might have with Congress, the President's guidelines on inflationary increases, Council on Economic Advisers, etc. No one sees any major problems. Dr Grove* was invited in to give an opinion. He stated that in light of our history in pricing actions, increases in the 8% range were easily defensible and would produce minimum problems. There would be no confrontation similar to steel or auto. *In response to TVL's request that he check with Newmyer in Washington, without mentioning any specifics, on the general temperature of the water relative to*

---

*David L. Grove, now Vice-President and Chief Economist.

our taking an action of this type, Dr Drove reported back later that there appeared to be no major concerns.' [Italics added.]

In the early seventies, the firm of Newmyer Associates Inc. were Washington P. R. consultants to IBM. If the passage above does not represent the results of a form of political lobbying, then the words have no meaning. But though Newmyer Associates are a legislative and administration listening post they are not officially lobbyists.

They fulfil many functions. For instance, IBM runs a local presentation centre, in which IBM hands down the message 'IBM is good for you' in a multi-media environment. To these sessions are invited politicians, their aides, members of the executive branch of government and the like. IBM also invites would-be customers and existing users—the latter, say some of those who have been to that centre, seem to be camouflage for the former. Newmyer staff are usually present.

The presentation centre is an idea that has been around for a long time in IBM. The most interesting such centre was in New York (1970) at Number Two Pennsylvania Plaza. It was designed by Charles Eames, was budgeted to cost $8 million and ended up costing another $6 million more—$14 million. A large portion of that sum was spent on specifically prepared films. It was the classic multi-media exercise buut with no expense spared: an octagonal room with two 35 mm film projectors behind each wall and slide projectors in profusion, all controlled by an IBM 1620 computer system. It had its own restaurant with its own chef (who was in the habit of using liquor in some of his dishes before IBM put a stop to that!).

Through that room have passed the same kind of people that IBM is still trying to influence. It had fifteen seats, and at each session all the chairs were occupied, at least five of them by IBM employees or executives. The visitors might know that; *what they did not know was that secretly peering at them from behind those walls were hidden TV cameras.* IBM wished to record and analyse audience reaction. The centre ran for six months before IBM closed it down. It has not, incidentally, featured in IBM's lobbying expenses.

But then the laws do not require that IBM nor anyone else report what it costs to cultivate those members of the administration thought to be worth cultivating, nor that it centrally report to any authority the efforts it makes to cultivate state legislators or members of other administrations, states, defence establishments or school boards. Nor do they require that IBM report its friendship with or hiring of a man who knows a man . . .

The policy of such hiring of winners is not confined to the junior levels of the marketing force; it applies particularly at and around board level. (As one former executive jocularly put it, it beats having to read *How to Win Friends and Influence People*, for a long time standard required reading in IBM.) Nobody has lied about IBM and politics, nobody has needed to. For if the hiring of a man who knows a man were an indictable offence, then much of modern business would crumble.

However, few companies have ever hired so many men who know so many other men, both at home and abroad—men from politics, men from the staider established and listened-to cor-poration and industrialists in America and elsewhere.   We had IBM. And at no time has it been more necessary to have such people onboard than since the start of the seventies. It would be stretching the bounds of credulity too far to believe that this has absolutely no connection with the trials and tribulations which legally and politically surround IBM.

Thus, if one compares the composition of the Board in 1971 and that of 1974, a number of changes become apparent. For a start, the Board has grown from eighteen to twenty-three members. To be realistic, however, the 1971 Board was eighteen members plus one temporary absentee: A. K. Watson had effectively taken leave of absence to become American Ambassador to France. Indeed, it is worth noting that IBM seems to regard that Embassy with a proprietorial eye: of the six men who have served the U.S.A. as Ambassadors to France through the sixties and seventies, three have a *direct* connection with IBM*. Amory Houghton Jnr is on IBM's Board; A. K. Watson had been on that Board and was to return; John Irwin II—who succeeded him—is brother-in-law to the two Watsons, one of the counsel of IBM who signed the 1956 Consent Decree on IBM's behalf and for nine months in 1970 a member of IBM's main Board.

In establishment terms, the 1971 line-up was impressive. Seven of the eighteen Board members were full-time IBM executives who

---

* One other had an indirect connection. See page 358.

had in the process, collected directorships of Continental Oil, Standard Oil, Mobil Oil, Bankers Trust, J. P. Morgan Guaranty, the Chemical Bank, and First National City Bank (it will be noticed that the Rockefeller interests here are large on the list). Also on the list were Carborundum, General Foods Corporation, Eli Lilly and Company, and Caterpillar Tractor.

All told, twelve members of the Board as a whole had connections with banks or investment houses, mostly of the first rank. The *external* directors included a former chairman of the Federal Reserve Board, a former president of the New York Stock Exchange, and other directors of some of the companies and banks noted above, among them Mobil, Chemical Bank, Caterpillar Tractor, and First National City Bank. Other interests included directorships of Bankers Trust—the Chairman; the Olin Corporation—the Chairman; Corning Glass—the Chairman; the United Fruit Company—also the Chairman;* Southern Pacific, Republic Steel, Avco, Metropolitan Life Insurance, New York Telephone, American Express, Dow Jones, General Foods, United States Steel Corporation, Royal Dutch Petroleum, National Biscuit, American Can, Fairchild Hiller and Pan American.

The eighteen between them also picked up the usual side interests, from a trusteeship of the Rockefeller Foundation (TJW Jnr) and of Vassar College, to worrying over the Salvation Army and the Boy Scouts of America. A company whose directors engaged in such pursuits could not be all bad.

A number of directors are deeply immersed in international trade through the International Chamber of Commerce and thus have some connection with politics, while two of its members had served past administrations in senior positions: Cyrus R. Vance, a Kennedy associate who had been Secretary of the Army and a former U.S. negotiator at the 1968–1969 Paris-held Vietnam Peace talks, and that other Kennedy associate, Nicholas de B. Katzenbach.

Other 1971 directors with interests in foreign affairs included Dr Grayson Kirk, President Emeritus of Columbia University, who was also President of the Council on Foreign Relations —publishers of that prestigious and influential journal *Foreign*

---

*They have now added the Chairmen of Du Pont and of Philip Morris Inc.

Affairs; and that retired Chairman of the Federal Reserve Board, William McChesney Martin, also a member of the Advisory Council of the School of International Studies. And, of course, Albert L. Williams had been Chairman of a Presidential Commission on International Trade, and John C. Folger was a former American Ambassador to Belgium.

Between 1971 and 1974, the line-up changed. During that time three directors left. Two were on that 1971 Board: the former American Ambassador to Belgium, and Emmanuel Piore, IBM's chief scientist. The third was an interesting retirement, one illustrating well IBM's close contacts with real central-to-American-interests money. He was Donald McNaughton, Chief Executive of Prudential Assurance, America's largest insurance company, and one with which IBM has been extensively involved almost throughout its growth. The cause of the resignation was his in a Prudential Investment in a subsidiary of that Plug-Compatible Manufacturer, Memorex. Memorex was suing IBM, and the Prudential had an interest in the outcome; it was owed around $20 million by Memorex and had shares in the company. That this was a straightforward clash of interests situation was made apparent in an IBM statement which also showed that Prudential headed a group of insurance companies which took in some $48 million of IBM money in 1973 under various IBM employee insurance plans. It showed too that IBM's long-term debt due to Prudential was then over $140 million.

Who then were the seven additional directors? The 1974 Board had seen the return of A. K. Watson and the promotion of three other IBM executives—Opel, Beitzel and Rizzo—so that ten of the members had now come up through IBM.

But the problem that faced the Watsons was that their full-time executive successors were all basically political innocents. They may have had beliefs, and made subscriptions (generally thought to be small) to party campaign funds at election times, but they had never really cultivated national politicians and had even less understanding of the in-trading that is the currency of politics (the only pressing of the flesh that IBM directors do is in the ritual of customer–supplier and employee–boss relationships, and those are differently motivated).

Looking after politics in its broadest sense was the job of the Watsons and of Al Williams: if the Watsons wished to leave IBM politically well connected, means must be found. A crash course in political friendship can be no substitute for what the Watsons gave IBM—the results and benefits of long and deep social involvement with politicians of all parties for more than thirty years.

The solution chosen was to involve politicians and political animals directly in the affairs of IBM, and it is in that light that the other three directors should be viewed. One was Harold Brown, President of California Institute of Technology, once director of Defense Research and Engineering, Department of Defense— another Kennedy appointment—and formerly Secretary of the Air Force under Johnson and delegate to the Strategic Arms Limitation Talks, a man who knew his way round Washington. The second, that ex-Congressman, former member of Presidential Commissions on this or that matter, and ex-Governor of Pennsylvania, William W. Scranton, probably knows it even better. Mr Scranton brought other qualifications to his post. He is also a former leader of the American delegation to the 1969 Intelsat talks, and satellites and communications are very much on IBM's mind.

He, too, was a director of Pan American World Airways, and so now was Tom Watson Jnr, which, with Cyrus Vance, brought IBM's Pan-Am representation—or vice versa—up to three. Co-operation, it seems, has its rewards.

But nothing brought out the new 1970s face of IBM more than the appointment of that third director, Patricia Harris, on the Board since 1971. Ms Harris, lawyer, ex-ambassador, black, former chair person of the 1972 Democratic Convention Credentials Committee, may initially seem to have been the ultimate in well-connected minority appointments, but that is still only on the surface.

It must not be forgotten that the Washington law firm which carries her name on its board also has that of Sargent Shriver. And Shriver, of course, besides once directing the Peace Corps and having been McGovern's eventual running mate in the 1972 Presidential election, is a Kennedy in-law; just to compound the Kennedy–Watson–Paris connection, he too has been Ambassador to France.

Patricia Harris, however, has other connections: she is on the board of the Chase Manhattan Bank and thus tied in to Rockefeller interests.

Ms Harris is but the latest manifestation of someone with a contact with those interests to surface within IBM, for the ties go back quite a way.

There is the ironic coincidence, the literary device connection; IBM was founded in the year that Standard Oil was broken up, 1911. There is the Rockefeller Institute Trusteeship of Tom Watson Jnr. And there is another connection not so far noted which pre-dates the arrival of Ms Harris by some eight years. That connection is through George Hinman, long Nelson Rockefeller's political campaign manager. Mr Hinman's other directorships are not quite as spectacular; his fortunes seem well involved with IBM's, for Scranton and McChesney Martin apart, he had the largest holding of any external director.

When dealing with the Rockefellers one deals with big money, and there is a large amount of Rockefeller money in-volved. There is, of course, the direct holding of the Rockefellers. IBM is the largest shareholding of the Rockefeller money* —reported to be $70 to $80 million in November 1974—next to Standard Oil (Exxon) and the Chase Manhattan Bank. The first is understandable; it is the basis of the family's fortunes in that grandfather founded it; of the second, one of the Rockefeller brothers owns 1% directly,† as well as being its Chief Executive. It was then to be expected that they would be represented on IBM—the third.

All this makes Patricia Harris's directorship of Chase Manhattan of interest. Its political bonus apart, it strengthens the ties of IBM to the Rockefellers and big 'Establishment' money generally.

Wall Street, it has long been noted, abhors a monopoly like nature abhors a vacuum; at the first opportunity it rushes to fill it. And Wall Street has had plenty of opportunity over the years to do so. The ties between IBM and what could be called 'Establishment' money are formidable. A *Fortune* listing of Institutional holdings in IBM stock as at the end of 1972 was very revealing, as are the directorships of IBM directors in those Institutions.

---

*Vice-President Nelson Rockefeller's and his dependents' trusts, according to the report of the Senate Committee enquiring into his investments prior to his clearance in November 1974, showed holdings of 103,635 shares in IBM, worth as of August 1974 nearly $20 million, or some 15% of his then total oil–industrial holdings.

†Rockefeller interests in the Chase Manhattan Bank all told add up to 2·5%.

Rank by Total Assets Managed	Investor	IBM Stock Held (in $ Value)	IBM Rank Among All Security Holdings
1	Morgan Guaranty	$2,094,000,000	1
2	Bankers Trust	*	1
3	First Nat. City Bank	1,028,000,000	1
4	Chase Manhattan	*	1
5	Manufacturers Hanover	769,000,000	1
6	Mellon Bank	468,000,000	2
7	First Nat. of Chicago	318,000,000	2
8	Continental Illinois	180,000,000	1
9	Harris Trust	254,000,000	1
10	First Nat. of Boston	474,000,000	1
11	Northern Trust	219,000,000	1
12	Chemical Bank	610,000,000	1
13	Bank of America	163,000,000	1
14	Bank of New York	422,000,000	1
15	Cleveland Trust	234,000,000	1
16	Girard Bank	208,000,000	1
17	St Louis Unions Trust	*	2
18	1000 investment co's.	2,366,000,000	1

*No $ amt. available

IBM is well represented in these institutions. IBM directors are also directors of five out of six of the major institutional shareholders in IBM stock. Frank Cary and Maersk McKinney Moller are directors of Morgan Guaranty, T. J. Watson Jnr and W. H. Moore of Bankers Trust, Amory Houghton and A. L. Williams of First National City Bank, Patricia Harris as previously noted of Chase Manhattan, T. V. Learson and G. Keith Funston of Chemical Bank. John R. Opel is a director of the eighth largest institutional holder of IBM stock, the Bank of New York.

Quid pro quos, indeed, abound all round. Thus two of the banks on that cross-related list, Morgan Guaranty and Bankers Trust, have much to do with IBM money. The first acts as one of IBM's district collection banks, receiving IBM monies; the second holds IBM's investment portfolio.

We cannot yet leave the new directors without listing other directorships they hold: Brown is a director of Schroeders, Scranton of Sun Oil, and both Scranton and Harris are directors of

Scott Paper. Other directors interlock on New York Telephone, while Learson has joined McChesney Martin at Caterpillar Tractor and has added Pepsi to his seats.

It can now be seen quite clearly that the list of directorships held by IBM directors welds the corporation quite firmly into the rest of the American financial establishment, particularly where no immediately glaring clash of interest can be seen. It ties IBM in to respectable money, to old money, though not necessarily always to the sort of economic performance that IBM likes to be associated with, but that is a small price to pay.

However, there are two not so obvious clashes of interest. That list of companies also reads like a listing of major IBM installations, which was to be expected. But even more interesting is the second possible clash of interest, for it is the result of a line taken by IBM in its legal argument about the structure of the market.

The line taken by IBM (see pages 398–402) is essentially that users could also be competitors; that companies with large computer installations could well come into the market and compete by offering time on their machines, machines which IBM has either sold or rented to them.

It didn't matter who supplied the machines, or which companies IBM chose to include or not to include in The Census. IBM itself has opened the door, and on that basis one could argue that as American companies are legally restricted from coming to market-sharing agreements, IBM cannot, therefore, in its turn, make any legal agreement with any company whereby that company is restricted from offering such computer services: IBM has set up a clash of interest situation in which there are very few commercial companies on whose boards IBM directors can also serve. But serve they do.

The political connections of some of these directors are, as the listing has shown, obvious. But what of the political connections of the Watsons? They are as many and as involved as were those of their father. Obviously, Dick Watson had such connections: one does not become Ambassador to France without them. Of the two, Dick Watson is the more faithful. Three months before he resigned from the IBM Board in April 1970, he called on Maurice Stans, then U.S. Secretary of Commerce. The problem IBM faced was concerned with 'the regulations then in force making it obligatory for American corporations operating overseas to repatriate a substantial proportion of their profits, profits which IBM preferred to leave abroad to enable it to finance as much of its growth from internal sources as possible.

Maurice Stans, it should not be forgotten, was also Nixon's chief fund raiser, and two years later appeared Dick Watson's $300,000 cheque for the re-election campaign.

TJW Jnr's politics are more involved. At some time or other he has supported Eisenhower, Kennedy, Johnson, Humphrey, Muskie, but then, in 1972, served as Vice-Chairman of Democrats for Nixon.

As we have seen, one politician really got hold of TJW Jnr, and that was Kennedy. Or, to be more accurate, he became involved with the whole Kennedy clan. That involvement ran deep: Bobby Kennedy at one point in the 1968 campaign was seriously considering bringing TJW Jnr on the ticket as candidate for the Vice-Presidency.

In 1974, informed specialists in the offices of the U.S. Congress and other Washington sources maintained that anyone who had a bad or questioning word to say about IBM, such as asking about its record and muttering the words anti-trust, would not get the chance to mention it to Senator Ted Kennedy.*

There was good reason. Nicholas Katzenbach's predecessor as IBM Counsel was Burke Marshall, who was also a close friend and legal adviser to the Kennedy family. He provided legal cover for Ted after Chappaquiddick. IBM aircraft also have been supplied to the Kennedy family at critical times, such as after Bobby's assassination.

That there is perhaps more than a nodding acquaintance between the Kennedys, their aides and friends, and IBM should by now have been well enough demonstrated. But this is not confined to politics. And here, without any implication of any wrong

---

* If that were true, then it adds a touch of irony to one much noted statement of Ted Kennedy: 'For at least a generation, few major pieces of legislation have moved through the House or Senate, few major administrative agency actions have been taken, that do not bear the brand of large campaign contributors with an interest in the outcome. Who really owns America? Is it the people, or is it a little group of big campaign contributors?'

He might usefully have added, 'or those who have assiduously and privately cultivated influential politicians and bound them with the bonds of friendship and private otherwise legitimate economic interests'.

intent, we need to turn to Mr Katzenbach's activities. Mr Katzenbach knows a lot of men, a lot of them lawyers, and why not? Many of them turn out to be favourably disposed towards IBM. It may be no more than that a company which employs Mr Katzenbach or one for which he pleads is bound to have something in its favour. But nevertheless it does lead to questions being asked, both in public and private. Among the latter have been those asked by Justice Department lawyers, who have looked at every bit of paper and correspondence that Mr Katzenbach wrote during his period at the Justice Department which might have a bearing on the case of Justice versus IBM. There is much interest, too, in Mr Katzenbach's associations with judges, not least with Judge Craig who ruled in IBM's favour in the Greyhound case (see Chapter 14). It turns out that the Judge, Mr Katzenbach, and Mr Barr among others are all sponsors of a legal aid to the poor nenenintion. It has also had been unknown for Mr Katzenbach to dine with Judges who have had something to do with cases in which IBM is involved.

It is all, no doubt, perfectly proper, just the courtesies being exchanged, but it is gossiped about within American legal circles, who also gossip about the trading that Mr Katzenbach does on his former place in Camelot and his period as Attorney General. There may be some sour grapes here. But even so, as there is no law against hiring a man who knows a man, there is also no law against hiring a lawyer who gets on with other lawyers, whether or not they are judges.

Up in the Supreme Court, one of the nine judges is that close friend of Mr Katzenbach's and former member of Camelot, Justice Byron ('Buzzer') White, who no doubt should any of the cases come before him will have little option but to declare an interest. He was after all influential in bringing Katzenbach into the Justice Department and is reputed to have close ties with his predecessor Burke Marshall.

And just to make the situation more difficult, at least two of the other Supreme Court Judges may well have to disqualify themselves should any case against IBM reach them, for they are also IBM shareholders (at the time of research). Indeed, indirectly almost all Judges are likely to have problems (as will many academics). To save themselves from conflict of interest problems, it is usual practice for federal judges to have their investments in

Mutual Funds and similar institutions in which their holdings are spread across many companies. The trouble is that most mutual funds in America are often substantial holders of IBM stock. Indeed the 'blue chip' status of IBM has been so high that even the present American Attorney General (late 1974) has had to disqualify himself from the prosecution of the Justice case against IBM, for his family trusts are substantially involved with IBM stock.

*   *   *

IBM's involvement with politicians is not confined to the United States. Wherever possible, it operates on similar lines abroad. Any politician who wishes to investigate computing can always do so as IBM's guest at one of IBM's facilities in some salubrious clime. But that is trivial; Germany, France, Britain, all have their legislators who are known to a few as the member for IBM, which does not necessarily mean that they have an IBM plant in their constituency.

IBM goes in for similar sorts of friendships abroad as it does at home. Thus in France, one of its directors was Olivier Giscard D'Estaing, brother of the President of France.

In the U.K., of course, IBM plays both sides. Thus, the Chairman of IBM U.K. was for a long time Lord Cromer, an ex-Governor of the Bank of England, former British Ambassador in Washington and a close friend of former Tory Prime Minister Ted Heath. On the Board sits that former Labour Minister (for Disarmament) Lord Chalfont. IBM for a time even employed Labour M.P. Roy Hattersley (who will not talk about it) as adviser. His job was to reconcile the Unions and IBM, but Armonk would have none of it.

All this obviously needs more investigation. It looks as if, in America at least, it will happen. For the case of Justice versus IBM has brought forth all kinds of allegations, with both IBM and Justice Department documents being filed with the court, and only the essence of IBM's being made available. IBM's documents show that IBM believes that the Justice Department has documents which involve former Attorney General John Mitchell and a former assistant Attorney General, Richard

McLaren, and that the documents discuss injuring IBM commercially, by trying to persuade users in the Federal Government not to obtain IBM equipment.

Whatever all this may have shown, it is not that IBM has little to do with politics, but the reverse. IBM's involvement with politics has been non-political in the sense that the activities of the Watsons have been of the kind which cover all possible options which run within the mainstream of America's political life.* And IBM operates similarly in the foreign countries in which it has its major investments. But covering all options can be read as just as political an action as covering some.

---

*And not only mainstream. There came a point in the late sixties where some 'underground' journals were said to be operating with IBM typewriters freely provided by IBM on permanent loan.

CHAPTER FOURTEEN

'A Lawsuit a Day keeps Justice at Bay'

'Mr Bond, we have a saying in Chicago. Once is happenstance, twice is coincidence, the third time it's enemy action.'

(Ian Fleming's *Goldfinger*)*

In the United States, anti-trust matters are regulated basically by the 1890 Sherman Act, as amended by the later Clayton and Robinson-Patman Acts. On the sidelines up till now has sat the Federal Trade Commission (FTC), which, though it has powers in the field of anti-trust, has in the past largely restricted itself to regulating trade between corporations and the ultimate consumer. To understand anti-trust regulation, therefore, one must really look to the Sherman Act.

The critical parts of the Sherman Act are the following:

Section one states that every contract, combination in the form of trust or otherwise, or conspiracy in restraint of trade or commerce among the several states, or with foreign nations, is illegal. (Exclusions here are minimum price contracts and agreements where free and open competition exists with goods of the same general class.)

Section two states that every person who shall conspire to monopolise or attempt to monopolise or conspire ... to monopolise any part of trade or commerce among the states or

---

*Coincidentally, the appeal judges in handing down a judgement in the Telex vs IBM case referred to IBM's SMASH plan as 'shades of James Bond'.

with other countries shall be deemed to be guilty of a misdemeanour.

Section three restricts every contract which is in restraint of trade or commerce within the United States, and between the United States and other countries.

The Sherman Act was later followed and amended by the Clayton Act, with its critical clauses numbered three and seven:

Section three makes it unlawful to have restrictive clauses in contracts and agreements which will restrict commerce, lessen competition and tend to create a monopoly.

Section seven restricts corporations from acquiring stock or other capital in other companies where the effect of that acquisition would be to lessen competition. It excepts the regulated utilities.

Later came the Robinson Patman Act. Section two, which makes illegal price discrimination where that competition will also lessen competition or tend to create a monopoly.

The thrust of the Sherman Act has in the past been that the conduct complained of should be intentional and not arising from events over which the party concerned has little control. (However, much U.S. legal opinion has been swinging round to the view that a monopoly *per se*, however acquired, is illegal.) But offences under the Clayton Act are usually easier to prove, as proof is only required of actions leading to a lessening of competition.

The Sherman Act, however, remains the core. But, as befits laws passed to regulate the power of the rich to get richer, the outcome has not always been that expected. The anti-trust laws are essentially political and legal processes, generally dependent upon action being initiated by the administration. That administration can be—and often is—subject to pressure: campaign contributions are more likely to come from those who fear that the law will be upheld and that they will be found wanting, than those expecting the reverse. Except for the great traumas, when America has indicated that politically it has had enough (of which the best-known example is the Standard Oil Case of 1911), the furtherance of anti-trust law is dependent upon the political whims and wishes of those in power.

Americans are fond of asking the question: can one get justice in a foreign country and foreign courts? The answer has usually been in the negative. But is a question which one might usefully turn round to ask: can one get justice in American courts? The only thing so far that seems proven in the anti-trust field is that one can get law; what is not established is whether a plaintiff can get justice. Most of the time, rich and powerful in America still often presumes right and legal.

This is a harsh judgement, one that should be viewed solely in the context of anti-trust law. An American might retort that he saw little evidence of anything different in Europe. Generally he would be right: few Europeans would, even in theory, dispute such a judgement. The European commitment to anti-trust regulation is more recent and, reflecting a different history, differs in emphasis. Industry has not grown up in the same environment; that the state has residual powers is part of the background history of Europe's industrial development. The state has not had to struggle to impose controls; rather, industry has had to struggle to free itself from state involvement. The office of public defender against monopolies and cartels, essentially the task undertaken by the anti-trust division of the Justice Department, almost a formalised moral crusade, really has as yet no well-established European counterpart.

The European concentration differs. It has long been concerned with market sharing and cartelisation agreements operating across national frontiers, and that, to put it crudely, usually poses a problem, in that the nation state containing the worst offender is also usually the one which is getting richer from the practice: someone else in some other country is getting the short end of the stick.

Strangely, however, IBM outrages European opinion on these matters even more than American. In Britain, for instance, 25% to 30% of the market is regarded as about the maximum company size if a corporation is to avoid being stigmatised and eventually brought before the British Monopolies Commission, though it needs to be pointed out that the powers of that Commission are minimal. For Europeans tend to think much more in terms of the concept of the dominant firm, and for that one need not be a 'monopolist' with more than fifty per cent of the market.

This leads to the point that American anti-trust laws must be judged by American standards, not by those of Europeans. Considered in this way, IBM supplies a few surprises.

Had Goldfinger ever examined a listing of IBM's brushes with Sherman *et al.*, he would long ago have come to the conclusion that what they say in Chicago has even more to commend it than he might originally have thought. He would no doubt have appreciated the skill with which the law has been used; how IBM has seemingly circumvented its intent; how, in fact, justice has not been just blind, but also seemingly deprived of all her other senses. Indeed, on examining the record he would, one suspects, have come to the conclusion that he was in the wrong business. For over the years a pattern of lies, evasion, half-truths and deception has been allowed to flourish with almost no penalty, and IBM has been permitted to continue to build and grow with seeming impunity.

IBM time after time has been able to present itself to the Court as the injured party, wearing the look of the born injured innocent on the face of its counsel, an expression which will be familiar to all old soldiers, the look of the old sweat troublemaker with the glib tongue. For if one is to believe IBM, its record was and is as spotless as its employees' shirts used to be white.

Yet once one begins to probe, the record is only remarkable for its length, not its diversity. For over the years, IBM has had three major brushes with the Justice Department, has been involved in suits at some time or other with almost all its major competitors, has run foul of many of its smaller ones, and almost always has been cast as defendant.

Interestingly enough, more often than not, the practices it is accused of in one case turn out to be repeat performances of the practices that brought it into trouble and which it agreed to abjure in the sometimes long-distant past.

But not all: some of the past tactics can no longer be practised. It is doubtful if, for instance, IBM would be allowed today to get away with filing a patent infringement suit, settling with licensing terms set so high that a company was forced into the hands of an official receiver, as Mr Watson Snr did to the Powers Tabulating Machine Company in 1922, thus for a time removing a major threat, as that company was the only other source of patents and know-how.

It would get short shrift from the Justice Department today if it tried to do anything as blatant as to threaten other companies that if they entered IBM's area of business IBM would enter theirs.

IBM did that to NCR in 1936, forcing it to abandon the development and marketing of a card-punching cash register by threatening that if it did not cease, IBM would in its turn enter the cash register business.

It would get even shorter shrift from European governments if it tried to acquire potential competitors, as it did in Germany in the twenties with Dehomag, in order to remove competition. Or as with France's Compagnie Machines Bull, a manufacturer of tabulators, when in the thirties IBM used the law to harrass CMB to try to prevent it from manufacturing IBM-compatible machines or punched cards. Then IBM went further—it tried to stop CMB's exports by buying up the Swiss company which had the rights to market CMB's machines outside France.

These were battles against competitors, in which the law was only a backstop. However, IBM's first courtroom encounter with anti-trust law and the regulatory power of the state was in 1932, when the suit filed by that federal organ, the Justice Department of the United States, concerned itself with what was to become the standard charge: infringing the Sherman and Clayton Acts.

Round One: The U.S.A. versus IBM—1932–1936

The charges brought in 1932 by the Justice Department were jointly against IBM and the then Remington Rand. They were charges under the Clayton Act and the provisions of that act which restricted what are known as tie-in sales. Justice alleged that users were tied to using cards produced by the two companies, and that if they went elsewhere the companies would charge higher rentals for their leased tabulators and sorters, for which in any case IBM/RR jointly agreed minimum prices.

The card trick the two were practising was analogous to that ancient routine followed in the past by some razor blade manufacturers. Give a razor away, but the razor can only take the manufacturer's blades, and those contain a much higher profit expectation than would otherwise be normal. Except that in the razor field, there are lots of manufacturers, and if you find the blades too expensive, it is not too difficult to come up with a cheaper combination: no one has a stranglehold on razor and blade patents.

Such was not the case with tabulators. The two companies also had an exclusive patent cross-licensing agreement, which restricted entry into the field. The companies also operated a tabulator lease-only policy, refusing to sell equipment.

The case that was finally heard by the courts in 1934 excluded patent cross-licensing, for by the time the case went to trial IBM/RR had dropped their joint agreement. (The origin of that agreement was curious in itself. It had been IBM which had effectively broken one of its major competitors, the Powers Accounting Machine Corporation. But it had been RR which had bought up its patents and RR was a much tougher proposition: so IBM and RR had got together and had carved up the resulting market between them. IBM had then 85% of the market, RR 15%.*)

The case was eventually to go to the Supreme Court, where IBM lost. But the verdict did not make it essential for IBM to sell machines; it was only barred from tying the user card purchase to IBM. This idea, however, was for all practical purposes academic ... IBM was allowed to devise the card specifications, and it then drew them so tight that, with its control of the best card manufacturing rotary presses in the business, no other would-be manufacturer could get in anyway.

Once a company has faced a Justice Department anti-trust suit, however, it can relax for a few years. Whatever it does, there is little likelihood that the Justice Department will go after it again immediately, and if it should, there is always the time it takes to get such a suit to the Courts. That first suit, though filed in 1932 and settled in 1936, was a relatively simple case by modern standards, yet it concerned practices some of which had been objected to in the early twenties.

Had anyone wanted to bring another suit, Mr Watson's support of Roosevelt, much appreciated as he was one of the few business leaders to do so, ensured that whatever was to happen would not happen just yet. The intervention of the war delayed it for a few years more. However, there was still unfinished business between IBM and Justice, and under President Truman's Attorney General, Thurman Arnold, action was to be taken.

---

*The figures were to haunt both companies yet again, for twenty-five years later, nearly similar market shares were to be achieved by both, this time, however, in computers—almost as if that market split were a law of nature. It is not; the market shares have changed yet again.

Round Two: The U.S.A. versus IBM—1946–1956

The investigation and legal in-fighting which led to what became known as the Consent Decree of 1956 needs considerably more attention given to it than the 1934 case, for the 1956 agreement in theory still applies yet has been extensively contravened by IBM.

Justice began to dig into IBM again in the late forties. In 1952, the Attorney General, J. Howard McGrath, once more filed actions under Sherman sections one and two—the same sections that have dogged IBM ever since.

Yet IBM was well and truly caught over the 1952 suit and had to settle for far worse than it expected. Four years later a Consent Decree was entered into, and then by TJW Jnr, not his father. For once the elder Mr Watson had been too clever. In January 1953, Eisenhower took over the Presidency: it was the worst thing that could have happened to IBM. The problem was not that Mr Watson and Eisenhower hated each other, much the reverse. It was Mr Watson who had arranged for Eisenhower's appointment to the presidency of Columbia University, and it was Watson who tried to talk Eisenhower into standing for the American Presidency. Indeed, within the space of five years Watson was to be pressing the Presidency on Eisenhower first for the Democrats, then for the Republicans.

But the consequences were that any really soft settlement between Justice and IBM was not politically possible this time, any settlement had to have some teeth to it, for there were enough companies and individuals interested to cry foul—and they were going to. In the four years between filing and settlement, the infant computer industry, particularly Remington Rand, managed to talk the Justice Department into extending its complaint against IBM to cover computers, something initially not presented. This was a remarkable extension, for it came less than four years after IBM had delivered its first computer.

The prescience of the 1956 Consent Decree, in fact, is quite remarkable when one considers the thrust of IBM effort in 1956 was still concerned with machines which are extensions of the punch card machines of old. At the start of 1956 IBM could note (in a progress report for the year 1955) that where 200 of its Series 650 machines had been installed—out of more than 1,000 on order—the actual figures for all its Series 700 computers were that over 180 had been ordered and 40 installed. At the time that the Decree was signed, world-wide IBM computer installations still numbered less than 100.

The complaint is a familiar litany of practices; IBM has violated and is violating sections one and two of the Act of Congress of 2 July 1890, otherwise known as the Sherman Act.

The all-encompassing complaint ran like this: IBM had attempted to monopolise, monopolised and is now monopolising inter-state and foreign trade and commerce in the tabulating industry, including new and used machines, machine parts and service, cards and service bureaus. IBM had entered into contracts, agreements and understandings leading to unreasonable restraint in both American and foreign trade in tabulating machines and cards. The result was that IBM dominated the manufacture and distribution of tabulators and the cards that were used in them, and IBM domination was in part maintained by IBM policies which sought to exclude would-be competitors, whether American or foreign.

The complaint then became more specific: almost every paragraph included the words restrained, excluded, prevented, or attempting to do these things. There was restraint of independent service bureaus, making it impossible for companies other than IBM to offer tabulator services to would-be users. There was restraint in that IBM made it impossible for anyone else to service its leased machines or to manufacture replacement parts for them. IBM systematically opposed all patent applications where those patents might indicate that a way round IBM's patents had been found. IBM varied machine prices to users, making them conditional on customer indications that they were going to continue renting from IBM. IBM installed free tabulators in situations where the user might otherwise go to a competitor. There was the IBM refusal to sell machines and a clause in the lease which prevented the user from attaching anything to his machine without IBM's approval. The result of these company policies was that IBM had around 90% of the tabulator installations in the United States and a percentage not far short of that in the rest of the world.

But perhaps the most interesting IBM offence was that it had broken the provisions of the 1936 judgement. It had been ordered to cease requiring users to have to rely on IBM cards, and it had done so in name but not in practice.

As we have seen, IBM had got round the 1936 provisions very simply. It did not require that the user buy his cards from IBM, simply that he buy cards to artificially high IBM specifications. IBM's volumes were such that it could obtain preferential terms for the paper of which its cards were made. It could play with prices, manipulating them in favour of certain customers so that they would not switch to using anybody else's cards. Then it bought up card production technology to make sure that no one else could get into the field. Many of these practices were still going on at the time the complaint was filed, many going on, indeed, almost to the day when IBM signed the Consent Decree.

There is one important difference between a Court Judgement and a Consent Decree. If Court proceedings result in findings of guilt, the Court can then rule accordingly. Consent Decrees, however, are arrived at to save the necessity of having a court battle. In this situation, the question of legal guilt or innocence cannot arise. Such was the position with IBM: the Decree carries the standard provision that IBM made no admission of fact or law.

But this can have one important effect. The complaint had tried to restrain IBM from indulging in the practices objected to in perpetuity. This is the cease-and-desist provision, a standard demand in major cases. But as there had been no admission of guilt, there was no such provision in the Decree. As important, the Decree dealt only with the position on the U.S. domestic market; foreign matters were excluded.

The complaint charged that IBM had used its patents unlawfully to effect and maintain its monopoly. The Decree directed IBM to make available its patents, both current and future, on an unrestricted non-exclusive basis. It was not allowed to charge for the existing patents; it was allowed to ask for reasonable royalties on new ones.

The Decree restrained IBM from pursuing any legal action in respect of existing patents which might have been infringed and restrained it also from exclusive patent licensing agreements. However, IBM was given a let-out: it was not made mandatory on IBM to grant any patent licence unless those seeking them were also willing to cross-license their own patents at 'reasonable' fees.

It is the sort of situation perfectly made for lawyers, and IBM was to make extensive use of the loopholes in a continual war to strengthen its patent position.

The Decree required that IBM offer for sale its equipment at a discounted price according to age of the equipment, and that the price bear a realistic relationship to the lease charges for new equipment. There was to be no discrimination in lease and purchase orders, which had to be handled on a first come, first served basis.

The provision which effectively put the purchase price of the equipment on a sliding scale according to its age was the first to be breached. In late 1963 IBM announced that, from 1st January 1964, there would be a policy change. Sale price would become list price, and there would be no allowance for age of equipment: if users wished to convert their leases to purchase, then they would have to pay in full. IBM was not offering to sell old equipment as new; it was taking the view that those who had leased could not expect to convert as if the rental they had paid was an advance on the purchase price. This is a point of view for which a lot can be said and a good defence can be made. As a consequence, a large number of users decided to purchase their existing equipment; to buy while the existing policy allowed the crediting of such rentals against purchase price. Among them was the Federal Government which purchased substantial numbers of 1400 and 7000 Series machines.

One does not have to be addicted to the literature of deception to spot what was to come next. In April 1964, less than four months after the policy change, IBM announced its Series 360, thus making obsolete all its previous computers. The joke was not lost on many of the buyers: the cash IBM had received for those lease-to-purchase conversions was in turn to be used to help IBM to finance the series which made that latterly purchased old equipment obsolete.

Said a government official: 'The one thing that taught me is that if IBM ever makes you an offer, you need to examine it very carefully. You can be sure that any proposal will be primarily in IBM's interest, and that somewhere along the line there will be a catch.'

IBM also was to get round the purchase-price, leasing-price ratios. The Justice Department had been concerned to ensure that they were not loaded one against the other so as to drive the market in a particular direction which might be in favour of IBM. Originally, that ratio had stood at around fifty-four months, fifty-four times the monthly rental being the purchase price. The leasing business that was to grow in the sixties was predicated on rentals of this length; indeed, the rapid IBM rate of investment recovery had made the independent leasing business possible.

But while IBM might find the alteration of lease/purchase price ratios on current product difficult to achieve, there was nothing to stop it changing the relationship on new. So, in the late sixties, as competition from the leasing companies became more serious, IBM began to play with ratios on new product. IBM would naturally prefer that users lease, but lease from IBM. Could it rescue some of its business from other hands? It could—the independent leasors had bought a substantial number of 360/30s, so IBM brought out the 360/25, and here the monthly rental-to-purchase ratio had been changed to eighty months. However, the 360/30 was functionally similar to the 360/25. So what had IBM done? Well, the would-be leasor might not object, it brought down his monthly rental. But the 360/25 was now priced in such a way as to make purchase financially unattractive. A further effect, of course, was that IBM dried up by the independent leasing companies' 360/30 lease markets, for the new rental had been carefully calculated to make the leasing company's borrowed money cost prohibitive. It left them with no margin with which to operate: there were to be few 360/25s in their hands.

The 1952 complaint also sought to separate IBM from what was known as its service bureau business, and the '56 Decree in theory did just that: it separated these activities and made them financially distinct.

The resultant business, to be named the Service Bureau Corporation, was to be run as a separate entity with separate 'books': it was not allowed to obtain its equipment from IBM at prices which were lower than IBM would charge its competitors.

The IBM interpretation of the Decree, however, seemed to be that the only services covered were those which had been provided by tabulators or equivalent services provided using computers. In 1964 IBM began to offer bureau facilities directly out of IBM, effectively competing with itself as sole owner of SBC. From 1966 the service included a time sharing (TS) capability, Call 360, operating out of IBM's Data Processing Division. Here it could be argued that IBM was providing a new information capability. More important, it gave IBM the opportunity to develop its TS capabilities using the real market, such operational information as it gained being fed back into trying to create effective computer systems which it could then offer as part of its major lease/sale computer business.

It was 1969 before three years of industry objections made IBM have second thoughts; however, it was not till after those objections had been much discussed in Washington, both in the administration and in Congress that IBM was willing to change. But by that time, IBM had obtained some of the basic TS experience it needed for the development of its own future product.

IBM was to make even more effective use of the SBC provisions of the Consent Decree in a way which had not been contemplated when that Decree was drawn up. The thrust of the provisions had been to ensure that IBM did not treat its bureau operations more favourably than it treated competitors. It was assumed that SBC would be as aggressively managed as before. From the middle sixties, however, IBM was to manage a singular switch. It was to manage *downwards:* IBM might be backward in time-sharing, but not quite as backward as SBC's time-sharing facilities were to imply.

For it was only SBC that was supposed to be policed, and SBC that had to be treated similarly to the way IBM treated its competition. IBM was now to turn that to its advantage. The pattern of IBM support for many of the customers offering time-sharing services based on IBM equipment was to vary from that given to other IBM customers.

Engineering support seemed less than equal, as was systems engineering. IBM was happy to obtain the sale of the original equipment, but IBM was not about freely to provide possible competitors with unlimited manuals—as it did all its other customers. The staff to support the bureau side of the IBM user-base seemed to be carrying a much larger workload than staff in other areas of the IBM market, reducing, some customers claimed, the quality of the service they were able to give.

Naturally, some bureau managements complained. What was the IBM answer? That this was the way that IBM treated SBC, and therefore it treated all other bureaus similarly!

So blatant did this discrimination policy become that in the late sixties, knowledgeable former IBM employees, entering the service bureau industry as independents, refused to have IBM kit unless they had to deal with other than that part of IBM's sales force which had been designated to cover the service bureau industry. They had no intention of being caught by a 'separate but unequal' policy. If IBM wanted their money, let IBM take it on the same terms as it took anyone else's. And IBM did.

The final Decree covered a host of other practices, with differing degrees of severity. The relief sought varied. Thus the complaint dealing with IBM's by now historic domination of the punched card market brought the toughest provisions of all. IBM was directed to sell up to thirty punched-card rotary presses a year for five years to those who wished to manufacture cards, and to sell excess card stock to those who wished to buy it. It was ordered to reduce its portion of the card market to 50% within seven years. IBM complied and did so with minimal fuss. This should have told everybody something; the card market as a major source of IBM profit was on the way out.

The Decree dealt with the IBM standard contract provision, the IBM restrictions on what customers did with their leased equipment. These 'what do you do with it' provisions were dropped from the standard IBM contract. IBM also could not require purchasers of its equipment to obtain maintenance from IBM, or to purchase any repair or replacement parts from IBM (though it continued to insist that leasors do so). It could not prevent its customers, whether purchasers or leasors, from experimenting with or attaching equipment to the machines they obtained from IBM. However, IBM might restrict those alterations and attachments if they interfered with normal operations or substantially increased the costs of maintenance.

Here IBM was to make use of the argument that such attachments did increase costs of maintenance, etc. It has taken some of its users to court on this issue, to make them remove such attachments, but almost everywhere the courts have said that IBM would have to use its 'best efforts'—another happy legal hunting ground—to continue maintaining the equipment.

However, the Decree made no mention of three of the major initial requests. The complaint—and the request for relief—had been specific: it had asked that IBM be ordered to separate the various charges which comprised the total monthly payment a leasor would have to make. All the Decree was to say about these covered purchased machines, and with purchase there was no legal way that IBM could bundle all the charges together. But that ability of IBM to conceal from the leasor exactly what he is paying for the service he gets—maintenance, repair and free instruction—still lies at the root of much of IBM's dominance and profit.

Second, the establishment of free and unfettered competition conditions. Third, the request that IBM be broken up (the phrase the complaint uses is 'divorcement divestiture and re-organisation with respect to the business and properties of the defendant, including its foreign and domestic manufacturing, selling and distributing facilities') were both treated in the same way as the request to 'cease and desist'; no court proceedings, no admission of guilt or conviction, and therefore no provision.

And in the end, the Justice Department even had to pay its own expenses.

A major cause of confusion since was to be the failure to obtain the requests the Decree lists with an 'in perpetuity' time stamp actually specified on them. The Decree is, whether by intent, oversight or design, surprisingly muddled as to the time the provisions are to last. Some of these provisions are limited to ten years or less, others carry no explicitly stated time period. With one exception, the phrase 'in perpetuity' is never used.

The result? The Decree has been interpreted by IBM to suit itself, for IBM has never been comfortable with a situation in which its competitive hands are tied so that it must operate exactly as if it were anyone else. Relief has not been had, to quote the twelfth request of the initial complaint, to dissipate the effects of the defendant's unlawful activities.

The actions of IBM in relation to the Consent Decree indeed are the stuff of which good journalism can be made, and like most such, there are kickers in the tail. The first comes from Request Fifteen, the only stated perpetual enjoinment in the Decree. This is concerned with the classic anti-trust provision; it seeks to stop IBM from entering into any form of market-sharing agreements with would-be competitors at any time and anywhere.

This has been specifically broken, but ironically without any evil intent. The provision may seem quite straightforward, the consequences that stemmed from it were not always so. Between 1963 and 1966, at the time that IBM was in panic mode, it was also exhibiting concern for some of its smaller competitors. Not, of course, across the entire field of manufacture/service, but down among the smaller brethren; among them, it was said, some in the service bureau area. What IBM was taking away with one hand it was in part giving back with another: its credit terms were sometimes quite generous. The IBM reasoning was simple; it might not want those competitors to grow, but it also could not afford a situation in which they went down, for that might be attributed to IBM and would bring more legal problems and costs than the decimation of those competitors was worth.

During this period there was also talk within the industry of IBM bailing out a couple of its competitors. Nobody could ever find out which ones, and the talk was thought by some industry specialists to be IBM inspired. But supposing it to be true, it would have been a clear breach of Request and Agreement Fifteen —whether or not the Justice Department had approved of it.

Yet one can well ask what else IBM could do. It was enjoined from acquiring competitors,* and had it done so its legal problems would have been compounded, yet it could not let them be seen to go down as the result of IBM action.

Kicker number two comes from the simple—and obvious —question which hindsight indicates it is necessary to ask. Why was IBM allowed to turn its tabulator monopoly into a computer monopoly? The answer is not simple, and here one must forego hindsight. Law depends not simply on the arrived-at precepts and standards of what is acceptable, but on human fallibility; the ability of people to see that the future will be different from the past. Anti-trust law, however, has to be more specific; before one can rule, one needs complaints or evidence of wrongdoing.

Sperry Rand's lawyers might be in and out of the Justice Department seemingly every five minutes, pressing for a stronger decree, but in the mid-fifties the complaints of IBM abusing its

---

*Between 1956 and 1974 IBM was to make only two acquisitions, neither of them central to its business: SRA in 1963, in many ways a test case to see whether IBM could acquire anything (and that was to bring howls that IBM was adding to its educational resources to make its offerings to customers more attractive, thus strengthening its hold over the market), and CML Inc., a company in which for the first time IBM did not insist on having a hundred per cent ownership interest. (See Chapters 7, 15 and Epilogue.)

position in the new field of computing were few. Indeed, they seemed largely confined to Sperry Rand, which had seen its initial lead already whittled away. But SR in a brilliant stroke (which IBM was later to emulate) had made sure that its complaints would be heard, and it was primarily as the result of SR's push that computing was inserted. The lawyer making representations on its behalf was not exactly unknown to the Justice Department. His name was Herbert Bergson and he had, before becoming involved with SR, been an Assistant Attorney General with responsibilities in the anti-trust field.

Naturally enough, IBM's counsel were, in their turn, screaming about the inclusion of computers: 'But we have not violated the law with respect to computers.' And they were right.

The initial complaint might be comprehensive, and the addition of computing controversial, but though the Justice Department sought to get the broadest coverage and relief possible, in line with the breadth of the complaint, it would not be unfair to state that some parts of the complaint were viewed with more seriousness than others. (It is in the nature of the anti-trust complaint and defence that extreme position will be taken up, to give both sides room for bargaining at a later stage.)

Certainly, Marcus Hollabaugh, the attorney in charge of the case for the Justice Department, was reasonably happy with what they had obtained. He regarded the abolition of the lease-only policy and the compulsory licensing of patents as the most important objectives, for they would have the greatest impact upon the user and would create opportunities for competitors.

The Justice Department was in a very strong position. For between 1952 and 1956, two cases had gone its way which were to immensely strengthen its hand. The first was the case of the Besser Manufacturing Company versus the U.S. The Justice argument here had been that Besser had monopolised the manufacture of machinery for making concrete blocks. It had been fought by Hollabaugh at the Supreme Court level, and he had finally won a judgement which required Besser to license its patents and cease its lease-only policies. The second case was that of the U.S. versus United Shoe Machinery Company. This is the case more normally quoted as apposite and important, for it too ended before the Supreme Court (in 1954), and the same sort of final judgement was given.

USM made equipment for shoe manufacture: it had between 75% and 85% of the U.S. market and operated a lease-only policy. The Court extended a decision made in a prior suit (that of Alcoa, with which we need not concern ourselves) and found that intent to maintain a dominant position was enough to convict under Sherman 2. 'Defendant having willed the means, has willed the end.'

And here with IBM was another lease-only situation. The IBM position was untenable, and naturally, building on a case that he had brought to a successful conclusion, Hollabaugh's first objective was to make IBM sell tabulators. But the prime patent objective was the tabulator patents, with IBM to produce a list of those at issue. Now, with the addition of computers to the complaints, the decree was widened to include computer patents.

As required, after the decree had been signed, IBM provided a list of the patents it held. Hollabaugh and the Justice Department now discovered that the tabulator patents were already much outnumbered (he talks nowadays of 'ten to one') by computing patents.

Hollabaugh was surprised, for that had not been apparent prior to the settlement. He could foresee that computing was going to lead to the creation of a new industry. After all, there were a number of major companies indicating that they were going to make computers. What he did not foresee was a situation in which most of the large corporations then expressing interest would, by 1975, no longer be in the computer manufacturing field. It is doubtful, however, if he foresaw computing growing at the rate it has, or its assuming the importance that it has within the organisations of the industry's users. Indeed, to expect that would have been to expect something most unusual, for hardly anyone else—even in IBM—saw it. It may be hard to credit it now, but credit it one must. After all, five years later, those expert American industry observers, the editors of *Fortune*, were to publish a book entitled *America in the Sixties*, in which they almost entirely missed the coming growth of the American computing industry, its shape, product and effects.

So why should Hollabaugh and his colleagues have been expected to be any different? In 1974, he said he thought that the case accomplished more than he expected, for the key to breaking the total hold of IBM was contained in the ability-to-purchase provision. As he puts it, in line with many past legal judgements: 'Once you buy, you have the right to tinker and to try to improve.' And it was that right that the 1956 settlement primarily obtained for users.

Yet the history of the computing industry since the Consent Decree leads to a question. If that Decree is in theory so powerful, however IBM might have treated it, why have we not heard more about it? Why has it not been more relied on in those seemingly neverending Everybody versus IBM anti-trust suits?

It has not been relied on, and cannot be relied on, largely because of the nature of a Consent Decree. Essentially, such decrees are an agreement between the U.S. Government and A. N. Other, and not a judicial judgement. A decree does not legally presume guilt or innocence. It is simply a legally binding agreement, and thus, though in theory the court is supposed to police it, the court, having little machinery at its disposal, must await effective enforcement by the government. This means that if a company digs its heels in, Justice will have to go through the processes of legal rigmarole which real enforcement will require.*

Here we come to an insoluble dilemma. It all sounds right in theory and principle: why should a corporation not have its day/week/months/years in court before a judgement is pronounced, whether for or against it? However, the other side of this is that the result is injustice: anti-trust consent decrees are arrived at because some competitor somewhere is aggrieved and thinks he is suffering. Yet one has the peculiarly dotty situation that almost no company will ever agree to a consent decree unless it can be proved that it was guilty of the practices initially complained of, and has come to the conclusion that even after the expense of much time and money it will be found guilty.

As we have seen, a consent decree can be the easy way out, the soft option. Yet having signed it, almost any corporation knows quite well that it can go ahead and break it if it so wishes, providing it does not do so too blatantly. The only people who can take effective action are the Justice Department. So, in signing that Decree, IBM proceeded to erect a block against those who might wish to take advantage of a legal judgement as the basis on

---

*It is possible for cases to be brought which seek a general enforcement of a decree—but this does not happen often.

which to sue. But as the decree is not a court judgement against a corporation, there is also another and parallel effect: other corporations are also barred from using it in their suits. So in CDC versus IBM, IBM managed to have references to the Consent Decree struck out of the final CDC complaint. Naturally, there were no references to it in the Telex case. So the public generally seems unaware of its existence.

The IBM settlement was to be Hollabaugh's last major case with Justice: he left in March 1956.* Yet, though he did not know it, IBM already had set in hand moves to circumvent what was considered one of the two major strands of the settlement. It was to make nonsense of the patents provisions by once more conspiring with Remington Rand (the word is not mine, it is used by the judge in the court case which follows) in a joint patent and know-how exchange agreement; theoretically non-exclusive, but in practice the reverse. Just to compound the deceit, Justice's lawyers were shown a copy, reviewed it, and decided that on the facts as stated there was nothing illegal in it, for the agreement on paper purported to be non-exclusive. (Indeed, Hollabaugh states that had he seen a copy he too might have approved, for it opened up the territory for Sperry Rand.) Its non-exclusiveness, however, depended upon management action—and there was to be no such action to let other companies know that it existed: much the reverse. This is not just my opinion, it is also that of the Judge, who summarised the joint IBM–SR action by stating that the parties had agreed to act so as to keep the agreement confidential.

Round Three: IBM's patent conspiracy

It brings us to His Honour Judge Roy Larson, U.S. District Court, District of Minnesota, Fourth Division, and the judgement he rendered.

What we are now dealing with is a patent case, one whose importance cannot be underestimated in any discussion of equitable solutions to the problems which plague the computer industry.

The critical word here, as throughout much of the rest of this

---

*After that he wisely kept away from IBM, computing and the Decree. The one thing he refuses to do is comment on the operation of the Decree: he has, he says, no knowledge.

book, is the use of the word 'equitable'. Now in almost every private anti-trust suit with which IBM has been involved, it has charged or put in a counter-claim concerned with what can broadly be described as its trade secrets, usually alleging that they have been unfairly used, pirated, stolen, depending on the case at issue. It did so in CDC, and in Telex it is indeed an almost automatic reflex action. But how has its own position been built? Why has it spent so little time re-inventing the wheel—when everybody else has had to? The case is to give some indications.

The case was between Honeywell Inc and the Sperry Rand Corporation, the first suing the second, once more under Sherman 2. (Also a party was a wholly-owned Sperry Rand subsidiary, Illinois Scientific Developments Inc., which, for all practical purposes, was an SR puppet, so I shall stick to SR throughout.)

At issue are the ENIAC patents to which SR was heir. Honeywell claimed that the patents are fraudulent and sought a judgement accordingly, for what is called 'the ENIAC patent'—a catch-all term—alleged to have exclusionary power; to make it possible for those who control it effectively to dominate the computer industry. The cause was the SR demand noted earlier (footnote, page 15) for $250 million from Honeywell.

IBM was not a party to the action, but IBM had one of the starring roles, and the Judge was to draw some quite startling conclusions about its behaviour, as well as to describe it in some detail.

The case went to trial in June 1971 and closed in March 1972 after 135 days in court. Seventy-seven witnesses appeared, eighty witnesses were present in deposition transcript, and there were nearly 33,000 exhibits, some of which were large. The documents relating to the ENIAC patent application occupied a four-drawer legal filing cabinet, while the famous patent itself consisted of ninety-one sheets of drawings and 232 columns of text.

All this data is contained in Judge Larson's judgement in October 1973: including references there are over 300 pages. It was a bitterly fought case; indeed, at one point in the judgement the Judge wrote of opposing counsel being 'less than kind to each other', the sort of phrase judges use only when lawyers are busy calling each other expletive-deleted liars.

Judge Larson overturned the ENIAC patent. He did so on a technicality, a grave technicality, basically that the machine was in public use* more than a year before the date on which the patent application was filed and there is therefore a bar in law. He also added for good measure that prior publication by John Von Neumann and derivation from Atasanoff also bar the patent.

But in the process, the Judge brought out that some of the applied-for patents, patents on which the position of both IBM and Sperry Rand have been built up, were not well founded in law or fact, and that both companies have known this for a considerable time. SR and IBM were referred to as conspirators and were told to watch out for the anti-trust implications.

The ENIAC patent application was filed in 1947, but the patent was not granted till 1964. The Court found that the delay had been deliberate: SR and IBM were trying to keep competitors out. Honeywell had had to expend considerable resources and time to try to get round the patents, when the ENIAC patents were not in fact valid.

During the years between the filing of the ENIAC application and the granting of the patent, SR was also filing patent infringement suits and interferences with the Patent Office. These are methods used to warn off other inventors, patent applicants, and would-be patent infringers. One with Bell Telephone Laboratories, eventually settled by a cross-licensing agreement between them and a short, one-day trial (which was to be another travesty of justice, for the trial happened *after* the patent cross-licensing agreement between SR and Bell had been made) was to cause Judge Larson to comment: 'Deliberately extending the expiration of a monopoly is a serious violation of the Constitution and the patent laws.' However, he found, 'with some reluctance', that this had not been the intention.

IBM entered the ENIAC game early: it filed an interference, a public use petition in 1946, a blocking move ruled premature. It filed again in February 1959, when it received an adverse ruling. But that, as we shall shortly see, was by then to be expected.

SR and IBM were to employ a number of different strategies over these patents. SR at one point hired an ex-government attorney who had been responsible for denying IBM access to

---

*In passing the Judge also brought out what had long been known but denied—for the dates at issue would have overturned the patents—that the ENIAC was used in feasibility calculations for the H-bomb.

government documents which might have helped IBM's claims. SR hired him with the intention of using him to help it with any further interferences and to win any prior public use proceedings that might be brought.

So eventually once more SR and IBM got together. They had been fighting over patents for years. There was, in fact, one legal fight still in progress (involving a patent clash between the ENIAC and IBM's SSEC). IBM told SR that neither would get a patent, so they agreed that it was in their joint interest to settle their differences. (To make sure that SR saw the force of the argument that it was necessary for them to come to an agreement, IBM shortly afterwards put in a counter-claim in the ENIAC v. SSEC suit, in its turn claiming patent infringement.)

The Consent Decree came into force on 25th January 1956. On 21st August 1956, IBM and SR entered into an agreement to cross-license each other their computing and calculating equipment patents and patent applications—including the ENIAC—and to exchange secret and proprietary computing and tabulator equipment know-how: probably the largest patent licence deal in history.

It was IBM which suggested that the deal include both tabulator and computing patents; all patents up to 1956, among them those for the ENIAC. What was proposed was, as the judge was to call it, a technological merger, and that was what was going to happen.

The judgement is quite clear on what this accomplished:

'15.25.11. The impact of the total EDP* and TAB system technological merger between IBM and SR in 1956 was stifling on the growth of EDP competitors and the EDP industry generally; since 1956, all EDP industry members except IBM and SR (and CDC to a limited degree) have been operating under artificial EDP market constraints imposed by having to compete against the combined technological portfolios of IBM and SR during the critical starting and developmental period of the EDP industry.'

Thus Honeywell spent more on R&D during the years 1955 to 1960 than it had computing turnover. The Judge continued. Honeywell has proven that it was injured in its business or property

---

* Throughout the judgement the phrase EDP, standing for electronic data processing, is used for computing.

by reason of that 1956 EDP cross-license between IBM and SR.

And at 15.25.24. 'The SR–IBM technological merger . . . injured competition in the EDP industry by *conspiratorially* allowing the perpetuation of the high combined market share of the two parties to the merger and tending to protect the proportion of each conspirator.' [Italics added.]

Both companies had the duty to seek out their competitors and tell them what was going on: neither fulfilled it. Indeed, the reverse happened. Both knew that the technological merger was 'fraught with anti-trust difficulties' (in IBM's case the Judge Bromley we have met before had said so clearly).

Throughout the negotiations between the two, IBM kept on reiterating that the two companies would have to provide the same know-how to all competitors who requested it. IBM was worried that any settlement with SR might be construed as admission of guilt to SR monopoly charges, particularly as IBM had agreed to pay SR $10 million under the terms of their settlement. But (according to the Judge): 'IBM did nothing effectual to implement this requirement.'

Now this happens to be a serious issue. The Consent Decree forbade IBM from exchanging technical information on an exclusive basis. Yet here was the same TJW Jnr, within months of signing that Decree, if not specifically and directly agreeing to break it, at least being legally responsible for it having been broken.

One would think that, after all this, Honeywell would have collected handsomely. Yet it lost its suit. It turned out that most of the disclosures in Court were time-barred: the Statute of Limitations obtained and Honeywell could not collect. The Judge was not very favourably disposed to Honeywell. At one point, he stated that 'plaintiff failed to act with any kind of diligence in the protection of its interests'.

Honeywell had actually known much of this story for a long time, if not as long as IBM and SR. Indeed, according to IBM claims, Honeywell was offered all the technical information made available to SR. Honeywell, it turns out, had signed its own agreement with IBM, though eight years after the SR–IBM deal. Its agreement called for cross-licensing between Honeywell and IBM of existing 'information handling' patents issued or to be filed prior to May 1968. Had Honeywell known, of course, it could have had access as of right, without any special negotiations. Yet because of the technological lock-out, Honeywell had been forced to obtain many of its peripheral devices from IBM, substantial quantities being leased by Honeywell and then re-leased to users.

Anyone signing an agreement with IBM, however, had better beware. At the end of 1964, IBM notified Honeywell that it would no longer lease for re-lease such items as card readers and punches: this meant that Honeywell would have to purchase at full list price and then have to go through the full cycle of getting its money back itself.

The Judge did not give the reason, but one can be inferred. It is the same reason we met earlier, the problems of IBM in funding 360 Series development and using every trick available to make other people pay for it.

The 1965 IBM agreement, it might be thought, was proof enough of intent to treat the law as something inconvenient to which only lip service be paid. But, as so often happens when organisations set out on the path of deception, they try to cover all options and get themselves into a situation where, should discovery result, they will look even worse.

By 1958, IBM had become concerned that there could be anti-trust implications. If it did not proceed further with its attack on the merit of ENIAC patents there might be talk of collusion. So IBM took measures, *in concert with SR*, to mount such an attack: the Judge was to call the acts surrounding this a conspiracy. The acts included the withholding from the court of evidence then in IBM's possession that the ENIAC patents were invalid because of provable prior public use.

IBM might not wish to let the courts know this, but that did not stop it from saying so to SR. But now, of course, having by design failed in its attempt at proving prior public use of the ENIAC patents, IBM had to go along with SR. IBM agreed to further pay-ment to SR of $1·1 million under a royalty against production agreement in force between the two companies. In April 1964 SR's ENIAC patents were finally granted. In November 1965, eighteen months later, SR and IBM extended their licensing agreements to cover all information handling patents up to those to be filed before November 1970. This now left each party free to infringe each other's patents without risk.

At this point in the story, the Judge commented: 'IBM was then and should be now, apprehensive about anti-trust law suits.'

What exactly had IBM accomplished? It had used the threat of patent suits—in conjunction with SR—to keep its other competitors at bay; to make them go the long way round, even though it knew it was doubtful that the patents relied on would be confirmed. IBM had known that the ENIAC patents were not valid but nevertheless had conspired with SR to present a front to the rest of the industry as if they were. The costs of that to the rest of the industry were incalculable.

It had gone into this quite freely, no one had pushed it. It was a clear case of violation of the law's intent. The point of the 1956 Consent Decree patent provisions had been to try to create a situation where the growth of would-be competitors could not be blocked by IBM's hold over patents; the intent had been to open up the industry to competition. Initially IBM had complied, yet almost within weeks it had set out to create in computing a similar situation to the one complained of in tabulators, a situation where IBM would once more have a complete coverage of all relevant patents, such patents being denied to all but one of its competitors. It had, in other words, behaved exactly as its past indicated one could expect it to behave, unethically and, as the Court was to rule, illegally. But what else did anyone expect?

Round Four: CDC versus IBM

Though IBM and CDC officially settled their differences on Friday, 12th January 1973, the events which led to the settlement were set in motion by IBM some eighteen months earlier. The settlement arose not from what IBM did in the market but as a result of what IBM executives had put down on paper. (It is a perfect illustration of the Max Bleecher proposition noted earlier.) In other words, it has its roots in IBM's methodology and marketplace tactics. The CDC suit had been filed in 1968 but little seemed to be happening until, in the summer of 1970, IBM began the processes of document search. It asked the Minneapolis Court for access to large numbers of CDC files and documents, some eighty millions of have—a number eventually to rise to one hundred and twenty million. The Court gave the go-ahead, and CDC were instructed to provide the documents within three months.

CDC came back in the September: they, in turn, requested between twenty and thirty million IBM documents, provision to be made in four months. We can get some idea of the problem from one IBM affidavit. What CDC sought at the first search turned out to be 17 million documents, taking up approximately 5,800 cubic feet (enough space for a reasonably sized three rooms plus kitchen and bath apartment), or as IBM Counsel put it: '. . . 6,300 boxes which equals 174,000 pounds or 87 tons'.

The task of finding the IBM documents was massive, took 305 man-days and involved going through the files of 103 executives, 60 departments and searches in the files of 30 branch offices, one district office, five regional headquarters, one plant HQ, Corporate HQ, DP Group HQ, and DPD, SDD and WTC HQs.

It was a mammoth undertaking for both sides, though even more for CDC than IBM. There is no way that quantities of documents of this order can be screened in the sort of time conl00 envisaged: privileged and incriminating documents may surface anywhere.

Though most of the legally privileged documents had been removed by the time that CDC's lawyers started to go through the originals, deciding on what to copy and what not, many IBM documents got through about which there was to be much argument: were they—or were they not—privileged legal work product? Among them was the Faw Memorandum (p. xvii), which turned up in CDC's search quite early, and was the cause of the real trouble. The procedure adopted was one in which CDC's lawyers did their search, had the selected documents copied on the spot, and left the originals out on top of the boxes that they had come in: this gave IBM a chance to see what had been copied.

A few days after the Faw memo had been uncovered, IBM became aware of the seriousness of the discovery. Thomas Barr and Frederick Schwartz of Cravath, Swaine and Moore turned up, and the conversation between them and CDC Counsel went something like this:

'We have,' they said, 'a problem.'

'We know,' said CDC Counsel.

'In future,' said IBM Counsel, 'unless you consent to our screening first, you cannot copy.'

'No way,' said CDC Counsel.

The issue was put before Judge Neville. Judge Neville heard argument and ruled against IBM. 'However,' he said, 'if I find privileged documents from here on in, I may rule.'

Document production finished in February 1971, and, almost immediately, IBM hit CDC with its counter-claim. The counter-claim was in part based on the use of some CDC confidential documents on which CDC itself would have preferred to claim privilege.

What one side can do, however, so can another. The CDC response in its turn included the use of documents on which IBM also would have preferred to claim privilege. There was Faw's memo, and there was a five-page memorandum written by George Turner of Cravath, Swaine and Moore, addressed to Burke Marshall, then IBM's House Counsel. That document has not yet been published; it is indeed one of that handful of documents which IBM was and is struggling desperately to keep private. But it has been widely discussed among anti-trust lawyers. For reports have it that it summarises and analyses some 4,000 IBM documents which had been submitted to the Justice Department by IBM during the processes leading up to the Justice Department suit. 'It is,' said one lawyer, 'a statement in conclusionary form concerned with the meaning of the documents submitted to Justice'—the conclusion seemingly being that IBM has been caught red-handed.

That April, Counsel for both sides went before Judge Neville. They were arguing through various pre-trial motions. Here CDC Counsel objected to IBM's use of privileged documents. IBM had fought long and bitterly to keep the seal of privilege on as many documents as possible. (At one time it was to claim such a seal on 40,000, which the Judge was eventually to reduce to 1,200.) Now, trying it on, Thomas Barr, lead Counsel for IBM, argued that privilege had been waived by CDC.

'All right,' said the CDC Counsel, 'then IBM must waive. Rule similarly for both sides.'

Judge Neville was angry at IBM and Barr, for having been put in that position.

'I am ruling both sides waived,' he said.

At which point, Nicholas Katzenbach, by now IBM Counsel, made his first floor appearance. He didn't address the Court, he addressed Barr. 'He stood there,' said an observer, 'poking his

finger in Barr's chest. Eventually they disappeared into the hall.'
On his return to Court, Thomas Barr asked if the judgement
was appealable. The Judge refused.

So began the battle. IBM quoted from CDC privileged
documents. CDC replied in the same manner, using Faw and
Turner. The second evidently caused more interest than the first.

'Let me see it,' said Judge Neville at one point. The IBM
documents in CDC hands were passed up, and he sat there for the
best part of fifteen minutes quietly reading. At the end of it, he
looked at IBM Counsel as if to say: 'My, Mr Barr', and handed
the documents back to him. He then kept the ruling on waiver in
effect and denied everybody everything.

IBM had manoeuvred itself into the very position it did not
want: and that was to have repercussions.

Soon after the court appearance, Justice intervened. It asked
CDC to produce microfilms of some of the IBM documents CDC
had filed and indexed. There was no formal objection by IBM
Counsel, just an insistence that they should first vet the
documents, excising or holding back those considered privileged.

Justice regarded that as unsatisfactory and, in view of Judge
Neville's Minnesota rulings, now approached Judge Edelstein in
New York, the judge with responsibility for the conduct of U.S.A.
v. IBM, to obtain court enforcement.

Edelstein now ruled that the documents were to be produced.
IBM refused, and he promptly fined them $150,000 a day, or
roughly 5% of IBM's then daily net profit, until they complied.
IBM appealed. By now, IBM had seen the mistake it had made
and gone back to Minneapolis to try to repair the damage, saying
to Judge Neville words to the effect that a little mistake had been
made in the case of CDC v. IBM, neither side had waived
privilege.

It was, however, too late. Eventually Justice were to obtain the
documents after the rejection of the IBM appeal.

The above may seem a digression. As will soon become apparent, it is not. For the Justice and CDC cases are in many ways
intertwined, beyond separation. Much of the evidence in the CDC
suit is also evidence in the Justice suit. As important, the two suits
were for a time joined together—with the suits of Greyhound
Computer Corporation and Telex—for document production,
which led IBM lawyers, among other comments, to complain

bitterly that CDC was doing Justice's work for it.

Now one would expect that a case involving the computer industry would find that industry making use of its own skills and products to improve legal performance. Both CDC and IBM did just that: indeed, the preparation on both sides is the first try-out of computer skills applied to case preparation on a massive scale.*

The systems that CDC and IBM developed to cope with document searching and retrieval are in essence simple to describe, but time- and resources-consuming to construct. Much more is known about the system devised by CDC for the reason that, as part of the CDC and IBM settlement, the first agreed to destroy the index to the legal data base that it had built. This caused a public row and a demand by the Court that the index be reconstructed. In its turn that caused journalists—among them the author—to scurry about seeking as much detail as possible.

The system that was developed is essentially based on the coding of documents, the input of the resultant selected data into a computer system, and a capability to search the data base that is then built up.

In mid-1974, Hugh P. Donahue, Assistant to CDC's Chairman William Norris, was to give a short description of some of the systems essentials before the Sub-Committee on Anti-Trust and Monopoly of the Judiciary Committee, U.S. Senate.

'... A para-legal staff of approximately 120 people were engaged in the discovery process, in screening between 25–40 million documents in various IBM files throughout the country. Of those, more than one million documents were copied on microfilm as being relevant to our allegations. An automated data base was established and software developed for an information retrieval system to provide access to relevant documents. Of the one million documents that were copied onto microfilm, 80–100,000 of these were put into the automated data base.' (Other sources indicate that those documents were on average five pages long.)

'This also required extensive coding, key punching, verifying

---

*IBM sent its lawyers on a computer appreciation/utilisation course: Project DELPHI. They became so enamoured of it that, at one point, they wanted to put an on-line terminal in the courtroom.

etc. We employed over 10 full-time lawyers on the case and had 20 additional lawyers available on a part-time basis. IBM employed about five times as many.

'For their part, we estimate that IBM reviewed over 120 million documents of Control Data's and they copied over 6 million of these as being relevant to either their defence or to a counterclaim that they had filed against Control Data.'

There is no breakdown available for what this cost IBM. However, in fighting off a later Telex complaint over the destruction of the index after IBM and CDC had settled, CDC were to note the following:

'It is estimated that in the course of reviewing the millions of documents produced by IBM, microfilming those of interest, converting the microfilm to hard copy, developing computer programs, "coding" the most important documents and entering such codes into the computer and making it (th)e(se) als, CDC spent approximately $3,000,000.'

CDC had as many as eighty people coding at any one time (where IBM had between three and four hundred). Essentially, what the coders had to do was to follow the instructions of the lawyers who had pre-screened the documents. A form had been devised which gave the documents identification number, date on which it was written, addresses, type of document and such similar identification information. Then it went into greater detail: persons and equipment mentioned; competitor or user; the practices the document dealt with, market share, paper machines and fighting ships, intent to monopolise, profit and loss, disparagement, unhooking, coercion, bait and switch, education allowance discount, Consent Decree and the like.

The data base, however, is only part of the legal system that can be built up with the use of a computer. Not long after the IBM–CDC settlement, CDC were cheekily to advertise the system in the legal press. The American Bar Association journal carried an advertisement, which under the heading of 'Lawsuit Support' listed the following facilities:

On site document review/selection
Data base design implementation
pre-filing support
case sizing

trial support
interrogatories
document support
logistics and scheduling
procedures and documentation
offensive document discovery
defensive document discovery
complaint development validation
topical indexing
document control
privilege document handling
privilege system
document demands/subpoenas
information retrieval
abstracting
logistical planning
deposition support.

The cheekiness is further compounded, for the advertisement continued:
'We put it all together.
'A fast and more economical means of handling litigation.
'An experienced non-legal professional work force with established tested procedures and legal support systems.' [Italics added.]

It is obvious that, used with care, such a system can be a quite powerful tool (though such systems have, as we shall see in the Telex suit, one defect: if one is not careful one can end up relying on them to a point where the human being who still has to do the courtroom operating will not have as good a grip as otherwise on the case's essentials). Its power and effectiveness were to be demonstrated in both the CDC and Justice cases, in the latter being used extensively in some of the early pre-trial preparations. Such a system has other uses besides enabling the user to look at the weight of evidence in any area or to engage in complex searches by subject. It can also be used to indicate what does not exist, to find holes in the decision-making flow of paper being searched, to look for gaps in such chains as company mandatory procedures, searching to see if what was supposed to be carried out, was carried out.

The computerised legal system had much to do with bringing the suit to a favourable conclusion for CDC. However, computers or no, it was not quite all plain sailing. As we have seen, IBM can devote much skill and attention to putting up distractions, to diverting the opposing party, and if possible the courts, from the nub of the case at issue. There were some prime examples of this in the CDC case.

IBM Counsel talked of getting the Judge in to go and look at IBM installations at NASA, even if he had to go to the President for permission.*

There is a possibly illegal combine in Europe to which CDC is a partner (though anyone but a lawyer would know that that possible combine has about as much strength to it as a cigarette paper: the combine to which CDC belonged then being a joint company with a number of other manufacturers concerned with common standards for their equipment, a combine somewhat marred at the time by the inability of the participants to agree on such difficult matters as what time of day it was, due in part to the clash of personalities of some of those involved. As for them agreeing on anything else . . .).

And there was the media-gagging diversion. If a judge can be got to agree, the law will sometimes allow a party to throw everybody into general confusion. Pre-trial order number 4 in U.S.A. v. IBM, (see page 343), at one time seemingly barred almost everbody in the computer industry from making any public comment about anything whatsoever. It began with IBM Counsel instancing press reporting of the fact among others that the press had talked of 25 million documents having had to be produced by IBM, with a contention that this was prejudicial to IBM. It turned out eventually that the figure reported had originally emanated from IBM.

These were all interesting. But the biggest diversion of all was of a different order. (The legal cause was to appear in the Greyhound case—see next section—but as it also featured in the CDC case, this is a good place to introduce it.)

One of the techniques long practised by IBM in its dealings

---

*The systems they saw were the four on-line 360/75s at NASA Houston: the stars in IBM's NASA showcase, as they are used for in-flight control. It is doubtful, however, if the Judge was told that their operating systems had been primarily created by NASA and not by IBM.

with outsiders, whether lawyers or journalists, is to send them off, if at all possible, scampering after rabbits, in the hopes that if IBM can put up enough rabbits they will lose sight of the fox. Many articles and books have been written, in which IBM figures, where this technique has been most successfully used.

Now one of the problems that faced IBM was that the evidence in CDC, Justice and Telex contained hordes of IBM market studies, memoranda, reports of meetings and just plain reports concerned with IBM's market share. They indicated how IBM viewed the market and the IBM share of it. Taken together, they could be held to indicate that IBM was a monopolist and knew quite well that it was a monopolist.

The practical problem that IBM's management and lawyers were concerned with was how best this could be obscured. The solution involved being able to go before the court and say in effect, 'Sorry, Judge: we may have operated on the basis that we had sixty, seventy or eighty plus per cent of the market at various times, but it really ain't like that at all, we were wrong. The market is in fact much wider, and with the court's help and permission we intend to prove it.'

They sold this notion to Judge Neville. Whatever else may be said about the late Judge Neville, it is not suggested that he really understood the issues before him, which may have been as much the fault of the lawyers as the Judge. The work-load required to reach understanding was heavy, and, say observers, he was never prepared to put the time in really to master the case. He was also, as so many judges would be when faced with a case of the size and importance of CDC versus IBM, much flattered by the deference with which a lot of very senior and influential corporation lawyers treated him; by being called to testify before a committee of Congress, and the like.

Judge Neville bought it. What was it he bought? The notion that there were more companies in the field than those which obtained all the publicity; that the competitive market-place was in fact much wider than was generally assumed, even by IBM.

But, to establish what the market was, there needed to be carried out what is popularly referred to in the trade as The Census: IBM deposed 3,300 companies, of whom 2,700 replied. A winnowing process reduced the list to nearly 1,800. (As well as confusing the issue, this is a further example of the Bromley protractor principle at work, for it adds to the time taken up by pre-trial proceedings and reduces the likelihood of an early trial date.)

The way it worked went like this: first IBM worked out the questions in collaboration with Greyhound Computer Leasing Corporation, for this was the legal occasion giving rise to the Census. Then the companies had to be contacted—a long, lengthy process as the forms asked for much intimate company data, including turnover, budgets and costs; all data which happens to be valuable market intelligence, and which was made available to IBM. Naturally, some companies objected to the court giving IBM this latitude and to letting IBM have all the data—data not made available to them. This led to further delay as the courts became even more involved. And after all the data has been collected, one needs to do analysis and draw conclusions.

So how had the Court been sold a pup? Well, the Census in cluded almost every company which had any connection with any form of computing whatsoever. Besides the well-known mainframe, mini-computer and peripheral manufacturers, the survey also included manufacturers of instrumentation, data-transmission equipment, and analog computers. It included, too, time-sharing and othe computer bureaus and even, at one point, such companies as General Motors, treating that company's computing power as something which GM could sell on the open market. And if it did so, then it could be presumed to compete with the products of IBM.

The pup that IBM sold Neville can be looked at in another way by transposing it to the transportation market-place. 'Your Honour,' said learned Counsel, 'what we are discussing is the movement of people and things, there is a general market-place covered by the idea of transportation. Therefore trains, supersonic aircraft, wheelbarrows, trucks, roller skates, aircraft, bicycles, motor cars, skate boards, helicopters, motor scooters, tractors, submarines, all forms of shipping, travelators and escalators, and even shoes, are all in this general transportation market-place and compete with each other.'

Of course Counsel in one sense is right. But it is not much use and comfort to a businessman manufacturing track shoes in Kansas City and faced with falling sales to be told that he is in a general transportation market-place and that part of the reason is that he is facing competition from Boeing 747s operated by the visiting airlines.

The reality is that these do not directly compete with each other: like competes with like and not with products at this abstract, almost ethereal level.

The logic from here on in is not simply crazy, it is positively absurd and could only have been devised by corporation lawyers. One of the prime interests of IBM in The Census was to discover the size of the leasing industry market and to put flesh on the computer machine-time market.

The logic works like this. Companies to whom computers have been sold or leased may well also be competitors in that they offer a machine-time capability on the market which impacts on the possible systems sales that IBM can then achieve. They then become possible competitors.

The water here does not get just deep, it becomes bottomless. For the consequences are that almost everybody with a computer could be a competitor not even simply those with IBM computers. The market is no longer one concerned with who sells or rents computer systems but available computer time. Yet that most of the competitors have obtained their computers from IBM is immaterial. By doing so, they become competitors.

The sublime craziness of this proposition creeps up on one rather slowly. Sublime? Well, consider the consequences. The more that IBM sells, the larger it gets; but the less it has of the market, the less dominant does it become, for in doing so it is increasing possible competition. Therefore, far from the measures that IBM has taken leading to a situation which strengthens the IBM monopoly, the situation is the reverse. Thus, by behaving like a monopolist, IBM is in fact reducing its market share. The defence rests and the various complaints should be thrown out. They did not, of course, actually say just that, but no one would have been surprised had they done so.

But there is another reality: to seek to discover the state of the market on this sort of scale will take time. Indeed, in the IBM case it took a few years. But the computer business is, as we have seen, a growing, changing business, and after two years the chances are that the material is no longer as up-to-date as it might be.

So now one comes back to the court and says: 'Judge, we have a further problem. The Census is now out of date. If it is out of

date, how can we all possibly go to trial when at the heart of the
case lies our defence that the market figures were all wrong, that
the market we are accused of dominating is not in reality the
market that exists?

'Please, Judge, can we take another Census?'

Round Five: Greyhound versus IBM: 'It's the nature of the system?'

A number of other plaintiffs were tied in to CDC in Minneapolis
for document searching, among them the Justice Department and
the Telex Corporation (dealt with later in this chapter),
DPFG—a company which was represented in its IBM suit by the
legal firm of which IBM director Mr Harris is now a partner, and
the Greyhound Computer Leasing Corporation.

The Greyhound case is a Sherman two case, monopolising or
attempting to monopolise. It lasted for twenty-four days of jury
trial and ended quickly in a directed verdict by the Court that
there was insufficient proof. Gratuitously and eccentrically the
Court added that the computer market prices were set 'by
economic factors over which the defendant had no control'—a
strange judgement to make since the plaintiff's arguments had not
yet been heard.

How did this happen? Greyhound was offered an early
trial—'there's this Judge down in Phoenix who can hear the
case'—and jumped at it. And why not? Judge Neville had ruled
that what Greyhound had discovered could be challenged on
grounds of relevance and materiality, not authenticity. The
ground was clear to proceed.

Judge Craig in Phoenix had different ideas. In my court, he
effectively said, you have to establish authenticity, which immediately opened up the territory to any delaying or dismissive
tactics that IBM chose to play. IBM played them—and won the
first round, and the case went to appeal.

The case is useful for one thing: it is a demonstration of the
first trial run of The Census. That showed, for what it was worth,
that the companies in the field had grown from 11 in 1952 to
1,757 in 1970 and that revenues had grown from $45 million to

$9·4 billion during the same period. This, and the growth in manufacturers of computers to the extent that by 1972 there were 62 in existence, was all to be made much of by IBM.

The problem with the Greyhound case, however, is that while the company was clearly affected by actions taken by IBM, the company record, say close observers, does not exactly reek of managerial brilliance. To discover how much of the Greyhound failure was due to IBM actions and how much by the actions of Greyhound management would require much more public investigation than the case has had. That IBM had set out to systematically break the leasing companies, Greyhound among them, was never really proven in court, though obvious on the market place. Nor was the case fought through with the resolution that one might expect.

(Indeed, the case represents the second major anti-trust disaster for the lawyer who fought it on behalf of Greyhound. His name is Edward A. Foote, and in the fifties he was assistant to Attorney General Herbert Brownell. Mr Foote has been in the news before: he was put in charge of the case of Justice versus AT&T in the fifties, one of the major anti-trust cases of all time. He then lacked experience in anti-trust action; in fact the job was taken from experienced lawyers so that he could handle it. Shortly afterwards he approached AT&T's general counsel saying that he also lacked confidence in the government's case and thought it therefore silly to take the case to trial. The issue ended up in front of a Congressional Committee, though not till after AT&T had agreed to a Consent Decree (1956) so weak that an AT&T executive was to scribble on the margin: 'It is only window dressing'.)

Judge Craig of Phoenix, appointed by Katzenbach to the bench during the latter's period as Attorney General and Greyhound attorney E. A. Foote between them tend to leave the case surrounded with confusion. It is not, therefore, a case that anyone—even IBM—is much interested in relying on; it is a diversion. Greyhound may have assembled the evidence, but as it never really got a chance to publicly discuss it and to properly connect it both with IBM management and the corresponding moves that IBM took on the market, little can be made of it.

What makes a suit of interest in this context is the light that it throws on the workings of IBM. To lay bare IBM's methods requires much skill and hard work. That skill, hard work, and the resultant light were to come in the Telex suit.

In his judgement in that case, Judge Sherman A. Christensen said this about IBM:

'. . . anything that was done by way of strategy was sophisticated, refined, highly organised and methodically processed and considered. But in this day and age such conduct is hardly less acceptable than the naked aggressions of yesterday's industrial powers if unlawfully directed against competition. The organised, selective, subtle and sophisticated approach, indeed, may pose more danger under modern conditions than instantly more obvious strategies.'

It is in Telex that the same sort of 'organised, selective, subtle and sophisticated' methodology begins to be seriously applied to the processes of the law.

Round Six: The Age of Aquarius: Telex versus IBM

The first-round triumph of Floyd Walker, attorney for Telex, over Thomas Barr, lead attorney for IBM, is essentially the triumph of man over machine, of individualist over quintessential organisation man. That is really a conclusion, for Telex did not choose to fight it in that way. They had little option but to do so: there were just not the resources around to mount an IBM-style assault.

The contest between Telex and IBM is interesting not solely in these terms but also because it tells us a lot about how IBM operates when faced with serious competition. It is interesting too because the Telex trial was also used by IBM as a test bed for its legal machine; it is almost a rehearsal for U.S.A. versus IBM.

The Telex case contest is, however, unlikely to be representative. There Floyd Walker was on a small expense retainer and a contingency fee organised on the basis of the larger the damages, the more he received. There was a point after the initial judgement where the belief was that Floyd Walker stood to make $60 million: after the amended judgement he stood to gain $52 million. Whatever Thomas Barr and his trial colleagues are paid by IBM, it is not that, nor if they lose, will they collect nothing.

The contrast between Walker and Barr is interesting. Walker is a shrewd Tulsa lawyer who cultivates his homespun accent and country lawyer image, an actor of considerable skill, with a trick of floundering in public while in reality taking his time to collect and organise his thoughts as he steadies on his next target.

He is as deceptive as his home base. Tulsa may look a bit like a large twentieth-century mid-west hick town, but appearances here too are deceptive. It is rich oil country, and to survive in the law in Tulsa one has to be capable, sometimes more capable than is imagined on either the East or West Coast. Oil, after all, is an international business.

Essentially, Floyd Walker is a loner. At the height of trial preparation he had up to fourteen attorneys helping in documents searching, the taking of depositions and the like, but it was essentially his case. He appeared in court at every stage, carrying the case in his head as best he could. Having picked his ground he had to stick to it. It is an old technique, and if the ground is well prepared a good trial lawyer, who will run with the fox he has picked and not be diverted by all the rabbits the opposition puts up, can have advantages.

Whatever else Floyd Walker would claim to be, he would not claim to be a great trial lawyer. But that is precisely Thomas Barr's reputation. He too is neither an East- nor West-Coaster born and bred. He is very much the self-made Missourian, an ex-Marine officer who has made his way in the big city, an actor—but of a different breed: brasher, more calculating. He is reputed to keep a suit especially prepared for jury trials. It has, so the story goes, loose stitching under one arm, so that when he raises that arm in addressing the jury, the old ladies can think, 'Look at that nice Mr Barr, dedicated, he works so hard in the defence of that company that he doesn't even notice his suit needs fixing'. (He didn't need the suit in Tulsa, there was no jury.)

If that were true, it would be in keeping with Thomas Barr's reputation as one of the best false-trail layers in the business. The archetypical Barr strategy, say observers, is to lay and overlay a case with false scents, smokescreens and general fol-de-rol until no one (except Thomas Barr) knows where they are.

It could then be inferred that Barr, the Cravath, Swaine and Moore team and IBM suit each other—they seem so mutually compatible. For the IBM method of fighting the Telex case was almost a carbon copy of the methodology that IBM employs in other fields: it could have come straight out of the IBM organisational handbooks.

The contrast between Walker and Barr is nowhere better brought out than here. If Walker had to keep the details of the case in his head, Barr did not, could not and should not have had to. (In any case, Barr was much too thinly spread: Telex was only one of the problems he faced, as he fronted for IBM in its other cases, including Justice.)

The reason that Barr should not have to do so is found in the adaptation of IBM's methodology to cope with law. First, there is the man organisation: here IBM does its standard routine of swamping the problem: whatever IBM is going to do, it is not going to go to court without having data at its command. There is at least one attorney to deal with each major area at issue. One attorney is detailed to deal with each witness, whether its own or those of the other side. In terms of people, this means that IBM will expect all witnesses to have been completely covered, there should be no surprises. Thus during the trial in Tulsa, there were three to four hundred people behind Thomas Barr solely devoted to that one lawsuit.

A large number were attorneys. Outside the trial appearances the Barr method of work consisted of running over what had happened that day with each of the specialists responsible, then doing the same for the next day, going through the witnesses who were to be called, the line of attack or defence, each attorney making sure that Barr was properly briefed: some of the after-court sessions were known to take four to six hours.

This is the jigsaw assembly method, time-consuming, swamping the problem with the know-how and data of dozens of skilled, hard-working people. 'I have never,' said one attorney, 'seen so many hard-working lawyers before.'

'The method,' said another lawyer, 'has one defect. It never gives Barr a chance to be really on top of his material. It may be pleasing to the ego to command those troops, but command itself is a distraction. There is still nothing like steeping yourself in a case and using the very limitations of the human intellect to concentrate your attention and energies.'

But behind those people, the visiting attorneys, the resident local law firm, the specially drafted-in IBM Communications office with its press handouts, there is also the second strand of IBM's legal machine, the extensions to the legal information retrieval system used during the CDC case preparation.

It is the first trial situation in which those computers have been used, and by all accounts the legal system proved itself handsomely. The system is no longer the elementary one used in CDC. That system itself had in part been a reaction to CDC, and the news that CDC was creating it had sent IBM off in a hurry to build, if possible, a larger and better one of its own.

It deals with most of the routines that the CDC systems also dealt with and has one major addition: it can cope rapidly with free text. This is not in fact very difficult to do: all it requires is what IBM has in plenty: time, resources and skills. However, it is in this context novel.

IBM set itself up in Tulsa almost immediately the trial date was fixed, some four to five months before, putting in Optical Character Recognition Readers into the offices of the local law firm which also represented it. These readers were on-line to the IBM Information Retrieval System Aquarius, and that contained every single piece of documentation connected with the case, the depositions, exhibits and legal documents of both sides. As one might expect, it was all indexed.

The free text addition was novel in that it allowed IBM to compare that day's testimony and court record with the other evidence. All the testimony could be put up quickly. The two sides were receiving the court transcripts on a twice-daily basis, after morning and afternoon sessions. In IBM's case, it was immediately put on microfiche and the details fed into the system. It gave them the capability of comparing that day's trial testimony with everything else that was held, on an instantaneous basis. This was a substantial advance, for it meant that IBM should have been in a position to discover not just glaring discrepancies between testimony and submitted evidence, but also the less obvious contradictions, and that almost as a matter of routine. It gave them the ability to prepare for the next day's court performance in a fashion that lawyers had nowhere been able to do previously.

This, then, is the machine that IBM wields. It should not be thought, however, that IBM was using simply its own techniques, or what would be the point of employing a smart-aleck New York law firm?

IBM and CSM between them have tricks apart from these. The combination of the two was to provide one or two stories for lawyers to discuss. All attorneys know that the use that can be made of the law can sometimes be questionable, and some questionable things were to be done in IBM's name.

Judge Christensen came late to the case. The originally assigned Judge was meant to be Judge Barrow. But in getting Judge Christensen, IBM outsmarted itself.

During the pre-trial proceedings, all applications were being heard before Judge Neville in Minneapolis. There came the time when Telex Counsel went before the Judge and asked for an injunction to stop IBM's memory 158/168 CPU price manipulation.

Before Judge Neville, IBM Counsel said words to this effect: 'Your Honour, there is no need for an injunction; this case will be ready for trial within six months, and then it can be tried on its merits. IBM will be ready to go to trial by 1st March 1973.'

So Judge Neville sent them all down to Tulsa to get a trial date fixed with Judge Barrow. IBM knew its judge, one with a reputation for lengthy preparation and also with a crowded calendar. The one thing he did not want was someone pressing for a case to be heard out of time, pleading that unless the case were heard early, plaintiff might be out of business, it might not be there to fight it. Which was what Telex was doing.

In front of Barrow, Barr was now to utter words to a different effect. 'Your Honour, we hear Mr Walker saying that this case will be ready in March. But as far as we are concerned this case will not be ready for trial for two years.'

Barr was to compound the error even further. He wrote both to Barrow and the Chief Judge of the Tenth Circuit stating that there were other cases that had been waiting longer than the Telex case, arguing that it should not be expedited.

Neville found out about it. Here was IBM making one set of representations in one court and a different set in another, in connection with the same case. He promptly sent the Chief Circuit Judge a copy of the transcript of the proceedings in his court. Within days, IBM suddenly found that Judge Neville (at, it is said, the urging of the multi-district litigation panel) had appointed a new trial judge: Sherman A. Christensen, and Telex had got its early trial.

What is interesting about the IBM depositions in both CDC

and Telex is how they seem to fit into a general pattern. The men at the top of IBM seem to co-operate freely—except over a very narrow territory (though not all, one was plainly scared).*

They co-operated not only in deposition. On the stand Frank Cary had to admit that while IBM was charging that Telex had hired IBM employees with the intent of making use of IBM confidential information, IBM had itself not so long before been hiring selected engineers from such companies as Bell Laboratories and Texas Instruments, both competitors of IBM. IBM had done so because IBM was lagging behind in the development of Field Effect Transistors. Now one can understand why Dr Piore's estimate of the time it would take IBM to get up to date with the technology was over-long.

But those at the bottom ...

The depositions in some cases are almost farcical, with IBM employees pleading the next best thing to the Fifth Amendment: I do not remember, please repeat the question, I do not understand the question, for hour after hour to the point where the only thing they would admit was number, rank and name.

Take, for example, the deposition of Ander Torgerson, an IBM staff financial analyst who was involved in the Memorex (a PCM) studies and did financial analysis on disc storage products.

Parts of the deposition have an almost surrealist charm to them, almost as if Estes Kefauver was still wielding his gavel. The quotation below is not an unfair or unrepresentative extract from the transcript, just one of the funnier parts:

'BY MR WALKER:

Q. In connection with performing your duties at IBM, have you had occasion to use or hear the term "PCM", or "plug compatible manufacture" used in any way?

A. [Mr Torgerson] I don't understand the question.

Q. In performing your duties at IBM, have you ever used the term "PCM" in referring to anything?

A. I don't understand the question.

Q. Do you have a recollection, Mr Torgerson, in your duties

---

* A similar pattern emerges in the Justice case, though there, the farther up the ladder the person deposed, the more specific the questions have to be—and the less specific are the answers.

there at IBM ever using the phrase "plug compatible competition"?

A. I don't understand the question.

Q. Can you tell me what it is you don't understand about the question so that I might better express myself?

    MR COOPER: Well, Mr Walker—

    MR WALKER: Now—

    MR COOPER: We are here to answer the questions, not to ask them.

    MR WALKER: This is a question:

BY MR WALKER:

Q. Will you tell me, Mr Torgerson, what it was about the last question that I asked you that you did not understand?

    ʍʀ ᴄᴏᴏᴘᴇʀ: I ⅃ ⅃⅃⅃⅃⅃⅃⅃⅃⅃⅃⅃⅃⅃⅃⅃⅃⅃⅃⅃⅃ ⅃⅃⅃⅃⅃ ⅃⅃ answer the questions, not help you ask them. If Mr Torgerson can't answer that question, if you can give him an example of what it is you don't understand in the question, all right this time, but there seems to be a problem in asking the questions. Go ahead.

    THE WITNESS: He is asking me within my duties have I ever used the terms. What is meant by "duties"?

BY MR WALKER:

Q. Mr Torgerson, do you have any recollection in performing any work for the IBM Company ever using the phrase "plug compatible competition"?

A. I don't recall.

Q. During the period of time that you have been employed by IBM since 1968, up to the present time, and whether it was then while you were performing work or not, have you ever heard the term "plug compatible competition" used?

A. I don't recall.

Q. Then are you familiar with the name Mallard?

A. Yes.

Q. Where did you hear the term "Mallard"?

A. It's a kind of a duck.

Q. In connection with the performing of any duty at IBM, have you ever heard, seen, written or used the term "Mallard"?
A. I don't understand the question.
   MR WALKER: Would you read the question to him?
   (Pending question read.)
   THE WITNESS: I don't understand the question.

BY MR WALKER:

Q. In connection with any work that you have ever performed at IBM, have you ever seen, used or heard or read the term "Mallard"?
   THE WITNESS: Would you read the question back?
   (Pending question read.)
   THE WITNESS: Yes.'

It is not by any means the funniest. That surely deserves to be an extract from the deposition of Gerard J. Fassig, an IBM analyst who had been involved in PCM studies. Counsel and Gerard J. Fassig are discussing the Memorex study—and what was and was not shown to IBM senior management.

'Q. Can you tell me whether or not any of the pages from 32 on through 69 was covered by you in your oral presentation to Mr Nern, Mr Cooley and Mr Powers?

Q. How about the page 33 and the pages following?
A. Page 33, I don't recall.
   Page 34, I don't recall in the context of that question.
Q. 35?
A. Page 35, I don't recall in the context of that question.
   Page 36, I don't recall in the context of that question.
   Page 37, I don't recall in the context of that question.
   (And so on, line after line, from page 38 onward through to page 69.)

It is in the light of these practices that one must view the IBM counter-claim. This was filed as late as possible—within the time the court allows. The object seems to have been to try to make Telex ask for a postponement; Barr and his colleagues figured that no lawyer would go to court with a counter-claim hanging over his head which alleged that his clients' case and claim for injury was in part based on information stolen from the defendants. (In fact, though Telex is no doubt quite capable of making its own defence, the one thing that does come out of the case is that Telex never managed to get any products based on such information to market, and its claims were not based on them.)

This was not the only delaying tactic. Any lawyer knows how to stretch out a deposition. One has an impression, an opinion only, but nevertheless one with some seeming foundation, that IBM management for a time were using their attorneys as part of their management effort to accomplish manoeuvres in the market, not solely in court.

This comes from the technique used in deposition: IBM simply dragged the depositions out. Telex were made to consume seven or eight days on depositions which would normally have taken a day or two.

But there was another reason for the tactic. IBM could spare the executives concerned; it has a depth of 'management' resources which few can match. Certainly not Telex. IBM was to keep Telex witnesses in court as long as possible, seemingly intentionally trying to tie up their time. Now there is a purpose to this tactic, as stated by Floyd Walker in one of the arguments between Counsel during a deposition.

'... we take the position that IBM is unnecessarily delaying and prolonging trial preparing by ... forcing us to go back to the Court on each individual witness to secure an order for the witness to answer questions involving matters that we have waived by the production of documents months and months ago, and something that has already been determined by the Court.

'I feel that it's just a means by which they prolong and unnecessarily delay trial preparation in this case.'

For a small company, with only a few key people, can be run into the ground. The situation became so bad the Judge had to rule that IBM simply had only a stipulated number of days left. If it had not asked all its questions by then, there was no more time allotted to it. Afterwards, the deposition process mysteriously and suddenly speeded up.

We cannot leave the depositions without recording one dubious incident, found in the deposition of Richard L. Martin, for a time President of Telex Computer Products. He was being shown documents purportedly taken from his files, and IBM documents at that. He denied then (and has denied it since) that the documents were ever in his files. He stated in the deposition that his memory might be poor, but not that poor. He maintains to this day, in public, a serious charge which has never been satisfactorily answered, that his documents were doctored.

IBM has other ways of tying up its opponents' time and resources. An IBM executive's files are deposed. So IBM provides them. But somehow those files seem to arrive at the plaintiffs so scrambled that putting them together is going to be time-consuming. This might be accidental; however, when it happens time after time, inferences can be, and were, drawn.

We cannot, however, leave the Telex case and this short resumé of some of the tactics of the IBM legal machine, without dealing with allegations of IBM intimidation of Telex witnesses.

This might seem a strong charge to make; but one witness has said it publicly, and the issue was to be raised by Telex with the Court and was never satisfactorily answered by IBM.

Telex deposed a clutch of witnesses, many of them formerly with IBM. Some of those witnesses had volunteered, some had been asked, all had initially agreed. It made little difference, they soon changed their minds. Telex affidavits in the record make revealing reading. They detail all sorts of peculiar events to follow . . .

There was the witness from White Weld and Company of New York, whose management knew—from unknown sources—that he was on the final Telex witness list even before Telex informed him of the fact. White Weld then informed him of their long-standing policy not to take sides in litigation. That same witness, according to one affidavit, was approached by an IBM attorney, wanting to discuss his testimony, if he was, in fact, to be a witness, and telling him that he did not have to be one if he did not want to.

Floyd Walker was to summarise what happened to the witnesses in a brief submitted to the Court, from which the following extracts are taken.

'. . . there has been developed certain information which

forms a pattern indicating an apparent concerted plan of tampering with witnesses.

'In August of 1972 Telex filed its tentative witness list containing names of witnesses which might be used at the trial of this action. Included therein were certain designated independent witnesses who were to testify based upon their extensive research and knowledge concerning financial information about IBM and Telex.

'After making the names of these witnesses known to IBM, there transpired a series of incidents so strange and coincidental, forming almost a pattern, as to cause Telex to inquire if there has not been a concerted effort on the part of IBM, its agents and attorneys, to impede the progress of pre-trial preparation by inducing and persuading witnesses not to testify. Telex believes that these witnesses have been induced to refuse to testify by pressures brought against them by IBM, its agents and attorneys, and that these matters should be called to the attention of the Court.

'As this brief is being written Telex has just been advised that John Schmidtt in the data processing department of the Midwest Stock Exchange Service Corp., who was listed as a prospective witness in the Telex final witness list, has been contacted by a sales representative of IBM and after such contact Mr Schmitt now states he does not want to be a witness at trial even though he had previously indicated his complete co-operation.

'The foregoing demonstrates a remarkable pattern of witness behaviour; a pattern that could not be formed without outside contact and interference. Telex inquired of IBM: Have witnesses and their employers been contacted and advised, suggested or in any manner urged not to testify? It should be emphasized that at one point prior to filing the final witness list, all these witnesses has indicated a willingness to testify and were actively co-operating in the taking of their depositions. Suddenly, after filing the final witness list, and without warning they have declined to testify. The importance of these witnesses cannot be overestimated. Of the ten (10) witnesses (outside of Telex employees and agents) designated to testify in person, four (4) have suddenly indicated an unwillingness to testify. Of the seven (7) designated to testify by deposition, three (3) have now declined. It is inconceivable that IBM had nothing to do with this new development.'

Has IBM done something illegal? In reply Barr filed a lengthy affidavit: in summation, that IBM had done nothing wrong, it simply used the processes of law available to it. Thomas Barr and his colleagues fought with every tool available to them, and one they had come up with is a classic: If a man is being deposed as an expert, then wanting proof of the basis of the expertise, they propose to depose documents from his employers on which his expertise is based. It is a good way of 'cooling' employers.

One witness who did not withdraw was Richard Whitcomb, also an ex-IBM employee. So IBM tried a new tack: if you cannot stop a man appearing, then you can aim to make him feel uncomfortable in the witness box. What better way of doing so than to bring some of his former fellow IBM workers, including his former direct superior, to sit in court while he gives testimony.

So IBM brought the superior, and three others, to sit in court: not to dispute testimony, but just to be there. The trick went wrong. Mr Whitcomb is evidently a man of mettle, he spotted them and told Floyd Walker.

They were not to sit there for long. It was time for Floyd Walker to have some gentle fun. He was not going to let their appearance go unmarked. Whitcomb was led around to discussing the people he had worked with in IBM and asked if there were any present.

When the expected answer duly came, he was asked to name them. Then Walker asked them to stand up in court and be identified.

It did not go unnoticed: they did not turn up in that courtroom again.

This run-through of some of the events which befell Telex when it took IBM to Court has been in the nature of a cautionary tale. Those who have ambitions to sue IBM must be prepared not only to meet with the IBM mechanics, they must also prepare themselves to face an organisation which will use every method that comes to hand and which has the resources to make things happen.

The rough housing that IBM subjected potential Telex witnesses may have been according to rule, but the Judge summed it up tidily when he commented that the measures IBM had taken tended to 'chill their availability.'

IBM pressuring has not had the same effect on all companies. One would expect that would-be litigants would consider the uphill fight they face and decide not to bother, to get out and look for some other business. This, however, has not been the case.

Round Seven: IBM versus Everybody

The legal costs incurred by IBM during the years 1952 to 1956, when IBM was fighting the complaint of the Justice Department which led to the Consent Decree, are stated to have been around $3 million a year—a considerable amount for the time but nothing compared to what would come later. Legal costs attri-
butable to litigation fell off sharply thereafter, as did the litigation itself. There were few court fights and those were mainly against small competitors: as a general rule, IBM won quite easily.

Expenses, however, began to rise again towards the end of the sixties (though internally they were quite low: a memorandum in evidence in the Justice suit describes the costs of IBM programming, key punching computer and man time to produce analyses of IBM's position—analyses to be used in discussions then going on with the Justice Department—as being $41,000 by January 1968).

The situation has since changed substantially. By early 1974, knowledgeable industry lawyers were discussing estimates of total IBM legal costs, the fees to CSM and other law firms, the use of internal IBM resources, the production of documents, etc., as totalling around $200 million since the start of the CDC case. These costs included those incurred in CDC, Greyhound, the taking of The Census, Justice, Telex and the other PCM cases. CDC alone, it is said, cost IBM $70 million on top of IBM's settlement expenses and much of that was for document production and document searching.

This is not surprising, for there is much at stake. In any case it must be remembered that it is all tax deductible; it does not come out of profits. Spread over the six years 1968 to 1973, it is a small annual charge for IBM to pay to protect the extra profits that the measures under dispute have made possible for IBM. IBM would much prefer that expenditure than to have to settle the claims against it—short of court decisions and action.

For the legal problems that IBM is faced with must be weighed against the problems it would face were it to settle prior to such court action, in terms of the precedent such settlement would create. IBM is well aware of this fact and is most worried about such precedent. Thus after the initial Telex case judgement, IBM twice approached Telex to see whether it could be bought off: was a settlement possible in the $5 to $15 million range? It was not, each time the offer was rejected.

The sum, in relationship to the initial judgement, may seem derisory, but IBM was quite serious. It was the precedent that the settlement would set which worried it. At all costs, any settlement made with any one of the PCMs must be small, so that any other settlements made with others would then be related to it, the whole in turn bearing some sort of relationship to the settlement made with CDC.

And again at all costs, any settlement made should insist that as much as possible of the record should be withdrawn. The one thing IBM does not want is a judicial decision against it which, having gone through the process of appeals, is then confirmed. The combination of an adverse judgement and an open court record could open the doors to damages of awesome proportions.

For the majority of the suits which IBM faced and still faces are treble-damage suits. On a finding of guilt, the Court will treble the damages it awards, the punitive element prescribed by law.

The magnitude of the damages that IBM could end up paying was calculated in December 1973 by Eugene Collins of the New York brokerage firm Evans & Co in a customer news letter. It was entitled The Telex Gamble. In it, he determined that the total IBM exposure then totalled seven billion dollars, of which nearly a third would go to the PCMs. On the basis of the Telex claim, itself initially for $1·2 billion, what the court actually awarded Telex, the way court's award for both loss of profit and loss of market share, and the share of the PCM market that Telex had at the time the measures complained of took place, Collins concluded that the IBM (Domestic) exposure in Telex carbon copy suits was nearly $440 million before any trebling took place. He then added the possibilities of claims in the foreign markets (where the issues had been severed) and increased likely damages by fifty per cent more, which after trebling brought the figure up to nearly two billion dollars.

All this providing that other courts awarded similar damages to those awarded in Telex, and that other cases were fought on the same grounds. If Telex finally won, then obviously there was a strong probability that they would be fought. If Telex lost, then, as the ground over which Telex fought was relatively narrow and did not by any means cover all the possible claims that could be made against IBM, the situation would be open again.

On the day that the report was published, Memorex alone—evidently having done similar calculations—set out to up the ante. It filed an anti-trust suit which, if granted in full, would have meant that after trebling Memorex would obtain punitive damages of $3·15 billion.

To put these possible damages and legal travails into proportion, it in perilous list of the events of the suits which IBM has faced or is facing, many of them not included in the Collins calculations. No doubt some will be settled before these pages appear in print, and some new ones will appear. However, what the following listing seeks is to give some idea of the breadth of the legal onslaught on IBM and its diversity. Not only have CDC, Greyhound, Justice, Telex and the legal processes around the census tied up IBM lawyers' time: IBM has faced a large number of other complainants since the beginning of the seventies.

First come the suits of individuals. There is the strange case of Vernon Bugg, a suit dismissed in 1974 because the statute of limitations was such that the case could no longer be heard. A pity—for Mr Buggs was a former IBM research engineer from the thirties who sued IBM and AT&T jointly, claiming that they had conspired to restrain trade in the teletype market and asking for $120 million in damages.

Mr Bugg maintained that IBM set out to impede his original patent application, effectively telling the patent office that it had been dropped. When he left IBM the prototypes were confiscated and put in the machine morgue at Endicott (the machine morgue actually exists: when IBM was running short of work space, employees were actually given it as premises for development work. It contains many of those heartbreaking developments which Mr Watson never took up, and those machines and devices which lost out in the internal what-shall-we-take-to-market competitions that were a familiar product of IBM's contention system). He claimed also to have been told that IBM had an agreement with AT&T not to enter the teletype business. Whether or not any of this is true, the fact is that IBM long had the skills and the opportunity to enter that business, yet stayed out of it, though it was a natural extension of both the tabulator and computer businesses.*

Just as strange is the tale of Marilehen Jones who joined IBM in 1962 and claimed to have been eased out in 1973. The attrition programme of the early seventies had, she claimed, resulted in her being shifted around the country and her rating being dropped from class 1 'far exceeding expectations', to class 5 'unsatisfactory' in the process. She sued IBM for $500 million damages in a class action and asked for another $500 million in punitive damages.

A similar class action was brought by some former SBC employees who were transferred to CDC without consultation. The first news they had of the transfer came when they were told that the deal had been done and their employment was being transferred to CDC. They were, however, much more conciliatory, still emotionally with IBM, and were asking for only $3 million in damages.

Whatever the legal merits or demerits of the cases that were brought under these individual headings, at best they show IBM being singularly high handed.

Then there are a miscellaneous bunch of suits which arise from IBM being simply IBM, a large corporation which makes claims for its products, claims which are not always borne out by what happens when the equipment is actually out in the field in service. Two examples will suffice here, one concerning a jewellery manufacturer in Rhode Island, Catamore Inc. IBM claimed that Catamore owed it nearly $70,000 in equipment rentals and filed suit to collect. Catamore in its turn counter-claimed that IBM had misrepresented aspects of its unbundling • policies, alleged

---

*Another story long current in IBM was that Mr Watson Snr had come to an agreement with one Mr Kearns to stay out of the teletypewriter business. So impressed had Mr Kearns and Mr Watson been with each other, that the former's son, David Kearns was sent to work for IBM. He in his turn rose so high within IBM that when he resigned a note of it appeared in IBM management minutes. He is now with Xerox.

monopolisation of software and systems markets and asked for
$62 million in damages.

The largest damage claim of all, however, arose from the case
of Equity Funding. It was claimed that a number of officers and
employees had used IBM systems to commit fraud by creating
fictitious insurance policies which were held on a computer and
transferred to other companies for cash; the cash was then used in
part to continue to pay the new owners the premiums. When these
events finally surfaced publicly, a group of shareholders sued
IBM on the grounds that they should have done something
to protect Equity's shareholders from the use of
their—IBM—product to commit 'fraud' and asked for $10
billion damages.

The above suits do not group into clear-cut classes. However,
IBM is faced with a set of actions which closely parallel the Telex
ones in their allegations of market monopoly. They come from
other peripheral manufacturers and leasing companies and are
generally thought of as carbon copy cases, though whether or not
they are going to be fought in the same way depends very much
on the final outcome of the Telex and IBM cross appeals.

Memorex and its $3·15 billion claim has already been men-
tioned. (This was, in fact, the second time that Memorex had sued
IBM. The first time was in 1971, the case ending early in 1972 in
an agreement between the two parties that neither should sue each
other for at least a year.) Other companies involved in peripherals
manufacture claiming injury from IBM's peripheral market activities include California Computer Products (otherwise known
as Calcomp—this faced an IBM counterclaim with the unique
IBM response that with less than $100 million revenues Calcomp
in its turn dominated the graphics systems market) whose case was
consolidated with four other companies for pre-trial discovery.
All were asking for injunctions to restrain IBM market practices,
and for divestiture, and between Calcomp, TransAmerica Computer Corporation, Hudson General Corporation, and Marshall
Industries (excluding Memorex) were seeking damages of $642
million. They were not the only peripherals companies affected,
out on its own was DPF Inc. seeking $45 million, while Forro Preci-
sion, a components manufacturer, sought for $36 million.

But these are not IBM's only legal travails. Still awaiting trial is
that long standing (late '60's) suit, the claim of VIP Systems of

Washington, a small bureau operation, for more that $40 million, contending that IBM and SBN were monopolising the computer services market.

Then there is the case of the Sanders companies, manufacturers of computer terminals. They claim $85 million, trebled to $255 million. The Sanders case is unusual in that they were the first to see a market for IBM compatible terminals in a similar way to which the PCMs had seen a market for tape and disc drives. Their 720 terminal competed with the IBM 2260. IBM eventually brought out its 3270 interactive display terminals, with different standards, built in the usual mid life kickers, and then announced that it would no longer provide software support for terminals which functioned on the 2260 standard.

According to the complaint IBM then exploited the lead time it now had 'by securing thousands of orders of 3270 terminals, even orders far in excess of its represented production capability'.

IBM's marketing force, according to the complaint, went around 'maliciously threatening customers that were they to attach non-IBM terminals to an IBM system, one or more of the following consequences would occur'. Foreign terminals meant that the integrity of the system was at risk and IBM guarantees could not be maintained, IBM could not service it with foreign terminals attached, the foreign equipment was defective and would not be compatible, a mixed system's operation would be impaired as IBM made hardware and software changes, operating deadlines required by the customer could not be met in this environment, and that it would not be possible to obtain in time components necessary to attach this foreign equipment to the IBM CPU.

And as I was writing this, there came the announcement of a $250 million suit by a New Jersey company not normally thought of as in the computer business: William Marrion Inc. It is not primarily in the computing business, rather it concentrates its activities in the business that IBM originally had before computers came along. William Marrion claimed that IBM was restraining trade in the secondhand punch card machine field when IBM pulled out of its maintenance agreements.

Meanwhile, as quietly as possible and without any great public fuss, IBM which tends to counter charge wherever possible that the complainant has been involved in activities which infringe its 'fairly' acquired know-how and patents, settled two patent disagreements. One was with a peripherals manufacturer Ampex where IBM stumped up $13 million, the other with Bunker Ramo, where a suit brought in 1974 was settled within a year. Bunker Ramo alleged patent infringement: the two settled with a cross license agreement and the payment by IBM of $7·5 million.

Without going into the merits of any of these cases, and leaving aside the rest discussed in this book, I have so far listed claims against IBM running at nearly $16 billion, and no doubt there are some more around that I have missed. Whatever the outcome, and whatever the merits of those claims, it is a lot of suits to have to face. But still these are not all inclusive. For we must discuss three areas in which IBM faces legal action, has faced legal action, or is likely to face legal action.

The first of these concerns loss in that suits for their own interest they are the users. Suits such as that of Catamore are unusual. Whatever one may write about IBM, the one thing it does not normally do is to make a total hash of it. It is unlikely that there will ever be similar suits in large number. What is more likely is perhaps even more interesting and arises from the suits being pressed by competing manufacturers. Whether or not IBM has done what the record so far has shown is unimportant, what is important is the outcome of these suits. For suppose that IBM were finally found guilty of 'monopoly practices', a broad umbrella term covering what the various suits are about, this could lead to damage suits by users. This area is wide open: it is unlikely that IBM would in fact be faced with many suits, the costs of pursuing them would be too great. However, it could be faced with the threat of such suits leading to a horde of out of court settlements. All it needs for this to happen is one manufacturer suit going against IBM and finding it guilty of monopoly practices. The grounds on which that could happen are wide, a finding of guilt in one of the leasing suits, or in one of the other manufacturer suits say in the case of add-on memory a finding that there was price manipulation of memory—CPU costs. Just one success would be enough to open up the territory. The key to that territory is a legal finding which can be built on to show that user costs rose as a result of monopoly practices. This could well result in a similar situation within board rooms as arose in Telex: a legal opinion that if the company does not sue it could be subject to stockholder charges of dereliction of duty.

IBM of course does not have to fear suits on every and all possible counts. The events which arose from the unbundling decisions of 1969 might well end up being time barred. (Though there are those who maintain that IBM's decision not to unbundle its operating systems could lead to legal problems.)

The second possible group of suits arise from events outside the United States. So far, for all practical purposes the current suits deal with IBM's practices in America. How IBM has behaved outside the United States and the implications of that behaviour, all this has been severed. The Justice Department at one stage did indicate that it would raise the foreign issues, but this did not feature in the list of issues in its pre-trial brief.

There are of course two legal ways of tackling IBM and its foreign interest. One through the American courts under the Sherman Acts, two through the courts of the countries concerned. IBM has been involved in few cases which transcend national boundaries, perhaps the best known one being add-on memory cases, cases arising from users buying add-on memory from other suppliers above and beyond the limits set by IBM for their particular IBM computers. Having done so, this has been countered by IBM withdrawing maintenance and service. Legal action in the U.S.A. has caused IBM to back down, while a similar suit in West Germany brought by a German publishing house went against IBM. Indeed in that case the judge was so struck by what he heard that the papers were handed over to West Germany's own anti-trust authorities.

IBM however is perhaps more worried by the possibility of action being taken by the Directorate for Competition of the European Community than by the likelihood of action by any individual foreign company or government.

The activities of IBM WTC have been under investigation by that Directorate since 1973, and its officials have made a number of trips to Washington to discuss what might be done with the Justice Department. That Directorate has wide powers which stem primarily from Articles 85 and 86 of the Treaty of Rome, and the many decisions made by the European Court which clarify those articles. To say that Community law is complicated is an understatement, for it tries to reconcile differing philosophies. The German and French approach to cartels for instance is very different, the Germans see those as a problem where the French do not, for the French police intensively. By contrast, the French and the British share similar attitudes to monopolies; a lack of belief in the proposition that monopoly as such is a bad thing and a further belief that monopolies can and should again be policed in the interests of society.

However, Articles 85 and 86 and the case law that has been built up point in different directions. They can be summed up as an evolution towards the concept of the dominant firm, in which the onus of proof need not be as great as that for a monopoly case under Sherman, a strong shift towards creating conditions of competition in which the test is what actually has been happening on the market. Indeed in a landmark decision in 1972 in a merger suit in a different industry, the European Court said something which has been with by indical probably in almost every disorderium undertakings boardroom in Europe '. . . Abuse may . . . exist if an undertaking in a dominant position so strengthens its position that the level of dominance achieved substantially restricts competition and that, therefore, only those undertakings the market behaviour of which depends on the dominant undertaking remain on the market . . . In actual fact, irrespective of any culpable act, it may be deemed to be an abuse if an undertaking occupies such a dominant position, that as a result of a fundamental change in the supply structure which may seriously endanger the consumer's freedom of choice on the market, the aims of the Treaty are circumvented'.

This of course leads one down the road of the problem of establishing what the market is. However legal sources within the Community make it quite clear that the fundamental nonsense of market share as proposed by IBM in America would not be accepted within Europe: IBM will not be allowed to plead the bigger we get, the smaller we are.

Indeed though it may be a long-term prospect, IBM perhaps faces more legal problems within Europe than it does in America, hence the Commission's known interest in IBM pricing in the Common Market countries. The only things that some IBM European prices have in common are that they are generally higher than American IBM prices. There have been many disparities in European prices between the Common Market countries which are not necessarily accounted for by differences in cost levels, thus putting IBM in danger under clause c of Article 86 of the Treaty: 'the application to parties to transactions of unequal terms in respect of equivalent supplies, thereby placing them at a competitive disadvantage . . .'

The third European approach to the problem of IBM meets with little favour in Washington, it is the approach which goes down the route of what are known as Non-Tarriff Trade Barriers: the restriction of areas of public funded purchase to European owned companies, the pouring of public money into the development of locally owned and locally controlled industry. It can be best thought of as economic engineering rather than law, an approach which rather than try to cut IBM down in present size tries to restrict its growth by building up countervailing forces. It is not liked in legislative Washington primarily because such policies do not impact solely on IBM but also on other American owned corporations competing in the same markets, and it is not simply the presumed monopolist which is affected. The European answer to that is that the solution is in American hands, but until a European sees any evidence that the economic power of IBM is brought under restraint within its own home country, few knowledgeable Europeans are going to worry too much. Until too, America opens up its own government funded market to foreign manufacturers.

The solution is in American hands . . . Which brings us to the case of Justice verses IBM. It is now (1975) nine years since CDC sent the Justice Department its memorandum requesting that the Anti-trust Division investigate and take action against IBM's anti-trust violations, and more than six years since Justice filed suit. In those six years IBM has used every possible delaying tactic in the book to stop the case from ever coming to trial.

The reasons for those delays was perhaps best put by the Executive Director of the Computer Industry Association A. G. W. Biddle in Senate Hearings on proposals for an Industrial Reorganisation Act: 'Each day's delay is worth $4.5 million net aftertax profits, so why not drag it out?' Clearly they have the ability to do so. The defendants legal staff outnumbers that of the Department of Justice by more than 10 to 1.

Obviously in a case involving depositions of more than 1000 companies, over 500 witnesses, and some 1,500,000 pages of evidentiary material, this imbalance gives IBM a distinct advantage over the Anti-trust Division of the Department of Justice.'

Well yes, on one hand it does. That hand consists of the abilities of IBM's lawyers to stretch things out. They may have good reason to, justice may require that they do and should not justice be seen to be done? But that dragging out has now taken a long time—and had the effect on IBM profits that Biddle noted. IBM's profits continue to mount while the IBM lawyers, it would not be unfair to write, also continue to play havoc with the court room performances of those lawyers Justice has assigned to the case. To watch the case of Justice versus IBM in action is much like watching a bumbling small weak man trying to fight a strong, cunning and clever big man, with the difference here that the Federal Government is cast in the first role.

But, and now we come to the other hand. The question has to be asked and answered, is there any way that the weakling can lose. The answer in none.

Which brings us in turn to the Judge who has been patiently presiding since legal proceedings began in 1969, Judge David N. Edelstein. The Judge presided over the last round which led to the Consent Decree of 1956, and gives the impression of regarding this case as the continuation of unfinished business. There is indeed an impression in some legal anti-trust circles that he is doing everything short of conducting the government's case for it: not necessarily that he has prejudged the case, but to see to it that this time there is a full open hearing. It is a feeling that some of those who have watched the case can sense, one of which a close observer has indicated IBM seems well aware. So much so that CSM and IBM are believed to have taken 'Fritz' Schwartz off the IBM defence for that reason: he and the judge it seems do not get on too well in court, and IBM has enough against it without adding that to its headaches.

And yet can the judge now be totally unbiased? There is for instance no question in the minds of the anti-trust lawyers I have talked to that the events which surround the CDC case find IBM with no real defence short of saying that the documents do not mean what they state and that the English language is not quite as clear and distinct as we all thought it was. IBM sold under cost, again no ifs or buts. Whatever the excuse this is a Sherman Act offence. One accepts that a case has to be presented in court, but this Judge at least is reputed to know some law, and Mr Katzenbach, Mr Barr and their colleagues must have a good opinion (in private if not in public) of the way at least part of the case is likely to go. (And if he did not? It has to be remembered that since 1969, about all that has been heard from have been Justice and IBM.)

But those more than 500 witnesses cover the American computer industry almost in its entirety among them many of those who have been keeping quiet. The major companies in that industry are well represented, among them, Control Data Corporation, Honeywell, National Cash Register, and Sperry Rand. These four spelt out the problem that faces the Justice Department, that faces them and other manufacturers at home and abroad, and in the end that faces other governments both as protectors of their own industries and as large scale computer users.

Before the settlement of its suit, CDC had proposed that IBM be made to divest itself of its components division, its terminal equipment, Service Bureau Corporation, Science Research Associates, Office Products, and its education and training business. Justice in October 1972 had also asked for divestiture: one year later the four companies were to go further.

They presented a joint memorandum to the court in which they argued that because of the complexity of the case, were IBM to be found to be guilty it would be necessary to almost immediately have some interim relief. The reason they wanted such relief is obvious. Even after judgement, the process of appeal and the time required for restructure would be such that IBM could continue to be dominant well into the eighties.

Though they did not put it this way, they wish to avoid the likelihood of a situation arising similar to that of the present. When initially brought—1968—the Justice case dealt with an IBM which had grossed a little under $7 billion and had earned NEBT of $1·8 billion. In the year prior to the case being scheduled to come to court—1974—IBM grossed over $12½ billion and earned nearly $3·5 billion.

The question is quite simple. If IBM is guilty, should it then be allowed to profit any further from its illegal acts after guilt has been established. Can a situation be allowed in which IBM can earn, as it did in the interval between filing and trial, well over $16 billion, some of which must have been the result of those acts. (It needs to be pointed out that on the basis of today's turnover, IBM's earnings might well double this over the next six or so years.)

A situation should also not be allowed to arise in which IBM uses that interval to change once more the basis of the technology on the market, so that it can then answer that the charges are only of historic interest, the business and business practices of IBM are by then different to the business and practices complained of.

This has already been the IBM answer in the Justice suit, where it sought to deal with the issues of the sixties by recounting events of the seventies. 'The action', says IBM, in its pre-trial brief' 'is at bottom an attack on IBM's success through competition on the merits.'

And yet in its lengthy and voluminous replies, it has really put the situation quite neatly. The burden of almost all the claims against IBM has been that IBM is not just another company, it is the environment and the standard. For in suggesting that one were at this stage to agree that the results had been achieved by competition on the merits, IBM has now moved itself into a situation where it is the standard and where it must behave accordingly.

As to the means, Goldfinger, it seems, was right.

CHAPTER FIFTEEN

Technology: the IBM Systems in Your Future

'Opel? He has been around saying that if you thought Series 360 was "you bet your company", Future Series is the largest technological undertaking in the history of man: far more complex than the space programme. Now with anybody else, I would say that they were just making rah rah noises for the troops. With Opel I would take it much more seriously: you'd better believe it.'

'Future Series? It's ambitious in the extreme, costly, and incredibly complex. This time they are really going to try to jump the technology to where no one can catch them. What's the phrase . . . Out of sight . . .?'

To understand computing one must understand IBM. To understand IBM one must understand IBM's technological record. This is necessary because the changes that are being brought about in society which can be attributed to the installation of computers are changes often attributable to IBM technological and marketing possibilities, plans and moves—not to the possibilities inherent in the computer *per se*. It has been so in the recent past, it is likely to be so for the foreseeable future.

To discuss the IBM product of the future, one must look at some of IBM's product record. For that Future Series (or FS, as it is generally known) about which Opel is so expansive is an attempt by IBM to overcome much of that past; it is an attempt by IBM management to justify for probably the first time the belief of its own employees—and most of its customers—that

428

IBM really understands advanced technology. Actually, that is unfair: IBM has long indicated that advanced technology was one subject it understood very well; during most of the sixties and early seventies it has seemed as if it wanted as little to do with it as conceivably possible.

Though this opinion runs counter to much of the prevailing conventional wisdom, it is not as individualistic as it might seem at first. It is an opinion shared, within IBM, by those who are in a position to know: Data Processing Commercial Analysis. That department exists to tell the truth, to enable IBM management to adjust its marketing policies and tactics to allow for the maximum market penetration, having taken into account IBM's technological shortcomings.

Commercial Analysis's opinions are not, of course, too widely disseminated within the corporation: the unexpurgated versions, which detail the full IBM product together and comparable with that of its competitors, market wide, are confined to the somewhat rarefied heights of PDG, DPD, and Corporate HQ. However, a QPLA (Quarterly Product Line Assessment) summary of August 1971 featured in the IBM Papers in the Telex suit. This listed Commercial Analysis's best judgement of IBM product in relationship to that of IBM's competitors on the basis of price performance as of that date (though the QPLA made it clear that it did not cover some recently announced price increases by UNIVAC and Honeywell).

The document contains seven pages of evaluations; the first of which is reproduced here. This is the really important page, for it lists IBM's major computer systems, the key product around which most of the rest are slung. It is not essential to understand it in all its fine detail—the critical part is the 'Assessment' column in the middle. And that, as the exhibit shows, lists only one of IBM's major systems as superior to that of the competition. That system, it must be noted, is the most recently announced of those listed.

The six pages which follow list fifty-five IBM products in relationship to those of the competition; of these more than half (29) are rated 'deficient', only eight are rated 'superior'—and, of these, two have no competitive equivalent to enable a rating to be established.

All this brings us to the contrast between the Galbraithian view

PRODUCT LINE ASSESSMENT SUMMARY

System/Product	Assessment	Competition
LARGE SYSTEMS		
	Deficient	CDC STAR–100
Model 195	Deficient	CDC CYBER 70 Mod. 76
Model 165	Equal	UNIVAC 1110
Model 155	Equal	Burroughs B6700
		HIS H6080
INTERMEDIATE SYSTEMS		
Model 145	Equal	RCA 6, HIS H6040
Model 135	Superior	RCA 2, NCR C–200
Model 30	Deficient	UNIVAC 9300/9400, NCR100
		Burroughs B2500, HIS H1015
Model 22	Deficient	NCR–200
Model 25	Deficient	UNIVAC 9200, NCR C—100 &
		C–200, Burroughs B2500,
		HIS H115–2
SYSTEM/370 ADVANCED FUNCTION		
Multiprocessing	Deficient	UNIVAC 1100 Series,
		Burroughs B6700/B7700
Relocate	Equal	RCA 3, RCA 7,
		Burroughs B6700/B7700
Sensor Base	Deficient	Control Data, Digital Equipment,
		Xerox Data Systems

of the large corporation as the driving force in the development, production, and bringing to market of advanced technological products, the supposed ability of the large firm to organise such technology; and the reality, that the largest firm in this industry has done no such thing.

As we have seen in the case of CDC, with large systems, or Telex and the other PCMs with peripherals, the advance in technology brought to market was not madè by the largest firm. (This is also true in other advanced areas of computing, parallel processing and multi-processing being good examples.) The issue, however, is really much more complex. Galbraith is right in so far as it (obviously) takes substantial resources to bring into being large complex technological systems, whether aircraft or computers. But the large firm needs to be distinguished from the dominant firm, or the monopolist.

The dominant firm in the computer industry behaves as classical economics teaches. The role of IBM, dominant company, in bringing advanced technology to market is two-fold and dependent upon the size and market position of the competitors it is facing. One, as we have seen earlier, it can legitimise the products of small and technologically advanced would-be competitors by deciding that it too will market an equivalent (or it can, of course, imperil the legitimacy of such a product by deciding that it will not market an equivalent); two, where the competitor is large and operating within the mainstream of its business (and thus aimed—in theory, if not in volumes—straight at its jugular, the markets that the dominant company considers critical to its survival) a technological advance by that competitor will be resisted as long as possible without commitment to major change until the dominant firm is so placed as to find the goading in-tolerable. This will happen, as it has happened with IBM, when that competition begins to make inroads into IBM's mainstream business, creaming-off the richer users, those with the most favourable long-term growth prospects. At this point the dominant firm is forced to consider making changes in the product which will require upgrading the technology. It will introduce as much of that technology as will suffice to stem the competition but not enough to disturb, more than need be, its main customer base.

This is a very different view of IBM to the one that it puts forward, its public face as represented in the media or by many of its customers. But it is not simply a view of IBM in the seventies, it is a view which could have been put forward at almost any time during the last twenty-five years. Two short periods excepted, IBM has generally been technologically backward.

Yet, it has been a critical part of the IBM defence in the Telex and other cases that, through 'exceptional diligence, technology, and discovery', IBM has been an innovator of new product and that this has merit in itself. One should not begrudge IBM its success in extracting this sentiment from a judge: it has after all worked hard enough through the courts to obtain it. But how true is it? We have seen from some of the examples of the fifties and sixties that IBM has in the past often lacked technological surety, a 'feel' for the direction in which the technology should evolve and a grip on the know-how to make it go in that direction.

What is quite surprising when one examines, say, the direct

technological antecedents of the main product of today, is the lack of critical IBM invention within it. Indeed, the general triviality of IBM-initiated technological advance on the market is more than merely surprising; it poses important questions about the role of IBM's massive R&D expenditure in the provision of technological answers to satisfy user needs.

It has been IBM's publicly expressed view of its competition, particularly in the suits brought by the Peripheral Compatible Manufacturers, that these companies are primarily in the business of copying IBM product. It is an odd accusation for a company to make, when its own past demonstrates a talent for copying and improvement besides which the Japanese of the thirties were bumbling unsystematic amateurs.

Almost all the critical invention which has made the growth of IBM possible has originated elsewhere: components almost generally, discs and disc drives, tapes and tape drives, most of the communications technology, and as we have seen almost all critical invention within central processor and memory technology. What has made IBM strong has been its ability to improve on the work of others, the very process that it tries to deny anyone else the right to do.

One can perhaps best illustrate this by going to the heart of IBM's main business: the IBM 370 Series systems with what IBM calls 'advanced function'—in The Papers called 'relocate'. The technique is better known as virtual memory, the IBM version of which was announced in 1972.

The IBM internal Advanced Function Marketing Guide does not sound like the sort of document in which revealing truths will be buried: but appearances are deceptive; once more IBM illustrates its capacity for self-deception.

'This revolutionary capability—the system-wide implementation of virtual concepts—has been created by an evolutionary addition to an existing system line.'

'System 370 with advanced function represents a new direction with full IBM commitment to virtual concepts as "our way of the future".'

'IBM . . . has been a leader in *marketing* [italics added] virtual storage since 1965, with the announcement of the System 360/67. Today's announcement reinforces this leadership role.'

IBM of course is quite right; the corporation has been a leader in marketing virtual storage since 1965. That, in the instance it records (the 360/67) IBM for many years could not make advanced function work with any worthwhile degree of efficiency, should not detain us. However, what the guide does not state is that the concept of virtual storage or memory owes very little to IBM. Virtual storage is the name for techniques which in part give a computer system the ability to behave as if it were a different computer system. The work originates out of development done by the University of Manchester and Britain's Ferranti Limited on a then large-scale machine called ATLAS. The initial development was sponsored and aided by Britain's government-financed National Research and Development Corporation, which has ever since been part owner of the resulting patents. The techniques were well-established in 1965 when IBM began to investigate virtual technology.

How then did IBM get into virtual memory? It has, and has done for years, an annual licence fee to the NRDC and the other inventor/owners. This is generally camouflaged within a general licence fee for a miscellaneous collection of NRDC patents including those dealing with virtual memory. But the patents concerned are critical and cannot be bypassed, however much IBM may since have built on and around them. Perhaps as important, by the time that IBM brought virtual to market, the system it used had long been surpassed by, among others, CDC, Burroughs, and UNIVAC.

Yet whether one considers the internal comparisons of IBM product *vis-à-vis* its competition, or the IBM inability to initiate technology which will actually appear on the market leaving IBM long dependent on research done elsewhere for its major technological advances, IBM's R&D expenditures are puzzlingly massive. Between the time of announcement of Series 360 and the date of the QPLA noted above, IBM claimed to have spent more than $3 billion on Research and Development (since when it has spent over $2·5 billion more), substantially more than the total R&D budget of the rest of the computer industry world-wide (even allowing for massive expenditure in Japan and Russia).

If one takes a more traditional comparison between IBM's annual R&D expenditures and those of its better-known individual competitors, then IBM has been spending at a rate which is, at a minimum, some four or five times the R&D expenditure that any of them have individually made in any one year.

But there is a twist to come: at the basic research level, IBM is now very competent, and no one should be in any doubt about it. If one looks formally at the output of IBM's research laboratories, the number of patents that IBM is granted, there is no question that IBM can originate. The bi-monthly IBM *Journal of Research and Development,* almost any issue, gives a good indication of IBM's research strength. Thus the May 1974 issue showed under 'Recent Patents' a total of 111 U.S. patents granted. And the listing continues, at this sort of rate, for issue after issue: July, 87; September, 116.*

Currently (1973–1975) IBM management may worry about its inability to attract to IBM research the brightest of the output of universities. It may internally indicate that it is disturbed by the ageing of its existing staff, who more and more seem middle-aged—if not older. Nevertheless, the results that its researchers have achieved, combined with the IBM ability to hire the best—once they have proven themselves elsewhere—or to retain as consultants the most creative members of the academic community† now make it possible for IBM to go in any direction it chooses.

'now make it possible . . .' 'now' is all important. One has to remember that the IBM direction is not set by current research nor the results of it which are now appearing in the professional literature: the direction is set by work done in the past. The Papers

---

*Of course, one needs to be very careful in linking invention and patents applied for and granted. Much of the corporate patent game consists of trying to protect data which is often general public knowledge, of putting a patent around something which is already in practice but which no one had previously formalised into a patent form. Since the overthrow of the ENIAC patents there are very few of the original patents left which are worth anything. No one challenges them, it is too time-consuming and expensive. No one defends them either, for the same reasons. Much of the patent game in the computer industry is really concerned with a bar to entry, though if anyone could be bothered to challenge, no doubt the averages would operate in computer patents as elsewhere: 70% of patents which are challenged in America are eventually overthrown.

†That it can hire the best there is no doubt. Over the years I have compiled a list of some forty or more gifted academics who engage in research in areas which interest IBM—from linguistics and mathematical theory to solid state physics and computer networks. They are spread as far wide as the University of California at Berkeley to research institutions in Austria. They are men whose continued insights into the possible are such that I keep returning to ask more questions. Significantly, a rough check indicates that nearly two out of every three are or have been IBM consultants. Not included in this list, but also at some time in IBM employment, have been at least two Nobel Prize winners.

have shown that IBM regards the time-span between invention and marketing to be about eleven years. (This may seem long: it is not. Most studies elsewhere have indicated that the industrial norm between invention and the mass market is more like fifteen years.) And as IBM research until the early sixties was not really regarded seriously, we should expect that the results of IBM invention should be beginning to appear on the market: they are, even if as yet only in a trickle.

Even were that research effort not to produce any new invention, however, IBM would still probably be safe into the eighties simply using its own internal resources. But, there is another phenomenon worth noting. One cannot look at IBM research in isolation. The consensus of opinion among observers of IBM's R&D is that it is now generally three to five years ahead of its major competitors, even if due to management decision the products on the market should often be technologically three to five years behind those same competitors.

This is not to imply that IBM research is ahead of everybody across the entire front: there is much work done elsewhere by industry, universities and government-financed laboratories which sometimes makes what IBM is doing seem singularly old-fashioned. Nor should this, conversely, be thought of as an attempt to decry the abilities of IBM scientists and development staff. Research emphases are the result of IBM management decision. IBM is primarily interested in a specific spectrum of activity. On top of this, there are areas where, though the results may bear on the problems that IBM management is prepared to try to have solved, research just will not be followed through. Management has definite ideas about the way the future should be shaped and has no wish to finance work in some areas, work, that is, which consists of more than a watching brief on the state of art. This is a precaution against the emergence somewhere of a critical invention which could make an impact on IBM's future product-lines and plans. Thus, for instance, IBM works intensively in communications research: it does not, however, seriously work in the area of what is known as distributed packet switching (a methodology of communications equivalent to sending data around almost as if it were letter post travelling at the speed of light, and chargeable as if it were letter post, with classes being distance independent). The reason it does not, of course, is that this method of working implies a breakdown of the standard hierarchy. But IBM is, as we have seen, classically hierarchical to the nth degree, and technology suited to hierarchical organisations of this mould is the basis of its business. One cannot expect an organisation to be much interested in a methodology, however promising, which runs counter to the basic beliefs of the men who run it.*

The research, then, has direction and that direction is obviously concerned with the problems that concern IBM. There is much work in solid state physics, enquiry into phenomena such as the Josephson effect (the change in nature of certain materials at very low temperatures which make them suitable for rapid switching and information storage) and into the properties of many forms of high-frequency signals, into lasers and other areas which could be basic to the improvement of computing, the ability to store and get at more information faster and faster—and cheaper and cheaper.

Essentially the work of IBM is primarily related to extending what computers can do when used by organisations, and has the limitations of such research. IBM too is interested in how to improve the performance of its own design, development, and manufacturing function and ways in which its technology will fit into product which will improve control within organisations. It shows surprisingly little interest in the problems of very fast computation with very large and complex data bases, the extension of the real-time calculation capability which interests many scientists and mathematicians. It has shown little interest also in what is known as Artificial Intelligence, giving the machine elementary capabilities, say, to be able to operate independently in a hostile environment, or in the direct linking of men with computers and with technological devices.

IBM's problem here is that it just cannot see how it can market in the IBM style—or make a profit: the classic problem of a project requiring as much management time and initiative for a market with a potential of a hundred million as for one of a billion dollars. As important, these possible markets do not seem to im-

---

*It is, in part, also due to the fact that the computers required for this method of working are small and relatively cheap, something again unlikely to be of much help in shifting iron.

pinge as yet on the general market as conceived by IBM, and IBM's organisation is not fitted to cope with them.

For the market of IBM is the organisation. There have been many attempts by IBM at management level to look into areas where computer techniques could be useful to people, sometimes at a seemingly trivial level. Television repair, electronic watches, home information retrieval (that one might eventually come in the future but is dependent upon a whole hos. of legal changes in the practices IBM is allowed to engage in) and the like. What defeat IBM are the marketing-cost and profit levels.

Up till the early seventies, IBM's reactions to the market and the competition which had faced it was to concentrate its technical attention on three things: reliability, achieved both by technological advance over its previous commercial product and the traditional high quality of IBM hand-holding, maintenance and service; change in the speed of the CPU and the units which surround it—thus, Series 370 in performance terms was initially, generally and roughly twice as fast as Series 360, and after the addition of virtual memory, twice as fast again; and an increase in the number of tasks that the computer could handle.

The third item was, of course, linked to that CPU speed increase, but just as important, the more the computer could be made to do, the more embedded within an organisation and critical to its activities would it become. And there would be added bonuses: a steady demand for the peripherals which during the sixties had become the main source of IBM's rental and purchase income—and, post-1969 and unbundling, the extra income which came from new software product.

This orientation continued into the early days of Series 370, though that, when initially announced in 1970, could initially best be described as a non-event. But this view ignored what was under the covers, the parts that were not originally made public, but for which the connections were present. Within a couple of years some of those connections were to be uncovered, and it became noticeable that IBM was evolving its users in a new direction.

First came virtual memory and its introduction to that large, tied IBM customer base. Given that you adopt a technical philosophy of having a large computer at the centre of operations in the creation of the large data bases and information retrieval systems, without which it is really impossible to embed the computer in the daily activities of an organisation, that concept was critical.

With the arrival of virtual, there came the second, also critical, element in the chain: communications.

Series 360 had been essentially batch, after-the-event information recording and after-the-event recall. Though IBM was later to claim a widespread communications capability inherent in Series 360, the facts of the market place belied it; IBM just was not pushing communications. For though IBM had long had experience with systems involving communications, it was generally in special classes of equipment. There were military systems—SAGE and its successors and derivations, and airborne computers for aircraft. There were like systems involved in air traffic control, and there were long existing airline reservation systems which IBM had been developing since the fifties with reservation terminals spread sometimes continent-wide.

With 370, however, IBM began to evolve (a term that IBM loves to use) its mainstream commercial users towards working in this different environment. If one could involve communications, one could in theory access those files centrally held on a computer directly from anywhere within the organisation (given that customer managements considered it useful and were willing to pay for it). And one could speed up remote data capture, and thus the timeliness of the information available; one could operate in 'real-time' controlling functions while they were happening. The new systems, then, gave the possibility of interacting with events as they unfolded and were not restricted to after-the-fact evaluation of where the organisation had gone wrong.

This was and is the route of an old humanitarian—in all its senses—dream.* That the computer and communications are intertwined, and that their interaction would result in something new, had been foreseen by science fiction writers, computer scientists and embryo futurists and prophets ever since the computer had been invented. Indeed, the literature concerning the threat of the computer—and the automation it made possible—to sterile, repetitive, boring routine work, was then extensive (and now is more so) and was dependent on this mix being achieved.

---

*It is the same dream which first got me hooked on the computer sciences, business and computing industry back in the fifties.

The threat, however, was for a long time interesting, fascinating —and irrelevant: it might exist in the abstract, but the computer industry was not in practice developing that way. Its main attack was being mounted on a different market place: the accounting, after-the-event function in the generally non-unionised, white-collar areas of industry.

However, the threat remained. What would cause it to become something more than an abstract (and for some, a highly lucrative) dream would come from the exhaustion of the conventional accounting/administration paper generation market place* as the source of sufficient long-term growth to sustain the computer industry in the future, a situation reached some time ago. For the threat to become reality, it would require that IBM devote some of its skills to industrial markets, markets not quite as simple to move into and organise. But gradually IBM began to shift. It took some of the individual schemes that it had worked on in the production area and began to market them in a much wider, if still muted, form: muted, because the adaptation of the technology to industrial production was nowhere near as well developed as it was on the office/management information side.

The dream is now well on the way to realisation, a process which tears one two ways. One cannot disapprove—there must, after all, be something better for people to do. But—and it is a large but—one also knows that in the process of realising it, the computer industry will change out of all recognition, and that without substantial change in the power balance within the industry, a change which will have to be externally enforced, it will be IBM which will grow and become rich from it: and IBM simply does not deserve it.

We can get some idea of one of the newer thrusts of IBM—the intermingling of computers, communications and 'real-time' working—from an IBM manufacturing industry management presentation put forward in 1973. What was being shown in the four-page extract (see Appendix One) was an approach to using computers, one which few companies are following and which IBM still has considerable difficulties in making work

---

*We can get some idea of the amount of paper that is computer generated and of the main uses to which computers are put from a 1973 American research report which indicated that 60% of all U.S. first class letter mail is either computer generated or bound for a computerised data base.

even for those who want it. However, IBM and the industry faced similar problems in the fifties and sixties in the automation and computerisation of basic routine office and administrative functions. What must be remembered is that this is one of the first signs of real change.

IBM is not, of course, going to let it stop there. It calls these systems which control on-going processes in factories and plants 'sensor based'—some sensor based working was discussed in the presentation—and such systems are critical to its view of the future. Sensor based systems are the first break-out from IBM's traditional business since it became involved with scientific computation. IBM began with a computer called System 7, at the small end of the range. IBM wishes eventually to go sensor based throughout the range, so that the largest of its offerings will be able to run sensor based applications.

Why should it want to do this? The one thing from IBM that is always worth listening to is its analysis of the coming market. SDD has put the reasons for going in this direction very well:

'The most significant reasons for developing and implementing a total sensor based plan are: To assist in achieving the total growth goals of the IBM Corporation.'

. . . . . .

'SDD foresees a rapid expansion in the use of real-time systems in the 1970's. This expected growth is of necessity and is based on basic changes in our social and economic environment.

'The relationship between costs and profits is probably the single most important generality concerning American Industry [and now also everbody else's]. Over the past several years, the labor content of a unit of real corporate product has risen sharply, driving up prices and putting a squeeze on corporate profits. In the 1962 to 1969 time period unit labor costs increased at three times the rate of non labor costs.

'. . . In 1955, eleven cents out of every capital invested dollar went for automated equipment and machinery . . . by 1980 the outlay is expected to reach 30 cents.'

Naturally, IBM wants a share of it. But to get it, IBM has to extend its capabilities in a number of ways. And it must enter as a major force at least one market in which it has had some experience but has not yet committed major resources—telecommunications. But why should IBM have been so slow in entering this field?

IBM may too often be number two in coming to market, but what has long interested IBM in its market entries has been getting its costs right. For instance, IBM saw in the early sixties that semi-conductor component production was the key to hardware costs and began to move as much of this in-house as possible, becoming the largest complex high quality integrated circuit manufacturer in the world. We can get some idea of the reason why this should be so when we remember that years later one of the IBM Papers indicated that 75% of the cost of manufacturing the 370/135 was taken up by components technology which, stated the document, was 'cost sensitive to quantity variations and yield percentages'. Or, in other words, up to certain limits the more you can manufacture, the more the ꙋꙋꙋꙛꙋꙛꙛꙇꙑ ꙋꙉ ꙓꙇꙇꙏꙇꙇ ꙉꙇꙇꙇ ꙏꙇꙇꙇ ꙇꙇ ꙏꙇꙇꙇ ꙉꙇꙇꙇꙋꙉ ꙁꙇꙇꙉ ꙓꙇꙇꙇ ꙉꙇꙇꙇ was so was understood by everybody; their problem was simply that they could not generate the volumes of sales to justify bringing production in-house to the same extent. That IBM has this strength is not generally understood, even by close IBM watchers. However, this is critical to IBM's future, for its development plans lead IBM down the road of creating what is thought of as a single level memory–CPU system, a black box in which the separated functions taken up by the CPU—main store, backing store, buffers—all this is LSI. And this, naturally, is something any manufacturer would prefer to have inhouse.

It is known from the professional literature that IBM can build up to 32K of store on a single LSI chip, and that is already generally well beyond the capabilities of any competitors. What is nowhere near as widely known is that IBM has had considerable success at 64K, an advance of a substantial order of magnitude, *over the capability of would-be competitors.*

That last is the key. The results of the many IBM task forces studying telecommunications—satellites, networking—seem to lead to one general conclusion: the future areas of cost savings and of profitable mark-up now lie within communications in the same way as they looked as if they would eventually lie in semi-conductor integration techniques.

In introducing communications IBM is attempting to change the business practices of those users whom IBM knows best: the least-efficient, regulated offices of the money men—the banks, insurance and financial companies—and the administrative organisations of those just as paper-bound organisations—governments, oil companies, major utilities, large manufacturers and retail chains.

The first group are least efficient by custom and practice, and the theory, often long-hallowed and established and reinforced by regulation, that a basic safeguard for depositors' and investors' money is to make sure that their funds are not eaten up by 'administration'. The rule seems generally to be that administrative costs should, at the maximum, be 2% of the investment funds which pass through their hands.

A maximum, of course, tends to become a general rule, which has in fact happened. But that rule became general in the days of paper control, accounting systems and their business machine replacements: it has little to do with the era of the new communications-based systems.

The rule does not apply to the second group, but generally they tend to follow the path of financial businesses, believing it to be good practice. The situation seems to invite exploitation but will require a major force to do so, a fact which IBM understands very well. And what better force than IBM itself, a company with a claim to understanding the processes of administration, what actually goes on inside offices?

IBM is building up to what we can call the total business of the systems and artefacts óf management control. It would like to do a clean sweep: the communications devices; the word-processing equipment, whether typewriters, copiers or facsimile transceivers; and the company information systems pulling in data from both production and administration; and the computers and associated kit on which they are run. It wants, in other words, to provide the office of the future. In order to do this IBM must radically change the products it markets and change itself to effectively produce and market them.

This is the direction in which IBM is evolving its users and their organisations. But IBM also understands the impact that such evolution will have on organisations, not least on itself. Back in 1970, Opel was to summarise the conflicts posed for IBM like this:

'The FS plan does not contemplate a DPG reorganization but

it is strongly felt that a reorganisation is necessary to pull it off. It should be a corporate-wide program and it will imply resource conflicts since current organizational definitions do not hold. *In addition, FS isn't capable of being stated as a normal product program and has no evolution to build on.'* (italics added).

The Future Series line was initially forecast in the summer of 1971 to be announced according to the dates given in the table below. The table is now out of date but gives a good indication of IBM's planning in action.*

Replacement Systems	115	125	135	145	155	165	195
FS Ann.*	6/78	12/77	12/76	12/76	12/76	12/76	12/76
FCS**	6/79	12/78	12/77	12/77	12/77	12/77	12/77

*Ann : Announce
**FCS: First Customer Shipment

FS was predicated on the notion that communications and computing are now inextricably intertwined. But there was a snag. The snag was that while IBM might make equipment for data communications, as IBM stood it was producing kit which would eventually end up supporting the income and profits of the telecommunications carriers. This was not the way IBM had been built: it was a situation which could not be allowed to continue.

For a long time the problem seemed insoluble. The world over, the telecommunications market is either state-owned and state regulated, or privately owned and state regulated. In either case that regulation is the price that has had to be paid for the handing over of a natural monopoly. And that regulation restricts tariffs and the profits that are allowed to be made.

That was one price IBM did not wish to pay. Was there a way out? After considering the problem for a very long time, IBM finally hit upon the solution. Getting that solution organised, however, was to take much effort and time.

---

*The table is now more than out of date. See Epilogue.

The chosen solution involved IBM's entry into the communications satellite business. At first there seemed to be no mechanism available to enable IBM to do so, for the decision could not be just a straight, simple, new product decision. It would involve either applying for a licence to operate, or getting hands on a corporation with an existing licence or some form of pending application.

The decision had been made too late for IBM to seek its own licence, for the time for applications was past.* So IBM approached companies who had such permission; reports have it that it sought control. To its chagrin it was rebuffed.

IBM was forced to consider various other schemes for getting into the business. There was, reputedly, an element of desperation: IBM, it seemed, could not get hold of an American domestic satellite operation. But if IBM could not have an American satellite, why not one under foreign registry? Why not seek a foreign collaborator, with IBM putting up the cash for a launch? IBM sources at one stage indicated that the corporation was trying to buy into a Canadian satellite operation.

In the end, this was not necessary. On Friday, 3rd July, in time for the long Independence Day weekend and no doubt in the hope that it would not be noticed, IBM announced its plans to join with America's Communications Satellite Corporation—COMSAT—in the communications business and filed an application before the government's regulatory body, the Federal Communications Commission in Washington, seeking approval for its entry and the appropriate licence.

The plan was for IBM and COMSAT General Corporation, a COMSAT subsidiary, to acquire a small Washington-based satellite operation—CML Satellite Corporation—a fifty-employee company which had filed for permission to put up a satellite 'for general and specialised purposes' but whose application was no longer pending, primarily because the original partners were then cash starved. The cost was not heavy—$5 million between the two—with the projected end result that IBM would hold 55% and COMSAT 45%. Almost immediately, the

---

*Indeed, there had been prior reports that when applications were being sought, IBM management had not noticed until the period had run out. Those responsible for IBM missing this boat were reputed to have been disciplined.

application was to be opposed by nearly everybody in sight. Few people doubted, however, that IBM would get some form of operational permission.

IBM had long had experience with staellite transmission of digital data. It had been a user early in the life of the communications satellite business. There were transatlantic computer-to-computer experiments between Endicott, New York, and La Gaude, in France, as far back as 1962. By 1967 IBM had gone much further than the simple investigation of possibilities. It now had further experience as the result of its involvement with N.A.S.A. and the U.S. Air Force. It had also mounted experiments mixing normal commercial internal U.S. communications between nine of its American sites, the Early Bird satellite, and a site in France, the tests being controlled from Raleigh, North Carolina.

By the early seventies, satellite transmission was a regular and routine daily operation. It had been built up into the internal IBM WTC information system RESPOND, a system created essentially as a management control tool tying in the sales offices to production and allowing management and the plants fast access to the current position of the order book as well as allowing for the rapid interchange of manufacturing change information between those internationally integrated plants.

The experiments had not been simply with satellite operation: IBM's consideration of the communications business had two preoccupations. There was the offering of communications proper, a problem over which the MRC had been struggling since the late sixties. Struggling, because IBM did extensive business with AT&T and had come to the conclusion that the price to be paid for any entry into a conventional communications business would be the loss of its trade with AT&T, a price it was not for a long time willing to pay. Any direct entry into the communications market then would have to be in an area which initially seemed to impact on AT&T as little as possible: the business IBM would have to go for would have to come primarily from growth which IBM initiated. Above all, it would have to stay away from the bedrock telephone business, or at least indicate that the business it was after would not be likely to impact on this base until some time so problematically into the future that AT&T executives could safely leave it to their successors to worry about.

These considerations also applied to non-computer-oriented communications equipment: IBM knew that were it to offer such equipment, it would also face the possibility that AT&T, with its very solid technical expertise, patents, experience and probably the best American communications/electronics research facility (Bell Labs, Murray Hills, near New York), would move down against it. And it would do so were IBM to enter at the mass market level, where Bell's marketing organisation was superior. For while IBM's experience of direct dealing with John Q. Public was limited, Bell's was not.

For these reasons the MRC had for many years agonised over the IBM-developed and manufactured computerised telephone exchange (initially the 2750, but 'up-graded' and re-announced in 1972 as the 3750, otherwise known in The Papers as CARNATION).

The problem was to reconcile the revenues and profits that IBM saw (as the market stood, $4 billion of the former and $1 billion of the latter for the 3750 within the U.S. alone) with the change that might happen on the general market place as the result of the introduction.

As the studies progressed, IBM began to discover more about the communications market place and the possible position of telecommunications satellites within it. Thus, an April 1970 report of a Satellite Communications Task Force (steered by the Corporate Technical Committee) stated in an MC report to the MRC: 'It appears that internally we could replace the common carriers with satellite, and gain both cost and performance advantages. The savings would appear to be in the neighbourhood of $5–$7 million per year.'

But otherwise, communications thinking continued along traditional lines. The Task Force report, for instance, was to recommend that the IBM 3750 exchange be marketed in the U.S.A. via a new division, Information Switching, as if it was just another new and different product. The recommendation was turned down.

For John Opel was beginning to take a different view of the future and pressing for change. He was coming round to the view that IBM should go for a total systems strategy, the result of which should eventually be what is otherwise known as 'the end to end system', a set of solutions which would lead IBM to produce a range of products and services to cover the information needs of an organisation in their entirety. IBM should be aiming its efforts at providing the systems for the office of the future. It should set out to create a situation in which the user could come to one supplier only: where eventually he would be able to look around his offices and find that the only equipment they contained—typewriters*, dictating machines, copiers, word processing and other terminals, exchanges, computers, storage, communications–all were provided by IBM. It would be a situation in which many of those artifacts would be differently organised to the way in which they generally are today. They would generally be on-line, connected via communications systems. Such systems would also link remote locations—plants, sales outlets or offices—and data would be collected automatically as changes occurred.

I think to the idea that undorlino ▪ ▪ ▪ ▪▪▪ ICTBTof I ▪▪▪▪▪▪▪▪▪▪▪ ▪ tion, F3 must differ quite radically, from current offerings. There is little idealism here; it has to. The main reason for the change is to be found in the level of complexity reached with present-day large computer systems, immense and intelluctually unbearable. IBM could not set out to add immensely to that complexity without first making sure that the existing confusion was reduced as much as possible—without any loss of information to those depending on the new systems. And this meant a radical re-think.

For though IBM and the rest of the computing industry make much of the increases in speed that technological change brings, those increases are not always marked by a corresponding change in throughput. By way of example, the 360/195 may in theory be thirty times as fast as the old Ferranti ATLAS,† the first of the virtual machines, but in practice comparing similar sorts of job mix (similar programs doing similar things and coping with similar volumes) the 360/195 can provide a throughput only three times as great. Which means that, as the 360/195 is well over twice as expensive as ATLAS, one is almost back to where one

---

* 'Typewriters' provided with on-line text-editing and correction facilities, one of the booming parts of the early '70's computing business.

† ATLAS is used as a scale by British Government agencies. The machines they obtain are rated in terms of ATLAS throughput, so many times ATLAS power.

started (though we are now in fact comparing situations some eight years apart).

We do not simply have to look at IBM's—or anyone else's—very large computers operating in the scientific environment. A more directly commercial example: fourteen airlines were, at the time of writing, getting together and comparing notes on the performance of their IBM computer installations. The one thing they all agreed on was that they were just not getting the performance which IBM had led them to expect and for which they had contracted. Instead they were talking in terms of 30% of promised performance.

Why should this be so? To understand that we need to look at the cause of that complexity, which derives from something not well understood outside the computer industry—sometimes, it seems, not well understood even within it.

Laymen tend to think of a computer as a collection of electronic devices. But that electronic nanny is more, and that 'more' is critical and not primarily electronic at all (though its operations are handled electronically). What determines what one can do with computers lies in a complex of skills known by the generic name of software.

The creation of software is not in practice as yet a science, one in which the rules age generally accepted and fully understood. The creation of computer systems is really a fraudulent occupation; fraudulent in the sense that those inhuman looking cabinets give the impression that their creation came about as the result of a coldly rational, logic-bound process, an objective process which seems to qualify as a branch of science.

In fact the reality is generally much different. For up till now we have built computer systems largely on an empirical basis. If it worked well enough, if a market for it could be foreseen, if cost and profit levels looked right, it went into production.

Then and only then did we get around to trying to organise its operating system: we have traded off the electronics against the software in a fashion which would be more familiar to an artist than a scientist. If there is an underlying logic to the processes of software creation, most of the industry often seems unaware of it. And when one considers the large so-called experienced commercial users, one too often finds that much if not most of their software activity consists of trying to convert software written for previous systems to run on their current systems.

Like all other manufacturers, IBM is well aware of this problem. Indeed, doing something about it has been a major IBM preoccupation throughout the years. Part of the answer is to be found in the creation of what are known as emulators, special software conversion aids which allow programs for previous systems to run on those presently installed. Indeed, in some long-term IBM user installations, the situation now existing has been described by one IBM software specialist as 'emulating eight levels up from the abacus'.

The result is a situation where the user has the feeling that the software written for his Series 700 system in the fifties has managed to survive unchanged through the Series 1400, Series 360, Series 370, 370 with virtual, and 370 with virtual and communications. He also has the surety that the newer software written in the interesting systems have been developed will also run on his current systems without requiring a total rethink. What he does not seem to appreciate is that those emulators eat up computer power. For the conversion is done by the system, with the result that it takes a far larger and faster—and more expensive—computer to produce the same results in the same time.

It would make more sense, it seems, to upend existing practices; to go back to first principles and the underlying theoretical structure which must exist (indeed, it does exist and we are beginning to have some understanding of it), and then to make use of it in the same way that the physicist uses the laws of physics: take the required subset and build on it. What is being suggested here is that the systems architecture is dictated by natural law, and not, as currently happens, by the building of computers once they have been made to work.

IBM expects to do this ultimately with Q. Q is the operating system, the critical software which makes everything happen, to go with Future Series. It is expected to be proprietary to IBM, for Q is much more than an operating system as these are now conceived.

Q can best be thought of as a software architecture which will determine and dictate what the electronics will do. The notion behind Q is really a recognition that we can now build in electronics almost any computer we care to. Q then is meant to be basic. It is IBM once more setting out on the road that it tried to go down with OS 360, and is expected to do what that could never do because IBM started at the wrong end, the electronics end.

The IBM Papers tell us that all current and future software releases are interim to Q and have been designed so as to be compatible with it and not to violate the general ground-rules which will determine what Q is to look like.

Series 360 systems will require emulation, but all System 370 software should run under Q. This is emulation carried to the extreme, emulation not simply using software techniques, for Q will be part software instructions as hitherto understood, part electronics. And Q is a basic challenge to the software professions in that programmers simply will not be able to understand what the operating system is about. This has the effect, of course, that only IBM can change it. As ever, good theory and IBM profits can be made to coincide.

The documents indicate that, for the unskilled user, Q will be transparent. It looks as if it will be a family of hierarchical systems-software which, at the point where the user comes into contact with it, will accept relatively unstructured plain language—initially, no doubt, the plain language of business.

What IBM wants to achieve is a set of systems which do not deter the layman, so that those without training in the esoterics of computing can use them. In this sense most business executives are laymen. Q, of course, will go much further than most current operating systems: much of the triggering, the guidance through the system, will be thrust onto the computer and initiated by it, instead of the user having to make most of the initiating moves, the present-day position.

This is a potted guide to the software environment. But what of the machines, the iron that IBM needs to shift to continue to grow? Future Series, of course, will be new in terms of hardware. There are indications in The Papers that though Q will run on all IBM systems of the future, the main thrust of IBM's effort will go into a parallel machine, LSI CPU's running side by side within one set of boxes. In late 1974 IBM was believed to be developing at least three such models: two CPU's, four CPU's and eight.*

If these can be made to work—and there is no reason why they

---

* The documents however disclosed the existence of four models code-named FS0, FS1, FS2 and a large system called THRUSH.

should not, for there is considerable experience in this area of computation—they will have a lot of advantages, notably in the way that they allow data to be treated. Currently IBM and everybody else do a lot of data compression, sorting and re-sorting and rearranging data into queues to be run through a computer. With Future Series, one should be able to take advantage of the falling costs of electronics and, where possible, sweep the problem through. It will not matter that one does not make optimum use of electronic resources, those will be cheap.

Which leads to the units with which the FS computers will be surrounded. It is the essence of FS that it should be what is thought of as a single level system, in which storage is generally on-line and the storage devices seem to act each as if they were part of CPU main memory.

The key to FS then lies in storage. Q will need virtual storage and will require very large and very fast memory capacity. Here, the falling costs of electronics allied with IBM's semi-conductor expertise and its design capability give it great advantages.

There is much argument within IBM about which devices and which technologies to push, with the producers of the various IBM memory technologies each taking the view that the future should be theirs. However, IBM does have some quite revolutionary memory devices under development. Probably nearest in time is what is jocularly referred to in the industry as IBM's 64 Mgb 'beer can', so named because that is roughly the size it is. This is an LSI memory, using some quite advanced reliability techniques, cheap to produce and very fast.

Coming up behind are such technologies as bubble memory and cryogenic memories in part based on the Josephson effect. There is not, however, any serious experience yet in the fabrica-tion of such devices on a mass scale; even supposing that the technologies were proved, their manufacture for the mass market must be considered some time off.

On the way, however, are more traditional devices. The Papers indicate that there will eventually be a 400 Mgb capacity disc drive, code named Apollo, to be announced with FS. And already on the market there is that mass storage device, the IBM 3850 tape library, which in its largest version holds 472,000 *million* characters of information, and which, as the data is transferred to the computer via a disc drive system, looks to the user as if it were such a system, and not the near-revolutionary device that it is (though even here it should be noted that IBM was not the first to bring such a system to market: that honour belongs to a little company in Boulder, Colorado, called Xytek).

But what are user organisations to do with all this storage that they do not do already? To consider that, one must consider the new devices and software that the user will have available.

The office of the future based on IBM equipment will obviously demand considerable interlinking of the equipment that is offered. The key to the use of FS will lie in the terminals that IBM is expected to offer. Many will be specific to industries. However, there is a general class of terminal based on what is called the touch wire principle, which allows information to be electronically flicked through at very high speed. IBM is expected to market colour video terminals fitted with light-pens and the technology that makes them operate. It is being so devised that a child could use it, and user dependence on the keyboard as a means of data input and output is being radically reduced.

The calculation, in effect, is that once the system can be made easy to use, then a much wider range of people will begin to use it, not least among them senior company managements. In taking this tack, IBM has struck a nerve: it is indeed going to try at long last to provide a solution to a problem in part of its own creation.

It is now almost a classic complaint of user managements, particularly those with long experience of computer operations, that IBM and the rest of the computer industry have provided the possibility of computer services for everybody in their organisation except themselves, the people who in the end make the real decisions and pay the bills. The company Chairman or President, according to this line, sits in his penthouse suite as ever surrounded by fog and dependent upon other people for his information. Naturally much of the time they tell him what he wants to hear. They are below him in the hierarchy; the systems were devised under their supervision to answer the questions that they feel should be asked; they interpret the print out. But this is not what those at the top may really want.

The problem that has faced the computer industry over the years, however, has been that if those who did the detailed work involved in the system's creation could really specify what senior management wanted, they would not in fact be devising the system at all: they would be in senior managment's shoes, far removed from that particular battle.

This has been a major handicap to the advance of computing among senior corporate management, even in IBM. For a time, IBM Corporate had its own management information system, complete with terminals in executive offices. It did not last long, for it was not being used. And the reason it was not being used was that the informaion kept on the system was not that which IBM senior executives wanted.

The next IBM stage was to create an information room. IBM executives could specify the information they were seeking, not to machines but to men. The requirement would then be translated by specialists with access to all IBM's information resources into the correlated information that the executive was seeking.

But that marginal interface, while an advance, was still not satisfactory. What was required was a system which would enable the executive to find out for himself. It is this market that IBM expects to seriously open up with FS and Q.

Of course this market has long been the obvious next move in the sense that fusion is the obvious next move after fission. Comparatively, however, the jump required is not as great, though it does demand that IBM commits extensive resources into seeking answers to some quite basic questions concerned with aspects of behaviour, the structuring of language, and of course much work which can not be easily summarised but is concerned with the interlinking of systems, both software and hardware.

With these sorts of possible systems, communications knowhow and skills become very critical. For on-line working has different characteristics to batch, and those characteristics can be a severe constraint on the market when the system is now directly operated by the very senior user. The difference in part comes from the time scale of operations. It is of the essence of a communications-dependent system that it becomes part of the organisation, one which must be present and working while the user is there in the same way as electricity must be present. It is just as critical, and the reliability must be of the same order.

IBM cannot, therefore, allow that system to be out of service, and FS is expected to provide a facility to make sure that it is not. IBM is eventually expected to propose a back-up service, one which will have the capability to transfer the user's computer files to working machines whenever there is a systems failure, so that the user can continue operating with a seeming semblance of normalcy while his systems are checked out, repaired, or even changed. That last, of course, is bound to happen: systems do not last for ever, and even FS will be subject to technological change.

But why wait for the systems to fail? One of the problems that IBM faces is that the costs of service and maintenance are ever mounting. This is because they are heavily manpower dependent. However, as computer systems have become more complex, so the industry has begun to make effective use of its products in replacing that manpower. It has developed diagnostic routines —effectively automated regular and frequent 'medicals', checks on the reliability and serviceability of the electronic systems and the software.

Gradually these have been built up to where the procedures can be recorded on tape or disc—as they are in the case of the 370/135. This has advantages, not the least of which is that IBM can quickly alter the diagnostics—as it alters the operating system—simply by sending the user a new disc.

But not as quickly as IBM would be able to do if those changes could be made directly on-line from an IBM master installation. IBM has been conducting experiments in long-range diagnostics over telecommunications lines with the user's computers linked to IBM service centres and checked out from these remote installations at regular intervals. These experiments have been made both in the U.S.A. and Germany. But it is not all experimental. American IBM has a service called RETAIN which enables its service engineers to check some users' equipment with an IBM computer at the end of a communications line.

But remote diagnostics are only part of the possibilities which communications make possible. The in-house satellite facility would give capabilities, among them it should enable IBM to offer other new services, such as direct computer-to-computer connection between the IBM user and his suppliers and customers, and this whether or not they both have an IBM system.

But to get to a situation in which IBM can let its imagination roam, IBM must also find methods of locking out other would-be suppliers, of creating even more user dependence on IBM. There are many ways to attain this end, but two are worth noting.

The first is to have a continuation of the situation in which IBM releases information to the rest of the industry at the same time as it ships its first units to customers (FCS). What the industry generally wants, however, is this release to other manufacturers at the time when IBM starts production. Given the tight technological time-window discussed earlier, one could easily end up with a situation whereby no one could compete, for by the time that the competitors have looked at the product, designed their equivalent version and brought it to market, IBM might have a three to five years lead and be ready to bring out that product's successor. By this means it makes itself a moving target.

The second is the scrambling of the interfaces. The Papers indicate an IBM intent to create a situation in which the only pieces which can fit together will be IBM pieces, as the crucial bits of the interfaces may be uniquely and differently placed in each case: in part through the use of electronics special and individual to each interface, in part due to scrambling of electronics and software. For it is possible to create interfaces which are more than matching plugs and sockets with the connectors and their values spelt out: interfaces in which the transfer of something is dependent upon instructions upon circuitry buried deep inside the CPU or one of the units being connected, and without access to these instructions a competitive product cannot be made to work.

Having locked out the competition, it is obvious that IBM would have locked the user in. And to make quite sure he stays there, the probable proprietory nature of the operating system and the way in which the programmer will have been cut off from access to it will ensure that the user is unable to tamper with what IBM offers; the possibility of self-improvement by the user (through PCM's, for example) will have gone.

The result of all this will probably be systems which give the user new capabilities, which enable managements to grapple in real time with events out in remote locations and the field. Taking into consideration all the elements of the system that IBM is developing, at least all those that are known and can be thought of, Opel is probably right. This is a more complex undertaking than the space programme. It is certainly the largest technological enterprise ever mounted by a non-governmental organisation in the history of man, and almost as certainly the most expensive, one, for instance, expected to far outstrip in cost what had been spent on the development and manufacture of the Anglo-French Concorde.

If IBM can pull it off, and that is much more dependent on IBM will than the forces on the market, then IBM will set in hand the transformation of the organisations which use these systems, and a little bit of the promise of the computer will be on the road to fruition.

Yet one cannot help but wish that it were all in a better cause: whereas IBM should, of course, obtain a fair reward for its endeavours, undoubtedly there is nothing in the history of IBM to make anybody think it will be content with that. It will want more: it will probably even want it all.

IBM technology may cause problems but not as many as IBM attitudes. It is that blinkered arrogance of innocence which causes societies and governments problems, and which we have to face.

CHAPTER SIXTEEN

And Tomorrow . . . the World?

To answer the question of what, if anything, çan be done about IBM, it is first necesary to pose and answer another question. Even given the IBM record in these pages, why should anything be done which involves more than administering a short, very sharp rap on the knuckles to IBM's management, making them—and IBM's shareholders— suffer appropriate financial penalties; and the creation of specific means of policing IBM to ensure that when IBM executives state that corporate IBM will behave itself, the promise is kept. (That last, of course, is a very tall order: as far as America is concerned, the IBM skills are still much greater than those of any 'policeman' operating under current rules and with the present resources that states will allow.)

To state that IBM has broken the law, has flouted the wishes of a society, has offended against the basic tenets laid down by the Founding Fathers, and that its corporate behaviour is often repugnant may all be true, but this is not the whole story. There are many examples of corporations which have behaved similarly, without anyone requiring that the attempts to police their behaviour should be of extraordinary rigour. The behaviour of IBM really needs to be discussed in terms of IBM's size in relation to the markets in which it operates. Here is a company which has for fifty years behaved almost as it likes, a company which for most of this time was really no size at all. It was 'dumb funny company', its behaviour seemed Chaplinesque: it managed simultaneously to be wildly nutty and totally, ruthlessly self-seeking.

It may continue to exhibit the same kinds of behaviour. While one may comfort oneself with the belief that all curves are eventually S-shaped ($\sim$), that what goes up must come down, no society in which there is any measure of free enterprise is really prepared for the type of large and rich corporate animal which can so radically change its business that the downward part of that curve will mainly affect other people.

Even with minimal growth expectations—the expected reduction where IBM only grows, say, by 10% a year throughout the rest of the seventies—one could expect that IBM would be a twenty billion dollar corporation by 1980 and a forty billion dollar corporation by 1990. (This is net growth at constant prices, it takes no account of inflation. There are indications in the IBM Papers that, faced with a choice between revenue growth and low profit and no revenue growth but increasingly high profit, IBM would take the latter every time.)

Those $20 and $40 billion minimal projections indicate in themselves that something will be done: there is no case in history of any commercial entity or corporation being allowed to grow so hugely in any field significant to society without its being brought under political control. But this, too, is not enough. Size apart, are there any good and compelling reasons why the industry that is information processing should not be left to be dominated by one major company, particularly when that company so obviously provides a level of service which, if found in other fields, would earn it citations from the most unbiased and commercially least self-interested parties?

There are good reasons, and they override any temporary and questionable benefits that IBM may have provided or may still provide. There are people, though, not all employees or in some way financially connected to IBM, who perhaps naively, regard IBM as 'a good thing'.

The computer business is now at the heart of a complex of skills, techniques and machines which place the industry in a critical position among the world's three most essential fields of activity (the other two being energy and food). Computing, however, transcends most industries; indeed, it can be stated that if we did not have computing we should have to invent it. The reason is to be found in the new volumes of people and of things—and as mathematicians, though not unfortunately politicians, have discovered, the volumes of our era breed a complexity which requires new mathematics to handle. The old mathematics just do not work unless society is prepared to accept the price—the sheer administrative inability to cope. This is a price which the societies of the West are not prepared to pay.

It follows that if the industry has this criticality, it has too much importance for society to allow it to be dominated by any one company, however well run. There has to be choice, and for choice there must be a viable industry, one which does not necessarily, as now, pace itself according to the moves that IBM is making. It is critical that IBM be reduced in total importance both to society and the individual user: that there be options offering as good if not better services by different routes. It is important that IBM, in fact, become just another company, one whose relationship to society is of the utmost importance, no more important than that of any of the oil companies.

What, then, can be done? There are a number of options. There are those which involve restructuring IBM, including alterations to the arrangements of its ownership. There are those concerned with its regulation, which acknowledge that the industry is a sensitive one and that it cannot be allowed to police itself, i.e., that the interests of the users are as important as the interests of the producers and purveyors of services. There are those which involve the policing of Corporate IBM in the same way that other corporations are policed. And lastly, there are those options of a longer-term nature, the setting of standards independent of the IBM's and their supporters, in the same fashion as we set rules and conventions for the creation, ownership and driving of motor vehicles, with society insisting that, yes, the product can do this, but it cannot do it without observing safeguards which bind everybody and do not give a preferential advantage to the already powerful.

It may well be, of course, that what we need to do is to take measures which come under all of these headings. Before we can get to that we need to see what the options presently available would involve.

The possible restructuring of IBM ranges all the way from a consent decree along the lines of that issued in 1956, to a total break-up into six, seven, ten or twelve divisions. All these possibilities have been canvassed with varying degrees of seriousness.

A 1956-type solution would have IBM sever itself from one or more divisions which are not critical to the core of its business, say Office Products. It would involve IBM giving undertakings to the Justice Department, probably on disclosure of information and its timing and would require that IBM operate under restrictions which would 'give its competition a break'.

A solution of this kind, however, poses problems. It would involve IBM in lengthy discussions with the Justice Department, at the end of which, no doubt, we would once more be in a situation in which IBM had admitted no guilt, so that the decree could not be used as the basis of suits by anyone else. It would also allow IBM to behave, if it chose to do so, in a similar fashion to the way it behaved in the early sixties, changing the nature of its business.

A consent decree would leave IBM in a position in which it could count on staving off further Justice onslaughts in to the 90s, by which time that $40 billion corporation would have arrived. It is doubtful if, at the time of writing, a consent decree is a political possibility, though there are believed to have been discussions about such a settlement between IBM Counsel and the then U.S. Attorney General William Saxbe, in the autumn of 1974. In any case it is even more doubtful that Justice lawyers would settle on terms as light as those of 1956. Some, it is said, are reputed to feel that any decree would require more divestiture than IBM would be willing to countenance. A decree might, of course, satisfy Justice's political masters, for it is unlikely that any of those look forward to a situation in which the Justice case drags on for years, a likely possibility.

In any case, a consent decree would be satisfactory only within the United States. Whatever settlement was achieved in respect of IBM World Trade, it would not preclude any other country in which IBM operates from taking what action it saw fit. Justice is in no position to come to any agreement that commits any Administration apart from America's.

Restructuring IBM is something else. Much energy has been expended on the possibility within the computer industry; there are, it seems, as many plans for the break-up of IBM as there are would-be competitors and many variants have been suggested.

The most major restructure operation of the twentieth century is, of course, Standard Oil—one company divided into thirty-four—more than sixty years ago, and that, one sometimes feels, was only accomplished because it was the first time that the anti-trust laws had ever been applied on a major scale. Since then all Administrations seem to have been aghast at the temerity of that decision. Nothing quite so major has since been attempted.

Stripped of subtleties, restructuring would involve the break-up of IBM into a number of independents, apportioning the assets between the new companies and restructuring the stock.

There are basically two plans here. One is to slice IBM vertically into four, five or six companies, each of which would be a mini-IBM in its own right. This solution seems to me to contribute little if anything to industrial advance or user solutions. It would result in an Almuth an industry with a dozen or so units competing with each other across the line for the same general market. This is precisely the sort of market split which leads to a situation in which executives get together cosily to hammer out agreements on pricing and shares; it is the perfect breeding ground for cartelisation.

The second split has much more to commend it. This is to break up IBM by function: Computers, Office Products, Federal Systems, Supplies and Components is one suggested separation.

Following this general route could lead in the direction of something more sensible. How about the following:

Office Products, including typewriters, copiers and any new allied devices that IBM may release on to the market.

Peripherals: it would probably require two companies to handle these. For peripherals include terminals, communications interfaces, storage (tape and disc drives), and add-on memory. Putting them all together into one would create a company which would still be a giant by the standards of the rest of the industry. Because of the volumes involved, a company which contained all IBM's peripherals would still be much larger than any other possible competitor: a split would probably need to be made between memory devices and the rest.

Federal Systems is a natural off on its own, as is Supplies —tapes, punch cards, discs and the like.

The rest of the IBM business could be further broken down.

There is here a natural successor to IBM's Software, Consultancy and Systems Design which, hived off on its own, would be a major force in the market.

This leaves communications and the computer proper. Were IBM not to be the monolith that it is today, the objections to IBM Satellite and Communications Corporation would disappear. As for computers, there are those who wish to anyway separate IBM's larger systems from its smaller, and Components from both. In fact, there is a strong case for arguing that in view of the coming changes in the technology, the dividing line between components manufacture and computer systems manufacture is now an artificial one—the two are naturally integrated; much of computing manufacture consists of no more than the design and creation of components later suitably gift-wrapped.

There are other possible permutations. However, the break-up of IBM could have a number of effects, some of which are unlikely to be the ones that IBM's most vociferous critics would welcome: restructuring on its own would not be enough.

The first effect would probably be that, having taken the wraps off management of the 'NewCo's,' as they are already known, the successor companies would no longer really have to worry about the threat of a Justice Department-initiated anti-trust action; the twenty-year interregnum 'rule' would apply, in practice if not in principle.

In support of that theory, people point to the events that followed the restructuring of Standard Oil. The main result of that was a release of managerial talent and initiative. The successor managements were enabled to expand in a way which had not been possible with the huge monolith, and by the twenties, the stock of each of the successor companies was valued as highly as the stock of Standard Oil had been before the break-up in 1911.

Against this, there is the possibility that in the case of IBM, the successor companies would require much more time to settle down. The shaping and organising of the NewCo's would require more management initiative than was necessary in Standard Oil. That, at least, was a break-up of production of a basic product into geographical areas; this would involve something very different—a break-up into product areas, all operating continent-wide. This would be unbundling carried to its logical conclusion and could be a traumatic experience all round, and not just for the NewCo's.

It would, of course, remove one threat to the survival of the rest of the industry, the threat that IBM gets the business simply because it is IMB: the mystique would no longer exist. But again, one suspects that would take much longer to happen than those who wish IBM to be broken up in these ways would expect.

None of this addresses the problem of IBM World Trade Corporation. It is obvious that any break-up of IBM without an order for some form of divestiture or restructuring of its foreign operations would leave a very muddled situation. But the possible future of WTC needs to be considered on its own.

At first sight, the notion of turning computer manufacture into a regulated industry has a lot to commend it. It would enable IBM practices to be policed. There is one trouble with regulation, however: it has a tendency to reinforce the existing situation at the time that such regulation is introduced. It would effectively legislate the existing monopoly situation. As important, one of the keys in the regulatory process is the control of prices, which in practice means the regulation of charges in favour of the least efficient, as has happened in other industries almost without number. All that regulation would achieve, then, would be a situation in which price competition would disappear. It is no doubt a price that IBM would be perfectly happy to pay, but one cannot say the same for anyone else.

And lastly, there is currently, and will continue to be throughout the seventies, one major objection to regulation: what exactly would the regulators regulate? As previously discussed, IBM is in the precess of changing the nature of its computer business; but in any case the business generally is in a transitional stage. Any regulation, therefore, which did not also take into account the technological change in the industry would fail.

The third group of possibilities, the policing of an IBM, whether achieved by the processes of a consent decree or a court judgement, is something which really cannot be divorced from politics. The events that have taken place since the 1956 Decree indicate quite clearly that IBM has not been effectively policed, by the Justice Department or by the court which approved the Decree, the same court which is hearing the Justice case now, nearly twenty years later.

The reasons why it has not been effectively policed have much to do with political process. In theory, Justice is independent; in practice, it never has enough funds. Its annual budgets have to be negotiated with the Office of Management of Budget, which controls investigative funds. And that, of course, is in practice an agency dominated by the White House and by politicians.

And yet, were the public utterances of U.S. Administration officials to be taken at their face value, effective measures could be devised to make the policing of corporations adjudged guilty of monopoly or anti-trust practices that much more effective: this, quite apart from seeing to it that there is full compliance with existing regulations and laws.

What America needs (and not just America) are effective independent policing institutions. These are not as difficult to achieve as might at first be thought.

Let us restrict ourselves to those who have been adjudged guilty by the courts; to cases in which there has been due legal process.

A possible solution would lie in an extension of the probationary principle. The court could decide to monitor the activities of the offender, either through the Anti-Trust Division of the Justice Department or some other agency, whether existing or new. It would pass an order that for the next x years, or for however long a period the court may determine, the activities of the offending corporation would be subject to investigation and monitoring. The responsible agency would have wide powers, in the same way that probation officers have powers, and would have to turn in regular reports to the court.

So far no new ground of principle has been broken. New ground, however, is broken by the following: finding of guilt here should give the courts power to make the offending corporation pay the costs of monitoring. The costs would be recovered from the offender's profits, specifically the part that would normally be remitted to shareholders. And, as it would also be mandatory for the progress reports to be made public, any obstructions could be noted.

Such a system would create a situation in which shareholders, particularly institutional shareholders, would have to think seriously about the conduct of the corporations in which their funds were invested. The mechanism would be recognised by any first-year cybernetics student as one of reinforcement for the principles that are publicly upheld by everybody but privately broken by those who can get away with it.

This, of course, is an after-the-event solution.*

Is it possible to add to the powers of deterrence that the courts can wield? One such proposal has come from Senator Gaylord Nelson, Chairman of the monopoly sub-committee of the Senate Small Business Committee. His proposed partial solution is to make violations of the Sherman Act a felony instead of a misdemeanour, raising the maximum penalty for those convicted, from one year to five years' imprisonment:†

'. . . corporate executives who conspire to fix prices and thereby overcharge consumers millions or even billions of dollars cannot be sentenced to [imprisonment] for more than one year. Often they are not convicted or sentenced at all. It is high time that we realised that the anti-trust criminal—despite his expensive suit, fancy car and polished appearance is one of the most harmful elements in our society.'

The Nelson proposals have much to commend them in terms of the threat they pose to executives. But they suffer from the difficulty of the policing proposals just put forward: they are an after-the-event punishment. They perhaps suffer, too, from the reluctance in the past of American courts to use whatever imprisonment powers they already have, however minimal they might be.

It is when one comes to deciding what a monopoly is—before its existence has resulted in legal proceedings—that one runs into difficulties. Unfortunately most monopolies are not of the kind that was found in the Alcoa case where Judge Learned Hand observed that 90% is a monopoly. He did not need to add that anyone would recognise 90% as a monopoly; that was obvious. It is not so simple in the case of IBM, where there is room for legal argument (as distinct from the arguments dealing with reality).

One solution has been proposed by Senator Philip A. Hart in his U.S. Industrial Reorganisation Act first put forward in 1972, one more attempt in a long list of attempts to get to grips with the issue of monopoly and to arrive at clear ground rules; to deal with monopolies before the event rather than after.

---

* Another after-the-event suggestion made on the Hill would be to adapt the principle used in smuggling cases—upon conviction not only is the contraband forfeit but Customs and Excise can claim up to three times the value of the goods involved.

† In December 1974, it became law. The penalty, however, was raised to only three years imprisonment.

The Act would seek to define monopoly power, using net rate of return on net worth after taxes, lack of price competition, and number of corporations in the affected field between them possessing 50% or more of the market, 50% being the target figure; and all these indicators requiring some consistency over time. The Act would allow a temporary monopoly to exist where this rests on valid patents, a clear attempt to allow for such situations as the advent of, say, a Polaroid or a Xerox. The Act would also create an Industrial Reorganisation Commission—which could well act as the policeman in the sense put forward already*—and would have behind it an Industrial Reorganisation Court.

But there is a snag, as the 1973–1974 hearings of the sub-committee showed: few economists can be found who would agree on what constitutes a monopoly in an industry or market. There is no general, clearly enunciated body of principle which would state how many companies holding what market shares in a market would constitute a monopoly either in fact or in law. There is no agreement on what the barriers to entry created by monopolists really are, or what their effects are. For every half dozen authorities on one side, one can quote another half dozen as impressive on the other. It does not take a genius to find six more who will agree on one thing (though they may not agree on anything else): that neither of the first two schools knows what it is talking about.

Nowhere is this more true than in the field of industries which are subject to technological change. There is even less generally accepted economic precept to deal with industries in which planned product obsolescence is the norm. Thus, as noted in Chapter 13, as far back as 1952, Galbraith was to be found discussing the large firm of modern industry as an agent for inducing technological change. Yet a major study reporting in the early sixties concerned with the weapons acquisition process found the reverse: entry largely occurs during marked advances in the evolution of technology, and the new entrants were often innovators. (That, too, is a statement of the obvious: innovation

---

*Indeed, section 205 of the proposed Bill (51167)—1973 version—contains a general provision for information reports which could usefully be expanded in this direction.

after all is a means of industrial and market entry.) To thoroughly confuse matters further, one could argue on the same grounds that the computer industry has lacked technological change; for since the early sixties, while new entrants to the overall computing market have been many, none have grown to any substantial size: the major units of the industry are to be found among those who were there before the advent of Series 360, if by major one means any which can point to a share of the market higher than 5%.

There is even less agreement, if that were possible, on what the effects of monopoly generally have been on the prices that purchasers have to pay. Depending upon which authority one reads, the effects vary from an increase in overall consumer costs of as little as 1%, up to . . . well, one can take any figure one likes. And if one tries to quantify, the figures vary from an imprecise few billion dollars to as many as $80 billion a year in the U.S. market alone —which, it would not be putting it too strongly to utter, is a wide variation.

Almost the only point on which there is general agreement is that monopoly is a condition that exists. Of course, one man's monopoly is another man's reward for thrift, hard work and enterprise, or, to come back to computing as TJW Jnr put it in a letter to *Datamation*, commenting on an article dealing with his retirement:

'The responsibility to make our competitors successful must lie with their managements, not ours.'

This might well be the epitaph for the state of economic knowledge and of the law on monopoly in a world of changing technology.

This is the legal and factual jungle one enters in dealing with monopoly *per se*, which makes one think that agreement on what a monopoly is will be difficult to obtain in principle. In the case of IBM, Justice will be forced back on the existing precedents of specific proof, including that of intent.

The last solution is the standards solution, and it is essentially a long term solution. For this is the trickiest of areas. The problem is that the IBM standard is the industry's *de facto* standard. Other people may have ways of doing things which fit more closely with natural law—data structures, methods of formatting which give easier solutions: but what are needed are standards which would lead to complete interchangeability between manufacturers, and not a situation in which companies devise their systems in the light of what IBM does: some going with it, others against.

Standards will not provide a solution to the immediate problems which plague users and the industry; they cannot, for we are yet nowhere near a situation where natural standards can be found in all the areas in which standards are required. Natural standards, of course, would not simply be standards for America; they would be standards for everybody else and would have to be accepted by everybody else. Experience with international standards so far has shown, particularly in Europe, that IBM is usually the odd man out. It can, however, manage still to go its own way, as few governments are willing to enforce standards, even where devised by their own laboratories and theoretically accepted by their own standards institutions. Why not—most computers in use are IBM models.

So far in this chapter we have looked at IBM primarily within the context of American society and American laws. Whatever the outcome of the cases that IBM is fighting, IBM's position in the outside world can also be expected to change and change radically.

IBM may be multi-faceted, what you see being dependent on the point from which you look, but outside America those facets have a number of characteristics in common. To most non-Americans, IBM is an American company and essentially 'foreign'.

To Americans generally, IBM is an example of what talent and energy can achieve. To some, a sizeable number of investors, IBM is good enough for them to invest their funds; if you challenge IBM you are challenging the safety of their cash—and their judgement. To other Americans, IBM is a remarkable company, but it would be even more remarkable were it to stop exporting jobs to foreigners. They forget that were IBM to bring those jobs back home, there is now no way in which IBM products could be exported in sufficient numbers to materially add to U.S. employment possibilities. As a matter of routine the countries which purchase the majority of the world's computers, the industrialised countries of Europe and Japan, are committed to supporting their own local computer industries. The only entry now possible for U.S. product would be through radically new systems, not simply variations of those which already exist.

But there is also another American view of IBM worth recording. These are Americans who regard IBM as *anational*. But, as has been shown, the way IBM is controlled and run clearly indicates that it is quintessentially American: the IBM ethic is the American corporate ethic writ large. IBM is probably the most interesting example one has of the corporation as supremely self-interested entity and certainly the best documented. It is run by a group whose concerns are specifically 'gut-American'.

However, the view of IBM as *anational* has been seriously argued by, for example, a leading American economist with a long acquaintance with anti-trust matters:

'. . . It is not a gimmick to think of IBM as a sort of State. It is possibly right to think of IBM as a supra national, anational, or indeed perhaps national (in its own behalf). But certainly it is not within the American only politic, it is not *our* IBM. But there's a tendency for Europeans to think of it as American and from observation of its behaviour I think that that is a mistake, which needs to be pointed out to European policy makers.

'They [IBM] could shift their headquarters to Trinidad, to Tahiti or to anywhere they need if it should ever become inconvenient to control it from within America.'

'Yes, but it would still be controlled by Americans,' I said.

'I am not sure,' he said, 'any more than you can be sure that the College of Cardinals will always be dominated by Italians. Think about the role of the Roman Church over the last three hundred years and you will get a better analogy. It is very like that: the people who are in it have some sort of emotional commitment to their nationality, to their language and group; the Frenchman working for IBM will always be somewhat French, the American will always be somewhat American, but he's also IBM. That's not unlike the person who is a Catholic but also a national of another State.' [This time the analogy is not mine!]

It expresses different sentiments to the official Washington view. For it is a viewpoint which seemingly is not held by the U.S. State Department. In the autumn of 1974, the rumour arose (out of Beirut) that somewhere within the oil-rich Middle East there were Arab investors wishing to obtain control of IBM. One need not worry whether or not the rumour was true; what was interesting was the State Department reaction—this would not be permitted: IBM was in a 'sensitive' industry and essential to national defence.

And so is everybody else's computer industry. Indeed, if non-Americans had wished for an example of the law which states that the one thing one should not expect Trojan horses to contain is Trojans, they could have wished for no better demonstration. However, while the defence issue is one which any politician in any country will understand, even if he acknowledges that he cannot always in practice do that much about it, it is not the only issue which puts at risk the existence of IBM WTC in any recognisable form.

First, there is the resurgence of the 'nationalist' spirit, whether in Europe, Latin America or Asia. In the case of Europe, this was to be expected; it is a natural reaction to decline in influence: it expresses itself in terms of the nationalism of the 'nation-state' variety, and of a nationalism of the 'European' variety, as expressed in the formation of the EEC.

Second, there is the growing realisation that computing is one of the key industries for the future, and what is more, an industry in which European companies had an early lead which lack of coherent policy allowed to be quickly whittled away, in large part by IBM.

Thirdly, there is a growing understanding of the way in which multinationals operate; of their ability to move their investment funds about without regard to the wishes of the countries concerned, of their manipulation of transfer prices which affect the taxes paid, of their distinct foreign corporate ethos, and of their power to blackmail what to them are foreign governments: 'let us do this or we do nothing at all'. In the case of IBM this expresses itself in an insistence on retaining 100% ownership wherever it operates, and in its control of plant location, siting plants in one country which are wanted by others or by all. This would not matter were there enough of the market left for other people to bring in such plants, but as there often is not ...

The consequence of that insistence on 100% control of foreign subsidiaries is that IBM can no longer operate in some countries in Latin America or in Asia. Furthermore, there is a growing likelihood that it will not be able to operate in this fashion in some countries in Europe within the next few years; probably the first country to object will be Sweden.

But these are not the only measures being taken. If IBM will not give, then from IBM must be taken. This is a twofold exercise.

First, there are the various attempts by European governments to try to help in the creation and support of local computer industries. In Britain this has taken place through a process of government-sponsored amalgamation and government provided investment and R&D funds—though the sums have not been large: so far, ICL, Britain's major entrant, has received little more than $100 million, and that spread over some four to five years. France, in seven years, has spent less than $200 million on its Compagnie Internationale de l'Informatique (CII); Germany has spent even less in direct support of Siemens and Telefunken.

With this, there has gone a willingness to back a European consortium made up of CII, Siemens and Holland's Philips. The creation of a common range of systems, when the three partners are separated by differing accounting practices, standards, languages and customs, is likely to be fraught with difficulty. And so it has proved.*

A different and more coherent attack on the problem posed by IBM, has been mounted by Japan. Japanese policy is much longer term: Japan does not allow short-term political and budgetary expediency to run counter to long-term ambitions. They have been content to mount a holding operation while going back to fundamentals: the creation of their own standards, extensive research in communications techniques and software, and a long-term development programme of large computers and their peripherals, most of which are not likely to be on the international market on any major scale before the late seventies.

The second strand of the war on IBM (and the other so-called multinationals) is the articulation of 'Buy European' or 'Buy national' policies, similar to the 'Buy American' policy of Washington. The Commission of the EEC is moving in this direction, but more importantly, so are the governments of Japan, France and especially the U.K., the most experienced in this area of policy formulation, having had such an embryo policy since 1967–68. (Germany is regarded by many Europeans as being in IBM's pocket. Perhaps this is unfair, but Bonn has over the years done everything except act.) In the case of the U.K., the policy is theoretically one of support for a British computer industry; in

---

* That willingness came partly unstuck in 1975 when the French Government allowed CII largely to go under, agreeing to its takeover by Honeywell.

practice it is primarily support of ICL in civil systems and of Marconi in defence and aerospace. The policy has only been publicly stated for the first, because in practice no government would allow defence-related work which goes to Marconi to be handled by any foreign company.

The ICL protection policy demands a 25% performance, and 10% price, differential between ICL and any competitors, before such competitors could obtain the contract.

Charges and counter charges have been made about this in the American and British press, but in practice all but a few of the orders that ICL obtained from the British government were obtained without requiring that the policy be exercised.

Basically, Europe's protection policies have proved a weak reed. There were, however, in 1974, clear indications that they will not remain so much longer, that the governments of Europe are going to get tougher. In the U.K., ICL is beginning to get more and more of the large systems orders on which IBM used to rely—and there are pressures on the civil non-government sector to make corporations buy British. Similar situations are expected to arise in France and in Germany; the *quid-pro-quo* that locally owned companies are demanding for staying in the computer business.

The days when questions by locals about ownership, control and direction could be satisfied by simplistic answers concerned with the numbers of locals employed and 'we try to be good citizens' are rapidly coming to an end. There is nothing like inflation, and a recession, to make people question a situation in which they see dicisions being made outside the national consensus.

It has been the thrust of the argument throughout this book that the political power of IBM is limited, that the notion of a multinational as a Sovereign State is naive. But if IBM is only a rich candy floss Super State, why should this book have been called *And Tomorrow ... The World?*

It is a fair question. This book is not an attack on size and should not be construed as such. If it is an onslaught on anything, it is on the world-wide policies pursued by a small group of men single-minded pursuing their own economic interest and status.

IBM is a corporation which is not simply peddling computers; it is, as we have seen, also peddling a particular view of the world, one I find singularly antipathetic. It is possible to find things in IBM of which to approve, indeed some of the uses to which it puts its resources have been nothing but admirable. But overall, the good that IBM has done is far outweighed by the bad effects it has had on increases in industrial costs and on the development of computing. It took IBM to turn a set of inventions and techniques which promised and still promise much, into something which is generally regarded by the majority either fearfully or with yawning boredom.

IBM has been allowed to do these things, because, till fairly recently, most people were unaware of the sort of corporate creature that IBM is. Even now we may have concerns of greater priority which will allow IBM to continue on its present lines, lines in which the only changes IBM make are cosmetic, changes in slope and not in step function.

But it is a change in step function that is needed. IBM has ceased to be 'dumb funny company'. In some cases indeed, IBM loyalty has passed the bounds of all good sense.

Senior IBM executives were dining after one conference with a known public opponent. How far, he wondered, would IBM take its opposition to his public arguments. He did his wondering aloud: supposing someone at the top expressed discontent. This would be translated at middle level as a desire for action which someone at the bottom would execute. But how far would it go? All the way . . . ?

Yes, replied one of the executives, he supposed it could. The threat was left hanging. Nobody mentioned that IBM management would be content with expressing the thought, but would not wish to enquire into what was done or how it was done. Nobody needed to. They all knew that American IBM can function in just that way.

But these, of course, are the sanctions of states. To quote Georges Clemenceau: 'I fear a peace without a victory.' To get the first, it is — as I hope these pages will have shown — now essential to have the second.

Epilogue

As seen from that battle command post, the hilltop above Armonk, the first quarter of 1975 must have seemed to have been developing like a good-news bad-news joke. Within the space of two months, IBM was to cancel Future Series, win the second round of the Telex suit, and be given permission by the FCC to enter the satellite business in every form except the one that it was apparent IBM wanted.

The Telex second-round judgement came first. The Denver Court of Appeals overturned the lower court's judgement, wiped out the more than $250 million awarded to Telex against IBM, but upheld the damages awarded against Telex. It was a stunning upset, one which had the immediate effect of transforming the stock market. Within the next four weeks, IBM stock was to rise on the market from $160 a share to $220 a share. Perhaps more importantly, the decision seemed to come as a signal to Wall Street: the rich were going to be protected. Almost all the other Blue Chip stocks began to rise as if the decision was not simply an award to IBM but an award to dominance and monopoly power generally.

The Appeal Court judgement immediately put the computer industry in uproar: it was to be criticised in private and public by many companies and individuals, and something needs to be written about it.

To call the judgement eccentric is to dignify eccentricity beyond all measure. It is not normal for an Appeal Court almost

entirely to rewrite the opinion of a lower court as to fact, to re-
interpret almost in its entirety what has been found in the court
below; but the court did so.

And in doing so, it found as fact 'facts' which, to those with any
experience of the computer business, were not facts at all.

It found that Judge Christensen had concluded that IBM had
only 35% of the market, though he had done no such thing.

It found that, on this basis, IBM was not therefore a
monopolist, and that accordingly IBM was not in violation of the
law, a part of the judgement which, if upheld, could lead to some
pretty peculiar behaviour in the future.

It found that few companies would have any difficulty in
creating interfaces to enable them to latch on to IBM product and
that the costs of doing so were slight. (I know of no technical
opinion in which I would have any confidence, within IBM or
outside, which could be found to agree with them.)

It would be possible to criticise the judgement line by line. It is
perhaps better to consider its overall tone. To this writer at least,
the judgement does not really read like a legal opinion at all. It
reads in truth much more as if it were a socio-economic document, one aimed at instilling confidence in a society facing a recession, rather than the judgement of a court seeking to find truth and
apportion responsibility. Indeed, some American lawyers say that
the authorities the court quotes in its support are often obscure
and are not much relied on generally. Nor can the same lawyers
understand why the judgement is so loaded in IBM's favour,
almost to the point where it sometimes seems to look as if the
judges have set out to destroy Telex.

Telex appealed. The appeal was rejected, so Telex set in hand
moves to appeal to the Supreme Court, the court which, from the
start, everybody expected would have the final say. At the time of
writing this appeal is still being progressed. However, whether or
not the Supreme Court chooses to hear it, that court has already
been put in an impossible position. For if, as the reality of the
market place has shown, the immediately prior court decided
wrongly in favour of IBM, then what is the Supreme Court to do?
If it hears the case, it will have to rule on the market issue. And if it
rules on the market issue, then it is really also deciding the outcome of a suit being tried elsewhere: Justice versus IBM before
Judge Edelstein. Mr Katzenbach could not have obtained a deci-

sion more likely to throw everybody and everything into confusion had he picked the time and the issue on which to do it.

But while this was going on, the Federal Communications Commission in Washington was quitely preparing a ruling on the IBM/COMSAT satellite proposals which, while not rewriting the past, was busy setting out guidelines concerned with the future, guidelines which would be unlikely to meet with the approval of Mr Katzenbach and his masters.

Since its application has been submitted, IBM had gone quite a long way in planning its satellite service. True, it might not yet have a license, but this had not stopped it from giving presentations to selected major users of IBM systems describing the essentials of the service it proposed to offer.

These presentations confirmed the satellite antenna on the roof of the user's premises (though whether IBM had told them of some of the subsidiary equipment, including its very high speed 60 Mgb communications interface, otherwise known as a modem, this writer could not discover), and the spread, the totality of service, that IBM intended to offer.

And then the FCC ruling went and spoilt it all: The FCC gave IBM what it wanted, permission to enter the satellite communications field, but it did so with reservations. It turned down the link with COMSTAT on the terms IBM had proposed and stated that IBM would have to enter either with more partners and on different terms, or go ahead on its own. But the sting in the tail came in the restrictions that the FCC imposed on IBM. Whatever IBM did, it would only be allowed to enter the field provided that the satellite corporation was totally separated from IBM's computing interests, and neither IBM (satellite) nor IBM (computing) would be allowed to market the services provided by the other. The relationship had to be total market separation.

It had been critical to IBM's satellite and Future Series plans that it be allowed to bundle communications and computing together technically and economically. Hence the encryption service IBM had up its sleeve to guarantee the security of customers' data required that the user take the whole package, computing and communications, from IBM. The service had been projected on the basis that IBM would charge the customer according to actual usage, metering the traffic that flowed through those satellite links. The traffic would be computer originated: it would no longer be a question of deciding to use telecommunications, rather of a request to the system generating—or not—telecommunications traffic according to where the data or appropriate computing power to answer the query was to be found.

But IBM was now restrained from bundling the two together: the user, ruled the FCC, had to be able to opt for another carrier, which obviously made nonsense of it all. IBM would have to continue to separate the charges it made for computing and computing services from those it proposed for telecommunications.

Almost within hours, IBM was saying that it would seek 'clarification': IBM was being treated like everybody else, and IBM was just not accustomed to being treated in this way.

The event which was to cause the industry the most problems, however, was yet to come, and this time it was IBM which was to initiate it. Since the existence of Future Series planning had become known in the spring of 1973, much of the rest of the industry, and many of its major customers, had been predicating their future product—and installations—on the basis that the change that FS would represent would come on the market in the late 1970s. On the 14th February, 1975, however, there occurred the largest upset in corporate future product planning in American history. It was soon to become widely known as ... The St Valentine's Day Massacre.

Here this account needs to become partly autobiographical, at least for a few paragraphs. At the time that the decision to kill FS was made—on the Friday with announcement to the divisions and subsidiaries scheduled for the following Monday, on the principle that those involved should at least be allowed a quiet week end—I was in Canada.

I arrived in the U.S.A. shortly afterwards. Within days, I knew that the decision had been made. I had gone to America to bring the manuscript of this book up to date, particularly that section concerned with the development of Future Series. Nearly two years had elapsed since the initial release of the news that FS was under development; the implications of FS were, when one thought of it, quite staggering, and I wanted to discover what progress had been made.

I knew that FS was running behind schedule and that some of the initial intentions had been changed. I was prepared for change, both of time and technology. I was not, however, prepared for what I found: disarray.

Now it is the essence of IBM that once a decision is made, IBM troops will move monolithically in the direction indicated, even if that direction is the reverse of the one in which they were all going yesterday. But this takes time to happen, there is an interval within IBM as there would be in any other organisation, a period in which no one is quite sure what is going to happen next, in which instructions to close down the work that is now aimed in the wrong direction are not necessarily in step with the feelings of those who were involved. It is not as easy to turn men off as it is to turn off money and resources, particularly when the new direction has not been spelt out.

Many of those who had been fully committed to FS were livid. 'Those jerks in Armonk wouldn't understand computing if a good system were thrust under their noses.' Perhaps even more were busy trying to find new positions to retreat to: 'I never believed in FS anyway, I thought it was going to fail.' Those high enough up the promotion ladder to have their careers affected were busy making sure that whoever got sent to the penalty box, it would be someone else. That someone, or even a lot of someones, would end up in the penalty box was obvious; that was the way that IBM worked.

I had arrived in the right place at the right time—that period in which no organisation is secure, a time in which people seek to unburden themselves, that interval in which they are retreating from one prepared position and have not yet had time to build a new one. A lot of people were talking to me. I knew it could not last long. I knew also that as there had been some 15,000 to 20,000 people who had had some involvement with aspects of FS, even if the majority of them had not understood its full implications, some were bound to know other journalists and would eventually talk.

I broke the news early in March, around the time that the IBM-sponsored annual television spectacular was being shown. With its usual sense of the apposite, the 1975 offering on the ABC network was a play starring Sir Laurence Olivier and Katherine Hepburn entitled 'Love Among the Ruins'. There was plenty of the latter if little of the former. IBM was left with individual product plans but no overall strategy. Naturally a strategy was what was sought and that quite quickly.

The time interval had been enough to bring back the old gang of traditional batch processing men. It had long been known that many people in IBM had been unhappy about the FS direction. They had grown up in the days when IBM simply sold hardware and when its progress could be measured one year against another by the amount of new hardware that had been shifted.

They were not attuned to the communications environment with all its complexities, and certainly not in tune with anything as radical as computing which had distributor elements to it. They would·be much happier with larger, faster, conventional after-the-event batch processors. And this was the proposal that almost immediately went forward: IBM should produce more of the same.

The FS story was in the old-fashioned sense a scoop, and any journalist can in time be forgiven for reliving the taste of it: stories of this magnitude, with all the ramifications they will have on the market, do not come every day of the week.

What had I discovered? According to the best estimates I could obtain, IBM had probably spent between eight hundred million and one billion dollars on the development of FS since the initial studies had been done in 1970. FS had been running into problems for the best part of a year and, instead of covering the entire IBM range, had been restricted to the top end, thus in part changing its revolutionary nature. IBM had reacted to the problems encountered in a typical visceral IBM fashion: if you have problems, devote more resources. So much so that towards the end of its life, almost the entire resources of SDD and ASDD had been committed to the solution of FS problems and the enhancement of existing product had been starved of funds and management effort. IBM thought it did not need to bother: if there were problems with existing product, FS would provide the solution. Indeed, it would be best if there were no real solution prior to FS.

And there were problems: by early 1975, world-wide, the better part of one hundred 370/168 installations, and at that mostly commercial installations, were 'running out of steam'. They were facing the same problems that were being faced by the airlines and some large users with IBM computer installations (see Chapter 15): the promised throughput just was not there. We can get some understanding of what was happening by noting that with some of these large systems one simple transaction could take up to 70,000 lines of code to execute. It is a lot of software to enable simple tasks to be done.

But FS was to solve all this . . .

That the cancellation of FS was made public was received with less than rapture by IBM management. The initial stories, in *O1 Informatique, Computer Digest,* and the *Financial Times,* brought forth a satement from IBM's Chairman Frank Cary:

'Recent press reports speculating about changes in IBM product plans and resulting write-offs that might result from such changes are grossly inaccurate. FS was a label that meant Future Systems: the label is no longer in use but that in no way implies that our development efforts on products for the future have stopped. While IBM does not comment on such speculation [Grossly inaccurate: the chairman of IBM has just done so. Author] changes in product development plans are being made all the time. Any assertion that these changes will result in write-offs are erroneous because production development expenditures are charged against income as they are incurred.'

It was a weak response, seeking to downgrade FS to just another product. It confused, perhaps purposely, the writing-off of cash within the financial year with the writing-off of that irreplaceable commodity, the deep involvement of much of IBM's best talent with FS for well over three years.

Almost immediately, IBM set out to hide the magnitude of the disaster that the cancellation of FS implied. After all, if those estimates I had obtained were right, then FS had cost IBM more than Ford lost on the Edsel, or GE and RCA combined had spent on their attempt to match IBM in the mainframe business. It was, to pick up a familiar IBM phrase a 'boo boo' of the first magnitude. And it was a much more interesting failure than the Ford, RCA, GE disasters, for it was with FS that IBM had applied the full range of its new management skills, the skills on which much of its reputation now rests.

Variants of a highly selective view of the truth were carefully leaked to journalists just as carefully selected, and the impression was generally given that FS was simply postponed, not cancelled. IBM even managed to turn the cancellation to its future market advantage. One line that was effectively peddled, sometimes to those who should have known better, was that IBM had run into serious problems with the organisation of LSIs. It had, but there were few problems there that were beyond IBM skills; the one thing that component specialists I knew in IBM were happy about was their expertise in the field.

So why was FS killed? Piecing together the evidence as best one can, the scenario which leads to the cancellation begins to look something like this.

First, there were some technical and market reasons. FS was running late and above budget, but it is in the nature of advanced technological developments that they take longer to bring to completion and cost more than originally expected, even after inflation has been taken into account. Indeed, there is even a rule to account for it: the greater the amount of technological advance a project requires, the greater the degree of overspending above budget that will also be required.

If there was a programme failure, it had much to do with Q, the operating system. IBM has long believed in the fallacy which is enshrined in the computer industry's version of Dobbins Law: when in doubt, build a bigger operating system. The problem with Q was that it threatened to be the biggest and most complex operating system ever conceived. It would be a system, too, which would have to cope with all those emulations: it might well be that the 70,000 lines of code needed to execute a transaction on System 370 loaded with all its bells and whistles would become a 100,000, or even more lines of code with FS.

But Q was not simply an operating system: it was the environment. And here IBM had made a fundamentally wrong decision. The search for a structure of knowledge which is basic and not limited to the subject-matter in hand has been a long one. It has much to do with computation, for after all if you can create a data structure which can be used irrespective of the data content, then you have done a once-and-for-all job; you do not have to keep reinventing and reworking. IBM has long had work in progress in that area; the work is on as relational data bases and its chief advocate was—and is—E. F. Codd, a senior IBM researcher at San Jose. Much of the world of computing is split concerning whether Codd is right or not, with most of his supporters being outside IBM and his detractors within it. As a consequence, the Codd ideas never had the support they should have had from IBM.

However, one thing was certain, Q had to be predicated on the ideas of Codd and the techniques he had developed if FS—or something similar—was to work effectively: there was just no other way. But, it was not. Yet, there was no other work of any depth in progress within IBM, which could have substituted for Codd's.

So Q grew, it became larger and larger and more and more ceased to bear any resemblance to the system which IBM had set out to create.

IBM also faced a set of market problems. Between the start of FS and its termination, IBM's market began to change. In part, it was IBM which caused it to do so; in part, it was user demand. That demand was for solutions to problems specific to individual industries. IBM researchers had long known that the more the salesman concentrated on one industry, the more he was likely to sell. So, in line with, though generally after, everybody else, IBM had been developing systems unique to individual industries.

None of the problems so far outlined were, however, insuperable. There was nothing in them which would not have been susceptible to a solution, *given that IBM could bring the technology to market in the way it wished.*

From here on in we enter the world of surmise, for the real reasons are unlikely to surface until some new litigant seeks the paper concerned from IBM and pulls it out into the public record. *Given that IBM could bring the technology to market in the way it wished* . . . IBM, one suspects, foresaw that it could not, and that is probably the real reason.

But why could it not? First, there was the cloud hanging over IBM's future existence as the IBM everybody knew and most did not love. At least one senior IBM director was saying in semi-private at the start of 1975 that IBM must settle with Justice, it must go for a Consent Decree, because he could not see how IBM could continue to operate in the atmosphere that the trial was likely to create, with the management time and effort that would have to be devoted to it. IBM was already beginning to feel the pressure that those who had sought to sue IBM in the past had felt from it.

But if IBM settled, it would have to settle on terms set by the Justice Department. And the Justice Department, it was made quite clear, sought a break-up of IBM. But how could you plan the future, how could you propose to bring anything quite so radically different as FS to the market when you did not know whether Justice would settle for a new IBM which would allow you to keep it? One could put it stronger than this: the likelihood that IBM would be allowed to keep to itself a system which involved—as did FS—the entire resources of the corporation in its manufacture and marketing was nil. And if it was nil, why should IBM continue to develop it?

The FCC decision had already given IBM a warning: FS would not be allowed to be created in a way which would permit the service to be bundled. But unless IBM could move into the telecommunication business in the way it wanted, FS was seriously compromised.

Even supposing that these problems did not exist, IBM faced others which management had not foreseen when the development of FS began. IBM's invention record might be derisory, but IBM's development record, particularly in the component its field, had been impressive. Management had been told for years that it was bringing down the costs of components. But it had not taken all the consequences to heart. And one of them was now beginning to appear. Much of the market growth which IBM management expected to come to IBM was in fact going to other people, not to conventional competitors, but to manufacturers of micro- and mini-computers, who found that the economics applied to them as they applied to IBM; manufacturers who did not have high expense levels of IBM to support.

The second problem was that IBM's major markets, those high-profit earners—the U.S., France, Germany, the U.K.— were all in the middle of a recession. That recession had one major effect; equipment orders had been cut back, and the IBM forecasts had all gone wrong. IBM was no longer on target, with the consequence that FS would at the very least have to be put back.

As if this was not enough, above IBM there hung a further long-term threat: was there a future for IBM World Trade as IBM and the world knew it? FS would mean extensive reorganisation; that much had already become apparent. The in-fighting between subsidiaries as to who was to produce what had already led to one casualty: with FS, the U.K. would no longer produce a major processor; that battle had been won by Germany.

But would governments accept any more that vital decisions

could be made in Armonk without their being consulted? The indications in Europe throughout the start of 1975 were that they would not, in that IBM was now seriously faced for the first time with a host of problems which arose from the rebirth of economic nationalism, and that now it had no cards left to play: nobody was really concerned whether IBM was there or not. If it went away, the vacuum would be filled by someone else, with just as good technology and probably at a more economic price. IBM, at least in Europe in 1975, operated on suffrance, a situation for which it was ill prepared.

It is these sorts of calculations which probably had more to do with the cancellation of FS than IBM's ability or inability to create it. In the end, IBM's attempt to develop a technology which would at least have delighted those executives who really understood technology, this was to be beaten, not by design or by superior forces on the market, but by the coming together almost accidentally of events over which IBM had no control. It was perhaps also beaten by a lack of IBM management ingenuity. IBM's efforts might not have been wholly in vain, but one thing was certain: FS was dead. For the technological time-window operates for IBM as for everybody else. If FS is to be revived, it will reappear in a different form, one offering different possibilities. It will not be this FS, it will be something quite different. And that it may be something as sensible is doubtful. It is unlikely that the next time IBM will be so inordinately ambitious: which is perhaps a pity.

Just before I left America, a colleague was discussing a Justice versus IBM pre-trial hearing. 'For the first time,' he said, 'the smiles on the faces of IBM's lawyers seemed a little strained.'

Could it be that they foresaw that 1975 was likely to be the start of the bad years? Having so far won almost every legal battle, perhaps IBM was starting to feel that it was all too good to last; IBM was beginning to consider, for the first time, the possibility that it might in the end lose the war.

APPENDIX ONE: DOCUMENTS

MEMORANDUM

August 28, 1963

Memorandum To: Messrs. A. L. Williams
T. V. Learson
H. W. Miller, Jr.
E. R. Piore
O. M. Scott
M. B. Smith
A. K. Watson

Last week CDC had a press conference during which they officially announced their 6600 system. I understand that in the laboratory developing this system there are only 34 people, "including the janitor." Of these, 14 are engineers and 4 are programmers, and only one person has a Ph.D., a relatively junior programmer. To the outsider, the laboratory appeared to be cost conscious, hard working and highly motivated.

Contrasting this modest effort with our own vast development activities, I fail to understand why we have lost our industry leadership position by letting someone else offer the world's most powerful computer. At Jenny Lake, I think top priority should be given to a discussion as to what we are doing wrong and how we should go about changing it immediately.

T. J. Watson, Jr.

TJW, Jr: jmc
cc: Mr. W. B. McWhirter

In this diagram, much of what has been made subject to computer control rests on an information base which is also dependent on computing for its creation and storage. For its effective, functioning, the system will depend on computerising (sic) and putting on line—so that the relationship is dynamic—order entry, shop floor activity data, material state (inventory) and billing, warehouse automation, machine state and performance monitoring, and movement, at its simplest conveyor belt control. Not shown but directly related will be the also part computer-dependent design, quality control, sales forecasting, financial, purchasing and personnel systems, all of which interact with the factory operation and will play their part in determining what is done there.

Although this is a future example of the sort of computerisation IBM hopes to make possible, it is a relatively trivial example of what could be possible. Even so, to cope with what is shown in the diagram will require a database containing information of the following type: stores, purchases, receipts, cost planning and control, engineering and production data, customer orders, forecasts, production schedule planning, inventory, manufacturing activity planning, plant monitoring, maintenance and order release.

FUTURE EXTENSION

AUTOMATED WAREHOUSE

SHIPPING DOCUMENTS

FURNACE CONTROL

PLATING CONTROL

PRODUCT TEST

JOB REPORTING

COMMUNICATION LOOP

DMC

PLANT COMPUTER

CORPORATE COMPUTER

MACHINE MONITORING

ATTENDANCE RECORDING

DNC

RECEIVING INSPECTION

TEST STAND MONITORING

The IBM passion for security is exemplified by its document control. The reprint below is of the cover page found on many of the study documents obtained from IBM during Telex's document search. It is a civil version of something met with daily in defence/intelligence reporting.

DOCUMENT NO.
RECIPIENTS EMPLOYEE NO.

Registered IBM Confidential

UNTIL_____(DATE)

☐ IBM CONFIDENTIAL THEREAFTER

☐ UNCLASSIFIED THEREAFTER

DOCUMENT DATE
COPY NUMBER

DOCUMENT TITLE		
ISSUED BY	NAME	DEPT.

THE ATTACHED DOCUMENT REQUIRES STRICT ACCOUNTABILITY AND SAFEKEEPING IN ACCORDANCE WITH EXISTING INSTRUCTIONS.

DO NOT DESTROY THIS DOCUMENT. WHEN IT IS NO LONGER REQUIRED, AND REMAINS REGISTERED IBM CONFIDENTIAL, RETURN IT TO THE LOCAL RECORDER OF REGISTERED DOCUMENTS.

DO NOT REPRODUCE THIS DOCUMENT. IF ADDITIONAL COPIES ARE REQUIRED, CONTACT THE LOCAL RECORDER.

THIS SHEET MUST REMAIN ATTACHED TO THE DOCUMENT.

COVER SHEET

APPENDIX TWO: SELECT BIBLIOGRAPHY

I have listed only those books which have a direct and immediate relevance, and which I have used as a starting point in my own enquiries or from which I have quoted directly.

I must, however, first acknowledge the help that three particular manuscripts—unpublished at the time of writing—have given me. One is by Professor Gerald Brock of the University of Arizona, and is concerned with the economic history of the computer industry, particularly market shares. The second is by a well-known American computer industry entrepreneur, whose business has been much affected by IBM action. It has had restricted U.S. circulation in draft form among those political and economic animals who have had to consider what, if anything, should be done about IBM. The third and last is an internal, though incomplete, listing of events in IBM's history which came into my hands some years ago but which since has been withdrawn from circulation.

Babbage, Charles, MA, FRS, etc. *Passages from the Life of a Philosopher.* Longman, Green, Longman, Roberts & Green. 1864.

Eames, Charles & Ray. *A Computer Perspective.* Harvard University Press. 1973.

Gilchrist, Bruce and Milton R. Wessel. *Government Regulation of the Computer Industry.* AFIPS Press. 1972.

Goulden, Joseph C. *Monopoly.* G. P. Putnam & Sons. 1968.

Green, Mark J. (with Beverly C. Moore Jr and Bruce Wasserstein). *The Closed Enterprise System.* Grossman. 1972.

Hoffman, Paul. *Lions in the Street.* Saturday Review Press/E.P. Dutton. 1973.

Kohlmeier, Louis M., Jr. *The Regulators.* Harper & Row. 1969.

Martin, James and Adrian R. D. Norman. *The Computerised Society.* Prentice Hall. 1970.

Randell, Brian (ed.). *The Origins of Digital Computers: Selected Papers*. Springer Verlag. 1973.

Rodgers, William. *Think*. Weidenfeld & Nicolson. 1969.

Sackman, Harold. *Computers, System Science and Evolving Society*. John Wiley and Sons. 1967.

Sharpe, William F. *The Economics of Computers*. Columbia University Press. 1969.

Stekler, Herman O. *The Structure and Performance of the Aerospace Industry*. University of California Press. 1965.

Turing, Sarah. *Alan M. Turing*. W. Heffer & Sons. 1959.

U.S. Government Printing Office. *Nomination of Nelson A. Rockefeller of New York to be Vice-President of the United States:* Report of the Committee on Rules and Administration. Washington, D.C. Dec. 3, 1974.

Watson, Thomas Jr. *A Business and its Beliefs. The Ideas that Helped Build IBM*. McGraw Hill. 1963.

Index

(Footnote references appear in italics.)